Psychology
Applied to Law

Mark Costanzo

Claremont McKenna College

THOMSON
™
WADSWORTH

Australia • Canada • Mexico • Singapore • Spain
United Kingdom • United States

DEB SCHUSTERMAN

Publisher: *Vicki Knight*
Acquisitions Editor: *Marianne Taflinger*
Assistant Editor: *Jennifer Wilkinson*
Editorial Assistant: *Nicole Root*
Marketing Manager: *Lori Grebe*
Marketing Assistant: *Laurel Anderson*
Advertising Project Manager: *Brian Chaffee*
Signing Representative: *Claire Lynch*
Print/Media Buyer: *Kristine Waller*
Permissions Editor: *Sarah Harkrader*

Production Service: *Stratford Publishing Services, Inc.*
Text Designer: *John Edeen*
Copy Editor: *Mary Jean Frank*
Cover Designer: *Ross Carron*
Cover Image: *Martin Barraud / Getty Images*
Compositor: *Stratford Publishing Services, Inc.*
Text and Cover Printer: *Webcom*

● ●

Printed in Canada
1 2 3 4 5 6 7 07 06 05 04 03

For more information about our products,
contact us at:
**Thomson Learning Academic
Resource Center
1-800-423-0563**
For permission to use material
from this text, contact us by:
Phone: 1-800-730-2214
Fax: 1-800-730-2215
Web: http://www.thomsonrights.com

Library of Congress Control Number:
2003102299

ISBN 0534366295

Wadsworth/Thomson Learning
10 Davis Drive
Belmont, CA 94002-3098
USA

Asia
Thomson Learning
5 Shenton Way #01-01
UIC Building
Singapore 068808

Australia/New Zealand
Thomson Learning
102 Dodds Street
Southbank, Victoria 3006
Australia

Canada
Nelson
1120 Birchmount Road
Toronto, Ontario M1K 5G4
Canada

Europe/Middle East/Africa
Thomson Learning
High Holborn House
50/51 Bedford Row
London WC1R 4LR
United Kingdom

Latin America
Thomson Learning
Seneca, 53
Colonia Polanco
11560 Mexico D.F.
Mexico

Spain/Portugal
Paraninfo
Calle/Magallanes, 25
28015 Madrid, Spain

to Sally,
of course

About the Author

●●●●●●●●●●●●●●●●●●●●●●●●●●●●●●●●●●●●●●

Sophia Costanzo and the Author

Mark Costanzo is Professor of Psychology and co-director of the Center for Applied Psychological Research at Claremont McKenna College. He has published research on a variety of law-related topics including jury decision making, sexual harassment, attorney argumentation, alternative dispute resolution, and the death penalty. He is author of *Just Revenge: Costs and Consequences of the Death Penalty* (St. Martin's Press, 1997) and co-editor (with Stuart Oskamp) of *Violence and the Law* (Sage Publications, 1994). Professor Costanzo has served as an expert witness and has appeared on national radio and television programs to discuss the applications of psychological science to the legal system. He serves on the editorial board of *Law and Human Behavior* and is co-organizer of the annual Claremont Symposium on Applied Psychology.

WHY I WROTE THIS BOOK
●●●●●●●●●●●●●●●●●●●●●●●●●●●●●●●●●●●●●●

For the past 12 years, I've taught a course in Psychology and Law. Like many (perhaps most) instructors, I don't assign a textbook. Instead, I assemble a book of readings containing journal articles on a variety of topics in psychology and law. This approach has some clear advantages—it exposes students to original research and teaches them to think like researchers. But I've also noticed some persistent problems. First, students often lack the background to get the full benefit of journal articles. And, journal articles are written for researchers and scholars, not students. Even when I think an article is fascinating and insightful, my students often find it dense, dry, and difficult to read. Despite these problems, I am reluctant to adopt a thick, expensive textbook that would make it difficult to also assign a significant number of additional readings. I wrote *Psychology Applied to Law* with these concerns in mind.

This book is designed to provide a brief, accessible, thorough introduction to the field. My hope is that this slim (relatively) inexpensive textbook will give instructors the flexibility to assign collections of articles or additional books. In addition, great care has been taken to write *Psychology Applied to Law* in a friendly, engaging style. Although the emphasis is on psychological research, the book makes extensive use of actual cases and real trials to draw students into the material and to illustrate the relevance of research findings. To improve clarity, every chapter draft was reviewed by students in my Psychology and Law class. Finally, this book introduces students to virtually every aspect of the legal system studied by psychologists. Drawing on research in social, cognitive, clinical, and developmental psychology, I have attempted to show how psychological science can be used to enhance the gathering of evidence, improve legal decision making, reduce crime, and promote justice.

To assist instructors, each chapter ends with a list of supplemental readings. A test bank for *Psychology Applied to Law* is available from the publisher.

ACKNOWLEDGMENTS

I wrote this book alone, but I had plenty of help revising it. Reviewers included both scholars and students. Several prominent psychology and law scholars generously agreed to read and comment on all or part of the book. Reviewers included Margaret Bull Kovera, Robert Mauro, Bradley McAuliff, Marc Patry, Steve Penrod, Kerri Pickle, Ronald Roesch, Brenda Russell, Cheryl Terrance, and Lawrence White. This book is much stronger because of their efforts. I am grateful for their insights and assistance.

This book was written for college students. So, I thought it might be useful to have my own students review it. I was right. Over the course of a year, two groups of students in my Seminar in Psychology and Law read drafts of each chapter. Their comments were invaluable in helping me to improve the clarity and readability of the text. The following students from the Claremont Colleges (Claremont McKenna, Harvey Mudd, Pitzer, Pomona, and Scripps) served as reviewers: Drew Bloomingdale, Erin Butler, Bree Byrne, Joe Carman, Selena Carsiotis, Alex Castillo, Fabiola Ceballos, Locky Chambers, Natasha Cunningham, Jennica Derksen, Allison Holmes, Dayna Kamimura, Tiffany Keith, Keith Mendes, Andrea Riddervold, Micah Sadoyama, Debbie Schild, Nisha Shah, Netta Shaked, Tamara Shuff, Sam Slayen, Rochelle Smith, Marilyn Springel, Meg Stiaszny, Amber Taylor, Ali Taysi, Jamie Terbeest, and Christopher Vandover. *Psychology Applied to Law* is much more student-friendly because of their efforts.

This book would probably not have been written if Marianne Taflinger—my editor at Wadsworth—hadn't persuaded me to write it. Marianne not only got me started, she provided much needed support and prodding along the way. Whenever I had questions about marketing, I was able to turn to Lori Grebe at Wadsworth. She was always helpful and enthusiastic. Finally, I thank my family. My wife, Sally—a lawyer with a Ph.D. in psychology—read every word of this book and commented on every chapter. She even read the glossary—something only a spouse is willing to do. Her gentle but relentless perfectionism has improved the book greatly. Our three daughters—Marina, Zoey, and Sophia—deserve thanks for their patience and understanding. This book frequently made their father unavailable for more important activities like going to the playground or the beach.

Mark Costanzo

Brief Contents

● ●

CHAPTER 1   Psychology and Law: An Ambivalent Alliance   1

CHAPTER 2   Interrogations, Confessions, and Lie Detection   31

CHAPTER 3   Profiles and Syndromes   65

CHAPTER 4   Competence and Insanity   95

CHAPTER 5   Juries and Judges   121

CHAPTER 6   Memory as Evidence: Eyewitness Testimony and Child Sexual Abuse   169

CHAPTER 7   Predicting Behavior: Risk Assessment and Child Custody Decisions   209

CHAPTER 8   Workplace Law: Harassment, Discrimination, and Fairness   239

CHAPTER 9   Sentencing, Imprisonment, and the Death Penalty   268

● ●

Glossary of Key Legal Terms   311

References   321

Name Index   357

Subject Index   365

Contents

● ●

A Few Useful Web Sites   xxi

CHAPTER **1**

Psychology and Law: An Ambivalent Alliance   1

A Brief History of Psychology and Law   3

A Clash of Cultures   8

Goals: Approximate Truth versus Approximate Justice   9

Methods: Rulings versus Data   11

Style of Inquiry: Advocacy versus Objectivity   12

The Importance of Bridging the Two Cultures   13

Roles Played by Psychologists Interested in Law   14

Psychologists as Advisors   14

Psychologists as Evaluators   15

Psychologists as Reformers   17

Pathways for Influencing the Legal System   18

Expert Testimony   18

Cross-Disciplinary Training   22

Amicus Curiae Briefs   24

Broad Dissemination of Research Findings   26

Influencing Legislatures and Public Policy   27

Has Psychology Influenced the Courts?   28

In Conclusion   29

CHAPTER 2
Interrogations, Confessions, and Lie Detection   31

The Power of a Confession   32

The Evolution of Interrogation Techniques   34

Inside the Modern Interrogation Room   37

False Confessions   41

Videotaped Confessions Presented at Trial   43

Should Police be Allowed to Lie?   44

LIE DETECTION USING THE POLYGRAPH   47

The Development of the Modern Polygraph   47

The Process of Polygraphing   49
    The Machine   49
    Questioning Procedure 1: The Relevant-Irrelevant
    Test (RIT)   50
    Questioning Procedure 2: The Control Question
    Test (CQT)   50

Weaknesses of Polygraphing Techniques   52

Research on the Polygraph   54

Legal Status of the Polygraph   56

An Alternative Polygraph-Based Technique:
The Guilty Knowledge Test (GKT)   58
    Weaknesses of the GKT   59

The Lie Detector as Coercion Device   60

How Jurors Respond to Polygraph Evidence   62

The Future of Lie Detection   63

CHAPTER 3
Profiles and Syndromes   65

The Process of Profiling   66

Characteristics of Serial Killers   68

Two Famous Profiles   69

Research on Profiling   72

Psychological Autopsies   73
   Legal Status of Psychological Autopsies   75

Precise Profiles or Sloppy Stereotypes?   76

SYNDROMES   79

Battered Woman Syndrome (BWS)   79
   BWS and the Legal System   82
   The Scientific Validity of BWS   85

Rape Trauma Syndrome (RTS)   86
   RTS Testimony in the Courtroom   89

Post Traumatic Stress Disorder (PTSD)   92

CHAPTER 4
Competence and Insanity   95

The Meaning of Legal Competence   97

How the Criminal Justice System Deals
with Incompetent Defendants   100

Tests and Techniques for Evaluating CST   103

THE INSANITY DEFENSE   107

The Evolution of Insanity Law   108

Three Important Cases and Their Consequences   109
    The McNaughton Case   109
    The Durham Case   110
    The Hinkley Case   112

Tests and Techniques for Assessing Insanity   114

How Jurors Define Insanity   115

The Larger Context of Insanity Laws   118

In Conclusion   119

CHAPTER 5
Juries and Judges   121

Assembling a Jury: Pools, Venires, and Voir Dire   123
    From Jury Pool to Venire   123
    Voir Dire   125
    Cognizable Groups   126

Using Stereotypes and Science to Select Jurors   128
    Scientific Jury Selection   129
    The Use of Trial Consultants   132
    Does Trial Consulting Work?   133

Juror Characteristics and Attitudes as Predictors
of Verdict   134
    General Personality Tendencies   135
    Attitudes about the Legal System   137
    Defendant-Juror Similarity   138

Basic Trial Procedure   140

Jurors as (Biased) Information Processors   141
    Pretrial Publicity   142
    Defendant Characteristics   143
    Inadmissible and Complex Evidence   143
    The Judge's Instructions as a Source of Confusion   146
    Models of Juror Decision Making   148

The Group Dynamics of Jury Deliberations   150

    Strong Jurors and the Power of the Majority   151

    Stages in the Deliberation Process   152

    The Size of the Jury   154

    Decision Rules (Unanimous or Majority Rule)   156

    Jury Nullification   158

Jury Reform   160

    Allowing Jury Discussion During Trial: The Arizona Project   162

Judges Compared to Juries   164

    Agreement between Juries and Judges   166

In Conclusion   168

CHAPTER 6
Memory as Evidence:
Eyewitness Testimony and Child Sexual Abuse

169

The Impact of Eyewitness Testimony   172

The Legal System's View of Eyewitness Testimony   173

    Exposing Eyewitness Bias at Trial   174

The Construction and Reconstruction
of Eyewitness Memories   175

    Cross-Racial Identifications   176

    Weapons Focus   178

    Unconscious Transference   178

    Leading or Suggestive Comments   179

    Preexisting Expectations   180

    Witness Confidence   181

    When the Eyewitness is a Child   183

Using Research Findings to Improve
Eyewitness Accuracy   183

    Rule 1: Blind Lineup Administrators   184

    Rule 2: Instructions to Eyewitnesses   185

    Rule 3: Unbiased Lineups   185

Rule 4: Confidence Ratings   186
Costs and Consequences of Following the Four Rules   186

Three More Eyewitness Safeguards   187
Sequential Lineups   187
Videotaping   188
Expert Testimony   188

Techniques for Refreshing the Memories of Witnesses   189
Hypnosis   189
The Cognitive Interview   192

MEMORIES OF CHILD SEXUAL ABUSE   193

The Memories of Young Children   194
The Day Care Center Cases   194
Testimony by Children at Trial   198

Recovered Memories of Sexual Abuse   200
The Ingram Case   200
Were the Memories Created or Recovered?   202
Research on Implanting False Memories   204

In Conclusion   207

CHAPTER 7
Predicting Behavior: Risk Assessment and
Child Custody Decisions   209

ASSESSING THE RISK OF FUTURE VIOLENCE   210

The Evolution of Research on Risk Assessment   213

The List of Risk Factors   218
Historical Markers   218
Dynamic Markers   219
Risk Management Markers   220
Helping Clinicians Use the Markers   221

Jurors' Reactions to Risk Assessment Evidence   222

Treatment to Reduce the Risk of Violence   223

CHILD CUSTODY AND PARENTAL COMPETENCE   225

The Evolution of Child Custody Standards   226

Research on Children's Responses to Divorce   229

The Psychologist's Contribution to Custody Decisions   232

Custody Mediation as an Alternative to Litigation   235

In Conclusion   237

CHAPTER 8
Workplace Law: Harassment, Discrimination, and Fairness   239

The Evolution of Sexual Discrimination Law   240

Sexual Harassment: Prevalence and Perceptions   242

The Legal Boundaries of Sexual Harassment   244

Current Status of Harassment Law   246
  Sexual Harassment Lawsuits   247

The Psychology of Sexual Harassment   250
  Some Causes   250
  Some Effects   251
  Prevention   252

A Broader Look at Workplace Discrimination   253
  Racial Discrimination in the Workplace   257

The Psychology of Perceived Fairness   260
  Three Models for Allocating Rewards   261
  Research on Perceptions of Fairness   264

In Conclusion   266

Chapter 9
Sentencing, Imprisonment, and the Death Penalty   268

SENTENCING DECISIONS   270

Disparities and Guidelines   270

IMPRISONMENT   274

The Goals of Imprisonment   276

The Evolution of the American Prison   277
The 1800s   278
The 1900s   281

Prisoner Rights and the Role of the Courts   283

Some Statistics on Prisons and Prisoners   284
Who Goes to Prison?   285
Gender   285
Race   286

The Distinctive Culture of Prison   286
The Power of the Prison Situation   287
The Harsh Realities of Prison Life   288
Violence and Threats of Violence   290
Gangs   291
Drugs   291

Does Prison Work?   292

Alternatives to Prison   295

THE DEATH PENALTY   297

Supreme Court Decisions   298
Research on Capital Murder Trials and the Court's Response   300
Juror Decision Making in the Penalty Phase   301

Racial Disparities and the Death Penalty   303

The Death Penalty as a Deterrent to Murder   305

Errors and Mistakes in Death Penalty Cases   307

In Conclusion   309

● ●

Glossary of Key Legal Terms   311

References   321

Name Index   357

Subject Index   365

A Few Useful Web Sites

• •

Academy of Behavioral Profiling . . . . www.profiling.org

American Academy of Forensic
Psychology . . . . www.abfp.com

American Academy of Psychiatry
and Law . . . . www.aapl.org

ABA Journal . . . . www.abanet.org

American Psychological Association
law links . . . . www.psyclaw.org

American Psychology-Law Society . . . . . www.unl.edu/ap-ls/

American Society of Trial Consultants . . . www.astcweb.org

Death Penalty Information Center . . . . . www.deathpenaltyinfo.org

Gary Wells's Eyewitness Site . . . . www.psychology.iastate
edu/faculty/gwells/

The Innocence Project . . . . www.innocenceproject.org

Links to Legal Resources . . . . www.findlaw.com

National Center for State Courts . . . . www.ncsconline.org

The Sentencing Project . . . . www.sentencingproject.org

U.S. Circuit Court Opinions . . . . www.law.emory.edu/
caselaw

U.S. Department of Justice . . . . www.usdoj.gov

U.S. Supreme Court . . . . www.supremecourtus.gov

U.S. Supreme Court Decisions . . . . http://supct.law.cornell.
edu/supct/

1

Psychology and Law: An Ambivalent Alliance

Chapter Outline

A Brief History of Psychology and Law

A Clash of Cultures

    Goals: Approximate Truth versus Approximate Justice

    Methods: Rulings versus Data

    Style of Inquiry: Advocacy versus Objectivity

The Importance of Bridging the Two Cultures

Roles Played by Psychologists Interested in Law

    Psychologists as Advisors

    Psychologists as Evaluators

    Psychologists as Reformers

Pathways for Influencing the Legal System

    Expert Testimony

    Cross-Disciplinary Training

    Amicus Curiae Briefs

    Broad Dissemination of Research Findings

    Influencing Legislatures

Has Psychology Influenced the Courts?

In Conclusion

A defendant is on trial for a terrible crime. Lawyers make opening statements, witnesses are called, secrets are revealed, motives are questioned. In their closing arguments, lawyers make impassioned pleas to the men and women of the jury. Jurors struggle to find the truth. In a hushed courtroom, thick with tension, the jury foreperson announces the verdict: "We find the defendant . . ."

The courtroom trial is a staple of great and trashy literature, of distinguished films and lousy television. This is so because the trial is a compelling psychological drama. There is the question of motivation—was it love, hate, fear, greed, or jealousy that caused the behavior of a criminal? There is persuasion—lawyers and witnesses attempt to influence a judge or jury and, during deliberations, jurors attempt to influence each other. Perceptual and cognitive processes come into play—eyewitnesses must remember and report what they saw, jurors must sift through evidence to reach conclusions. Finally, there is decision making: The goal is to reach a decision, a verdict. And, if the verdict is guilty, there is a choice about what punishment is appropriate.

The trial is the most visible piece of our justice system. But it is only a small piece. When we look beyond the trial, we find that the legal system is saturated with psychological concerns. Every area of psychology (e.g., developmental, social, clinical, cognitive) is relevant to some aspect of law. Here are a few examples:

Developmental Psychology—Following a divorce, which kind of custody arrangement will promote healthy development of the child? Can a child who commits a murder fully appreciate the nature and consequences of his or her crime?

Social Psychology—How do police interrogators make use of principles of coercion and persuasion to induce suspects to confess to a crime? Do the group dynamics of juries influence their verdict decisions?

Clinical Psychology—How can we decide whether or not a mentally ill person is competent to stand trial? Is it possible to predict whether a mentally ill person will become violent in the future?

Cognitive Psychology—How accurate is the testimony of eyewitnesses? Under what conditions are eyewitnesses able to remember what they saw? Do jurors understand jury instructions in the way that lawyers and judges intend the instructions to be understood?

In the abstract, psychology and law seem like perfect partners. Both focus on human behavior, both strive to reveal the truth, and both attempt to solve human problems and improve the human condition. Yet the relationship between the two has always been somewhat rocky and the interactions between law and psychology have seldom been smooth or satisfying to either partner.

A BRIEF HISTORY OF PSYCHOLOGY AND LAW

Scholarly disciplines seldom have clear starting points. It is only in retrospect that we can look back and identify the small streams that eventually converge to form a strong intellectual current. What is clear is that a full appreciation of the possible applications of psychology to the legal system began to emerge in the early years of the twentieth century. In 1906, Sigmund Freud gave a speech in which he cautioned Austrian judges that their decisions were influenced by unconscious processes (Freud, 1906). He also noted that insights from his theory could be used to understand criminal behavior and to improve the legal system. However, it was two other events that triggered a broad recognition among psychologists that their ideas might be used to transform the legal system. One event was the publication of a book called *On the Witness Stand*. The author was an experimental psychologist named Hugo Munsterberg. He had been a student of Wilhelm Wundt (the person generally regarded as the founder of modern psychology) and he had been invited by William James to move from Germany to direct the Psychological Laboratory at Harvard.

Munsterberg wrote *On the Witness Stand* with the purpose of "turning the attention of serious men to an absurdly neglected field which demands the full attention of the social community" (Munsterberg, 1908, p. 12). His book succeeded in getting the attention of the legal community, although it was not the kind of attention he had hoped for. In 1909, John H. Wigmore, a leading legal scholar of the time, published a savagely satirical critique of what he considered to be Munsterberg's exaggerated claims for psychology. In the article, Munsterberg was put on trial for libel, cross-examined, and found guilty (Wigmore,

1909). Not only did *On The Witness Stand* receive an icy reception from legal scholars, it failed to mobilize research psychologists. Despite his achievements, Munsterberg is only begrudgingly acknowledged as the founding father of psychology and law.

The second important event came in the case of *Muller v. Oregon*. In 1907, the United States Supreme Court ruled that the workday of any woman employed in a laundry or factory could be limited to 10 hours. Lawyer Louis Brandeis (who later became a Supreme Court Justice) filed his famous "Brandeis Brief" in that case. His basic argument was as follows:

> When the health of women has been injured by long hours, not only is the working efficiency of the community impaired, but the deterioration is handed down to succeeding generations. Infant mortality rises, while the children of married working-women, who survive, are injured by inevitable neglect. The overwork of future mothers thus directly attacks the welfare of the nation (*Muller v. Oregon,* 1907).

The *Muller* decision was a major victory for the progressive movement, which sought to reduce work hours, improve wages, and restrict child labor. Most important for psychology, Brandeis's brief opened the door for the use of social scientific evidence by American courts. Ironically, the "social science" cited by Brandeis would not be considered valid science by modern standards—it was little more than unsystematic observations and the casual use of medical and labor statistics. But the important point is that, later, far more rigorous research would enter through the door pushed open by Brandeis.

During the two decades following the Brandeis Brief, the legal system showed little interest in social science. Then, in the late 1920s and into the 1930s, the "Legal Realism" movement reenergized the dormant field of social science and law. Legal realists reacted against the established order represented by "natural law." According to proponents of natural law, judicial decisions were thought to reflect principles found in nature. The task of judges was to deduce—through careful logic—the single correct decision in a particular case. In contrast, the realists believed that judges actively constructed the law through their interpretations of evidence and precedent. Further, these constructions of the law served particular social policy goals. In one of the first critiques of classical jurisprudence, Oliver Wendell Holmes wrote that the law,

. . . cannot be dealt with as if it contained only the axioms and corollaries of a book of mathematics. . . .The very considerations which judges most rarely mention, and always with an apology, are the secret root from which the law draws all the juices of life. I mean, of course, considerations of what is expedient for the community concerned. Every important principle which is developed by litigation is in fact and at bottom the result of more or less definitely understood views of public policy (Holmes, 1881, pp. 2–3).

These were revolutionary ideas at the time. Holmes and other legal scholars argued that law was not merely rules and precedents—it was the means through which policy ends were achieved. The legal realists argued that the social context and social effects of laws were as important as the mechanical application of logic. Realist scholars sought to look beneath "legal fictions," formalisms, and symbols to examine the actual behavior of lawyers and judges.

In 1927, the Dean of Yale Law School appointed a psychologist to the faculty of the Law School in an effort to ". . . make clear the part of the law in the prediction and control of behavior" (Schlegel, 1979, p. 493). Optimism about the potential for a fruitful partnership between psychology and law was widespread in the writings of the time. In 1930, the American Bar Association (ABA) journal proclaimed that, "The time has arrived when the grim hard facts of modern psychological inquiry must be recognized by our lawmakers despite the havoc they may create in the established institutions" (Cantor, 1930, p. 386).

The realist movement was an early example of the influence of psychology on the law. The two towering psychologist-philosophers of the time—William James and John Dewey—had already championed the ideas of pragmatism, induction, and scientific approaches to the study of social issues (James, 1907; Dewey, 1929). Legal realists embraced the idea that the law needed to pragmatically promote the common good and make use of social scientific research. By 1931, Karl Llewellyn, a leader of the realist movement, enumerated several core principles: (1) because society is always in flux faster than the law, laws must be continually reexamined to make sure they serve society well; (2) law is "a means to social ends and not an end in itself," and (3) law must be evaluated in terms of its effects (Llewellyn, p. 72). Realism's reconceptualization of the law was an enormous success. Llewellyn's fundamental principles now enjoy almost universal acceptance among the legal community.

Although the Realists set in motion a revolution in how people thought about the functions of law, the movement was much less successful in promoting the use of research findings. Curiously, almost none of the Legal Realists had collaborated with psychologists or other social scientists. The enthusiasm of the Legal Realists was based on rather naïve assumptions about the nature of psychological science. Following the 1930s, disillusionment about the utility of social science set in. Finding the answers to psychological questions proved to be more complicated and arduous than the Realists had supposed. Even worse, the answers provided by social scientists tended to be equivocal and probabilistic. Disenchantment and disengagement seemed to settle in for more than a decade.

In May 1954, in the case of *Brown v. Board of Education,* the U.S. Supreme Court voted unanimously that keeping black and white children segregated in separate schools was a violation of the Fourteenth Amendment's guarantee of "equal protection under the law." That historic decision—widely regarded as one of the most important Supreme Court rulings of the twentieth century—was a milestone in the slowly developing relationship between social science and the law. The ruling was not only monumental in its impact on American society, it was the first to explicitly make use of research provided by social scientists. The legal briefs submitted to the Court included a document entitled, *The Effect of Segregation and the Consequences of Desegregation: A Social Science Statement.* It was signed by 32 prominent social scientists. Many of the sources provided in that statement were cited in footnote 11 of the Court's decision and a few key passages from *Brown* echo the arguments made in the *Social Science Statement.* Chief Justice Earl Warren wrote,

> . . . the policy of separating the races is usually interpreted as denoting the inferiority of the Negro group. A sense of inferiority affects the motivation of a child to learn. Segregation with the sanction of law, therefore, has a tendency to retard the educational and mental development of Negro children and to deprive them of some of the benefits they would receive in a racially integrated school system (*Brown v. Board of Education,* 1954).

The Court further concluded that separating black children merely because of their race, ". . . generates a feeling of inferiority as to their status in the community that may affect their hearts and minds in a way unlikely to ever be undone" (*Brown v. Board of Education,* 1954,

p. 488). Although the true impact of social science in the *Brown* decision has been questioned, there is little doubt that it raised the hopes of social scientists (Hafemeister & Melton, 1987). *Brown* held out the promise that the highest court in the land would be receptive to social scientific research.

The social and intellectual climate of the late 1960s nurtured the fledgling field of psychology and law. In 1966, Harry Kalven (a lawyer) and Hans Zeisel (a sociologist) published an influential book entitled *The American Jury*. This seminal work (discussed more fully in Chapter 5) summarized a multiyear study of how juries and judges reach their decisions. Karl Menninger's book, *The Crime of Punishment,* also published in 1966, advocated much greater use of therapeutic methods to rehabilitate criminals. These books gave psychology and law a much-needed boost. There was great enthusiasm about psychology's potential for improving the legal system.

Within the broader psychological community, there was a growing eagerness to find ways of applying theory and research to areas such as law. In his 1969 presidential address to the American Psychological Association, George Miller (a distinguished cognitive psychologist who had spent virtually all of his career conducting basic research in the laboratory) called for "giving psychology away"—using psychological knowledge to address pressing social problems (Miller, 1969). In the same year, Donald Campbell called for much more extensive use of the research methods he and other scientists had pioneered. The opening sentence of his 1969 article neatly sums up his approach and conveys the optimism of the time:

> The United States and other modern nations should be ready for an experimental approach to social reform, an approach in which we try out new programs designed to cure specific social problems, in which we learn whether or not these programs are effective, and in which we retain, imitate, modify, or discard them on the basis of apparent effectiveness on the multiple imperfect criteria available (Campbell, 1969, p. 409).

Psychologists interested in the legal system were also feeling optimistic about psychology's possibilities. In 1969, they established The American Psychology-Law Society (AP-LS), proclaiming that, ". . . there are few interdisciplinary areas with so much potential for improving the human condition" (Grisso, 1991).

The intermittent flirtations between psychology and law did not mature into a steady relationship until the late 1970s. The first issue of the American Psychology-Law Society's major journal—*Law and Human Behavior*—appeared in 1977. Since then, several other journals that feature psycholegal research and theory have appeared (e.g., *Law and Society Review; Criminal Justice and Behavior; Behavioral Sciences and the Law;* and *Psychology, Public Policy, and Law*). Scientific organizations other than APLS (e.g., the Law and Society Association, the American Board of Forensic Psychology) have law and social science as their main concern. There are even a handful of "double doctorate" programs that award PhDs in psychology and JDs in law, and roughly 60% of university psychology departments now offer an undergraduate course in psychology and law (Bersoff et al., 1997). The relationship between the two disciplines has expanded and deepened over the past 25 years. This is clearly a boom time for the field. The future is uncertain, but there is reason for optimism.

A CLASH OF CULTURES

Many scholars have found it useful to think of psychology and law as fundamentally different cultures (Goldberg, 1994; Carroll, 1980; Bersoff, 1999). This section explores the nature and consequences of these cultural differences. The concept of "culture" has been defined in a variety of ways. Harry Triandis, a pioneer in cross-cultural psychology wrote that, "Culture is reflected in shared cognitions, standard operating procedures, and unexamined assumptions" (Triandis, 1996, p. 407). Culture has also been defined as ". . . the set of attitudes, values, beliefs, and behaviors shared by a group of people, and communicated from one generation to the next" (Matsumoto, 1997, pp. 4–5). People from a particular culture tend to share basic assumptions about the relative importance of competing goals, how disputes should be resolved, and what procedures to follow in striving for goals.

When anthropologists and psychologists contrast different cultures, they focus on the strength of tendencies in one direction or the other. Different cultures don't fit neatly into discrete categories; they fall along different points on a continuum. By comparing the cultural tendencies of law and psychology, we can understand why psychology and law have sometimes become frustrated with each other and we can see how the two disciplines might work together more productively. Many of the difficulties in the interactions between psychology and law can be traced to underlying differences in goals, methods, and styles of inquiry.

Goals: Approximate Truth versus Approximate Justice.   In a thorough discussion of the many points of tension between psychology and law, Craig Haney points out that "psychology is descriptive and law is prescriptive" (Haney, 1981). That is, psychology tells us how people actually behave; the law tells us how people ought to behave. The primary goal of psychological science is to provide a full and accurate explanation of human behavior. The primary goal of the law is to regulate human behavior. And, if someone behaves in a way that the law forbids, the law provides for punishment. Put somewhat idealistically, psychological science is mainly interested in finding truth, and the legal system is mainly interested in rendering justice. Although neither absolute truth nor perfect justice is fully attainable, scientists must strive for an approximation of truth and courts must strive for an approximation of justice.

In his classic study of cultural differences, Geert Hofstede found that cultures could be usefully differentiated on the dimension of "uncertainty avoidance" (Hofstede, 1991). Cultures high on this dimension develop elaborate rules and rituals in an effort to promote clarity and stability. Legal culture ranks high on uncertainty avoidance. Because people expect the courts to resolve disputes, the legal system must assimilate the ambiguities of a case and render a final, unambiguous decision. Putting an end to a dispute requires a clear, binding ruling. People are found guilty or set free, companies are forced to pay damages, child custody is decided, and criminals are sent to prison. While it is true that an investigation or a courtroom trial can be characterized as a search for the truth, that search is conducted in service of a judgment: guilty or not guilty. And, if the verdict is guilty, the judgment then becomes one of consequences: How much money should the defendant pay in damages? What kind of probation should be imposed? How long should the prison sentence be? To resolve a conflict, a conclusion must be reached. Because the legal system can never achieve perfect justice, it must settle for approximate justice in the form of conflict resolution. And, in a democracy, it is crucial that disputes are resolved in a way that *appears* fair and promotes social stability. Although citizens may disagree with many specific decisions of the courts, they must have faith in the overall fairness of the system.

In contrast, uncertainty is intrinsic to the scientific process. No single research study is ever conclusive, and no finding is truly definitive. Over time, uncertainty is reduced, but all conclusions can be revised or reversed by contrary data. The scientific process emphasizes the use of testable hypotheses, valid and reliable measures, statistical standards for accepting a conclusion, and replications of findings over time. The ultimate "truth" of a particular explanation of human behavior may be unknowable but, over time and multiple investigations, theories are revised and psychologists are able to construct increasingly useful explanations of human behavior. Judgments made by scientists are not dichotomous (like guilty or not guilty); they are probabilistic. That is, scientific conclusions are stated in terms of probabilities. Indeed, the tendency for psychological scientists to talk in terms of likelihoods and to couch their conclusions in caveats and qualifiers is something the courts (and the general public) sometimes find frustrating. In science, no conclusion is final and current understandings are tentative and subject to revision.

Another implication of the differing goals of psychological science and the legal system is that psychology emphasizes the characteristics of groups, while the law emphasizes individual cases (Goldberg, 1994; Haney, 1981). Psychological scientists conduct research to uncover general principles of human behavior. Because individuals are idiosyncratic, knowing how one person behaves doesn't necessarily tell us how everyone else behaves in the same situation. The reverse is also true— knowing how people behave in general doesn't necessarily tell us why a specific defendant behaved in a particular way. This often creates problems. If a 10-year-old boy walks into his fourth grade classroom with a loaded gun and shoots one of his classmates, a psychologist might be called to testify. A developmental psychologist might testify about the cognitive abilities and moral reasoning of 10-year-olds. A social psychologist might summarize the results of research about how children are affected by watching violence on television or in movies. But, in court, the essential questions must be: "Why did *this boy* kill another child?" and "What should happen to reform or punish *this boy*?"

As John Carroll notes, "The law emphasizes the application of abstract principles to specific cases" (Carroll, 1980). Lawyers, plaintiffs, and defendants can't bring an idea to court and ask the court for a ruling. They must bring a specific case with particular characteristics. A ruling by a judge may set an important new precedent, but the immediate goal is to make a decision about a specific case. Consequently, the law evolves one case at a time. The law's emphasis on the individual defendant or plaintiff explains why courts have been more receptive to clinical psychologists than to other types of psychologists. Clinicians examine and draw conclusions about a particular person. Like lawyers, they are oriented toward the individual case.

Methods: Rulings versus Data.   The law is based on authority, psychology is based on empiricism (Goldberg, 1994). Whereas law advances through the accumulation of rulings produced by courts, psychology advances through the accumulation of data produced by scientists.

Because cultures differ in the amount of deference and obedience given to people in positions of authority, this dimension (sometimes called "power distance") is often used to differentiate cultures. The legal system is explicitly hierarchical (i.e., it would rank high on power distance). If a court of appeals overrules the decision of a lower court, the lower court must accept the ruling. Higher courts simply have more authority. And if the U.S. Supreme Court issues a ruling, the matter is settled—at least until the high court agrees to take up the issue again. In comparison, psychology is much more egalitarian. Although there are power relations within scientific communities (e.g., editors of prestigious journals and directors of funding agencies hold considerable power), the structure is far more democratic. Any researcher, even a low-status one, can conduct a study that challenges a prevailing theory of human behavior. If the data are compelling, the theory must be modified.

Part of the method of law involves deference for past rulings. All cultures are shaped by history, but they differ in how much value they place on history. In some cultures, people make offerings to the spirits of their ancestors and believe that those ancestors actively intervene in the affairs of the living. Although lawyers and judges don't pray to their ancestors for guidance, the past is an active force in their professional lives. As Oliver Wendell Holmes observed, "Law is the government of the living by the dead" (Holmes, 1897, p. 469). Attorneys and judges are obliged to place current facts in the context of past rulings; they must link the present to the past. When lawyers argue in front of judges, they cite precedents: past decisions on legal issues in cases that are as similar as possible to the current case. The persuasiveness of a legal argument rests to a substantial extent on whether the argument can be tied to existing precedents. In making their rulings, judges are strongly constrained by the doctrine of *stare decisis* or "let the decision stand." The idea is not to move too far from established precedent. As Karl Llewellyn noted, each precedent is ". . . a statement simultaneously of how a court *has* held, and how future courts *ought* to hold" (Llewellyn, 1931, p. 72).

In contrast, psychological scientists live in a more future-oriented culture. They believe that our current understanding of human behavior can and should be continually revised in light of new and more extensive data. Scientific theories are made to be broken. New techniques, better measures, and more inclusive sampling of participants continually force psychologists to modify their explanations of human behavior. Change and progress may be slow at times, but, as long as research continues, it is inevitable.

Style of Inquiry: Advocacy versus Objectivity.

In the American legal system, a judge or jury makes the decision of guilt or liability after hearing evidence and arguments. In an effort to reveal the truth to the judge or jury, lawyers take an adversarial stance. A fundamental assumption of the American system is that truth will emerge from a contest between opposing counsel. Lawyers advocate for a particular version of events and a particular interpretation of evidence and actively promote a one-sided view of the facts. Attorneys make opening statements and closing arguments to advance their version of the evidence, they call witnesses who will support that version, they challenge the assertions of witnesses called by the opposing side, they raise objections, and they try to rattle witnesses and undermine their credibility. Lawyers even do a bit of acting at times—for example, feigning disbelief or outrage at the testimony of a witness who challenges their version of events.

Indeed, attorneys *must* be advocates for their clients. The ABA Code of Professional Responsibility requires that lawyers "represent their clients zealously within the bounds of the law." One lawyer puts it even more bluntly:

> Lawyers make claims not because they believe them to be true, but because they believe them to be legally efficacious. If they happen to be true, then all the better; but the lawyer who is concerned primarily with the truth value of the statements he makes on behalf of clients is soon going to find himself unable to fulfill his professional obligation to zealously represent those clients. Another way of putting this is to say that inauthenticity is essential to authentic legal thought (Campos, 1998).

Of course, there are ethical limits on zealousness. Lawyers cannot knowingly permit witnesses to lie under oath (this is called "suborning perjury"). But the fact that lawyers are sometimes required to vigorously defend people or corporations that have done terrible things is one reason that lawyers, as a group, are not held in high esteem among members of the general public.

In contrast, scientists must strive for objectivity. Of course, humans are not capable of perfect objectivity. It is not uncommon for researchers to disagree about the correct interpretation of data or to zealously defend a theoretical point of view. In this sense, scientists sometimes behave as advocates. It is also true that values infiltrate the research process—values influence which topics scientists choose to investigate, how they interpret their data, where they publish their findings, and whether they attempt to apply their findings. Science is a human process that is shaped by human choices. Whenever choices are made, values and biases inevitably come into play. However, even if a particular researcher strays from an objective reading of his or her data, others who view the data will be more dispassionate (or at least biased in a different direction). And, if a researcher collects data using biased methods, the findings are unlikely to be published or taken seriously by others in the scientific community.

Objectivity is an ideal that resides not only in the individual researcher but, more importantly, in the scientific community as a whole. Individual researchers strive for an objective reading of their data. And, although a particular scientist may be too invested in a particular theory to be fully objective, science is an ongoing, public, self-correcting process. Research findings are published as articles or presented at conferences and subjected to criticism by other scientists. Scientists' confidence in the validity of a conclusion rests on the findings of multiple researchers using different research methods. It is only over time, through the sustained, collective efforts of many scientists, that the ideal of objectivity is achieved.

THE IMPORTANCE OF BRIDGING THE TWO CULTURES

Given the fundamental differences in the cultures of psychology and law and the difficulty of changing the legal system, why bother trying? After all, many psychologists have the luxury of choosing which topics to investigate. Research questions are often guided by the curiosities of the individual researcher. And, other areas of applied research—for example, business and education—are often more welcoming to the insights and techniques of psychologists. So why take on the extra burden of trying to influence the legal system?

There are good reasons. First, law is important. The law shapes our lives from womb to tomb. It dictates how our births, marriages, and deaths are recorded. It regulates our social interactions at school, at work, and at home. The legal system has the authority to impose fines, to forbid certain behaviors, to send people to prison, and even to kill people in the execution chamber. It employs millions of people and consumes billions of dollars. Second, many issues confronted by the legal system are inescapably psychological. Questions about what people consider fair, why people commit crimes, and how the behavior of criminals can be changed are all essentially psychological questions. They are also largely empirical questions—questions that can be answered by conducting research and analyzing data. Because the legal system is so pervasive and powerful, many social scientists believe that we are ethically obliged to help ensure that the consequential decisions meted out by the courts are based on the best available scientific knowledge. Although the two cultures of psychology and law continue to clash at times, there are now many examples of fruitful interaction.

ROLES PLAYED BY PSYCHOLOGISTS INTERESTED IN LAW

Given the fundamental differences in the cultures of law and psychology, how should the two interact? If both cultures can be enriched through contact, how might this contact occur? Three broad forms of interaction are possible. Though conceptually distinct, the three roles are complementary rather than exclusive. Each highlights a different means by which psychological science makes contact with the legal system.

Psychologists as Advisors.   Sometimes lawyers and judges welcome the perspectives of psychologists through the vehicle of expert testimony. Lawyers simply hire a psychologist to testify on some aspect of a case. For example, clinical psychologists have testified about whether a particular defendant meets the legal definition of insanity, whether a defendant is competent to stand trial, and whether a defendant is likely to be dangerous in the future. This type of relationship is easy because it requires no major accommodations from the legal system: The nature and boundaries of the relationship are predefined by the legal system. Psychologists simply fill the role they have been asked to fill.

Psychologists acting as trial consultants also serve as advisors to the legal system. In this capacity, psychologists are hired by attorneys to help with jury selection, witness preparation, or trial strategy. In general, trial consultants use psychological knowledge to attempt to shape the trial process in ways that produce favorable outcomes for paying clients. Like psychological experts who are hired to testify at trial, trial consultants are hired to provide expertise in the service of litigants. For example, if a company that manufactures household appliances is being sued for making toaster ovens that tend to explode and cause fires, the company might hire trial consultants to identify jurors that will be sympathetic to the company's case. The effectiveness and ethical implications of trial consulting are covered in Chapter 5.

If a case is appealed to a higher court, it is possible for psychologists to contribute to written arguments (called "briefs") submitted to the court. Such briefs might summarize the findings and conclusions of research conducted by psychologists. These briefs can be excellent vehicles for major professional organizations (e.g., the American Psychological Society or the American Psychological Association) to provide well-considered, data-based conclusions to the courts. As such, they are valuable opportunities for influence. Yet, here as well, the law defines how and on what terms psychological research will be used.

Psychologists as Evaluators. What has been called "program evaluation" or "evaluation research" is one of the fastest-growing areas in the social sciences. The basic proposition is that any social program ought to be evaluated as to its effectiveness. Programs are put in place to achieve social goals, and it's only fair (some would say it is ethically necessary) to ask if those goals are being achieved. For example, if a community puts in place a program where police officers attempt to reduce drug use by talking to elementary school students about the dangers of drugs, it is fair to ask whether students exposed to the program are less likely to use drugs than students who are not exposed to the program. If we decide to send juvenile offenders to boot camps or chain gangs, it is worth asking whether those offenders are less likely to continue a life of crime than juveniles who are placed on probation or sent to a juvenile detention facility. If the instructions given to jurors are intended to help jurors understand and follow the law, it is crucial to determine if jurors understand the instructions. More than a century ago, Oliver Wendell Holmes asked the pointed question: "What have we better than a blind guess to show that the criminal law in its present form does more good than harm? Does punishment deter? Do we deal with criminals on proper principles?" (Holmes, 1897, p. 469).

Most evaluation research asks questions about a specific legal practice or policy. For example, do executions deter potential murderers? Does "pornography" offend community standards? Usually, the research conducted to answer these types of questions is initiated by social scientists. Although it is essential to ask, "Does it work?" the question is more complex than it first appears. A particular part of the legal system may have multiple goals, and some of these goals may be in conflict. Consider prisons. When we send a criminal to prison, we may have multiple goals—to remove the criminal from civilized society; to punish the criminal for the pains he caused to others; to rehabilitate the criminal so that when he returns to society, he won't revert to a life of crime. While abusive, unpleasant prisons may serve the goal of punishment, they may militate against the goal of rehabilitation and even make criminals more dangerous. Should the goal of punishment or the goal of rehabilitation take priority? Also, as noted earlier, one of the goals of the legal system is to inspire confidence in the public. This raises another question: What if an ineffective or harmful practice enjoys broad public support? Should that practice be retained or abandoned?

Evaluators distinguish between formative and summative evaluations (Donaldson & Scriven, 2003). Formative evaluations provide ongoing information about the effectiveness of a program so that adjustments can be made. The information gathered from formative evaluations is used to guide program development and help the program become successful. In contrast, summative evaluations attempt to sum up how well a program has met its goals. Often, summative evaluations judge overall effectiveness and recommend whether a program should be continued or abandoned. In the legal system, the approach is usually formative—the issue is not whether to continue or abandon a practice, but how that practice can be improved or fine-tuned. So, evaluation researchers not only try to discover *if* a program works, but *how* a program works. Making wise decisions about which components of a program need to be modified presupposes a clear understanding of how that program works.

Many social scientists take a more expansive view of the legal system—sociologists, political scientists, anthropologists, criminologists, and a few psychologists have attempted to critically evaluate law as a system embedded within the larger society. This more encompassing perspective allows for the asking of big, fundamental questions: Why are some acts defined as criminal while other injurious behaviors are not? Why are some types of crimes aggressively prosecuted while other types are not? How do legal procedures come to be viewed as legitimate or illegitimate by citizens in a given culture? Whose interests are served by the legal system? Which outcomes are just? There are both disciplinary and methodological reasons why sociologists, criminologists, and anthropologists have been more likely than psychologists to address such questions. First, psychologists generally take the individual or the small group as their level of analysis. They tend not to look at large systems or whole societies. Second, psychology still tends to be a science that places high value on controlled experimentation and careful measurement. Larger questions are often regarded as messier and less amenable to controlled, systematic research.

Psychologists as Reformers. If we use psychological theory and research to find out which aspects of the legal system need to be improved, the next step is to improve them. Evaluation and understanding without any attempt at reform is an empty exercise. Still, many psychologists are uncomfortable playing the role of reformer. Many researchers are trained in a "basic" or "pure" science model. This means that they ask questions to satisfy their own curiosity or to test the propositions of a theory. The practical application of whatever knowledge is generated is left to others. To actively promote change in the legal system, the psychologist must step away from the role of objective scientist. And, the farther the scientist moves from that role, the more uncomfortable he or she is likely to become.

There is also the issue of *when* psychologists have sufficient confidence in their findings to advocate a particular change in the legal system. Of course, scientists are fallible and what we believe is true today might not be regarded as true tomorrow. Still, if we wait for absolute certainty before communicating our findings or arguing for a position, we will wait forever (Ellsworth, 1991). Even though psychological science can only provide incomplete answers, the procedures and practices of the legal system ought to be based on the best information currently available. It is important to remember that much legal practice is based on little more than tradition, convenience, and the untested intuition of legislators and judges. The real question is not whether our research findings are final or infallible, it is whether the current state of knowledge based on carefully conducted research is an improvement over current practice in the legal system. Though social scientists cannot provide absolute answers, we can often suggest ways of improving current practices.

A field of study is perhaps best defined by the activities of people working in that field. Given the three roles described above, our working definition of psychology and law will be, "the use of psychological knowledge or research methods to advise, evaluate, or reform the legal system."

PATHWAYS FOR INFLUENCING THE LEGAL SYSTEM

Knowledge generated by social scientists enters the law through several routes. The next section describes some pathways used by social scientists to make contact with and influence the legal system.

Expert Testimony.   Jurors, judges, and legislators can't be expected to know everything. So, people who have acquired specialized knowledge through education and experience—experts—are called upon to testify in courts or in front of legislative bodies. In courts, the process usually works like this: An attorney representing one side or the other in a trial proposes that a particular expert be allowed to testify and the presiding judge decides whether or not to allow the testimony. The lawyer believes that the expert will strengthen his or her case. The judge has other concerns. He or she must decide if hearing the expert testify will help juries discover the true facts in a particular case. Juries are the "triers of fact." If a judge decides that ordinary jurors already know what the expert has to say, or decides that the proposed testimony would only confuse jurors, or decides that the expert testimony would have too much impact on the jurors, the judge can refuse to allow the testimony. Rule 702 of the *Federal Rules of Evidence* sets the legal standard for permitting expert testimony in federal cases:

> If scientific, technical, or other specialized knowledge will assist the trier of fact to understand the evidence or to determine a fact in issue, a witness qualified as an expert by knowledge, skill, experience, training or education may testify thereto in the form of an opinion or otherwise.

In practice, this standard gives enormous discretion to judges in deciding whether or not to allow expert testimony.

In 1993, in the case of *Daubert v. Merrell Dow Pharmaceuticals, Inc.,* the U.S. Supreme Court held that judges must serve as "gatekeepers" for scientific testimony. In effect, judges were told to assess the scientific validity of potential testimony before allowing the purportedly scientific evidence to be heard at trial.

To assist judges, the Court listed four criteria to be used when deciding if purportedly scientific testimony should be admitted: (1) the testability or "falsifiability" of the theory or technique (whether the technique can be proven false through data collection), (2) whether the scientific findings have been subjected to peer review (generally through publication in a peer-reviewed journal), (3) whether there is a known rate of error, and (4) whether the conclusions are generally accepted in the relevant scientific community. Of course, these criteria leave plenty of room for discretion. If two judges are considering the same expert testimony, one might decide the testimony is admissible and the other might decide that it does not meet the *Daubert* standard of admissibility.

Not everyone agrees that judges are well equipped to play the role of gatekeeper. In the minority opinion, Justice Rehnquist complained that the *Daubert* decision obliged judges to become "amateur scientists," a role beyond their training and expertise. Indeed, recent research demonstrates that judges are not especially skilled at distinguishing between high-quality and low-quality research. For example, Margaret Bull Kovera and Bradley McAuliff (2000) asked 144 circuit court judges to evaluate psychological evidence in a sexual harassment case. Although the researchers systematically varied the methodological quality of the research presented to judges, methodological quality did not influence the judges' evaluations of the study's quality or their decision to admit the evidence. Both weak and strong research was admitted at the same low rate (17% of judges admitted the research), indicating a lack of scientific sophistication among judges (and perhaps a general bias against psychological research). Other research supports this general finding. Sophia Gatowski and her colleagues conducted a survey of 400 state court judges (Gatowski et al., 2001). Although 91% of the judges supported the "gatekeeping" role established by *Daubert,* the vast majority could not adequately define the four guidelines for admissibility elaborated by *Daubert* (testability, peer review, error rate, and general acceptance). Two of the guidelines were reasonably well understood by judges and two were poorly understood. Seventy-one percent of the judges understood the scientific peer review process and 82% also demonstrated a clear understanding of general acceptance. However, only 6% understood the meaning of testability and only 4% clearly understood the concept of "error rate." Judges' limited understanding of scientific methods is troubling. Clearly, if judges are to assume the role of effective gatekeepers, they need to assume the responsibility of learning about scientific methods.

Ideally, expert witnesses educate the court—they summarize research findings in a clear, impartial manner. One of the ethical dilemmas posed by expert testimony is that psychologists can too easily be swept into the currents of the adversary system. Experts are not supplied to lawyers, they are almost always chosen by lawyers representing a particular side in a specific case. Naturally, in their role as adversaries, lawyers often "shop around" to find an expert who will support their side. They turn to experts who have done well for them in prior cases, they call other lawyers and ask for the names of experts who might provide favorable testimony, and they may have telephone conversations (a better term might be interviews) with a few potential experts to get a sense of who might provide the strongest testimony.

Once a suitable expert is found, he or she may be "prepared" for trial. During this preparation, experts may be seduced into thinking of themselves as part of an adversarial team. It is in the interest of lawyers to create this mind-set. Sometimes subtly and sometimes bluntly, lawyers frequently let their experts know that they are working on behalf of a just cause and that the opposing team is misguided or untrustworthy. Once an expert is hired, lawyers often try to find the strongest form of testimony that witness is willing to give. Because lawyers acting as advocates for their client's interests usually choose their expert witnesses, they tend to prefer experts who will make unambiguous statements and reach clear conclusions in support of their side of the case.

In a seminal article on expert witnesses, Michael J. Saks described three roles that might be assumed by expert psychological witnesses. The *Conduit-Educator* strives to present a full and accurate picture of the current state of psychological knowledge. He or she realizes that, "To do this may be to be a mere technocrat, rather than a human being concerned with the moral implications of what I say and with the greater good of society. The central difficulty of this role is whether it is all right for me to contribute hard-won knowledge to causes I would just as soon see lose" (Saks, 1990, p. 295). In this role, the expert faithfully represents a field of knowledge. In the second type of role, the *Philosopher-Advocate,* the expert makes concessions to the adversarial climate of the courtroom and allows personal values to shape testimony. He or she might say, "There is a greater good at stake in this case, and that is (fill in the blank: desegregating schools, seeing to it that this child goes to the right home, keeping people from being executed, seeing to it that people are executed, etc.). I must advocate for those outcomes, and that obviously means giving testimony that involves clever editing, selecting, shading, exaggerating, or glossing over" (p. 296). In the final role, that of *Hired Gun,* the expert essentially "sells out" and capitulates to the adversarial demands of the courtroom. Hired guns intentionally shape their testimony to help the side of the hiring attorney.

Many commentators have excoriated experts who are willing to assume the role of hired gun. Margaret Hagen, an experimental psychologist, has written a scorching indictment of clinical psychologists and other mental health professionals who have testified in court as experts. In her book—*Whores of the Court*—Hagen cites several cases where psychotherapists, social workers, and psychiatrists have made unequivocal statements that have no research support (e.g., it is possible to tell if a particular young child is lying, if a particular memory is accurate, or if someone is faking post traumatic stress syndrome). She argues that these "witchdoctors" and "self-styled psychoexperts" are often motivated by the money they receive for their testimony or by a missionary-like zeal to promote a particular cause (Hagen, 1997).

It is extremely rare for an expert witness who shades or misrepresents research findings to be prosecuted for misconduct. Perjury requires lying about verifiable facts. Experts are called to offer expert opinions. And because opinions are neither true nor false, even highly unusual opinions cannot be described as lies. An expert may be biased, or igno-rant about relevant research, or incompetent, but that is not the same as being a liar. As one state supreme court put it, "It is virtually impos-sible to prosecute an expert witness for perjury" (*Sears v. Rutishauser*, 1984, p. 212).

While it is true that unscrupulous "experts" have sometimes testified in court, the ethical guidelines established by psychologists conform rather closely to Sak's *Conduit-Educator* role. Here are a few quotes from the guidelines:

> . . . psychologists realize that their public role as "expert to the court" or as "expert representing the profession" confers upon them a special responsibility for fairness and accuracy in their public statements" (Roesch, Hart, & Ogloff, 1999, p. 434).

> Psychologists must not, ". . . participate in partisan attempts to avoid, deny, or subvert the presentation of evidence contrary to their own posi-tion" (Roesch, Hart, & Ogloff, 1999, p. 434).

> When ". . . their own personal values, moral beliefs, or personal relation-ships with parties to a legal proceeding interfere with their ability to prac-tice competently, . . . they are obliged to decline participation or limit their assistance in a manner consistent with professional obligations" (Roesch, Hart, & Ogloff, 1999, p. 427).

Clearly, psychologists' primary loyalty must be to their discipline. They must strive to accurately report the current state of scientific knowledge.

Cross-Disciplinary Training.   One way to increase the use of social science by the legal system is through education. It is during post-graduate training (graduate school or law school) that students fully commit themselves to careers in psychology or law. The impact of a solid introduction to the law (for graduate students in psychology) or a solid introduction to social science (for law students) may be felt long after school has ended. Exposure to social science is likely to make lawyers and judges more receptive to social scientific research and testi-mony by psychologists. It is also likely to make judges and lawyers less receptive to testimony based on shoddy science or testimony lacking a solid scientific foundation. Conversely, exposing psychologists to legal training is likely to have beneficial effects. Psychologists with a sophisti-cated understanding of law are better equipped to ask questions and seek answers that are useful to the legal system. They may also be more likely to communicate their findings to legal professionals.

The best arrangement for obtaining dual training in the disciplines of psychology and law is a matter of some controversy. Some have argued for double doctorate programs that lead to both a J.D. in law and a Ph.D. in psychology. Unfortunately, such programs generally require about seven years of graduate study. Also, to earn a J.D., students must take a full complement of law classes, some of which (e.g., Corporations, Tax, Wills and Trusts, Property) have limited relevance to the study of psychology and law. One former director of a double doctorate program reached the conclusion that, "Having both degrees is unnecessary for making a contribution to psycholegal studies. Indeed, expertise in one discipline with a basic knowledge in the other is probably sufficient" (Melton, 1987, p. 492). Those Ph.D. programs that offer specialization in psychology and law include substantial training in areas of criminal and civil law that are of interest to psychologists. A final training model involves encouraging psychologists who already have their Ph.D. to earn a one-year master's degree in legal studies. Unfortunately, few law schools offer such programs.

Lawyers with an interest in enhancing their knowledge of psychology can select from scores of masters programs in psychology offered at universities across the country. However, because many lawyers lack the requisite background in statistics and research methods, significant remedial work may be necessary. An understanding of the social scientific approach to generating valid knowledge is critical for applying psychology to the legal system. Three psychologists who work in law schools (Gary Melton, John Monahan, & Michael Saks) put it this way,

> Much law rests on empirical as well as philosophical foundations that, if not known, must be assumed. Although psychologists may not always be able to answer the law's ubiquitous questions about human behavior, they at least can provide a sophisticated and realistic appreciation of what it would take to discover an adequate answer, and they can instill appropriate caution in making assumptions about social reality (Melton, Monahan, & Saks, 1987, p. 507).

There are now efforts under way to educate judges about scientific reasoning and to train judges to be critical consumers of scientific research. In response to the Supreme Court's ruling in *Daubert,* the Federal Judicial Center (the research arm of the federal courts) established several training programs to help judges responsibly fill their expanded role as gatekeepers. Some states and a few universities (e.g., the National Judicial College in Reno, Nevada, or the Adjudication Center at Duke University) offer judges week-long workshops on scientific evidence. These workshops are designed to teach judges how to evaluate the validity of the science behind various types of expert testimony. Judges without the time or inclination to attend classes can turn to a reference book that makes scientific testimony accessible to judges (Faigman, Kaye, Saks, & Sanders, 1997).

***Amicus Curiae* Briefs.** The *amicus curiae* ("friend of the court") brief has proven to be a useful tool for educating judges about relevant psychological research. The "friends" are interested and knowledgeable parties that do not have direct involvement in the case. The goal of such briefs is to summarize the relevant body of research and clarify the overall meaning of a set of findings. The American Psychological Association, through its Committee on Legal Issues (COLI), has filed *amicus* briefs in a wide range of cases dealing with issues as diverse as jury size, the death penalty, gay rights, abortion, the prediction of dangerousness, rights of mentally ill patients, the effects of employment discrimination, sexual behavior, and the courtroom testimony of child witnesses. The contents of several of these briefs will be discussed later in this book.

The involvement of scientists in *amicus* briefs can be controversial. Here, as in other areas, some believe that scientists too easily slip into becoming advocates when presenting research via *amicus* briefs. Some scholars describe briefs as ranging along a continuum, with "science translation" at one pole and "advocacy" at the other. That is, we can dispassionately report and clarify relevant research findings, or we can take a strong position. Gary Melton and Michael Saks (1990) recommend that the writing of an *amicus* brief should be guided by ". . . an honest desire to share with the courts a faithful picture of the available psychological knowledge, and to interpret the research only to the extent that doing so will clarify its meaning" (p. 5).

But even a science translation brief may have an undercurrent of advocacy. This is because the accumulated research often supports a particular judicial decision. A group of psychologists who have extensive experience in developing *amicus* briefs offer the following guidance:

> It is possible to be scientific without being neutral, to be objective yet form an opinion about the implications of the research. If the data warrant a

particular conclusion, then it may be reasonable for brief writers to advocate for a legal decision that would reflect the knowledge gained from the research (Roesch, Golding, Hans, & Reppucci, 1991, p. 12).

An interesting recent example of an *amicus* brief was submitted to the Supreme Court in the 1999 case of *Kumho Tire Co. Ltd. v. Carmichael*. The case involved eight members of the Carmichael family who were riding in their minivan. When a tire blew out, the minivan crashed, killing one member of the Carmichael family and injuring seven others. In support of their case against Kumho Tires, the Carmichaels had hoped to have the testimony of a "tire failure expert" admitted at trial. The trial judge excluded that testimony. In a unanimous decision, the Supreme Court ruled in favor of the tire company, holding that federal court judges have broad discretion in exercising their responsibilities as gatekeepers for expert scientific testimony.

The *amicus* brief—authored by Neil Vidmar and 17 other social scientists—had nothing to do with minivans or tire failure. It addressed the issue of how juries respond to expert testimony. Tire company attorneys had submitted documents asserting that juries ". . . give great (and sometimes undue) deference to expert testimony," that ". . . an expert frequently ends up confusing jurors and effectively takes the jury's place if they believe him," and that ". . . jurors often abdicate their fact-finding obligation and simply adopt the expert's opinion" (Vidmar et al., 2000, p. 385). The *amicus* brief submitted by the group of social scientists reviewed the evidence on jury decision making and reached a contrary conclusion: "The great weight of evidence challenges the view that jurors abdicate their responsibilities as fact finders when faced with expert evidence or that they are pro-plaintiff, anti-defendant, or anti-business. . . . the data tend to indicate that jurors are often skeptical of plaintiff claims" . . . and that jurors do not . . . "suspend critical reasoning skills whenever experts testify at trial" (p. 388).

Briefs offer some advantages over expert testimony: They are typically written by a team of researchers, they are often reviewed by a professional organization (although this review may be rushed), and the research studies that form the basis for the brief are listed in a reference section. Sometimes scholars must point out that research is inconclusive or that definitive answers are not yet available. Other times, a body of research allows clear conclusions and recommendations.

Finally, it should be emphasized that an *amicus* brief is only one factor influencing a judicial decision. Legal and practical considerations are typically given more weight than social scientific evidence. For example, in a 1976 sex discrimination case, the Supreme Court was candid about its resistance to social scientific evidence:

> Providing broad sociological propositions by statistics is a dubious business, and one that inevitably is in tension with the normative philosophy that underlies the Equal Protection Clause . . . it is unrealistic to expect either members of the judiciary or state officials to be well versed in the rigors of experimental or statistical technique (*Craig v. Boren,* 1976, p. 193).

Broad Dissemination of Research Findings. Some psychologists argue that social scientists' greatest impact may be indirect—that is, if research findings are widely disseminated through the popular media, they eventually come to be regarded as cultural truisms (Ellsworth & Getman, 1987). Judges and lawyers don't live in caves set off from the larger world. They are part of the larger culture and receive most of their information about social science informally, through newspapers, magazines, television, and the Internet. As one researcher put it, ". . . the mention of findings of a particular study or group of studies in *Time* may have a substantially greater impact on the law than publication in a prestigious social science journal will" (Melton, 1987, p. 492). Indeed, studies show that judges are far more likely to read *Psychology Today* than law or social science journals (Melton, 1987). Judges' reading about the legal profession and legal issues tends to be limited to popularized magazines like *American Bar Association Journal.* Even when psychologists actively try to disseminate the results of their research to decision makers in the legal system, the path to reform is neither clear nor well established. While it is essential to make sure that research findings reach legal professionals in a form they can understand and use effectively, the impact of that understanding on the legal system is not likely to be immediate.

Efforts to disseminate research findings should not be limited to lawyers and judges. In a democratic society, it is ultimately the public who must place their trust in the legal system. If scientists want the public to understand psychological knowledge, we must intensify our efforts to educate the public. One scholar puts it this way,

> . . . too little attention has been paid over the last decade or so to elevating the level of popular discourse and understanding. . . . Elites—whether they are legal decision makers or academic change agents—ignore the public at their peril. When they do so, as I believe they have over the

last decade and a half, then the public can be counted upon to reverse whatever changes have been effected in their absence or without their consent. . . . it matters what "the people" think. Indeed, it matters even if they are incorrect in their beliefs (Haney, 1993).

Influencing Legislatures and Public Policy.   Much of the effort to bring psychology to the legal system has focused on the courts. But, of course, legislatures also make law. Sometimes, psychologists try to influence the thinking of legislators on a specific issue. For example, over the past 30 years, hundreds of studies have explored the conditions under which eyewitnesses are likely to provide accurate reports about crimes they have observed (see Chapter 6). Many psychologists serving as expert witnesses have summarized these findings for judges and juries in individual cases. Such testimony is an effective means of educating jurors and judges about factors influencing the accuracy of eyewitness identifications. However, expert testimony comes after an identification (possibly mistaken) has already been made. Research findings would have a greater impact on the legal system if they were taken into account as identifications were being made. In 1998, a team of psychologists translated the voluminous research on eyewitness testimony into a series of recommendations for use by police, lawyers, and judges (Wells et al., 1998). Working with the National Institute of Justice, the psychologists formulated several specific, research-based procedures for gathering eyewitness evidence. Use of these procedures dramatically improves the accuracy of identifications by eyewitnesses (see Chapter 6), and considerable progress has been made in persuading police departments to adopt the guidelines (Kolata & Peterson, 2001).

Finally, psychologists and other social scientists make direct attempts to influence legislatures through the lobbying efforts of their professional associations (e.g., the American Psychological Association and the American Psychological Society). These lobbying efforts are generally aimed at obtaining better funding for initiatives of special interest to psychologists—e.g., graduate training and basic research, promotion of mental health, prevention and treatment of violent behavior, improvement of childhood education and services for children, the development of fair and effective testing practices in school and work settings. In addition to lobbying for particular funding priorities, psychologists frequently testify before the U.S. Congress, and sometimes advise senators and representatives while serving on legislative staffs.

HAS PSYCHOLOGY INFLUENCED THE COURTS?

The results of psychology's attempts to influence the legal system have been mixed. In some cases, it appears that there has been a substantial impact. For example, in an examination of the impact of *amicus* briefs submitted by the APA on the Supreme Court, Charles Tremper (1987) found that the Court's opinion often mirrored the reasoning and language of the briefs. Other times, it appears that judges have made use of social scientific evidence only when it was supportive of the ruling a judge wants to make anyway. And, sometimes, the courts have ignored, dismissed, or misrepresented the findings of social scientific research. In a particularly distressing quote from the case of *Ballew v. Georgia* (1978), Justice Lewis Powell responded to a social science-based argument made by Justice Blackmun:

> I have reservations as to the wisdom—as well as the necessity—of Mr. Justice Blackmun's heavy reliance on numerology derived from statistical studies. Moreover, neither the validity nor the methodology employed by the studies cited was subjected to the traditional testing mechanisms of the adversary process (p. 256).

It can be argued that, for the most part, the presentation of social science evidence raises the consciousness of judges and forces them to take research evidence seriously. An interesting perspective offered by Thomas Grisso and Michael Saks (1991) is that the presentation of research evidence to the courts "keeps judges honest" by forcing them to clearly articulate the basis for their decisions even when they rule in a way that contradicts that evidence. They argue that, "Psychology's input may compel judges to act like judges, stating clearly the fundamental values and normative premises on which their decisions are grounded, rather than hiding behind empirical errors or uncertainties. In this sense, we can regard psychology's recent efforts as successes" (p. 396).

J. Alexander Tanford (1990) suggests that judges are often reluctant to embrace the findings of social scientific research for both intellectual and personal reasons. Intellectually, judges know little about empirical research and are unable (or perhaps unwilling) to make sense of it. Indeed, as noted earlier, legal and social scientific views of the world are often in conflict. But the resistance is not only intellectual. There are also personal reasons behind the reluctance of judges. Judges tend to be self-confident, politically conservative, and protective of their prestige and power. When confronted with empirical research, they are likely to feel that they do not need help from social scientists, they are likely to suspect that social scientists are politically liberal, and they may view social science as undermining their power. Efforts to increase the receptivity of courts may need to target both the intellectual and personal forms of resistance.

IN CONCLUSION

This opening chapter was an attempt to show you the big picture—a sort of aerial view of the field. Each chapter that follows will focus on a specific region of the legal landscape. However, not all areas of the legal system have received equal attention from social scientists. Some areas (e.g., eyewitness identification) have received intense scientific scrutiny, while other areas (e.g., antitrust law, product liability) have been largely ignored. This should not be surprising. Just as film and literature tend to focus on only the most dramatic aspects of the law—for example, the courtroom trial or police investigations—psychologists tend to focus on topics that are psychologically rich and interesting. Our map of psychological processes in the legal system is incomplete. Some territories have been well charted by researchers, some areas have barely been explored, and some territories are still uncharted.

Readings to Supplement This Chapter

Articles

Brigham, J. C. (1999). What is forensic psychology anyway? *Law and Human Behavior, 23,* 273–298.

Darley, J. M. (2001). Citizens' sense of justice and the legal system. *Current Directions in Psychological Science, 10,* 10–13.

Ogloff, J. R. P. (2000). Two steps forward and one step backward: The law and psychology movement(s) in the 20th century. *Law and Human Behavior, 24,* 457–484.

Risinger, D. M., Saks, M. J., Thompson, W. C., & Rosenthal, R. (2002). The Daubert/ Kumho implications of observer effects in forensic science: Hidden problems of expectation and suggestion. *California Law Review, 90,* 1–56.

Vidmar, N., Lempert, R., Diamond, S., Hans, V., Landsman, S., MacCoun, R., Sanders, J., Hosch, H., Kassin, S., Galanter, M., Eisenberg, T., Daniels, S., Greene, E., Martin, J., Penrod, S., Richardson, J., Heuer, L., & Horowitz, I. (2000). Amicus Brief: Kumho Tire v. Carmichael. *Law and Human Behavior, 24,* 387–400.

Books

Faigman, D. L. (1999). *Legal alchemy: The use and misuse of science in the law.* New York: W.H. Freeman and Company.

Wrightsman, L. S. (1999). *Judicial decision-making: Is psychology relevant?* New York: Plenum.

2

Interrogations, Confessions, and Lie Detection

Chapter Outline
● ●

The Power of a Confession
The Evolution of Interrogation Techniques
Inside the Modern Interrogation Room
False Confessions
Videotaped Confessions Presented at Trial
Should Police be Allowed to Lie?

LIE DETECTION USING THE POLYGRAPH

The Development of the Modern Polygraph
The Process of Polygraphing
    The Machine
    Questioning Procedure 1: The Relevant-Irrelevant Test (RIT)
    Questioning Procedure 2: The Control Question Test (CQT)
Weaknesses of Polygraphing Techniques
Research on the Polygraph
Legal Status of the Polygraph
An Alternative Polygraph-Based Technique:
The Guilty Knowledge Test (GKT)
    Weaknesses of the GKT
The Lie Detector as Coercion Device
How Jurors Respond to Polygraph Evidence
The Future of Lie Detection

On an October evening in 1995, Susan Smith served a pizza dinner to her two young sons, Michael, age 3, and Alex, age 14 months. Like any good mother she strapped her boys into their protective car seats before going for a drive after dinner. She drove to John Long Lake, got out of her car, shut the door, and let the car roll downhill into the dark water of the lake. The car slowly sank and both boys drowned.

But that is not the story she told the police. When questioned, Ms. Smith gave a very different account of the night's events. She reported that she had been carjacked by a young African American man who pulled her from her car and drove off with her children. She appeared on national television sobbing and begging the fictitious carjacker to release her two boys. A composite sketch of the carjacker appeared in newspapers and magazines across the country.

For days, Ms. Smith stuck to her story. But, as the investigation proceeded, some police officers began to doubt her story. They began to suspect that she might be responsible for her sons' disappearance. In an effort to get at the truth, the local sheriff told her a lie: He said that on the night of the crime his officers were conducting a drug stakeout near the location where the alleged carjacking occurred. What those officers saw indicated that Smith was not telling the truth. Faced with this bogus information, Susan Smith finally broke down and confessed to killing her sons.

The ability to tell lies is only one of several psychological tools the police have at their disposal during an interrogation of a suspect. These powerful tools sometimes enable police to persuade guilty suspects to confess their crimes. At other times, these same tools lead vulnerable but innocent suspects to confess to crimes they did not commit.

THE POWER OF A CONFESSION

The job of the police is to find people who commit crimes and gather evidence strong enough to secure convictions. Careful analysis of a crime scene might turn up physical evidence, but it is the leads and evidence uncovered through the questioning of witnesses and suspects that often results in a conviction. If the police believe someone may be responsible for a crime—that is, if the person is a suspect—the goal of the questioning is to elicit a confession. A handful of studies have examined how frequently interrogations culminate in confessions. Somewhere between 39% to 48% of suspects make full confessions when interviewed by police, and an additional 13% to 16% of suspects make damaging statements or partial admissions (Moston, Stephenson, & Williamson, 1992; Softley, 1980).

For good reasons, police prefer confessions to other types of evidence. First, confessions save time. Trials can be avoided because suspects who confess usually plead guilty. The slow, tedious process of gathering evidence, analyzing evidence, and finding and questioning witnesses can be compressed or even circumvented. Because suspects who confess often tell interrogators where crucial evidence can be found (e.g., where a gun is hidden), additional evidence becomes less essential. Second, and most important, a confession is the closest prosecutors can get to a guaranteed conviction. Understandably, juries almost always convict defendants who have confessed to committing a crime. In effect, a confession puts the suspect on the fast track to conviction.

Research attests to the power of confessions. In a study of the impact of a confession, Saul Kassin and Katherine Neumann (1997) had mock jurors read summaries of four types of criminal trials: a theft, an assault, a rape, and a murder. Each trial contained weak circumstantial evidence plus either a confession, an eyewitness identification, or character witness testimony. Confessions led to a conviction rate of 73%, significantly higher than the 59% conviction rate produced by the next most powerful type of evidence (eyewitness testimony). In two follow-up studies, confessions were rated as significantly more incriminating than any other form of evidence, and were also rated as the piece of evidence that most powerfully influenced verdicts.

Many legal scholars have also taken note of the surpassing power of confessions. In the case of *Colorado v. Connelly,* Justice William Brennan wrote that, "Triers of fact accord confession such heavy weight in their determinations that the introduction of a confession makes the other aspects of a trial in court superfluous, and the real trial, for all practical purposes, occurs when the confession is obtained" (*Colorado v. Connelly,* 1986, p. 173).

Sometimes defense attorneys argue that a confession was coerced by police and should not be admitted at trial. If the defense argues that a confession was not voluntary, a judge will be asked to rule on the admissibility of the confession. The judge may rule that a confession was coerced and therefore inadmissible. But such rulings are rare. If, instead, the judge rules that the confession is admissible, it is presented to the jury with other evidence. In some states, jurors are instructed to judge for themselves whether the confession was voluntary, and to disregard any statements they believe were coerced. However, even if jurors decide that a confession was coerced, it is still likely to have an impact on their verdict.

In one of a series of studies, Saul Kassin and Holly Sukel (1997) examined whether people are able to discount coerced confessions. Mock jurors read transcripts involving no confession, a low-pressure confession, or a high-pressure confession. In the low-pressure versions of the transcript, the suspect confessed right after police started questioning him. In the high-pressure version, the suspect was said to be in pain, his hands cuffed behind his back, and one of the police officers waved his gun in a menacing manner. Mock jurors had no problem recognizing that the high-pressure confession was coerced, and they reported that they disregarded the involuntary confession. But the verdicts indicated otherwise: In the low-pressure condition, 62% of the jurors found the defendant guilty; in the high-pressure condition, 50% of the jurors voted guilty; and in the no-confession condition, only 19% voted for conviction. Put differently, a coerced confession boosted the rate of conviction by 31%. This finding is consistent with other research on the power of confessions.

For obvious reasons, guilty suspects usually resist confessing their crimes to police. Police try to break down this resistance through the process of interrogation.

THE EVOLUTION OF INTERROGATION TECHNIQUES

Police interrogation techniques have evolved over more than a century. The arsenal of interrogation techniques has been thinned by laws governing police use of force, and refined by police experience. Richard Leo (1992) has noted that these techniques have become increasingly sophisticated, moving from direct physical violence (the traditional third degree), to covert physical torture that leaves no trace (covert third degree), to purely psychological means of coercion (psychological third degree).

Early forms of physical abuse used by police officers were sometimes quite imaginative. Prior to 1930, police frequently used beatings and brutality to extract confessions. Varieties of physical torture included beating suspects with fists, gun handles, rubber hoses, and blackjacks; burning the skin with cigars and cigarettes; using electric shocks; twisting a man's testicles; and dragging or lifting female subjects by their hair (Skolnick & Fyfe, 1993).

In 1931, a government commission headed by Attorney General George Wickersham produced a report that became a major catalyst for change. The *Report on Lawlessness in Law Enforcement* documented widespread abuses by police and focused attention on the treatment of suspects in police custody. The publicity and legislation that followed led to a decline in direct physical abuse of suspects and a shift toward forms of abuse that leave no physical trace. These covert forms of abuse included the "water cure," which involved pushing a suspect's head into a toilet almost to the point of drowning, or pouring water into the nostrils of a suspect lying on his back. An uncooperative suspect could be held upside down out of a high window or in a tall stairwell. Phone books could be stacked on the head of a suspect so that when the books were hit with a nightstick it would produce excruciating pain but leave no bruises. Suspects might also be forced to stand upright for hours at a stretch or have their faces pressed against a dead body in the morgue (Leo, 1992). Physical abuse could be combined with deprivation, isolation, and intimidation. Sleep deprivation is an especially effective means of lowering the resistance of suspects, and withholding food, water, and toilet privileges can also make a suspect more willing to talk. Isolation in a cold, dark cell (called an "incommunicado" cell) was sometimes used to persuade the suspect to confess.

Just as the *Report on Lawlessness in Law Enforcement* provided the impetus for the move away from direct brutality toward covert physical brutality, a series of legal decisions (especially during the 1960s) pushed police away from covert physical abuse toward more psychological forms of coercion. Since 1961, confessions have generally been ruled as inadmissible if judged to be the result of physical force, sleep or food deprivation, prolonged isolation, threats of violence, promises of lenient sentences, or promises of immunity from prosecution (*Culombe v. Connecticut,* 1961; *Reck v. Pate,* 1961; *Townsend v. Swain,* 1963; *Davis v. North Carolina,* 1966).

Since the *Miranda v. Arizona* decision of 1966, all suspects must be informed of their constitutional rights to remain silent and to have an attorney present during questioning. If you've spent any time watching police dramas on television, the process of reading suspects their Miranda rights is probably familiar to you. There are four parts: (1) "You have the right to remain silent. Anything you say can be used against you in a court of law; (2) You have the right to have an attorney present during questioning; (3) If you cannot afford an attorney, you have the right to have an attorney appointed to you prior to questioning; and (4) Do you understand these rights as I have explained them to you?" If the suspect has not been "Mirandized," any subsequent confession can be excluded at trial.

Surprisingly, only about 20% of suspects in police custody choose to exercise their Miranda rights. The remaining 80% waive their rights and submit to a full interrogation without an attorney present (Leo, 1996). It is not entirely clear why so many people waive their Miranda rights, but it is clear that we are accustomed to waiving our rights. We do it often—we sign waivers when we open bank accounts, we sign waivers when we change physicians or dentists, and we routinely click on the "agree" button following the long, legalistic privacy agreements on Web sites. Police detectives who want suspects to answer their questions have developed ways of de-emphasizing Miranda warnings to improve the probability of a waiver. Richard Leo puts it this way, ". . . police routinely deliver the Miranda warnings in a perfunctory tone of voice and ritualistic manner, effectively conveying that these warnings are little more than a bureaucratic triviality" (Leo, 1992, p. 44). Truly innocent suspects may waive their rights because they feel they have nothing to hide, and guilty suspects may not want to appear uncooperative. Finally, most suspects are probably not calm and clear-thinking when they are being taken into custody. Many may not fully realize they are waiving their rights.

The rulings cited above may give the impression that only a fully voluntary confession can be used against a defendant. This is true only if we use an expansive definition of "voluntary." To evaluate "voluntariness," the Supreme Court has held that courts must look at the "totality of circumstances" surrounding the confession (*Culombe v. Connecticut*, 1961). In a series of rulings over the past 30 years, the courts have permitted the police to use a variety of creative lies and theatrical tricks to persuade suspects to confess. Police have been permitted to: assemble a phony lineup and tell the suspect that a fictional eyewitness identified him (*People v. McRae,* 1978), tell a suspect in a murder case that the victim had "pulled through" and identified him as the attacker (*Collins v. Brierly,* 1974), have a police informer pose as a prison inmate and promise his cellmate-suspect that he would provide protection from violent prisoners in exchange for a confession (*Arizona v. Fulminante,* 1991), and hold a suspect in a cell without visitors or phone calls for 16 days (*Davis v. North Carolina,* 1966).

Individual judges must decide whether a particular confession was coerced and whether it should be admitted at trial. While all courts might agree that confessions obtained by physical brutality are illegal, what constitutes psychological coercion is far more ambiguous. And whether or not coercion occurred is seldom clear based on the information provided to judges. If a defendant claims that police threatened or intimidated him, and the police deny his allegations, it is difficult for the judge to take the word of the defendant. Lawyers refer to such disputes as "swearing contests" (police swear there was no coercion and the defendant swears there was). Police usually win such contests.

INSIDE THE MODERN INTERROGATION ROOM

Although it is still possible to find instances of physical mistreatment of suspects in police custody, it is far more common for police to rely on purely psychological techniques for extracting confessions. Early forms of psychological coercion rested on the implied threat of physical violence. For example, suspects might "overhear" feigned screams and cries of pain from an adjacent interrogation room. In the "good cop–bad cop" approach, the "bad" cop (typically the larger, more intimidating member of the pair) implies through words and behavior that he might hurt or beat the suspect. The officer playing the good cop role will begin the interrogation using a sympathetic, understanding approach but eventually express disappointment that the suspect is continuing to lie about his or her involvement in a crime. At that point, the bad cop will enter the room and scold the good cop for wasting time with the lying suspect. The good cop then leaves the room, pretending to be hurt by the bad cop's remarks. Alone with the suspect, the bad cop will insult and berate the suspect and maybe even throw a chair across the room. The good cop will re-enter the room and ask the bad cop to leave. The angry display of the bad cop induces many suspects to take the opportunity to confess to the good cop (Skolnick & Fyfe, 1993).

Officers read manuals on effective interrogation techniques and receive extensive training about how to extract confessions from uncooperative suspects. In the most widely used guide for police officers, Fred Inbau, John Reid, Joseph Buckley, and Brian Jayne (2001) offer detailed advice on every aspect of the interrogation process, including how to set up the interrogation room, what questions to ask, the non-verbal behavior of the interrogator, how to respond to questions or denials by a suspect, and how to handle passive or defiant suspects. Even peripheral details such as furniture receive serious attention:

> The chairs should be of the type normally used as office equipment. Straightback chairs should be used for the suspect as well as the interrogator. Other types of chairs induce slouching or leaning back, and such positions are psychologically undesirable. . . . the seating arrangement should be such that both the interrogator and the suspect are on the same eye level. Most certainly, to be scrupulously avoided are chairs with lowered front legs or other deviations that place the suspect in an "inferior" posture or prevent him from making normal adjustments in sitting (p. 30).

At the heart of the Inbau, Reid, Buckley, and Jayne approach are "the nine steps of interrogation." First, interrogators confront the suspect with a summary of the crime and evidence (real or fabricated) indicating that he or she is involved in the crime. In step 2, the interrogator offers the suspect some possible excuses for the crime. The goal here is to allow the suspect to place moral blame on someone else (e.g., an accomplice or the victim). Next, in step 3, interrogators persistently cut off attempts by the suspect to deny involvement in the crime, returning to the moral excuses offered earlier. Step 4 involves overcoming the explanations offered by the suspect to support their denials. For example, someone accused of an armed robbery might claim that he doesn't own a gun, or that he didn't need money, or that his strong religious upbringing would prevent him from committing such a crime. Step 5 is an effort to hold the attention of the suspect, who may have become withdrawn after an extended and intense period of questioning. At this stage, the officer must appear sincere and understanding. He or she may move closer to the suspect and use touching such as ". . . a pat on the shoulder, or in the case of a female, a gentle holding of the suspect's hand" (p. 80). By the time the process reaches step 6, suspects are usually showing visible signs of "giving up" and the interrogator is directed to maintain eye contact and to move the suspect toward an admission of guilt. Step 7 involves reframing the issue as a choice between having committed the crime for a good reason or having committed a crime for a bad reason. The final two steps involve eliciting a full confession (step 8) and writing out the confession (step 9) so that it can be signed by the suspect.

While this step-by-step procedure captures the general flow of the interrogation, several psychologically powerful aspects of the process deserve attention. In an analysis of interrogation tactics, Saul Kassin and Karlyn McNall (1991) identified two underlying strategies used by police officers: maximization and minimization. Maximization involves emphasizing the strength of the evidence against the suspect and suggesting that the punishment might be especially severe if he fails to admit his crime. Minimization consists of telling the suspect that his crimes were understandable and justifiable. These two strategies avoid direct promises of leniency ("the judge will go easy on you if you just admit you did it") and direct threats of punishment ("if you don't admit you did it, the judge is going to lock you up and throw away the key"). Instead, maximization *implies* a threat of severe punishment and minimization *implies* a promise of leniency.

Maximization often involves impressing suspects with the strength of the evidence against them. Sometimes there is actual evidence (e.g., an eyewitness who places the suspect at the scene) that implicates the suspect. If no real evidence exists, police often lie about the existence of evidence. They may claim to have an eyewitness, or fingerprints, or hair samples, or tire tracks that link the suspect to the crime. Police can be highly creative in their efforts to convince suspects that the evidence against them is overwhelming. Richard Ofshe and Richard Leo (1997) have documented some of these creative efforts. They note that ". . . an investigator is constrained only by the limits of his imagination and his ability to lie convincingly" (p. 1033). For example, one interrogator claimed to have satellite photos showing a defendant leaving the house where the crime had been committed. Another interrogator scraped the trigger finger of a young man accused of shooting two people, then told the young man that by testing the scraping using a "neutron-proton-negligence-intelligence test" he could detect whether the suspect fired the gun. A third interrogator told a murder suspect that the last image seen by the murder victim is forever imprinted on the retina of the victim. That image—which would likely show the suspect—was being developed like a photographic negative. These seemingly scientific claims are very difficult for suspects to refute. A suspect might be sure that he wasn't seen by anyone near the scene of the crime, but he can't be sure he wasn't seen by a satellite floating high above.

Minimization typically involves suggesting alternative, less morally repugnant, motives for committing a crime. For example, someone sus-pected of committing an armed robbery might be asked questions that suggest honorable explanations of the crime, "Did you plan this, or did it just happen on the spur of the moment?" or "Was this your own idea or did someone talk you into it?" or "I'm sure this money was for your fam-ily, for some bills at home. It was for your family's sake wasn't it?" (Inbau et al., 2001, p.167). Even with repugnant crimes such as rape and child molestation, the interrogator is taught to sympathize with the suspect, for example, by suggesting that anyone, under similar circumstances, might have acted the same way the criminal did. For sex crimes, Inbau and his associates urge interrogators to make comments such as:

> We humans are accustomed to thinking of ourselves as far removed from animals, but we're only kidding ourselves. In matters of sex, we're very close to most animals, so don't think you're the only human being—or that you're one of very few—who ever did anything like this. There are plenty others, and these things happen every day (p. 99).
>
> Joe, this girl was having a lot of fun for herself by letting you kiss her and feel her breast. For her, that would have been sufficient. But men aren't built the same way. There's a limit to the teasing and excitement they can take; then something's got to give. A female ought to realize this, and if she's not willing to go all the way, she ought to stop way short of what this gal did to you (p. 109).

Such justifications make the crimes seem almost mundane (e.g., "these things happen everyday") and deflect blame from the criminal to others (e.g., "what she did to you"). The implication is that the crimi-nal's actions were reasonable and the consequences may not be that serious. Suspects are offered a limited choice, ". . . a choice between an inexcusable or repulsive motivation for committing the crime and one that is attributable to error or the frailty of human nature" (p. 165).

The interrogation is a tightly controlled, psychologically powerful situation. The suspect is socially isolated in a barren, unfamiliar setting where police control everything from the lighting and layout of the room to the content and pacing of the conversation. Although the interrogator may seem reasonable or even sympathetic, suspects are subjected to concentrated, unrelenting pressure. If police believe a suspect is guilty, everything about their demeanor conveys a simple message: We know you did it, it is futile to deny your guilt, and any jury that sees the evidence will vote to convict you. To lower the resistance of the suspect, police offer face-saving excuses: Perhaps the suspect was under the influence of drugs, perhaps the victim provoked him, maybe he "blacked out" during the crime. Maybe he even suffers from a sort of multiple personality disorder and his crime was committed by a submerged personality. There may even be appeals to the suspect's sense of honor, suggesting that a full confession is the moral or manly thing to do.

These interrogation tactics are likely to cause a guilty suspect "to recognize that the game is over and that he is caught," and to cause an innocent suspect "to perceive his situation as frustrating, unreal, desperate, and tending toward hopeless" (Ofshe & Leo, 1997, p. 1010). This unreal, hopeless situation leads some innocent suspects to confess.

FALSE CONFESSIONS
• •

It is extremely difficult for most of us to imagine confessing to a crime we did not commit. To understand how false confessions can happen, it is instructive to look at the case of Thomas Sawyer.

Thomas Sawyer was a golf course groundskeeper whose neighbor was murdered by strangulation. Sawyer suffered from severe social anxiety, so when police questioned him he blushed, fidgeted, avoided eye contact, and began to sweat profusely. This behavior made police suspicious. They had learned that Mr. Sawyer was an avid fan of TV police shows and they invited him to come to the police station to "assist" with the investigation. He was happy to help. The investigating officers asked Sawyer to help them imagine different scenarios of how the murder might have occurred. Only then did the interrogators accuse him of being the murderer. At first, Sawyer vigorously denied having committed the crime. But, over the course of a 16-hour interrogation he came to believe that he was the killer.

To prove his innocence, Sawyer submitted to a polygraph examination (i.e., a lie detector test) and provided hair and fingerprint samples to the police. It shook his confidence badly when the police lied to him and told him that he had flunked the polygraph test. Still, he couldn't remember raping and killing the woman next door. During the time that Sawyer was "helping" the police, he had confided that he was an alcoholic. Knowing this, police suggested that he might have experienced an alcoholic "blackout" during the murder. This would account for his memory loss. A final lie from the interrogators led to a full confession—his hair sample matched hairs found on the victim's body. Confronted with this information, Sawyer became reluctantly convinced of his own guilt: "I guess all the evidence is in," he said, "I guess I must have done it." During the final phase of the 16-hour interrogation, police shaped and reshaped Sawyer's memory of the murder by providing him with details and urging Sawyer to incorporate those details in his account of the murder (Ofshe, 1989).

We do not know—and it may be impossible to know—how many confessions are truly false. Many defendants are convicted solely on the basis of their confession. Some claim during and after trial that their confessions were actually false—the result of police trickery, intimidation, or abuse. Sometimes these confessions are later revealed as false when physical evidence proves the innocence of the confessor or identifies the actual perpetrator of the crime. But far more often, the conviction stands. It is usually impossible to know if a person proclaiming his innocence from a prison cell is truly innocent. Because of the difficulty of a precise accounting, estimates of false confessions vary wildly from as few as 30 to as many as 600 per year (Kassin, 1997).

What we do know is that most documented false confessions are the result of vulnerable people being subjected to powerful situational forces. Suspects can be vulnerable in a variety of ways. They may be young, inexperienced, naive, easily dominated, under the influence of drugs, submissive to authority, of low intelligence, mentally ill, sleep deprived, or simply terrified. Gisli Gudjonsson, a psychological researcher who used to be a police officer, has developed a questionnaire to assess interrogation suggestibility and has shown that some people known to have falsely confessed score significantly higher on suggestibility than people who do not falsely confess (Gudjonsson, 1992). Of course, police don't screen suspects for vulnerability and then treat highly suggestive suspects more gently. As illustrated in the case of Thomas Sawyer, if someone is suspected of committing a crime, his or her vulnerabilities are sought out and fully exploited.

VIDEOTAPED CONFESSIONS PRESENTED AT TRIAL

One way to help jurors decide how much coercion occurred during questioning of a defendant is to let the jurors see a videotape of the interrogation. According to a national survey of police practices, roughly a third of large police departments videotape *some* interrogations (Kassin, 1997). The practice is more common in serious cases, for example, those involving assault, rape, or murder. The videotaping of confessions has many potential benefits—instead of hearing testimony about what happened in the interrogation room, judges and jurors can see for themselves what happened. Subtleties of what was said as well as *how* it was said (gestures, tone of voice, facial expressions) can be captured on camera. If interrogators were abusive or threatening or intimidating, it should be apparent in the videotape. Aside from providing a more complete record of the interrogation and confession, videotaping might have a beneficial deterrent effect—interrogators who are being videotaped might be more careful to avoid questionable behavior or outright misconduct. Yet, although the use of video cameras may eventually provide full and accurate video records of confessions, there are currently two problems with videotaping: technical and psychological.

Technical problems concern sound quality, picture quality, lighting, and the limited area that can be captured by the lens of a single video camera. If sound and pictures are of poor quality, subtleties of language and gestures won't be apparent to the judges or jurors who eventually view the videotape. And, if interrogators move around the room, they won't be visible at all times. These technical problems may have technical solutions. Clear lighting combined with the use of multiple cameras and microphones mounted at several key locations in the interrogation room would greatly improve the quality of the audiovisual record. Still, even a well-designed interrogation room outfitted with the latest equipment can be circumvented by determined police officers. Cameras may simply be turned off at key points or started only midway into the interrogation process. Even more important, some questioning of suspects happens outside the interrogation room. Suspects can be questioned in their homes, on the streets, in police cars, and at other locations outside the police station. The portion of the questioning captured on camera may be only a segment—and maybe not the crucial segment—of the interrogation process.

Psychological problems concern the impact of videotaped confessions on the people who view them. Jurors may interpret videotaped confessions differently depending on how they are presented at trial. Typically a relatively brief (e.g., half-hour) segment of the video is shown at trial. This brief "recap" may misrepresent what actually happened during a long (often multi-hour) interrogation. The video recap shown to jurors typically contains the clearest admission of guilt the police were able to obtain. Any admission is likely to weigh heavily in the decision making of jurors or judges. But the video recap, taken out of context, is likely to be especially influential. The recap may exclude hours of pressure or intimidation that occurred prior to the admission. By the time a partial admission or full confession is made, the suspect is likely to look exhausted and defeated. The defendant's exhaustion and lack of expressiveness may convey to jurors the impression that the defendant is a cold, remorseless criminal (Lassiter, Slaw, Briggs, & Scanlan, 1992; Lassiter, 2002).

A specific potential bias concerns who the camera is pointed at, that is, the camera's point-of-view. If the camera is aimed at the suspect, viewers of the video can only attend to the suspect. They cannot focus their attention on the interrogators. Psychological research has shown that people who are more visually salient in a videotape are viewed as more influential (Fiske & Taylor, 1991). In one experiment, people viewed a confession that had been videotaped from three camera angles: One showed only the suspect, another showed only the interrogator, and a third showed both the detective and the suspect. Researchers found that those who saw the "suspect only" videotape rated the confession as much less coerced than those who viewed the other versions (Lassiter & Irvine, 1986). Perceptually salient behavior (like a suspect looking straight into the camera and confessing) is viewed as especially revealing of a person's real feelings and less a result of situational forces (e.g., fatigue or intimidation by police officers).

SHOULD POLICE BE ALLOWED TO LIE?

In the Susan Smith case described at the beginning of this chapter, a lie told by an interrogator led to a truthful confession by a murderer. But even if lying sometimes works, should it be permitted? Would Smith have eventually confessed even if the interrogators did not mislead her? Several lies told to Thomas Sawyer led to a false confession. Would there be fewer false confessions if police weren't able to tell lies in the interrogation room? And would banning the use of lies and trickery result in large numbers of guilty criminals avoiding conviction?

England and Wales restrict police behavior during interrogations far more than does the United States. In 1986, enactment of the *Police and Criminal Evidence Act* (PACE) made it illegal to trick suspects or lie about evidence as a means of inducing suspects to confess. All interviews with suspects conducted at police stations must be audiotaped so that they can be evaluated by lawyers (called "solicitors" in England), judges, and jurors. Bullying, threats, and intimidation are not permitted, and police are required to call in an appropriate adult to witness the interview of any suspect who is deemed "vulnerable" (usually because of youth or low intelligence).

These reforms were set in motion by a few sensational cases involving false confessions. One such case came to be known as the "Guildford Four." In the fall of 1974, members of the Irish Republican Army exploded bombs in two pubs in the city of Guildford. Five people were killed and 57 were injured. Just over a month later, the police interviewed an Irishman named Paul Hill. He signed a written confession and implicated his friend Gerry Conlon. Mr. Conlon confessed and implicated several other people, including two (Carole Richardson and Paddy Armstrong) who made partial admissions while in police custody. Despite the lack of any physical evidence or any eyewitness linking these four defendants to the bombings, all four were convicted and sentenced to life imprisonment. All four ended up being released from prison after serving 15 years. The long investigation that led to the eventual release of the Guildford Four found that fear of the police, intimidation by interrogators, lies told by the police, isolation of the suspects during interrogations, and police fabrication of key evidence caused the four false confessions.

It is not yet clear whether the reforms established by the PACE Act have helped or hurt the ability of the police to elicit *true* confessions. One study found that although pressure tactics, intimidation, and trickery have declined substantially, the number of admissions of guilt during police interviews is not significantly lower than it was before the PACE reforms (Irving & McKenzie, 1989). However, another study found that prohibited tactics such as the use of threats, lies, and promises have merely been moved outside the interrogation room. That is, before the audiotaped interview begins, police are likely to have "off the record" conversations outside the police station (McConville, 1992). These conversations may incorporate many of the old-style pressure tactics previously used by police.

Back in the United States, courts have given the police permission to lie during interrogations. There is little doubt that lying is a potent weapon in the arsenal of police interrogators. However, looking beyond the interrogation room, some observers worry that lying by police may undermine public confidence in the police and reduce the willingness of citizens to cooperate with law enforcement (Slobogin, 1997). The approval of lying during interrogations may even remove inhibitions against lying in other important settings such as testifying in court. If it is justifiable to lie to a suspect for the purpose of securing a confession, it may not be that large a step to believe that it is justifiable to lie during courtroom testimony for the purpose of securing a conviction.

Both the police and the public want to prevent false confessions. But how might the number of false confessions be reduced? Although no single reform is likely to prevent all false confessions, several potentially effective reforms follow directly from the research summarized above. We could require that all interrogations be videotaped. Two states—Alaska and Minnesota—have already taken the step of requiring that all interrogations be audiotaped (*Stephan v. State,* 1985; *State v. Scales,* 1994). In cases where there is reason to believe a confession might be false, we could carefully compare the known facts of the crime with information provided by the suspect to see if there are inconsistencies (this can only be done if the interrogation is recorded). Suspects who may have confessed falsely could be tested for suggestibility (e.g., using the scale developed by Gudjonsson). We could prohibit lying or trickery by police interrogators. Finally, at trial, it may be advisable to allow expert psychological testimony on interrogations so that jurors can better understand the pressures brought to bear on criminal suspects.

Of course, police and prosecutors are likely to resist such reforms based on their belief that changing current practices will lead to fewer true confessions and fewer convictions of guilty criminals.

LIE DETECTION USING THE POLYGRAPH

During the interrogation process, part of an officer's job is to act as a sort of human lie detector—to scrutinize the suspect's nonverbal behavior, to look for inconsistencies in the suspect's story, and to decide whether the suspect is telling the truth. Sometimes, crime investigators make use of a mechanical lie detector, more formally known as a polygraph.

Long before there were polygraph machines, there were many primitive attempts to detect lying by criminal suspects. In one early form of "trial by ordeal," a suspect who denied committing a crime was required to plunge his arm into a pot of boiling water and pull out a stone. The arm was then bandaged. If, after three days, the burns were not infected, the person was judged to be telling the truth (Hans & Vidmar, 1986). The assumption was that God would intervene on the side of the innocent person and reveal the truth by preventing infection. Although investigators no longer rely on divine intervention to reveal liars, they sometimes put their faith in the polygraph.

The hope for an infallible device that can reveal if someone is lying is understandable. Such a device could revolutionize crime investigation, plea bargaining, and trials. Police could simply hook suspects up to a lie detector machine and ask questions like, "Did you kill him?" or "Did you rape her?" or "Did you rob the convenience store?" Because the job of jurors in most trials is to decide if a defendant committed the crime in question, most trials might be streamlined or even eliminated. The machine could do the difficult job of deciding who is telling the truth. Of course, the hope for such a magical device is far from being realized, and will probably never be realized.

THE DEVELOPMENT OF THE MODERN POLYGRAPH

The polygraph was invented and developed in the United States and is used only rarely in other countries, although it has been used in Israel, Japan, South Korea, and Turkey. It is estimated that about 40,000 polygraph tests are given each year in the United States (Barland, 1988).

The person generally credited with developing the first modern lie detector was William M. Marston, a flamboyant lawyer and psychologist who believed that measurable changes in blood pressure could reveal whether or not someone was lying. The optimistic Dr. Marston declared that his discovery of physiological reactions correlated with lying signaled ". . . the end of man's long, futile striving for a means of distinguishing truth-telling from deception" (1938, p. 45). In his spare time, Marston created the comic book character Wonder Woman. Like other super heroes, Wonder Woman wore a cape and fought crime. She also carried a magic lasso that served as a lie detector—any criminal cinched up in her lasso was compelled to tell the truth.

Although Marston considered himself a scientist, he was not above making wild claims about his device or using it for financial gain. A 1938 magazine ad for Gillette razor blades bears the heading, "New Facts About Shaving Revealed by Lie Detector" and displays a blood pressure chart of a man while using a Gillette razor on one side of his face and an unnamed "inferior" razor on the other side. The text of the ad tells of an experiment where hundreds of men are "Strapped to Lie Detectors, the same scientific instruments used by G-men and police officers throughout the country." The men shaved ". . . under the piercing eye of Dr. William Moulton Marston, eminent psychologist and originator of the famous Lie Detector test." The reader is informed that the Lie Detector "tells all," ". . . reveals the innermost thoughts and feelings," and "lays bare the emotions." The findings of the shaving study were apparently quite dramatic: the superiority of the Gillette blade was "revealed by the involuntary emotions of the shaver himself" ("New facts," 1938, p. 27).

The hyperbolic claims of the 1938 shaving ad illustrate a continuing problem that plagues the use of the lie detector. There is still a split between practitioners who have great faith in the polygraph and scientists who are interested in a dispassionate evaluation of its validity. Practitioners tend to have confidence in the validity of the polygraph and in their own ability to tell when someone is lying (Ben-Shakhar, Bar-Hillel, & Kremnitzer, 2002). A lack of clear feedback allows examiners to preserve their confidence. If a suspect they have labeled as "deceptive" later confesses, or is found guilty, their suspicions are confirmed. They were right. But if a suspect they have labeled as "deceptive" fails to confess or is acquitted, a polygrapher can still conclude that the suspect merely beat the rap.

During the 1960s, 1970s, and much of the 1980s, use of the polygraph was a lucrative business. Independent polygraph contractors offered employers a quick and seemingly scientific method for deciding who to hire and who to fire. People who were being considered for a job could be asked to submit to a lie detector test before they were hired. Once the job candidate was strapped into the lie detector, they might be asked about whether they had ever used illegal drugs, whether they had ever lied to a former boss, whether they had told the truth on every question on the job application, or whether they had stolen money or office supplies from a previous employer. People "caught" lying were unlikely to receive a job offer. Preemployment screening using the polygraph was often supplemented by post-employment polygraph testing. When employers were losing money because of employee pilfering, a polygrapher could be called in to test the suspected workers and find the thief. To meet the surging demand for lie detectors, training schools were established across the United States. Most offered short programs (a few weeks to a few months) that granted students certification in polygraphing. During this period, more than two million people per year submitted to polygraph testing (Lykken, 1998). Entrepreneurs had created a multimillion dollar industry.

The use of the lie detector as a method of deciding who gets a job and who keeps a job was nearly abolished by the federal Polygraph Protection Act of 1988. That Act prohibited *most private* employers from using polygraphs for the purpose of making decisions about who gets or keeps a job. However, public employers are exempt. Police departments, the Central Intelligence Agency (CIA), the Federal Bureau of Investigation (FBI), the National Security Administration (NSA), the Drug Enforcement Administration (DEA), and the Secret Service still routinely use lie detectors for employment screening. There are also exemptions for some commercial businesses. For example, businesses that supply security personnel to facilities that may affect public safety (e.g., nuclear power plants or public water supplies) are usually exempt.

THE PROCESS OF POLYGRAPHING

The Machine. Lie detection devices monitor physiological changes. People hooked up to a lie detector usually have a blood pressure cuff attached to the bicep, a pneumatic tube stretched across the chest, and metal electrodes on the fingers of one hand. The machine tracks changes in physiological reactions with multiple pens that write on a moving strip of graph paper. (These changes can also be displayed on a computer screen.) The Greek word poly means "many" and the Greek word "grapho" means write. The polygraph writes out many physiological responses to questions asked by an examiner. The theory of the polygraph test is simple: The act of lying will create physiological arousal. Specifically, the theory holds that when people lie their hearts beat faster, their breathing quickens, their blood pressure rises, and their skin moisture increases.

Questioning Procedure 1: The Relevant-Irrelevant Test (RIT).

John A. Larson of the Berkeley, California, Police Department developed the first systematic questioning procedure for use with the polygraph machine. The Relevant-Irrelevant Test (RIT) made use of three types of questions: (1) nonarousing questions that are not relevant to the behavior being investigated (e.g., "What day of the week is it?" or "What city are we in?"), (2) arousing questions that are not relevant to the behavior being investigated (e.g., "Have you ever watched a sexually explicit movie?" or "Have you ever lied to a member of your family?"), and (3) relevant questions that are especially arousing for the person who actually committed the crime ("Did you kill Joe Doe?" or "Did you steal the money?"). The three types of questions are asked in a predetermined sequence: a nonarousing irrelevant question, then a relevant question, then an arousing irrelevant question. What is of interest to the examiner is the *difference* in the strength of the physiological responses when the suspect answers each type of question. If a guilty suspect denies involvement in the crime, his reactions to the relevant questions should be stronger than reactions to the arousing irrelevant questions. Such a response pattern will be classified as deceptive. Only a few research studies have evaluated the RIT. Those studies show a disturbingly high rate of a particular type of error: false positives. That is, innocent people are very likely to be misclassified as guilty (an average false positive rate of 71%) (Horowitz, Kircher, Honts, & Raskin, 1997).

Questioning Procedure 2: The Control Question Test (CQT).

A second questioning technique—the control question test (CQT)—was designed to correct some of the problems associated with the older RIT. Variations of CQT are by far the most frequently used techniques for polygraphing (Iacono & Patrick, 1999). Like the RIT, the CQT relies on the measurement of *relative arousal*. That is, it is assumed that physiological reactions while lying will be elevated as compared to physiological reactions while telling the truth. The name CQT highlights the importance of the "control question." These questions involve behaviors that are uncomfortable for suspects but not directly related to the crime under investigation. For example, a suspect might be asked, "During the first 20 years of your life, did you ever take something that did not belong to you?" or "Before age 21, did you ever do something dishonest or illegal?" or "Have you ever lied to get out of trouble or to cause a problem for someone else?" These questions are deliberately broad so that anyone who answers "no" is assumed to be lying. Indeed, control questions are sometimes referred to as "known lie" questions. Reactions to control questions are compared to reactions to "relevant" questions about the specific crime being investigated. The basic proposition of the CQT is that innocent suspects will react more strongly to the control questions, and that guilty suspects will respond more strongly to the relevant questions about the crime. Examiners who use the CQT want suspects to answer "no" to the control questions, but they also want the examinee to feel uncomfortable about their denials. Because of the importance of control questions, the CQT relies on the skill and stage-managing ability of the examiner. The examiner must persuade the suspect that the polygraph can detect lies so that the suspect will be nervous about lying.

Scoring of the polygraph charts is done numerically. The scale runs from –3 to +3. No difference between a particular control question and the relevant question with which it is paired is coded as "0." Noticeable differences are coded as "1," strong differences are coded as "2," and dramatic differences are coded as "3." If reactions to a relevant question are stronger than reactions to a control question, a negative number is assigned. The opposite pattern leads to a positive number. Negative scores are thought to indicate deception while more positive scores indicate truthfulness. If three relevant questions are compared to three control questions, a total score of –6 or lower would lead the polygrapher to conclude that the suspect was deceptive (Lykken, 1998).

Although the CQT is an improvement over the older RIT, it places a heavy burden on the skills of examiners. Examiners must be able to formulate a delicately calibrated series of control questions that elicit stronger reactions than relevant questions if the suspect is innocent, but weaker reactions than relevant questions if the suspect is guilty. An alternative form of the CQT called the Positive Control Test (PCT) uses the relevant question as its own control. That is, the relevant question (e.g., in a rape case "Did you use physical force to make her have sex with you?") is asked twice. The alleged rapist is instructed to tell the truth once and to tell a lie once. This allows for a direct comparison of responses to the same question (Iacono & Patrick, 1999).

WEAKNESSES OF POLYGRAPHING TECHNIQUES

There are several general problems with any approach to lie detection using the polygraph. David Lykken—a leading polygraph researcher and leading critic of traditional lie detection—points out several problems relating to the person being tested. First, some people are so emotionally nonreactive (e.g., psychopathic or fearless or controlled) that lying produces little physiological response. Second, there is no guarantee that innocent people won't react strongly to questions about whether they committed a crime. Indeed, a jaded criminal may be less likely to react to lying than an innocent person being accused of a terrible crime. Third, if the person being tested does not have faith in the validity of the polygraph, he or she will not respond in the way examiners suppose. Guilty people who have no faith may not be concerned about lying because they have no fear of detection. Innocent people who have no faith may be especially anxious while answering relevant questions because they fear being accused of a crime they didn't commit (Iacono & Patrick, 1999).

The polygrapher must typically convince the suspect that the tube and electrodes recording his reactions are flawless detectors of deception. To pull this off, examiners sometimes resort to magic show theatrics. One famous technique is to use a deck of cards, with 52 identical cards (e.g., the queen of hearts). The deck is fanned out face down on a table and the suspect picks a card, looks at it, and places it in his or her pocket. All the other cards are gathered up and set aside. Then, the suspect is told to answer "no" to a series of questions: Is it a red card? Is it a face card? Is it the king of hearts? Is it the queen of hearts? The examiner pretends to inspect the polygraph charts and then declares that the polygraph has revealed that the card picked by the suspect was the queen of hearts. There are other less contrived ways of demonstrating the sensitivity of the lie detector. Polygraphers generally have considerable background information at their disposal. Factual information about an employee or job applicant can sometimes be gleaned from personnel files. Information about a suspect in a criminal investigation can be pulled from police case files. The person being examined can be asked to lie in response to a series of direct questions about his or her background (Were you born in Madison, Wisconsin? Have you ever been convicted of burglary? Are you 25 years old?). The examiner will then tell the suspect exactly which answers were lies. This bogus demonstration is often enough to convince the examinee that the machine is virtually infallible.

Another problem is lack of standardization. The content of questions, the number of questions, the demeanor of the examiner, and the scoring all vary from one polygraph test to another. Relevant questions must vary depending on the nature of the crime being investigated, and even control questions can vary. It is extremely difficult to standardize the behavior of all polygraphers. Some examiners induce more anxiety than others, and many let their suspicions about a suspect's guilt influence their interpretation of the polygraph charts. Moreover, there is considerable subjectivity in the scoring. There is no precise point at which the difference between control responses and relevant responses cross over from "noticeable" to "strong" or from "strong" to "dramatic." The polygrapher must make a judgment call. Although computer technology can now measure extremely small differences in arousal, and make scoring more precise, the final judgment is a dichotomous one: Was the suspect lying or telling the truth?

Suspects may attempt to fool the polygraph through a variety of "self-stimulation" strategies. Lie detection depends on the measurement of relative arousal—a comparison between the amount of arousal following relevant questions and the amount of arousal following irrelevant or control questions. There are two ways to reduce the discrepancy between the two levels of arousal—either elevate arousal during control questions, or suppress arousal during relevant questions. In one experiment, researchers trained guilty subjects who committed a minor theft to augment their physiological responses to control questions by either biting their tongues, or pressing their toes to the floor. These techniques for fooling the polygraph—called "countermeasures"—reduced the detection of guilty suspects by 50%. Moreover, examiners were not able to tell that the suspects were manipulating their own arousal (Honts, Raskin, & Kircher, 1994). Other countermeasures, such as taking tranquilizers to suppress arousal, or using mental countermeasures (e.g., counting backward from 200 by increments of seven) are especially unlikely to be detected by examiners but appear to be somewhat less effective in fooling the polygraph (Gudjonsson, 1988).

A final criticism of polygraph techniques is ethical rather than scientific: The questioning techniques invade the privacy of anyone being examined. To create anxiety and establish baseline measures of physiological arousal, polygraph examiners must ask personal questions (e.g., questions about the suspect's past behavior, use of drugs, and sexual preferences). Some people reject use of the polygraph on purely ethical grounds.

RESEARCH ON THE POLYGRAPH

It is not unusual for proponents of the polygraph to claim impressively high accuracy rates ranging from 90% to 99%. But these rates may not be as impressive as they first seem. Suppose a local branch of a bank employs 100 people. Over the course of a few months, two of those employees, working together, steal several thousand dollars from the bank. Every employee is given a polygraph to find out who stole the money. Results indicate that two employees (Sandy and Sam) are the thieves. But the real thieves are actually Mandy and Max. The results of the polygraph have cleared two guilty people and caused two innocent people to be falsely accused. But even though the results of the polygraph were terribly wrong, the polygrapher can still claim an accuracy rate of 96%. All but four people were correctly classified.

A second general point concerns chance accuracy of judgments based on the polygraph or other techniques. Let's say we have 100 suspects: Half are truly innocent, half are truly guilty, but all deny having committed the crime. One examiner uses a polygraph to try to detect which suspects are guilty. A second examiner simply flips a coin for every suspect using the rule that "heads" means innocent, and "tails" means guilty. By chance alone, the coin-flipping examiner will be right 50% of the time. Fifty suspects will be correctly classified. This means that to demonstrate its utility, the polygraph must achieve a significantly higher rate of accuracy than the 50% rate we could get by chance alone.

Empirical studies attempting to test the accuracy of the polygraph fall into two categories: laboratory studies and field studies. Laboratory studies make use of "mock crimes." People participating in such studies are randomly assigned to be either guilty suspects or innocent suspects. Guilty suspects are instructed to commit a prearranged crime, for example, stealing an object from a store or office. All suspects are told to deny any involvement in the crime. Both innocent suspects and guilty suspects then submit to a polygraph test. The great advantage of laboratory studies is that because we know for certain who is telling the truth and who is lying, we know for certain if polygraphers were right or wrong in their judgments. Field studies use situations where people are actual suspects in real crimes. Many were conducted during the 1980s when employees were frequently being tested in cases of suspected theft. Other field studies have used polygraphs administered during police investigations of serious felonies (e.g., rape, murder). The great advantage of field studies is realism. The consequences of failing the test are very serious—suspects might lose a job or be charged with a serious crime. Because the stakes are so high, the emotional arousal measured by the polygraph is likely to be quite high. Unfortunately, in field studies, we can't be certain who is really lying: Sometimes innocent suspects are misclassified as guilty, and sometimes guilty suspects are misclassified as innocent by polygraphers. No matter what we use as the criterion of accuracy—confessions, convictions, or judgments by panels of experts—field studies have some error built into their judgments of accuracy.

During the past 15 years, there have been several major reviews of research on the accuracy of polygraph testing. These reviews include a total of 63 studies (44 laboratory studies and 19 field studies) using the control question technique (Ekman, 1985; Honts, 1995; Kircher, Horowitz, & Raskin, 1988; Ben-Shakhar & Furedy, 1990). Reviewers included only the best studies—those that used careful, valid research designs. Here is a breakdown of the overall accuracy rates averaging across all 63 studies:

Guilty suspects *correctly* classified as guilty	78.5% (true positives)
Innocent suspects *correctly* classified as innocent	69.7% (true negatives)
Guilty suspects *incorrectly* classified as innocent	9.7% (false negatives)
Innocent suspects *incorrectly* classified as guilty	15.5% (false positives)
Guilty suspects that cannot be classified	11.8% (inconclusive)
Innocent suspects that cannot be classified	14.8% (inconclusive)

Under carefully controlled conditions, polygraphers appear to be able to catch about 78% of the guilty suspects and are able to exonerate nearly 70% of innocent suspects. They fail to catch about 21% of guilty suspects, and they falsely accuse nearly 16% of innocent suspects. These rates of accuracy are clearly better than chance, but are they strong enough to have practical utility for the legal system? Probably not. First, most polygraph tests given in the course of actual criminal investigations are not done under carefully controlled conditions. For example, there is usually no blind review of polygraph charts (i.e., someone other than the polygrapher, who was not present during the polygraph exam, does not interpret the charts). Second, although we can point to an overall accuracy rate of 70% for identifying guilty suspects, we can't say whether a particular suspect who flunks a polygraph test belongs in the true positive category or the false positive category. If that suspect becomes a defendant in a criminal trial, is it fair to let a jury hear that he or she flunked the test? Again, probably not. Our legal system is based, in part, on the idea that it is better to let 10 guilty people go free than to convict one innocent person.

LEGAL STATUS OF THE POLYGRAPH

Although most Americans seem to believe that the results of polygraph tests are strictly inadmissible as evidence in court, the truth is more complicated. Twenty-three states have banned the use of polygraph evidence in court, but many states allow for the use of polygraph evidence under special circumstances. Only one state—New Mexico—routinely permits the results of polygraph tests to be presented at trial (*State v. Dorsey*, 1975). The 1993 U.S. Supreme Court Decision in *Daubert v. Merrell Dow Pharmaceuticals* (described in Chapter 1) did not specifically address the admissibility of polygraph evidence, but it did rule that the admissibility of scientific evidence could be determined on a case-by-case basis. Evidentiary hearings can now be held to decide whether the results of lie detector tests meet standards of scientific validity. In the 1998 case of *United States v. Scheffer*, Justice Clarence Thomas clearly expressed the legal system's two major concerns about polygraphing. First, he noted the lack of consensus about scientific validity: ". . . the scientific community remains extremely polarized about the reliability of polygraph evidence" (p. 1264). Second, he expressed the concern that allowing lie detector evidence into the courtroom would usurp the role of the jury: "A fundamental premise of our criminal trial system is that the jury is the lie detector" (p. 1266).

In 1995, just two years after the *Daubert* decision, polygraph evidence was admitted in a case involving an insurance claim (*Ulmer v. State Farm*). When their house burned to the ground, Robert Savoie and Jessie Ulmer submitted a claim to State Farm insurance company. State Farm initially denied the claim, alleging that the fire had been intentionally set by the homeowners (or by someone they hired) for the purpose of collecting insurance money. As part of his investigation into the alleged arson, the state fire marshal asked Robert and Jessie to take polygraph tests. They agreed. Results indicated that they did not set the fire and did not hire anyone else to do it. State Farm was not convinced, and sought to suppress the polygraph evidence, arguing that it was not scientifically reliable. However, the judge decided to allow the polygraph evidence at trial. The basis for his decision was that polygraphs had been the subject of numerous scientific studies published in peer-reviewed journals, that many scientists believe the results are more accurate than chance, and that the polygraph evidence was essential to Robert and Jessie's claim of innocence.

Results of a lie detector test may be especially crucial *before* trial: They may be used to decide whether a case is pursued, or used to help police extract a confession. In cases where physical evidence is inconclusive or too weak to justify a trial, the decision about whether to devote resources to a case or charge a suspect with a crime may hinge on a polygraph test. If prosecutors have a weak case, they have little to lose if the suspect passes, and they gain considerable leverage if the suspect fails. For example, in a case of date rape—where a man says that sexual intercourse following a date was consensual and a woman says it was the result of physical force—police may ask one or both parties to submit to a lie detector before any further investigation is pursued or abandoned. In a case of sexual harassment in the workplace, where the accounts of an alleged victim and alleged harasser diverge wildly, attorneys for both parties may suggest lie detector tests, with each side stipulating in advance that the results will be admissible in court. In such instances, the polygraph is being used (or misused) to establish the credibility of a potential witness.

AN ALTERNATIVE POLYGRAPH-BASED TECHNIQUE: THE GUILTY KNOWLEDGE TEST (GKT)

A final technique that makes use of polygraph equipment does not attempt to detect lies. Instead, the Guilty Knowledge Test (GKT) is intended to detect whether or not someone knows things only a criminal would know. The logic is that a guilty person will recognize scenes and events from the crime that an innocent person will not recognize. This recognition will be reflected in elevated physiological arousal. For example, two suspects in a murder case could be shown 10 photographs, one of which is a photograph of the murder victim. Only the actual killer should react strongly to the photo of the victim. This fundamentally different approach to identifying guilty suspects was developed by David Lykken.

Lykken describes how a GKT might have been created to detect whether O. J. Simpson killed his ex-wife. In the most sensational trial of the past few decades, O. J. Simpson was tried for the murders of his former wife Nicole Brown and her friend Ronald Goldman. On a June night in 1994, Nicole Brown was brutally murdered just inside the front gate of her Brentwood condominium. Her throat was slashed. The wound was so deep that her head was nearly severed from her body. Mr. Goldman was killed in the same entryway, stabbed more than 30 times. Ms. Brown was wearing a black halter sundress. A bloody glove was found at the scene. Here are four questions from a 10-question hypothetical GKT devised by Professor Lykken (1998):

> 1. You know that Nicole has been found murdered, Mr. Simpson. How was she killed? Was she drowned? Was she hit on the head with something? Was she shot? Was she beaten to death? Was she stabbed? Was she strangled?
>
> 2. Where did we find her body? Was it: In the living room? In the driveway? By the front gate? In the kitchen? In the bedroom? By the pool?
>
> 3. I'm going to show you six pictures of Nicole's body. One of them shows her just as we found her. In the other five pictures her body has been transposed to other locations, places where we might have found her but did not. Which one of these pictures show Nicole where we found her? Is it: This one? This one? This one?. . . etc. [Note: The body is not actually moved, computer-altered photographs are used]
>
> 4. Nicole was dressed in one main color when we found her. What color was she dressed in? Was it: White? Black? Pink? Blue? Green? Tan?

Notice that each question has six multiple-choice answer options. For each question, physiological responses to the first answer option are thrown out. Responses to this "unscored buffer" question are discarded because people tend to react more strongly to the first item in a series. In a well-constructed GKT, each question should be followed by at least five good alternative answers. That is, all five options will seem equally plausible to an innocent suspect, and an innocent suspect will have a one-in-five chance of reacting most strongly to the correct option. In the simplest version of scoring, anyone with a stronger physiological response to six of the 10 correct options is classified as having guilty knowledge of the crime.

Experimental findings on the validity of the GKT are quite promising. Most of the research on the GKT has been conducted in the laboratory using mock crimes. For example, in a study conducted by Lykken and his colleagues, people committed a mock theft. They waited until a particular office was unoccupied, snuck into that office, rifled through a few drawers, and stole something of value (they were told what to steal). The stolen object was then hidden in an empty locker in a nearby hallway. Both innocent and guilty subjects were then interrogated using the GKT technique. Looking across eight such studies, Lykken (1998) found an impressive hit rate: 96.7% of innocent subjects were correctly classified as innocent, and 88.2% of guilty subjects were correctly classified as guilty. In a study using a GKT in actual criminal investigations in Israel, Eitan Elaad and his colleagues (1992) found that they could correctly identify 97% of innocent subjects and 76% of guilty subjects. Clearly, the GKT seems to be highly accurate in correctly identifying innocent suspects and thereby avoiding false positive errors.

Weaknesses of the GKT.   Although the GKT is the most promising polygraph-based technique to be studied, there are clear limits to its usefulness. First, there must be a sufficient number of crime facts from a well-preserved crime scene so that valid GKT questions can be constructed. Second, these facts (e.g., where a body was found) must not be widely publicized until after suspects have been questioned, so that only guilty suspects will know the facts. Police, interrogators, and (in high-profile cases) the media must keep the critical information secret. Third, the guilty person must remember details surrounding the crime. While it is probably reasonable to assume that a murderer will remember whether he stabbed or shot his victim, he may not remember the color of the victim's clothes. While he is likely to know that he killed someone in the woods, he may not know that he left behind a bloody glove. Memory is not always reliable under the best of circumstances. Murderers and other criminals are likely to be rushed, their capacity to perceive and remember may be clouded by fear or rage. They frequently commit their crimes while under the influence of alcohol or drugs. What criminals don't know can't hurt them on the GKT.

While promising, the GKT may not be applicable to a large number of crimes. If a husband comes home to find his wife dead on the kitchen floor, he knows much of what the murderer knows. Both he and the murderer will have guilty knowledge. If a man and his accomplice rape and kill a woman, both know the details of the crime but only one may be guilty of murder. A man accused of rape may admit to having sex with a woman but will often claim that the sex was consensual. In each of these cases, it may not be possible to construct a reliable GKT. One study examined the files of 61 FBI criminal cases where the CQT polygraph test had been used. The researchers concluded that the GKT could have been used effectively in only 13% to 18% of these cases (Podlesny, 1995).

A final limitation has nothing to do with the GKT itself, but with the resistance of professional polygraphers. Currently, polygraphers are often granted considerable latitude in devising questions, conducting interviews, and interpreting polygraph charts. Part of the skill of examiners lies in convincing suspects that the machine is infallible, and in intuiting which suspects are trying to hide something. As Lykken (1998) points out, routine use of the GKT would reduce polygraphers to "mere technicians." Ideally, the person who hooked up suspects to the lie detector would simply read questions (or show pictures of the crime scene) without any knowledge of which answers are correct. The activities and prestige of the polygrapher would be greatly reduced. Understandably, polygraphers are reluctant to lower their status.

THE LIE DETECTOR AS COERCION DEVICE

Towards the end of his career, John A. Larson—developer of the RIT questioning technique—became disillusioned with the widespread misuse of the lie detector: "The lie detector, as used in many places, is nothing more than a psychological third degree aimed at extorting confessions as much as the old physical beatings were" (cited in Skolnick,

1961, p. 703). Even today, polygraphs are frequently used as means of inducing suspects to confess. If you are being interrogated as a suspect in a criminal investigation, police officers may suggest that you take a polygraph. This is usually presented as an opportunity to "prove your innocence." According to police interrogation manuals, whether you agree to take the test or resist taking the test is diagnostic of guilt: "If he [the suspect] agrees and seems willing to take the test as soon as possible, this usually is an indication of possible innocence. . . . A guilty person to whom a proposal has been made for a polygraph test will usually seek to avoid or at least delay submission to the test . . . [attempts to avoid or delay] are usually strong indications that the suspect is guilty" (Inbau et al., 2001, p.151). But even if you agree to take the test and tell the whole truth, interrogators may inform you that the machine indicates that you are being deceptive.

Indeed, sometimes the polygraph plays a key role in eliciting a false confession. Eighteen-year-old Peter Reilly returned home one night to find his mother beaten, bloodied, and near death, collapsed on her bedroom floor. He phoned 9-1-1 for help but by the time the ambulance arrived his mother had died. He was asked to sit outside in a squad car while police looked for clues to solve the murder. He was later taken to the police station where he was interrogated and took a lie detector test. The police told him he had "failed" the test and that he must have beaten and killed his mother. Here is an excerpt from the portion of the tape-recorded interrogation where Reilly was confronted with the results of the polygraph:

Peter Reilly: The [polygraph] test is giving me doubts right now. Disregarding the test, I still don't think I hurt my mother.

Police Sergeant: You're so damned ashamed of last night that you're trying to just block it out of your mind.

Peter Reilly: I'm not purposely denying it. If I did it, I wish I knew I'd done it. I'd be more happy to admit it if I knew it. If I could remember it. But I don't remember it. . . . Have you ever been proven totally wrong? A person, just from nervousness responds that way?

Police Sergeant: No, the polygraph can never be wrong, because it's only a recording instrument, recording from you.

Peter Reilly: But if I did it, and I didn't realize it, there's got to be some clue in the house.

Police Sergeant: I've got this clue here [the polygraph charts]. This is a recording of your mind.

Peter Reilly: Would it definitely be me? Could it be someone else?

Police Sergeant: No way. Not from these reactions (Barthel, 1976, pp. 38–39).

In many cases, a polygraph is used as just another tactic for pressuring suspects to confess. In their research on false confessions, Richard Ofshe and Richard Leo found that, "While the nominal purpose of a lie detection test is to diagnose the subject as truthful or deceptive, the primary function of any lie detector test administered during an interrogation is to induce confession" (1997, p. 1036).

HOW JURORS RESPOND TO POLYGRAPH EVIDENCE

When juries are permitted to hear about the results of polygraph tests, it appears they generally find the results persuasive. Consider the case of Buzz Fay. Fay was released from prison after serving two years of a life sentence. He was sent to prison for aggravated murder, convicted of shooting Fred Ery during the robbery of a liquor store. After being shot, Mr. Ery was rushed to a hospital, given pain medication and, while still conscious, asked about who shot him. While suffering from loss of blood and dying in a hospital room, Mr. Ery first replied, "It looked like Buzz, but it couldn't have been." However, just before death he said, "Buzz did it." Realizing their case was weak—there was no physical evidence implicating Fay and only the contradictory testimony of a dying, sedated man—the police made Fay's attorney an offer: They would drop all charges if Fay passed a lie detector test. Of course, everyone would need to agree in advance that the results would be admissible in court. Because Fay was innocent, the offer seemed like a quick way to put the matter to rest. But Fay failed the test. Then he failed a second test. Fay was convicted by a jury and sent to prison primarily on the results of his polygraph test (Cimerman, 1981).

This is not the only case in which the results of the lie detector appear to have changed the outcome of a criminal trial. Although there is little systematic research on how much weight jurors attach to polygraph evidence, the few studies available suggest that jurors take such evidence seriously. For example, in one study mock jurors were presented with the case of a mentally disturbed defendant who had a history of confessing to crimes he did not commit. Even though testimony by psychiatrists indicated that the defendant was prone to false confessions, 52% of mock jurors voted to convict him of murder. However, when testimony about the results of a lie detector test showed that the defendant had lied about committing the crime, only 28% voted to convict. When the researchers added a statement by the judge that the polygraph was "only 80% accurate," 40% voted not guilty (Cavoukian, 1979). In another study, 20 law student mock jurors who reviewed relevant evidence found a defendant not guilty. They were later given an opportunity to change their verdict when given the information that the polygraph is 99.5% accurate and that the defendant had failed the test. Given this additional information, 85% of the mock jurors changed their minds and voted guilty (Lykken, 1998).

These studies are quite limited and more research is clearly needed. What is clear is that several people have been sent to prison because of polygraph results and that mock jurors can be strongly influenced by the results of a lie detector test. Whether or not jurors are swayed by polygraph evidence is likely to depend on several factors: how persuasive the polygrapher is when testifying in court, the amount and persuasiveness of rebuttal testimony, the strength of other evidence, the sophistication of jurors, and the instructions given by the judge.

THE FUTURE OF LIE DETECTION

Use of the polygraph has been controversial for decades. What is not controversial is that small, subtle physiological changes can be detected and recorded by sophisticated measuring equipment. Each year, advances in technology make such measurements more precise. And more numerous. Blood pressure was the first measure to be touted as a means of detecting deception, and heart rate, respiration, and skin moisture were later added to the list. Technological advances now make it possible to electronically monitor modulations in the voice, dilation of the pupil, tension in the facial muscles, and neural activity in the brain. It is conceivable that more and more sensitive physiological measures will eventually permit us to tell when someone is lying. However, the enduring problem is that there appears to be no distinctive set of physiological responses associated with lying. There is no unique tone of voice, no distinctive rhythm to the heartbeat, no precise change in blood pressure, and no peculiar pattern of neural excitation in the brain. Although the technology of physiological monitoring is likely to become more accurate and impressive, if there is no clear signal to detect, these advances cannot produce a fully trustworthy method of detecting lies.

Readings to Supplement This Chapter

Articles

Ben-Shakhar, G., Bar-Hillel, M., & Kremnitzer, M. (2002). Trial by polygraph: Reconsidering the use of the guilty knowledge technique in court. *Law and Human Behavior, 26,* 527–541.

Gudjonsson, G. H. (1994). Investigative interviewing: Recent developments and some fundamental issues. *International Review of Psychiatry, 6,* 237–245.

Kassin, S. (1997). The psychology of confession evidence. *American Psychologist, 52,* 221–233.

Leo, R. A. (1996). Miranda's revenge: Police interrogation as a confidence game. *Law and Society Review, 30,* 259–288.

Meissner, C. A., & Kassin, S. M. (2002). He's guilty!: Investigator bias in judgments of truth and deception. *Law and Human Behavior, 26,* 469–480.

Books

Lykken, D. T. (1998). *A tremor in the blood: Uses and abuses of the lie detector.* New York: Plenum Trade.

Skolnick, J. H., & Fyfe, J. J. (1993). *Above the law.* New York: The Free Press.

3
Profiles and Syndromes

Chapter Outline

The Process of Profiling
Characteristics of Serial Killers
Two Famous Profiles
Research on Profiling
Psychological Autopsies
 Legal Status of Psychological Autopsies
Precise Profiles or Sloppy Stereotypes?

SYNDROMES

Battered Woman Syndrome (BWS)
 BWS and the Legal System
 The Scientific Validity of BWS
Rape Trauma Syndrome (RTS)
RTS Testimony in the Courtroom
Post Traumatic Stress Disorder (PTSD)

Much of the public was introduced to the practice of criminal profiling by the 1991 film, *The Silence of the Lambs*. In that film, a young FBI agent (named Starling) and her boss are on the trail of a serial killer who murders young white women and cuts away large pieces of their skin. In one scene, Starling's skills are tested when her boss asks her to look at photographs of the victims and speculate about the killer's identity:

Boss: Look at these [photographs] Starling. Tell me what you see.

Starling: Well, he's a white male; serial killers tend to kill within their own ethnic groups. He's not a drifter, he's got his own house somewhere, not an apartment.

Boss: Why?

Starling: What he does with them takes privacy. He's in his 30s or 40s. He's got real physical strength, combined with an older man's self control. He's cautious, precise. He's never impulsive, he'll never stop.

Boss: Why not?

Starling: He's got a real taste for it now, he's getting better at his work.

Boss: Not bad, Starling.

Starling's profile of the killer turns out to be dead on. But, of course, she's a fictional character, and *The Silence of the Lambs* is only a movie. Is it really possible to make valid inferences about a criminal's age, race, gender, living circumstances, and personality based only on information from a crime scene?

THE PROCESS OF PROFILING

The techniques of criminal profiling were pioneered by the FBI's Profiling and Behavioral Assessment Unit (formerly called the Behavioral Science Unit) in Quantico, Virginia. Only about 14 profilers work at the FBI Unit. The profiling techniques (also known as retroclassification or criminal investigative analysis) used by the FBI have been most usefully and famously applied to cases involving serial killers—murderers who kill three or more people in separate events with a cooling-off period between murders. To build a foundation for generating profiles, FBI agents interviewed more than 40 imprisoned serial killers and entered their traits and the characteristics of their crimes into a computer database. To create a specific profile, investigators analyze the crime scenes, gather information about the victims, and study both police reports and autopsy reports. Information from these sources is used to create a description or "profile" of the criminal. Profiles are used to provide leads for police and to focus the efforts of investigators. For example, officers might be told to look for a white male in his 20s who works nights and lives in a particular part of a city. A profile might also be used to set a trap for the criminal. For example, if police are looking for a serial killer who preys on young prostitutes with long dark hair, an officer may pose as a prostitute in an effort to attract and entrap the killer.

Profilers who have worked at the FBI emphasize the importance of the "signature aspect of the crime." The "signature" is the distinctive, personal aspect of the crime that presumably reveals the personality of the killer (e.g., the particular form of torture used or particular sexual activity engaged in by a specific serial killer). According to John Douglas, one of the agents who developed the FBI's system, the methods used to abduct, transport, or dispose of victims may change, but the signature will remain relatively constant because it is ". . . why he does it: the thing that fulfills him emotionally. . . . the emotional reason he's committing the crime in the first place" (Douglas & Olshaker, 1997, p. 26).

Although the profiling of serial killers has captured the imagination of Hollywood and the general public, it remains a largely untested technique. How profilers move from raw data about a crime to a useful profile of the criminal is not systematic or clearly articulated. According to Douglas, "The key attribute necessary to be a good profiler is judgment—a judgment based not primarily on the analysis of facts and figures, but on instinct. . . . and ultimately, it comes down to the individual analyst's judgment rather than any objective scale or test" (p. 17). Douglas further explains that, ". . . it's very important to get into the mind of not only the killer, but into the mind of the victim at the time the crime occurred. That's the only way you're going to be able to understand the dynamics of the crime—what was going on between the victim and the offender" (p. 15). Indeed, part of the mystique of the profiling process is that it appears to rely on the skilled intuition of a particular profiler. In movie and television depictions of the technique, profilers seem to be as much psychics as investigators. They often enter a trance-like state where they are able to inhabit the mind of a serial killer, to see what he saw and felt at the time of the killing.

Because profiling techniques have been most notably used to find serial killers, it is useful to briefly review research on people who commit multiple murders.

CHARACTERISTICS OF SERIAL KILLERS

There is no list of characteristics that describes all serial killers. However, research has revealed some recurring patterns. Many suffer from some form of brain injury that impairs rational thinking. Most have also experienced some combination of physical, sexual, and/or psychological abuse during childhood (Hickey, 1997). Maladjustment during their childhood sometimes expresses itself in cruelty towards animals. Nearly all are white males and they are typically of average intelligence. Most seek to dominate their victims before killing them. They tend not to kill using guns, preferring more intimate methods such as strangulation, stabbing, or even torture. Before killing, they often drink alcohol or use other drugs, perhaps to desensitize themselves and to lower inhibitions (Hickey, 1997). They tend to select victims of a particular type, for example, only light-skinned young women. Serial killers often show an obsessive interest in violent pornography and serial killing is usually a highly sexualized crime. A killer's violent sexual fantasies may serve as rehearsals for his crimes and many serial killers replay past killings in their minds as a means of sexual self-stimulation. Some have even made videotapes of their killings so that they could watch them repeatedly. To feed their fantasy life, some keep souvenirs from their victims (e.g., a lock of hair) and collect newspaper clippings that describe their crimes (Fox & Levin, 1998).

Profilers sometimes distinguish between organized and disorganized murderers (Ressler, Burgess, & Douglas, 1988). Organized killers carefully select their victims and plan out what they will do to their victims. They show patience and self-control by waiting for the right opportunity and cleaning up evidence after the murder. They also tend to use more elaborate rituals that involve torturing the victim and dismembering the corpse. In contrast, disorganized killers tend to be impulsive, acting on sudden rage or following commands to kill from voices in their heads. Disorganized killers are more likely to use any weapon that happens to be available, to leave the weapon at the crime scene, and to use the dead body for sexual purposes.

A more differentiated classification scheme has been proposed by Ronald Holmes. Holmes groups serial killers into four types: visionary, mission-oriented, hedonistic, and power-oriented. Visionary types are usually psychotic. They have visions or believe they hear voices from God or spirits instructing them to kill certain types of people. Mission-oriented types are less likely to be psychotic but they are motivated by a desire to kill people they regard as evil or unworthy (e.g., one set out to kill all physicians who performed abortions). Hedonistic types kill for thrills and take sadistic sexual pleasure in the torture of their victims. The fourth type—power-oriented—gets satisfaction from capturing and controlling the victim before killing. Although these four categories overlap somewhat, they offer some insight into the varied motives behind these rare but hideous crimes (Holmes & DeBurger, 1988). Holmes developed his typology by looking closely at the characteristics of known serial killers, so there is clear evidence that many such killers fall into each of the four categories. However, it is not yet clear whether all serial killers fall into one of these four categories or perhaps other categories that have yet to be identified.

TWO FAMOUS PROFILES
• •

Although profiling has been most famously applied to cases involving serial killers, profiling techniques have been used—with varying levels of success—in the investigation of many other types of crimes, including rape, arson, skyjacking, and bombing. One notorious profile was produced in response to a bomb explosion during the 1996 Summer Olympics in Atlanta, Georgia. Based on evidence uncovered at the scene of the bombing and on their database of past bombings at public events, the FBI instructed police to search for a single, white, middle-class male with an intense interest in police work and law enforcement (what investigators sometimes call a "police buff" or "cop wannabe"). Within days, the police focused their attentions on Richard Jewell, a security guard at the Olympic Park who fit the profile in every respect.

Mr. Jewell became the target of intense investigation. Because of the need to reassure people that the Olympics were safe, Jewell's name and photograph appeared in newspapers across the country and his face was shown on television news programs in several countries. It appeared that the bomber had been caught. Only after three months—long after the Olympics had ended—did the FBI admit that they had uncovered no evidence linking Jewell to the bombing. Of course, the damage to Mr. Jewell's life and reputation could not be easily undone. In 1998, after much additional investigation, the FBI finally charged Eric Rudolph with the Olympic bombing. Rudolph was an anti-abortion activist who was wanted in connection with the bombing of abortion clinics in two states (Sack, 1998).

One of the first systematic profiles ever produced was also one of the most detailed. It was used to solve the "Mad Bomber" case in 1957. In 1940, an unexploded bomb was found on a windowsill of the building occupied by the Consolidated Edison Company. The note attached to the bomb explained "Con Edison crooks, this is for you." The person who became known as the "Mad Bomber" managed to terrorize the public by successfully planting (and sometimes detonating) bombs in locations dispersed across New York City. He sent several letters and placed a few phone calls to the New York police and *The New York Times*. Just after the United States entered World War II in 1941, the Mad Bomber sent a letter to the police declaring that because of his "patriotic feelings" he would ". . . make no more bomb units for the duration of the war" (Brussel, 1968, p. 21). He was true to his word. No more bombs were found until 1950. But in the same letter that informed police that his patriotism had inspired him to suspend bombings, he also declared that he would later return to "bring Con Edison to justice" and make them "pay for their dastardly deeds" (Brussel, 1968, p. 23).

Despite their best efforts, the police were baffled. In 1956, they consulted a prominent local psychiatrist named James Brussel in a desperate attempt to generate new leads. Dr. Brussel reviewed the Mad Bomber's letters as well as all the other information in the possession of the police. Brussel directed police to look for a man who was between 40 and 50, Roman Catholic, foreign-born, single, and living with a brother or sister. He would be suffering from progressive paranoia and would be a "present or former Consolidated Edison worker." In an especially precise but odd detail, Brussel told police that, "When you find him, chances are he'll be wearing a double-breasted suit. Buttoned" (Brussel, 1968, p. 47). The man the police eventually arrested—George Metesky—was a single, unemployed, 54-year-old former employee of Con Edison who was living with two older sisters. When the police took him into custody, he was wearing a double-breasted blue suit. Buttoned.

Metesky eventually confessed to the bombings. The profile of the Mad Bomber turned out to be eerily accurate and crucial to solving the case. However, in addition to the accurate details that were helpful to police, the elaborate profile constructed by Dr. Brussel also contained inaccurate details and wild psychoanalytic speculations. For example, noting that the Mad Bomber had cut open the underside of theater seats to stuff his bombs into the cushion, Brussel (1968) offered the following conclusion: "Could the seat symbolize the pelvic region of the human body? In plunging a knife upward into it, had the bomber been symbolically penetrating a woman? Or castrating a man?. . . . In this act he gave expression to a submerged wish to penetrate his mother or castrate his father. Thereby rendering the father powerless. . . ." (p. 63). Brussel went on to say that the bomber's yearning for what he called "justice" was truly a belief that people were ". . . trying to deprive him of something that was rightfully his . . . the love of his mother" (p. 39).

Finally, it is important to note that it was not his preference for double-breasted suits that helped police locate George Metesky. Police did not stake out men's clothing stores. The crucial information in Brussel's famous profile was that the bomber was a resentful employee or former employee at Con Edison. It was a search of employee records that led to the identification of Metesky, a worker who had been injured by a boiler at Con Edison. His disability claim (he claimed that the accident had given him tuberculosis) was denied and he was eventually fired from his job. It appears that Brussel's profile merely prompted the police to do what they should have done in 1940 when the first bomb was discovered: search the employee records of Con Edison to try to identify someone who may have felt wronged by the company. Indeed, if modern-day police officers found a bomb with a note about "Con Edison crooks" they would almost certainly examine employee records to generate a list of disgruntled former employees. Of course, that task is far simpler today than it was in 1957 because most employment records are now preserved on computers.

RESEARCH ON PROFILING

Despite surging interest in profiling and well-publicized anecdotal evidence suggesting that profiling is effective, systematic research is sparse. The most widely cited study was conducted by Anthony Pinizzotto and Norman Finkel in 1990. The study compared the accuracy of profiles produced by five different groups: undergraduate college students, clinical psychologists with no profiling experience, police detectives without training in profiling techniques, and police detectives who had taken a one-year profiling training program offered by the FBI. All groups evaluated two actual cases—a homicide and a sex offense. The crimes had already been solved, so the true characteristics of the offenders were known. All groups evaluated the same evidence: crime scene photographs, information about the victim, autopsy reports, and reports written by officers on the scene and detectives investigating the case. There were differences between the groups. The biggest differences were between the trained profiler group and all other groups. The experts studied the materials more closely, spent more time writing their reports, wrote longer reports, and made more specific inferences about the characteristics of the offender. But their profiles were significantly more accurate only for the sex offender case. For the sex offense case, the profiles constructed by the profilers were twice as accurate as the profiles constructed by the police detectives, and several times more accurate than the profiles created by college students. Although the findings of this well-conducted study are important, they are not conclusive. There were only six people in each of the groups that evaluated the crimes, and the profilers may have been more strongly motivated than the other groups to offer a detailed and accurate profile.

Researchers who have reviewed the few systematic studies on profiling highlight some intriguing tentative findings that need further investigation. First, it appears that crime scenes can often be accurately classified into broad categories (e.g., impulsive or planned) and may sometimes reveal information about a murderer (e.g., whether or not he knew the victim) (Homant & Kennedy, 1998). Second, profiling may be most useful in solving crimes with a strong sexual component, for example, serial killings or serial rapes. This may be because the psychopathology revealed in a killer's "signature" activities (e.g., sadistic torture or mutilation of the corpse) may provide useful leads for investigators. A third tentative conclusion is that, because profiling is not currently based on clear, systematic procedures, different profilers may produce very different profiles (Homant & Kennedy, 1998). The completeness and accuracy of profiles produced by different profilers vary considerably.

At present, we have no good estimates of how often profiles have been useful and how often they have been useless or even counterproductive. We don't know the error rates or the rates of success. Some profiles have led to the arrest of guilty suspects, some profiles have led to the arrest of innocent people, some profiles have pointed police in the right direction, and some profiles have led police astray and wasted time and resources. And, if police are looking in the wrong direction, the trail of the real criminal can grow cold.

The improvement of profiling techniques will only come with enhanced databases for many types of crimes, systematic research that reveals the conditions under which profiles reliably lead to productive use of investigator resources, and the development of standardized procedures for training profilers and creating profiles. Although profiling has been a promising investigative tool for decades, the promise is as yet unfulfilled. The President of the Academy of Behavioral Profiling put it bluntly in 2001:

> ". . . there are currently no accepted educational requirements for criminal profilers, no ethical guidelines, no peer review; nor in many quarters are any of these parameters welcome. . . . The reality is that no research or substantial evidence exists to confirm the validity of one type of profiling over another, or one specific educational experience over another . . . the field of criminal profiling has seen little significant advancement in nearly two decades" (McGrath, 2001, p. 2).

PSYCHOLOGICAL AUTOPSIES
• •

The psychological autopsy is an interesting variant of profiling techniques. Suppose a man is driving alone on a winding stretch of highway that skirts the edge of a high cliff. His car veers off the road, plunges several hundred feet, crashes into the rocks below, and bursts into flames. The man is killed. This is an example of an equivocal death. That is, it is not clear why the car fell from the cliff. One possibility is that the man's death was accidental—perhaps he was tired and dozed off for a second or two, perhaps he had been drinking, perhaps his attention lapsed while he was trying to find the CD he wanted to play. A second possibility is that the man committed suicide—he knew that the fall was certain to kill him but he wanted to make it look like an accident so that his wife and children would receive an insurance payment of several hundred thousand dollars (many life insurance policies do not pay survivors if a death was a suicide). A third possibility is that the death was actually a murder disguised to look like an accident—perhaps someone who knew that the man would be driving that stretch of highway tampered with the brakes or steering of his car.

Just as the name implies, a psychological autopsy is an effort to dissect and examine the psychological state of a person prior to his or her death. Of course, the analogy between physical and psychological autopsies is not perfect. Injuries on a dead body can be closely examined. A corpse can be cut open; body parts can be weighed, measured, and chemically analyzed. There is no comparable "psychological corpse" to examine. The autopsy-like psychological analysis must rely on less direct sources of evidence. Typically, these sources include any records left behind by the deceased (letters, emails, journal entries, audio or video recordings, bank accounts, student or employee records), as well as data about the person gathered from interviews with friends, family members, or coworkers who were in contact with the deceased prior to his or her death. The goal is to reconstruct the dead person's emotional state, personality, thoughts, and lifestyle. Inferences about the deceased person's intentions and emotional state just prior to death are crucial to the analysis.

Researchers have developed a checklist to assist medical examiners in distinguishing between suicide and accidental death. The checklist emphasizes two basic criteria: whether the death might have been self-inflicted, and whether there were clear indications of an intention to die (Jobes, Casey, Berman, & Wright, 1991). In many cases, the determination of whether the death could have been self-inflicted is straightforward. It is possible to poison yourself, jump from a tall building, or drive your car off a high cliff. It is even possible to drown yourself. But it is difficult to beat yourself to death with a baseball bat or shoot yourself from across a room. If investigators conclude that a death was self-inflicted, they must then determine if that death was accidental or intentional. For example, psychologists would be more likely to conclude that the man who drove off a cliff had committed suicide if he had been noticeably depressed, if he had made an effort to "put his affairs in order," if he had been experiencing serious emotional or physical pain, if he had severe financial problems, if he had made previous suicide threats or attempts, if he had made attempts to say goodbye to people close to him, or if he had expressed a desire to die.

Often, the findings of a psychological autopsy are equivocal—if the man who drove his car off a cliff had been depressed, we may lean slightly toward a judgment of suicide, but we can't be sure. Sometimes, the available evidence, though not overwhelming or conclusive, may be sufficient to settle the legal issue at stake. If the driver showed no clear signs of being suicidal, his wife and children will probably receive the insurance money.

Legal Status of Psychological Autopsies.   Courts have been receptive to expert testimony based on a form of psychological autopsy in some civil cases. When the distribution of assets specified in a will is challenged in court, the conflict usually turns on whether the deceased person was legally competent when the will was written or revised. An investigation or "autopsy" of the state of mind and intentions of a person at the time his or her will was drawn up is critical to a decision as to whether the will is legally binding. If medical records and testimony from friends and family members indicate that the deceased was suffering from some form of dementia, the will may be ruled invalid. This limited form of psychological autopsy is routinely allowed in court.

In contrast, in criminal cases, courts have generally been reluctant to allow expert testimony based on psychological autopsies. However, in one criminal case—*Jackson v. State of Florida* (1989)—psychological autopsy testimony was not only admitted, but, on appeal, the trial court's decision to allow the testimony was upheld. The case involved a spectacularly bad mother named Theresa Jackson and her 17-year-old daughter, Tina Mancini. Unemployed and struggling to meet her financial obligations, Ms. Jackson encouraged her underage daughter to take a job as a nude dancer in a nearby strip club. To get around the law, Ms. Jackson changed the birth date on her daughter's birth certificate and forged the signature of a notary. Tina's dancing earned her several hundred dollars a week but her mother charged Tina more than $300 a week for rent and living expenses. The nude dancing job was a continuing source of conflict between mother and daughter—Jackson wanted Tina to work more, Tina wanted to quit. Ms. Jackson told her daughter that if she did quit, she would report her to the police for underage dancing. Tina Mancini committed suicide before her 18th birthday.

Following her daughter's death, Theresa Jackson was tried and convicted of forgery, procuring sexual performance by a child, and child abuse. At trial, a psychiatrist concluded that the psychologically abusive relationship between mother and daughter had contributed to Tina Mancini's suicide. Jackson appealed the conviction, claiming that the trial judge should not have permitted psychological autopsy testimony about her daughter. In upholding the lower court's decision, the appellate court found that allowing testimony about the mental state of someone who died of suicide is not qualitatively different from allowing testimony about the sanity of someone accused of murder, or allowing testimony about the mental competence of someone who had written a will.

PRECISE PROFILES OR SLOPPY STEREOTYPES?

Examples of loose, subjective profiles can be found in many parts of the legal system. At the extreme, what have been called "profiles" are little more than biased stereotypes. Decisions about who becomes a suspect, who should be interrogated, who should be prosecuted, what evidence is relevant, and who should be convicted are sometimes based on the intuitive profiles held by police officers, attorneys, judges, and jurors. For example, in his classic analysis of police culture and behavior, Jerome Skolnick found that because police officers often find themselves in life-threatening situations, they tend to be alert to ". . . people who may not be engaging in criminal activity, but whose conduct suggests that they might be, or might be the sort of people who would if they could" (Skolnick & Fyfe, 1993, p. 97). That is, some people become suspects because they stand out, "as persons whose gestures, language, or attire the police have come to identify as being potentially threatening or dangerous" (p. 97). In essence, police sometimes rely on intuitive profiles to *predict* criminal behavior. Sometimes these predictions are accurate, sometimes they are not.

Race has sometimes been one of the characteristics that police investigators have used to identify suspects. Racial profiling—using race as an indicator of who might be engaged in criminal activity—has led to several lawsuits. An important early case involved a profile of a serial murderer used by the San Francisco Police Department (*Williams, Bazille et al. v. Alioto et al.,* 1977). In an attempt to catch the killer, the police detained more than 600 black men because they fit a vague profile—a black male, slender to medium build, five feet eight inches to six feet tall, 20 to 30 years old, who was traveling either by foot or car between the hours of 8:00 pm and midnight. A court eventually issued an injunction preventing police from stopping black men merely because they fit this broad profile. Another lawsuit arose from the following facts: although only 17% of drivers on Maryland's highway I-95 were black, 70% of drivers pulled over and searched for drugs by Maryland State Troopers were black. At the time, 71% of drivers on the same stretch of highway were white, but only 23% of the drivers who were pulled over and searched were white (Janofsky, 1998).

The use of stereotypes or vague profiles can also create problems at trial. In deciding whether to admit testimony at trial, courts must weigh the probative value of the testimony against the potentially prejudicial impact of that testimony. Probative evidence provides information that is useful in assessing whether or not a person committed a crime. Should information about whether a defendant fits a profile be admissible in court? Should a defendant's "fit" with a profile be considered evidence?

Deborah Davis and William Follette (2002) describe the case of a man on trial for the murder of his wife. His wife was driving a snowmobile and he was riding on back. The woman lost control of the snowmobile and crashed into a ditch. The man and woman were found shortly after the crash. She was found face down in a pool of water at the bottom of the ditch. She was dead, apparently drowned. The man was found face up, alive but unconscious. The prosecutor alleged that what appeared to be an accidental death was actually a murder: the man had caused the snowmobile to crash, held his wife's head underwater until she drowned, and pretended to be unconscious until the rescue. The prosecution was allowed to present evidence that the husband "fit the profile" of a spouse murderer. That "profile evidence" was: (1) that the husband would stand to benefit from his wife's death because of an insurance policy purchased about a year prior to the snowmobile crash, and (2) the husband had had several extramarital affairs during the course of their marriage. The implication was that the man had killed his wife to collect insurance money, and that he may have wanted his wife dead so that he could be free to pursue other women.

To statistically evaluate the probative value of this evidence, Davis and Follette collected estimates such as the number of men who are unfaithful to their wives (260,000 per million) and the number of men who murder their wives (240 per million) and calculated the probability that a man who has extramarital affairs is more likely to murder his wife. They concluded that ". . . at maximum, it is .0923% (less than one tenth of one percent) more likely that an unfaithful man will murder his wife at some point in their marriage than it is that a faithful man will murder his wife" (p. 138). Put differently, an inference that a man killed his wife *because* he is unfaithful will be wrong more than 99% of the time. The snowmobile case illustrates how inferences drawn from dubious profiles make their way into the courtroom. Judges' decisions about whether to admit or exclude evidence are often partly based on their own subjective profiles about which characteristics are associated with criminal behaviors. In essence, "The judge assesses relevance and admits the evidence based on his or her intuitive profile of persons or situations associated with the crime, and then the jury uses that evidence in combination with their own intuitive profiles to render a verdict" (p.151).

Sometimes the courts take notice of the misuse of unscientific stereotype evidence. In *State of Oregon v. Hansen* (1987), the conviction of a high school teacher who had engaged in a sexual affair with one of her students was overturned. The appeals court held that it was an error for the trial judge to allow a police detective to testify that Ms. Hansen fit the profile of a child molester:

> Detective Robson testified to what might be described as a "profile" of a nonviolent child abuser who is unrelated to the child: physical and psychological "testing" of the child, giving gifts, showing affection, praising, making the child feel comfortable in the abuser's presence, etc. That child abusers use these techniques has no bearing on whether a person who does these things is a child abuser. For example, it is probably accurate to say that the vast majority of persons who abuse children sexually are male. This says little, if anything, however, about whether a particular male defendant has sexually abused a child. . . . Given the lack of probative value of Detective Robson's testimony on this point, the danger of unfair prejudice to defendant from the unwarranted inference that because the defendant engages in acts that sexual child abusers engage in, she, too, is a sexual child abuser is simply too great. It was an error to admit this testimony (p. 157).

When based on extensive data, profiles may serve as important investigative tools that steer investigations in the right direction and improve the probability of catching a guilty criminal. However, the misuse of profiles poses clear dangers. Mistaken profiles can lead police investigators astray. Subjective or simply inaccurate profiles may lead prosecutors to charge suspects with crimes despite insufficient evidence. Judges may use their own profiles to decide which testimony to admit into evidence, and jurors may be guided by subjective profiles that lead them to conclusions not supported by the evidence.

SYNDROMES

Syndromes, like profiles, are clusters of behaviors or traits that tend to describe groups of similar people. In the legal system, the term "profile" is generally used to describe criminal suspects, while the term "syndrome" is typically used to describe the psychological reactions of crime victims. The word "syndrome" comes from medical or psychiatric settings. When someone is described as suffering from a syndrome, it means that he or she displays a cluster of related symptoms. In psychology, the concept of a syndrome helps therapists understand and treat people with specific mental and emotional disorders. Two psychological syndromes have become especially prominent in the legal system: One explains the behavior of women who have been physically abused by their husbands or partners (Battered Woman Syndrome), and the other describes how women respond to the trauma of being raped (Rape Trauma Syndrome).

BATTERED WOMAN SYNDROME (BWS)

Until the second half of the nineteenth century, wife battering was treated much less seriously than most other forms of violence. Prior to that time, laws regulating domestic violence were strongly influenced by the concepts of property and privacy. Wives (like children) were akin to property. What a man did with his wife was largely a private matter, and if he thought it necessary to "discipline" her with a "moderate" beating, the law did not interfere. The common expression "rule of thumb" derives from a law established in the American colonies to restrict wife beating. That rule stipulated that a man could beat his wife, but only with a stick or weapon no thicker than his thumb (Koss & House-Higgins, 2000). There were other broad limits. A beating that led to disfigurement or death would usually be prosecuted.

Because physical abuse between spouses or other couples usually occurs in private and is often kept secret, it is difficult to know how often it occurs. Some experts estimate that some form of physical violence occurs in one-quarter to one-third of all intimate couples (Strauss & Gelles, 1988). Although men in intimate relationships are sometimes physically beaten by their female or male partners, violence against women by their male partners is far more frequent. Also, men are more likely to seriously injure or kill their female partners, and it is male-against-female violence that is most likely to make contact with the legal system.

The idea that women who have been victims of long-term abuse suffer from an identifiable cluster of symptoms was first hypothesized in 1979 in a book by Lenore Walker. Walker based her conclusions on interviews with 400 battered women. She argued that the typical abusive relationship moves through a recurring three-phase cycle: tension-building, battering, and contrition. During the first phase, there is an accumulation of emotional tension and "minor" incidents of abuse. Although the woman tries to placate her abuser, these smaller incidents eventually erupt in a serious incident of abuse. This is the second, "acute battering" phase. During the third phase, the batterer is overcome with remorse. He treats his victim with kindness, expresses his regret for hurting her, and promises never to hurt her again. Especially during the early stages in the relationship, the woman may be successful in temporarily placating her abuser, and there may be long periods of time when the man does not beat her. Although this temporary success may lead her to hope that she can change his behavior, the cycle of abuse eventually resumes and the beatings become more severe and more frequent. According to Walker, women caught in such relationships experience "learned helplessness" and become submissive. That is, over time, women who endure long-term abuse become resigned to their suffering and fail to resist or leave their abuser.

Walker also identified a set of traits she thought were shared by most battered women. These traits include traditional sex role attitudes (such as the belief that women should be submissive to their husbands), poor self-image, and a tendency to accept responsibility for the abuse. Because the battered woman is likely to believe that she brought the abuse on herself, she will feel shame and attempt to conceal the abuse from others. Consequently, over time, she is likely to become socially isolated and increasingly dependent on her abuser. She will see few alternatives to staying with him and will become less able to extricate herself from the relationship (Schuller, 1994).

Sometimes, a battered woman will kill the man who is abusing her. Below is a description of such a case.

> Rita Felton's 23-year marriage ended when she shot and killed her sleeping husband using his own rifle. Prior to the murder, her husband had beaten and sexually abused her over the course of two decades. He once punched her so hard in the face that her dentures broke, he beat her while she was pregnant, he once held her down and threatened her with a blowtorch, and he forced her to engage in painful and degrading sex acts. He also beat their children and, on several occasions, he threatened to kill her. Although Mrs. Felton had sought help from her community—she called the police to her home several times and she confided in her minister—little help was provided. The police were unable to stop the beatings and the minister advised her to "try to be a better wife." She once separated from her husband for a period of 10 months, but because of financial problems and her belief that the children would be better off if they were living with their father, she reunited with her husband. The beatings resumed. Three weeks before she killed her husband, Rita Felton unsuccessfully attempted to kill herself. On the day she shot her husband, Mr. Felton had beaten both her and their 15-year-old daughter. Rita Felton waited for her husband to fall asleep before she shot him. At trial, she was convicted of second-degree murder (Ewing, 1987).

In part, BWS is an attempt to explain why a woman fails to leave a man who frequently beats her. According to Walker, part of her inability to leave stems from a fear that if she does leave, her husband will track her down and kill her. Indeed, many abusers explicitly threaten to kill their victims if they try to escape. Also, because the violence often follows a cycle where a husband beats up his wife, then apologizes and expresses remorse, then becomes violent again, the abused woman may perceive an imminent threat even when he is not abusing her. That is, although he may appear temporarily calm, she knows that he will eventually erupt in anger. The battered woman learns to anticipate her partner's violent behavior by carefully attending to his verbal and nonverbal cues, searching for signals of impending violence. This heightened attentiveness to the abuser's subtle behaviors is called "hypervigilance."

A battered woman is likely to feel trapped for other reasons as well. She may not have the financial resources to survive on her own, and because she may not have received help from police or the courts in the past, she may not feel that the legal system can help or protect her. It may be realistic for battered women to believe that the legal system won't give them much assistance. Several studies have found that police are reluctant to arrest batterers, and that restraining orders against violent boyfriends and husbands are frequently violated (Mundy, 1997). Fortunately, this seems to be changing. Many states now require police to make an arrest if they have reason to believe that physical violence has occurred between intimate partners, and the Federal Violence Against Women Act of 1994 made it possible for victims of domestic abuse or rape to sue for compensatory and punitive damages.

But what about the man who does the battering? Although there is no diagnosis of "battering man syndrome," there have been attempts to describe the traits and behaviors of men who abuse their partners. Donald Dutton (2000) has distinguished between two basic types of abusers. The first type of batterer tends to be extremely jealous and fearful of abandonment. These feelings lead him to be suspicious of his wife's friends and family. Fear and jealousy motivate him to exert strict control over her social contacts and to restrict her outside activities. Dutton has also argued that many batterers can be classified as suffering from borderline personality disorder, a serious disorder characterized by unstable relationships, dramatic mood swings, manipulativeness, intense fear of abandonment, and impulsive outbursts. A man suffering from this disorder may appear superficially normal but his jealousy and volatility will surface in intimate relationships. The second type of batterer—psychopathic abusers—is less selectively violent. They are generally predisposed to violent behavior against the people around them. They tend to be antisocial, prone to impulsive behavior, and dependent on alcohol or other drugs (Dutton, 1995). The first type of batterer is less likely to raise the suspicions of friends and coworkers.

BWS and the Legal System.   If a woman who has been repeatedly abused by her husband manages to kill him *while* he is violently attacking her, she can plead self-defense and she will have a good chance of being successful. But, realistically, a woman who is smaller and weaker than her mate will have a difficult time fighting him off during an attack. Instead, it is almost always the case that when a battered woman kills her abusive boyfriend or husband, she will do it when he is most vulnerable—for example, when he is asleep or in a drunken daze. If that woman then stands trial for the murder, her attorneys will typically use one of two strategies: self-defense or insanity. Proving self-defense in such a case is difficult. The traditional legal definition of self-defense permits one person to kill another person only if the killer reasonably believes that killing is a necessary response to a physical attack that is likely to cause serious injury or death. Self-defense is a form of justifiable homicide.

The alternative to self-defense is the insanity defense. To prove insanity, a battered woman would need to show that she was unable to distinguish between right and wrong at the time of the murder. An insanity defense is seldom used in cases where battered women kill their partners, in part, because the insanity defense is seldom successful (see Chapter 4). However, in a study by Marilyn Kasian and her colleagues, it was found that a variant of the insanity defense led to more "not guilty" verdicts than self-defense. The specific defense used was that the stress of the abusive relationship combined with a head injury the woman received from a battering caused her to slip into a dissociated mental state that rendered her unable to appreciate the wrongfulness of the murder (Kasian, Spanos, Terrance, & Peebles, 1993).

In cases where an abused woman who killed her abuser is on trial, it is natural for jurors to raise the question, "Why didn't she just leave him?" As part of either a self-defense or an insanity defense, attorneys will usually try to include expert testimony on BWS. Testimony on BWS is generally presented at trial to explain two facts that jurors are likely to find puzzling: (1) that a woman who suffers long-term abuse at the hands of a husband or partner fails to leave the abuser, and (2) that a battered woman might kill her abuser at a time when he poses no imminent danger. Testimony on BWS is intended to provide jurors with a framework for making sense of the woman's behavior (Monahan & Walker, 1998). By explaining how the woman perceived her situation, her failure to leave becomes easier to understand. BWS testimony attempts to illuminate a woman's state of mind at the time of the killing and helps jurors to understand why the woman may have believed she was in imminent danger even though she was not actually under attack when she killed her abuser. Still, jurors are likely to be skeptical (Dodge & Greene, 1991).

Like jurors, prosecutors at trial are likely to raise the question, "Why didn't she just leave him?" and to question the truthfulness of the defendant's account. Here is a quote from the closing argument of a prosecutor:

> I wish Joe [the murdered husband] were here to tell us his side of the story. I don't portray Joe as being a perfect individual, but I question if he was as bad as the picture that has been painted of him. . . . Ask yourself this question: If Joe was all that bad, if he did all those things, why didn't the defendant divorce him? Why didn't she leave him? If she was truly afraid for her life, why didn't she go to Idaho Falls, and visit with her family there? . . . her father said, "I love my daughter. The home is always open to her" (Ewing, 1987, p. 111).

Research shows that jurors tend not to go easy on battered women who kill their abusers. In the largest study of case outcomes, Charles Patrick Ewing examined the outcomes of 100 cases where battered women were charged with homicide. Twelve of the cases did not make it to trial: In three cases the charges were dropped and in nine cases the women pled guilty. In another three cases, the defendants were found not guilty by reason of insanity. The remaining 85 cases went to trial, with attorneys arguing that the women killed in self-defense. Sixty-three (74%) of the women were convicted. Twelve were sentenced to life in prison, one was sentenced to 50 years, and the others received sentences ranging from four years to 25 years (Ewing, 1987). A separate study of 41 additional court cases corroborated Ewing's findings. In the smaller study, 24% of battered women were acquitted or had charges dropped before trial, and 76% were convicted. The longest sentence was 50 years (Browne, 1987).

Based on the available research, the presence of expert testimony about BWS does not appear to have a powerful effect on verdicts. For example, in a series of three experimental studies, Regina Schuller (1994) found that including expert testimony on BWS in simulated trials produced only a modest shift in verdict choice away from murder and toward manslaughter. In addition to looking at verdicts, Schuller recorded the deliberations of mock jurors. Analyses of these recorded deliberations revealed a slight shift in tone: Mock jurors who heard an expert testify about BWS made more statements sympathetic to the perceptions and actions of the defendant. Other studies have found similarly weak effects (e.g., Follingstad et al., 1989).

The Scientific Validity of BWS.   Although BWS appears to enjoy acceptance among many mental health professionals, the scientific validity of the concept has been criticized by many researchers. Most of the research supporting the existence of BWS was based on interviews with battered women living in shelters. It is likely that many of these women received information about BWS from therapists and through conversations with other battered women living at the shelter. When such women report experiencing all of the symptoms associated with BWS, we can't be sure whether they have reinterpreted their experiences and symptoms in light of their knowledge about the syndrome. To date, there has been no systematic comparison of the symptoms exhibited by battered women, nonbattered women, and women who suffer other forms of trauma.

In a critique of the scientific validity and legal utility of BWS, Mary Ann Dutton has argued that BWS does not accurately or fully capture the experience of women who suffer from violent abuse. Dutton (2000) points out several limitations of the concept. First, there is considerable variability among the psychological and behavioral symptoms displayed by battered women. How a woman reacts is likely to depend on the woman's age, resources, experiences, the nature and frequency of the violent abuse, and whether or not there are children in the home. Second, BWS is vague. There is no well-established measure for deciding whether or not a woman should be diagnosed as suffering from BWS. Labeling a woman as suffering from BWS may not be the best way to help judges and jurors understand what happened. Indeed, the focus on BWS may limit the analysis and exclude consideration of other important concerns. Dutton argues that it is more important to understand the dynamics of the violence, what the woman did to "resist, avoid, escape, or stop" the violence, and the effect of the woman's efforts over time. A variety of situational factors also need to be taken into account—the woman's economic dependence on her abuser, her prior experience with abuse, and the amount of social support she received from friends, family, police, and medical professionals.

A final criticism of BWS it that it locates the problem in the mind of the battered woman. By focusing on the internal "disease" of the woman, blame for the violence is directed away from the man who batters and away from the failures of the legal system to deal effectively with domestic violence. For example, Mary Ann Dutton (2000) argues that using the term BWS, ". . . may inadvertently communicate to the jury or judge the misguided notion of an 'abuse excuse' and perpetuate stereotypic images of battered women" (p. 2).

Despite the serious scientific limitations of BWS, the concept of BWS has had an important impact on the legal system. David Faigman—a law professor who has been highly critical of the scientific validity of BWS—notes that the use of BWS has had several positive effects. It has raised awareness of the frequency of domestic violence, spurred research on the interpersonal dynamics of violence in intimate relationships, and been instrumental in exposing the limitations of the traditional, somewhat sexist legal doctrine of self-defense:

> The law of self-defense is largely driven by male conceptions of violence. Hence, in most jurisdictions, the defendant must show that she used a proportional amount of force and only to respond to an imminent harm. This is an idealized version of the way men fight. But a woman who is physically smaller than a man must defend herself in different ways. Whatever the validity of the notion of a "fair fight" for men, it cannot serve as a model of fairness for women. (Faigman, 1999, p. 73).

RAPE TRAUMA SYNDROME (RTS)

In 1974, Ann Burgess and Lynda Holmstrom published a research study describing how victims respond to the trauma of being raped. Burgess and Holmstrom interviewed 92 rape victims who had been admitted to a hospital for treatment. Each victim was interviewed within an hour of admission and then interviewed again about a month later. The term Rape Trauma Syndrome (RTS) was invented to describe the cluster of symptoms shared by the women in their sample. In their original conceptualization, Burgess and Holmstrom described recovery from rape as a two-stage process moving through an acute crisis phase to a longer-term reorganization phase. The "crisis" phase typically lasts a few weeks and includes severe physical symptoms (e.g., sleeplessness, loss of appetite, trembling, numbness, or pain), as well as severe emotional disturbance manifested in symptoms such as extreme fear, persistent nightmares, depression, or even suicide attempts. In the days and weeks following the rape, a rape victim's intellectual functioning is also likely to be impaired. The victim may seem dazed, confused, out of touch with her immediate environment, or "in shock." The psychological aftermath of rape is captured in the following quote from a college student's description of her reactions to being raped by the resident advisor in her dormitory:

> There's no way to describe what was going on inside me. I was losing control and I'd never been so terrified and helpless in my life. I felt as if my whole world had been kicked out from under me and I had been left to drift all alone in the darkness. I had horrible nightmares in which I relived the rape and others which were even worse. I was terrified of being with people and terrified of being alone. I couldn't concentrate on anything and began failing several classes. Deciding what to wear in the morning was enough to make me panic and cry uncontrollably. I was convinced I was going crazy. . . . (Allison & Wrightsman, 1993, p. 153).

The length of phase one varies, but eventually the rape victim moves into phase two. Whereas phase one is an intense reaction to the trauma of being raped, phase two involves a long-term process of recovery from rape. Rape victims often respond by blaming themselves for not having been able to prevent or stop the rape. They might castigate themselves for walking through a bad area of town, or for leaving a window open or a door unlocked. They might blame themselves for not having been able to fight off or run away from the attacker (Rowland, 1985). One survivor wrote:

> People tell me I shouldn't feel like that, it wasn't my fault, but still I feel like it was. Perhaps I should just have fought harder and not been afraid. Perhaps I shouldn't have let him do this to me" (Rape Survivors, 2001).

Rape has an enduring impact on victims. Women who have been the victims of sexual assault are at greater risk of becoming unemployed and divorced. One study found that, although 74% of rape victims reported that they had returned to normal functioning about five years after the rape, the other 26% reported that they had not yet recovered (Burgess & Holmstrom, 1979). Although there is recovery, it is important to note that recovery is not a process of "getting over" the rape. Instead, it involves finding ways to integrate the experience of rape into one's life to minimize negative after-effects (Frazier, Conlon, & Glaser, 2001). One rape survivor described the impact of rape on her life 12 years later:

> It becomes part of your person as anything, any type of huge change in your life. . . . I am a different person than I was 12 years ago. And it will never go away. You learn to live around it. . . . You try to take it and use it to go in a positive direction but it never goes away (Thompson, 1998).

Although the concept of RTS has served the important function of drawing attention to the effects of rape, the research evidence on RTS is inconclusive. Burgess and Holmstrom's initial research was quite limited. Only rape victims who were admitted to a hospital were studied, so the sample was somewhat unrepresentative. Many rapes—especially those committed by dates or acquaintances—go unreported. Also, because there was no control group (e.g., a comparison group of women who had not experienced a trauma or a comparison group of women who experienced another form of trauma), it was not clear which symptoms were specific to rape victims. Finally, the follow-up interviews did not extend beyond one month. More recent research demonstrates that some symptoms are strongly associated with rape victims but that the two-stage recovery process hypothesized by Burgess and Holmstrom is not typical (Frazier, Conlon, & Glaser, 2001).

Among the symptoms most strongly associated with rape are fear, anxiety, depression, self-blame, disturbed social relationships, and sexual dysfunction. These reactions tend to be especially intense during the three or four months following the rape (Frazier & Borgida, 1992). Although these same reactions may be associated with other types of trauma, the symptoms are likely to take a particular form in rape victims. For example, in rape victims, fear and anxiety are likely to be most strongly felt in situations or settings similar to the one in which the rape occurred. Also, rape survivors are especially likely to experience a loss of sexual desire and decreased enjoyment of sex with their partners (Becker et al., 1984). Like other victims of trauma, rape victims face the long-term challenge of regaining a sense of safety and a sense of control over their environment.

Of course, not every rape survivor experiences the same symptoms with the same intensity. In their comprehensive discussion of the factors affecting responses to rape, Mary Koss and Mary Harvey (1991) describe four broad classes of variables that modulate the responses of rape survivors: (1) characteristics of the person (e.g., age, maturity, coping capabilities, ability to make use of social support), (2) characteristics of the event itself (e.g., the violence of the rape, the duration of the rape), (3) the victim's environment (e.g., support of friends and family, attitudes of surrounding community, physical and emotional safety), and (4) the therapeutic intervention (if any) used (e.g., timing of the intervention, how effectively the intervention empowers the survivor). These resources—both personal and environmental—strongly influence how effectively victims cope with the psychological effects of rape.

RTS Testimony in the Courtroom.   The concept of RTS (like the concept of BWS) was created to serve as a therapeutic tool—to help victims come to terms with their experience, and to help therapists assist rape victims during therapy. But, like BWS, it has been appropriated for use in the courtroom.

The role of the expert who testifies about RTS is to educate jurors about the reactions of rape victims. A secondary purpose of expert testimony about RTS may be to disabuse jurors of common misconceptions about rape. These so-called "rape myths" include the following: that women don't really mean it when they say they don't want sex when a man initiates sexual activity, that the typical rape is committed by someone unknown to the victim (in fact, most rapists are acquaintances of the victim and only about 15% of rapes are committed by strangers), and that it is impossible to rape a woman who is unwilling (Koss & Harvey, 1991).

Rape trials usually turn on the issue of consent. Most defendants do not deny having sex with the alleged victim, but they do claim that the sex was consensual. To counter a defendant's claim that sex was consensual, prosecutors have imported RTS into the courtroom. Psychological experts testifying for the prosecution will point out that the symptoms being experienced by the alleged victim closely match the emotional and behavioral responses predicted by RTS. Used in this way, expert testimony about RTS is intended to bolster the credibility of the alleged victim and thereby improve the odds of convicting the defendant. Conversely, psychological experts testifying for the defense may point out that the alleged victim's behavior was not consistent with how women typically respond to rape. Any lack of fit between the behaviors displayed by the alleged victim and the behaviors predicted by RTS invites jurors to infer that the woman consented to sex with the defendant.

Sometimes victims respond to rape in unexpected or counterintuitive ways. In cases where an alleged rape victim exhibits puzzling behavior, psychological experts may use RTS as a way of explaining that behavior (Faigman, 1999). In the case of *People v. Taylor* (1990), a 19-year-old woman reported that she had been raped and sodomized at gunpoint on a secluded beach near her home in Long Island. Around 11:00 pm, she returned home, woke up her mother, and told her about the rape. The mother called the police. Initially, the young woman told her mother she didn't know who the attacker was. When questioned by police, she again reported that she did not know who her attacker was. However, just a couple hours later, at about 1:15 am, she told her mother that she had been raped by John Taylor, a man she had known for several years. Mr. Taylor was arrested and put on trial for rape. In fact, he had two trials. During the first trial, no testimony about RTS was allowed. The jury failed to reach a unanimous verdict. During the second trial, the judge decided to allow testimony about RTS. The prosecution used that testimony to help explain two puzzling aspects of the alleged victim's behavior: her reluctance to identify her rapist for more than two hours after the rape, and her apparent calmness in the hours following the rape. The defense had argued that these behaviors were highly uncharacteristic of rape victims. At trial, a counselor who had worked with victims of sexual assault testified that, because of fear and shock, rape victims sometimes appear calm and dazed during the first few hours following the attack. The counselor also testified that during this period, rape victims are sometimes unwilling to identify their attackers. The jury who heard this testimony convicted John Taylor.

Judges must make decisions about admissibility based on an assessment of the scientific validity of the testimony, the helpfulness of the testimony to the jury, and the possible prejudicial impact of the testimony (Frazier & Borgida, 1992). Many questions have been raised about the scientific validity of RTS. At its core, RTS predicts that rape victims will show a distinctive pattern of responses and move through a two-stage process. But, as noted earlier, the responses of rape victims are not uniform or universal. Just because a victim shows symptoms consistent or inconsistent with RTS does not tell us whether or not she (or he) was raped. Consequently, it is problematic to use RTS as a means of assessing the credibility of a woman who claims to have been raped. Some women who have been raped do not show the symptoms specified by RTS and some women who falsely claim that they were raped show many of the symptoms associated with RTS. For these reasons, the closeness of the "match" between an alleged rape victim's symptoms and the symptoms specified by RTS is not a reliable indicator of rape. It is impossible to tell a genuine rape victim from someone who had sex voluntarily merely on the basis of her post-event behavior.

A second question a judge must consider is whether RTS is outside the common knowledge of the jurors. If the judge believes that such testimony won't provide the jury with new and relevant information, he or she is not likely to admit the testimony. According to the rules of evidence, helpfulness is a basic requirement for admitting scientific evidence. Scientific testimony should not be allowed unless it adds "precision or depth to the jury's ability to reach conclusions about that subject" (*State v. Helterbridle,* 1980). Some judges decide not to admit testimony because it is deemed to be part of the common knowledge of the average juror. Only information judged to be "beyond the ken" of jurors is admitted.

Third, a judge might decide that allowing RTS testimony might be prejudicial—that is, it might improperly bias the jury against the defendant. Judges are required to guard the role of the jury as fact-finder. It is the jury that must reach conclusions about the credibility of witnesses and it is the jury that must decide whether a defendant is guilty or not guilty. Some judges have refused to admit RTS testimony because they believe it will interfere with the jury's essential role as fact-finder (it will "invade the province of the jury" or "usurp the role of the jury" as it is sometimes put). Judges may believe that allowing an expert to testify about RTS is equivalent to allowing a witness to say that the woman was raped. Some critics have argued that use of the word "rape" in RTS necessarily implies that a rape did occur. In court, saying that a woman suffers from RTS may unfairly bolster her credibility with jurors.

If a judge does allow RTS testimony, there is a further complication: RTS testimony may open the door to more extensive questioning of the rape victim at trial (Faigman, 1999). Prior to the 1970s, alleged victims of rape could be subjected to extensive questioning about their past sexual experiences. At that time, the reasoning was that a jury needed to know whether a woman was promiscuous to determine whether sexual intercourse was consensual. During the 1970s, so-called "rape shield laws" were passed to prevent lawyers from delving into the sexual histories of alleged rape victims at trial. An unintended consequence of allowing RTS testimony is that if a prosecution expert testifies that the alleged victim of rape suffers from RTS, it can open the door to an examination of the victim's past. That is, a defense attorney may be permitted to ask the plaintiff about her sexual history in an effort to prove that what appears to be RTS may in fact be a response to other events in her past (e.g., sexual abuse prior to the alleged rape).

POST TRAUMATIC STRESS DISORDER (PTSD)

The DSM-IV (short for the *Diagnostic and Statistical Manual of Mental Disorders,* 4th edition), the book that provides a comprehensive listing of the diagnostic categories used by clinical psychologists, lists PTSD as the primary diagnosis for people suffering from the after-effects of extreme trauma. The diagnosis of PTSD is reserved for people who have "experienced, witnessed, or were confronted with an event or events that involved actual or threatened death or serious injury, or a threat to the physical integrity of self or others," and who have responded with "intense fear, helplessness, or horror" (DSM-IV, p. 128). The diagnosis includes four other criteria: (1) re-experiencing the event (e.g., recurrent nightmares or memories of the event); (2) avoidance of stimuli associated with the event (e.g., a victim of rape might move out of the house or apartment where she was raped); (3) heightened arousal (e.g., insomnia, fear, or difficulty concentrating); and (4) persistent symptoms that last more than a month. Although PTSD was originally formulated to describe psychological symptoms experienced by combat veterans returning from the Vietnam War, rape survivors are now the largest group classified as suffering from PTSD (Norris, 1992).

Some researchers have argued that it might be useful to use the more general term PTSD instead of either RTS or BWS when providing testimony about the responses of trauma victims. Using PTSD would have several advantages: PTSD is already an established diagnostic category in the DSM-IV; there are several tests and structured interviews used to assess PTSD; and, in the case of RTS, use of the word "rape" could be avoided. However, others have suggested that some symptoms specific to rape victims—for example, depression, sexual dysfunction, reduced sexual satisfaction, guilt and self-blame—are not well captured by the more general diagnostic category of PTSD. Eventually, it may be possible to create a single large diagnostic category that manages to capture typical responses to a variety of traumatic events, as well as more specific reactions to particular types of events like rape. Others have suggested developing more differentiated subcategories of PTSD, for example, a subcategory for people who have experienced chronic interpersonal violence such as wife abuse or incest (Herman, 1992). After a thorough analysis of the problems with using RTS in the court-room, Laura Boeschen, Bruce Sales, and Mary Koss (1998) reached the following conclusion:

> Although RTS has historical importance, it makes for confusing and potentially unscientific expert testimony and should no longer be used in the courtroom. PTSD, although far from being a perfect diagnosis for rape survivors, looks to be a more reliable and valid diagnosis for expert testimony, especially when accompanied by a description of the additional post rape symptoms absent from the PTSD diagnostic criteria. . . . If used cautiously and appropriately, expert testimony on PTSD can help to edu-cate the judge or jury about common reactions to rape (p. 428).

The same arguments could be made about the use of BWS in the courtroom. Both RTS and BWS might be usefully assimilated into the more expansive diagnostic category of PTSD. Use of that broader, bet-ter validated category may solve some of the persistent problems associ-ated with the use of specialized syndromes like BWS and RTS.

Readings to Supplement This Chapter

Articles

Davis, D., & Follette, W. (2002). Rethinking the probative value of evidence: Base rates, intuitive profiling, and the "postdiction" of behavior. *Law and Human Behavior, 26,* 133–158.

Frazier, P., Conlon, A., & Glaser, T. (2001). Positive and negative life changes following sexual assault. *Journal of Consulting and Clinical Psychology, 69,* 1048–1055.

Holtzworth-Munroe, A. (2000). A typology of men who are violent toward their female partners: Making sense of the heterogeneity in husband violence. *Current Directions in Psychological Science, 9,* 140–143.

Salfati, C. G., & Canter, D. (1999). Differentiating stranger murders: Profiling offender characteristics from behavioral styles. *Behavioral Sciences and the Law, 17,* 391–406.

Terrance, C. A., Matheson, K., & Spanos, N. P. (2000). Effects of judicial instructions and case characteristics in a mock jury trial of battered women who kill. *Law and Human Behavior, 24,* 207–230.

Books

Jackson, J. L., & Bekerian, D. A. (Eds.). (1997). *Offender profiling: Theory, research and practice.* New York: Wiley.

4

Competence and Insanity

Chapter Outline

● ●

The Meaning of Legal Competence
How the Criminal Justice System Deals
with Incompetent Defendants
Tests and Techniques for Evaluating CST

THE INSANITY DEFENSE

The Evolution of Insanity Law
Three Important Cases and Their Consequences
    The McNaughton Case
    The Durham Case
    The Hinkley Case
Tests and Techniques for Assessing Insanity
How Jurors Define Insanity
The Larger Context of Insanity Law
In Conclusion

On a summer morning in 2001, Andrea Yates filled the bathtub in her home and called her children to the bathroom one by one. Her 3-year-old son Paul was the first to be called. She forced Paul into the bathtub and held his head underwater until he stopped breathing. She carried his soaked body to the bedroom, laid him down, and covered him with a sheet. Then her sons Luke, age 2, and John, age 5, were killed in the same way. Yates's 6-month-old daughter Mary—who was on the bathroom floor crying while her three brothers were killed—was the next to be held underwater. Just as Yates was lifting her daughter's lifeless body from the tub, her oldest child Noah (age 7) walked in and asked what was wrong with his little sister. When Yates tried to grab Noah, he ran away. She chased him down a hallway, dragged him to the bathroom, and drowned him next to his sister.

After killing all five of her children, Andrea Yates called 911 and told the operator that she was ill and that she needed an ambulance. She also called her husband Russell and told him to come home. "It's time," she told him, "I finally did it." Then she hung up. When police arrived at the scene, Noah was found floating face down in the tub; his brothers and sister were found laid out in the same bed. Mary's head was resting on the shoulder of her brother John. His mother had placed his arms around the body of his sister. She told police that she had been thinking about killing her children "ever since I realized that I have not been a good mother to them." She said that the children "weren't developing correctly." To the surprise of many, the grieving husband refused to condemn his wife. "I don't blame her a bit," he said, "If she received the medical treatment she deserved, then the kids would be alive and well. And Andrea would be well on her way to recovery" (Springer, 2002).

When Andrea Yates went on trial in 2002, two keys facts were undisputed: She had killed her five children, and she was mentally ill. Before the trial, a hearing was held to consider whether Yates was competent to stand trial on murder charges. Based on testimony by psychologists who had interviewed Yates and studied her history, she was deemed competent to stand trial. As the trial began, she entered a plea of not guilty by reason of insanity. Because Yates had confessed to the murders, and because the physical evidence against her was overwhelming, the trial focused on whether she was legally insane. After listening to weeks of complex expert testimony, a jury of eight women and four men deliberated for three hours and 40 minutes before finding

Andrea Yates guilty. They apparently agreed with the prosecutor in the case, who argued that Yates "made the choice knowing that it was a sin in the eyes of God and a crime in the eyes of the state" (Stack, 2002, p. A18). Her defense attorney reacted bitterly to the verdict, "If this woman doesn't meet the standard for insanity, nobody does. We might as well wipe it off the books" (p. A18). But all the expert testimony about Yates's mental illness may have influenced the sentence she received. When asked to choose between life in prison or the death penalty, jurors took less than an hour to decide to send Andrea Yates to prison.

In the trial of Andrea Yates and many other trials, decisions about "competence" and "insanity" are at the heart of legal proceedings. Because these decisions require judgments about the psychological functioning of a defendant, clinical psychologists—those who study and treat various forms of psychological dysfunction and mental illness—are often crucial to the legal process in such cases. But when clinical psychologists are called upon to evaluate competence or insanity, they must force their psychological diagnoses to fit into the specific categories provided by the law.

THE MEANING OF LEGAL COMPETENCE

Defendants have the most to lose during criminal proceedings. It is their liberty that is at stake. Consequently, it is important that they understand what is going on at every stage in the criminal justice process, from arrest to sentencing. A defendant charged with a serious crime has a right to a trial. But what if the defendant can't understand what is going on before or during trial? Perhaps the accused lacks the mental capacity to understand the complexities of a legal proceeding. Perhaps he or she is substantially impaired by mental illness. But if we judge some people to be too impaired to stand trial, how much impairment is too much? Does it matter if the defendant can understand much but not all of what happens in court? These are some of the difficult questions surrounding the legal concept of "competence."

There are several reasons to be concerned about competence. One set of concerns involves fairness to the defendant. Full participation of the defendant in his or her own defense improves the probability of a just verdict. In an adversarial system, defendants must be able to provide their lawyers with information about the crime and about the witnesses who testify at trial. Without the assistance of the defendant, the attorney is less able to mount an effective defense. That makes mistaken convictions more likely. And, even though a lawyer handles the defense, the defendant remains ultimately responsible for several key decisions: whether to plead guilty, whether to waive a trial by jury, whether to testify, and whether to accept a plea bargain offered by the prosecution (Winick, 1996). A second set of concerns has to do with public respect for the criminal justice system. To use the full power of the state to try, convict, and punish defendants who do not understand the nature of the legal proceedings against them undermines the perceived legitimacy of the legal system. It would simply not seem fair. A related but less central concern is that unruly behavior in court by a mentally disturbed defendant disrupts the dignity of legal proceedings.

The legal doctrine of incompetence originated in English common law of the seventeenth century. Competence was considered critical because, at the time, defendants usually had to argue their own case. At present, the most frequently evaluated form of competence is called competence to stand trial (CST). It was defined by the U.S. Supreme Court in the 1960 case of *Dusky v. United States* and refers to the defendant's ". . . sufficient present ability to consult with his attorney with a reasonable degree of rational understanding and whether he has a rational as well as factual understanding of the proceedings against him." Notice the word *present* in the definition. CST refers to the psychological state of the defendant *at the time of trial*. The defendant's psychological state at the time of the crime is not relevant to a determination of CST (although it is relevant to a determination of insanity). During the 1990s, the Supreme Court held that there should be a presumption of competence. That is, the defense bears the burden of proving that the defendant is incompetent. But the standard of proof is a "preponderance of the evidence." Using this standard, the defense must show that it is more likely than not that the defendant is incompetent (*Cooper v. Oklahoma*, 1996; *Medina v. California*, 1992).

It is essential to recognize that CST is a legal, not a psychological, concept. Being judged CST does not certify robust mental health or even normal mental functioning. It merely means that a defendant meets the minimal standard of being able to cooperate with an attorney, and is aware of the nature and possible consequences of the proceedings against him or her. Even people suffering from psychosis or mental retardation can be judged CST. In addition, CST is a somewhat flexible standard—a defendant facing very serious charges in a case with complex facts may need to be more competent than someone facing less serious charges and a simpler legal proceeding. Also, if the defendant has many friends and family members who can provide information helpful to the defense, the competence of the defendant may be seen as less crucial.

Although CST is by far the most frequently assessed form of competence, issues of competence can arise well before and long after trial. The issue of competence may surface during a suspect's first encounter with the police. Children or adolescents, adults who are mentally impaired, or mentally ill suspects may not be competent to waive their Miranda rights or to provide a voluntary and accurate confession. Next, at arraignment, there may be an issue of whether the defendant is competent to decide to plead guilty. In an early decision (*Johnson v. Zerbst*, 1938), the Supreme Court held that a guilty plea must be "knowing, voluntary, and intelligent." In part, this means that defendants must understand the charges against them, as well as the potential consequences of a conviction (e.g., spending several years in prison). Judges are required to question the defendant to make sure he or she understands that by entering a plea of guilty, important constitutional rights are forfeited: the right to a trial by jury, the right to remain silent, and the right to confront one's accusers. Later, at the trial stage, a defendant may decide to serve as his or her own attorney. Here again the issue of competence can be raised. Do such defendants fully understand the consequences of waiving their right to an attorney? You have probably heard the old saying that "anyone who serves as their own lawyer has a fool for a client." Some lawyers argue that simply asking to represent oneself is evidence of incompetence. However, the law only requires that the decision to serve as one's own attorney is voluntary and made "with understanding" (*Faretta v. California*, 1975).

A rare situation involving the assessment of competence involves prisoners sentenced to die in the execution chamber. Although the Supreme Court has ruled that executions do not violate the Eighth Amendment's prohibition against cruel and unusual punishment, it has also ruled that it would be cruel and unusual to execute an incompetent prisoner who does not understand why he or she is being executed (*Ford v. Wainwright*, 1986). In some instances, mental health professionals have been enlisted in the ethically troubling process of restoring prisoners to competence so that they can then be executed (see Chapter 9).

Although courts and psychologists use somewhat different standards to judge different forms of competence, in the 1993 case of *Godinez v. Moran,* the Supreme Court endorsed a single standard of competence. That decision permits states to develop separate standards for different types of competence but requires that the *Dusky* standard be used as the minimum requirement.

HOW THE CRIMINAL JUSTICE SYSTEM DEALS WITH INCOMPETENT DEFENDANTS

Even if a defendant does not want to raise the question of competence, ethical guidelines require lawyers to tell the presiding judge if they believe that a defendant may be incompetent. Usually the defense lawyer raises the issue, but prosecutors and judges are also ethically obliged to be vigilant for incompetent defendants. Further, if either attorney raises the issue of the defendant's competence, the presiding judge almost always orders a psychological evaluation. Unlike most other issues decided in court, there tends to be little dispute about providing a competence evaluation when it is requested. Prosecutors seldom object to requests for competency evaluations, and judges rarely deny such requests (Roesch & Golding, 1987).

The issue of CST is typically raised at a pretrial hearing but can be ordered by the judge at any time during the trial. At least one, and occasionally more than one, mental health professional—usually a psychiatrist, clinical psychologist, or social worker—is asked to serve as an evaluator. The evaluator (or evaluators) will usually interview the defendant, administer psychological tests, review the defendant's history, and write a report. That report will summarize the evaluator's findings and offer a conclusion about the defendant's ability to participate in his or her trial and cooperate with his or her attorney. The evaluation can be done on either an "inpatient" or an "outpatient" basis. Inpatient evaluations involve holding a defendant in a mental institution for a period usually ranging from a few days to a few weeks. An advantage of evaluations in institutional settings is that they provide multiple opportunities to observe the defendant's behavior over time. Outpatient evaluations are those that occur outside of mental institutions. They are usually conducted in jails or local clinics and are now much more common than inpatient evaluations. Usually, a written report is all that is required by the court. But, it is not uncommon for a judge to ask a psychologist to testify about his or her findings.

It is estimated that somewhere between 25,000 and 39,000 criminal defendants are evaluated for CST every year (Zapf & Roesch, 2000). That is roughly 5% of all defendants. Of those defendants who are referred for a competence evaluation, only about 12% are actually found to be incompetent (Melton, Petrila, Poythress, & Slobogin, 1997). It is quite rare for a judge to reject the conclusion of an evaluator—especially if the defendant has been found incompetent. Research on defendants judged to be incompetent has revealed that such defendants tend to live on the fringes of society. As a group, they tend to have a history of treatment for mental illness, to show obvious symptoms of current mental illness, to have a history of drug abuse, and to be charged with a serious crime (about half are accused of violent crimes). They also tend to be socially isolated, unmarried, unemployed, poorly educated, and below average in intelligence (Nicholson & Kugler, 1991; Nestor, Daggett, Haycosck, & Price, 1999). If an evaluator reaches the conclusion that a defendant is incompetent, the report will usually contain recommendations for treatments that might restore the defendant's competence.

Prior to the 1972 decision in *Jackson v. Indiana,* defendants judged to be incompetent could be held in mental hospitals for indefinite periods. Indeed, just prior to that decision, researchers found that about half of people found incompetent spent the rest of their lives in mental institutions (McGarry, 1971). Hospital stays often exceeded the amount of time defendants would have served in prison if they had been found guilty of the crime. The *Jackson* ruling limited the period of confinement to the time necessary to determine if the defendant could be returned to competence in the "foreseeable future." As a result of the *Jackson* decision, most states now limit confinement to somewhere between four and 18 months. If, after that period, the defendant is still judged to be incompetent, an extension of several more months can be granted. Significant problems and uncertainties arise if, even after this extended hospital stay, the defendant has still not been restored to competence. Sometimes involuntary civil commitment proceedings are initiated. But to commit someone to an institution against his or her will using involuntary civil commitment laws is difficult. The person must either be shown to be "gravely disabled" (unable to care for him/herself and to provide for basic needs like food or shelter) or to be "imminently dangerous to self or others" (LaFond, 1996).

Even if an incompetent defendant is hospitalized, it is not certain that he or she will receive the kind of treatment that will restore competence. The quality of treatment at mental health facilities varies considerably and sometimes there is little emphasis on restoring legal competence. However, a study conducted by Alex Siegel and Amiran Elwork (1990) suggests that training specifically designed to explain courtroom rules and procedures can help to restore CST. Those researchers used two groups of defendants who had been judged to be incompetent and who were confined in psychiatric hospitals. The treatment group was given information about courtroom rules, personnel, and procedures by means of videotapes, lectures, and discussions. The control group received more standard forms of therapy. By the time the training ended, hospital staff judged 43% of the treatment group to be CST, but only 15% of the control group to be CST.

Occasionally lawyers may request competence evaluations for purely strategic reasons, that is, to gain some advantage. For example, a competence evaluation may be requested by either side to delay the trial. A competence evaluation may postpone trial for a few weeks and give attorneys more time to prepare. Also, prosecutors may request a competence evaluation to prevent the defendant from being released on bail, and either side may seek an evaluation to gain information about the feasibility of an insanity defense (Winick, 1996). Information gathered during a competency evaluation cannot be introduced at trial *unless* the defendant places his or her mental state into evidence, for example, by pleading not guilty by reason of insanity (*Estelle v. Smith,* 1981).

Judgments about competence may be especially sensitive when the defendant is under 18 years of age. One prominent forensic psychologist—Thomas Grisso—has argued that competence evaluations should be automatically triggered for juveniles if the defendant: is 12 years old or younger, has been previously diagnosed as mentally retarded or suffering from mental illness, has a learning disability, is of low or "borderline" intelligence, or if there are significant deficits in attention, memory, or understanding of reality (Grisso, 1997). If CST is controversial in a given case, two experts may be asked to perform evaluations and a formal competency hearing will be held. At such a hearing, both experts will be questioned by prosecutors and defenders.

An interesting issue related to competence was decided in the 1992 case of *Riggins v. Nevada.* David Riggins was mentally ill. While he was waiting to be tried for robbery and murder, he complained of hearing voices and severe insomnia. A psychiatrist acting on behalf of the court prescribed an antipsychotic drug (Mellaril) and a relaxant (Dilantin). Riggins had suffered from similar problems in the past and had been treated before using these same medications. The drugs were successful in stabilizing Riggins's behavior and he was declared CST. However, because Riggins was relying on an insanity defense, he asked that he not be forced to take Mellaril during his trial. He argued that the drug made him unable to assist his defense lawyer and that the jury should be able to observe him in his unmedicated state—the state he was in when he committed the murder. The judge refused his request and the jury convicted him and sentenced him to death. However, on appeal, the U.S. Supreme Court ruled that forcing Riggins to take medication deprived him of due process. The ruling held that involuntary medication was only permissible to achieve essential state interests—such as a fair trial or safety of the defendant or others.

TESTS AND TECHNIQUES FOR EVALUATING CST

Because competence to stand trial refers to psychological states and mental capacities, it makes sense to consult clinical psychologists and other mental health professionals when trying to assess the competence of a particular defendant. But, because the law does not prescribe a particular method of evaluation, the specific assessment techniques used by a particular clinician tend to be a function of his or her training, orientation, experience, and sophistication. Up until the early 1970s, mental health professionals often attempted to measure CST through the use of techniques designed for other purposes. Then, beginning in 1971, researchers began to develop tests specifically designed to evaluate CST.

In 1971, researchers at the Harvard Laboratory of Community Psychiatry introduced the Competency Screening Test. People taking this test are asked to complete 22 sentence fragments such as, "When I go to court, the lawyer will _____" and "If the jury finds me guilty, I will _____." Responses are scored as "0" (incompetent), "1" (uncertain competence), or "2" (competent). One weakness of this early approach is that, because of the wide-open nature of the responses, significant training was required to interpret and score the responses of the person being examined (Lipsitt, Lelos, & McGarry, 1971). A second approach developed by the Harvard group (the Competency

Assessment Instrument) uses a systematic one-hour interview. The Competency Assessment Instrument was noteworthy for its attention to several components of CST including: the ability to communicate with an attorney; awareness of defenses that are realistically available; understanding of the roles played by people in the courtroom; understanding of the charges and their seriousness; understanding of the sequence and purpose of trial procedures; awareness of the likely outcome of the trial and the potential penalties if convicted; ability to inform the defense attorney of relevant facts and distortions in the testimony of prosecution witnesses; and the capacity to provide useful testimony on one's own behalf (if necessary).

Since the pioneering work of the Harvard Laboratory in the 1970s, several tests have been developed to improve the evaluation of competence. The Fitness Interview Test-Revised (FIT-R) was developed by researchers in Canada to assess both legal knowledge and psychopathology (Roesch, Zapf, Eaves, & Webster, 1998). The Computer-Assisted Determination of Competence to Proceed (CADCOMP) aims to provide a fuller assessment of a defendant's psychological functioning. A defendant's answers to 272 questions can be scored and distilled into a narrative report on competence by a computer program (Barnard et al., 1991). Because some studies have suggested that existing tests may have difficulty assessing mentally impaired defendants, Carol Everington (1990) devised a technique called the Competence Assessment for Standing Trial for Defendants with Mental Retardation (CAST-MR). It uses both open-response and multiple-choice questions to assess basic legal requirements like the ability to assist defense counsel, and understanding of how a case moves through the criminal justice system.

The term "adjudicative competence" is often used to capture the various types of abilities needed to participate effectively in all stages of the legal process. In 1993, Richard Bonnie wrote an influential paper arguing that adjudicative competence consists of two underlying components. The first component—foundational competence—involves the capacity to assist counsel and is essential for ensuring the fairness, dignity, and accuracy of the criminal justice system. Foundational competence implies a basic understanding of the trial process as well as the capacity to provide a lawyer with information relevant to the trial. If a defendant is competent to assist counsel, then the second component—decisional competence—comes into play. This component has to do with the capacity to make informed, independent decisions. Based in part on Bonnie's distinction, a national network of researchers (funded by the MacArthur Foundation) developed the MacArthur Structured Assessment of the Competencies of Criminal Defendants (MacSAC-CD). An unusual feature of this test is that most of its questions are structured around a hypothetical vignette involving a bar fight:

"Two men, Fred and Reggie, are playing pool at a bar and get into a fight. Fred hits Reggie with a pool stick. Reggie falls and hits his head on the floor so hard that he nearly dies" (Hoge et al., 1997). CST is assessed by presenting variants of this basic scenario and asking defendants to decide how Fred should respond to questions and assist his lawyer. If the defendant being evaluated can't answer a particular question correctly, he or she is told the correct answer and then asked more open-ended questions to see if the misunderstanding has been corrected. Following the open-ended questions, a few true-false questions are asked to further clarify which areas the defendant may not understand. Three abilities are assessed: understanding of the legal system, reasoning skills, and the defendant's appreciation of his or her own circumstances. Two versions of "Mac" are available. The 82-item MacSAC-CD takes about two hours and is used primarily for research purposes. The much shorter (22-item) MacArthur Competence Assessment Tool-Criminal Adjudication (MacCAT-CA) takes about 30 minutes and is designed to be used by clinicians who are often asked to make quick judgments about competence (Hoge et al., 1997).

Modern tests that focus on legal competence have several advantages over more general tests of psychological functioning. The newer, more focused techniques are able to assess understanding of specific legal issues and allow for efficient outpatient assessment of CST. Also, if the test is widely used, it can serve as a common frame of reference for professionals evaluating competence. In using such tests, many forensic psychologists have emphasized the importance of being guided by a "contextual" or "functional" approach when evaluating competence (Zapf & Roesch, 2000). Such an approach requires that evaluators keep in mind the specific demands of the particular legal case. For example, Stephen Golding and Ronald Roesch (1988) have argued that to be judged incompetent, a defendant must not only be severely disturbed:

> . . . it must be further demonstrated that such severe disturbance in *this* defendant, facing *these* charges, *in light of existing* evidence, anticipating the substantial effort of a *particular* attorney with a *relationship of*

known characteristics, results in the defendant being unable to rationally assist the attorney or to comprehend the nature of the proceedings and their likely outcome (p. 79).

Sometimes psychologists or lawyers suspect that a defendant is faking incompetence to avoid going to trial. For example, a defendant who is facing a murder trial might claim to be suffering from amnesia. If that defendant really can't remember anything about the crime, he or she would have a very difficult time assisting his or her attorney. But some courts have held that because claims of amnesia may be fraudulent, severe memory loss alone does not mean that a defendant should be ruled incompetent (*Morrow v. Maryland,* 1982). The problem of faking mental illness or disability is known as "malingering." Specifically, malingering is the deliberate feigning of physical or psychological symptoms in order to gain something positive (e.g., an insurance payment or compensatory damages) or to avoid something negative (e.g., a long prison sentence). Malingering can be difficult to detect. Some psychological tests contain questions designed to expose malingering, and a few specific tests have been developed to help psychologists detect people who are faking their symptoms.

Just as it may be possible to fake incompetence, it may also be possible to fake insanity. One of the most extreme examples of malingering ever recorded involved a serial killer named Kenneth Bianchi. Over a period of five months in 1977 and 1978, Bianchi (who was dubbed the "Hillside Strangler") raped and strangled several young women and left their bodies on the hillsides above Los Angeles. When apprehended, Bianchi denied any involvement in the murders. However, while under hypnosis, his evil alter ego "Steve" surfaced and confessed to the murders. Two psychiatrists who examined Bianchi became convinced that he suffered from multiple personality disorder and that "Ken" was not aware of or responsible for "Steve's" horrible crimes. Eventually Bianchi exhibited a total of five separate personalities and his lawyers filed an insanity plea. It took an expert on hypnosis (Martin Orne) to discover that Bianchi was pretending to be hypnotized and consciously inventing multiple personalities (O'Brien, 1985). Bianchi changed his plea to "guilty" and was convicted of several murders in California and Washington.

THE INSANITY DEFENSE
• •

Unlike competence, the concept of insanity refers to the criminal's state of mind *at the time the crime was committed.* Insanity is not a scientific concept used by modern psychologists. It is a legal judgment that is decided in court. Legal definitions of insanity are crafted not by psychologists or psychiatrists, but by legislators and judges. The label of "insanity" does not correspond to any established psychiatric diagnosis and many mental health professionals are deeply conflicted about being asked to decide whether or not a defendant was legally insane at the time the criminal act was committed.

Even people who clearly suffer from mental illness may not qualify as "insane" using the legal definition of insanity. Andrea Yates is a good example. There was ample evidence that Andrea Yates was psychotic. Following the birth of her first son, Noah, in 1994, Yates began to experience what she called "visions." Then, after the birth of her son Luke in 1999, the visions became stronger and more frequent. She had told psychologists that "there was a voice, then an image of the knife. I had a vision in my mind, get a knife, get a knife. . . . I had a vision of this person getting stabbed, and the after-effects" (Springer, 2002). The visions became so disturbing that, in 1999, Yates attempted to kill herself by swallowing more than 40 sleeping pills. On another occasion, she pressed the blade of a steak knife to her neck and threatened to cut her own throat before her husband managed to disarm her. Yates was diagnosed with postpartum depression with psychotic features. That is, she was severely depressed, her depression deepened following the birth of each child, she was plagued by feelings of overwhelming anxiety, and she was sometimes out of touch with reality. She had four stays in a psychiatric hospital because of severe psychological disturbance. Following a suicide attempt, Yates told a psychiatrist that "I had a fear I would hurt somebody. . . . I thought it better to end my own life and prevent it" (Springer, 2002).

Andrea Yates was given a prescription for Zoloft, a powerful antidepressant. She improved, but not for long. She began staying in bed all day, she scratched four bald spots on her head, developed sores from picking at her nose, and scraped lines on her arms and legs with nails. She seldom spoke, even to her family, and psychiatrists described her as "mute." Child Protective Services visited her home, conducted a brief investigation of the Yates family and concluded that the children were safe and adequately cared for. Russell Yates said that after the birth of Mary, their fifth child, the death of Andrea Yates's father "sent her spiraling down." She once attempted to scratch the number "666" (the sign of Satan) into her scalp, and sometimes she believed that cartoon characters were talking to her from the television programs she watched with her children. As she awaited trial, she could still hear Satan "growling" and she saw satanic images hidden in the walls of her jail cell (Roche, 2002). But, at trial, the crucial question was not whether Andrea Yates was mentally ill. Rather, in accordance with the legal definition of insanity used in many states, the crucial question was whether or not she knew the difference between right and wrong at the time she killed her five children.

THE EVOLUTION OF INSANITY LAW

To understand the evolution of the insanity defense, it is critical to appreciate two facts: First, the principle that people who commit crimes without full awareness should not be held fully responsible for their crimes can be traced back several centuries and is fundamental to most legal systems. The underlying logic is that it is immoral to convict and punish people who are not responsible for their criminal behavior. Second, to a much greater extent than other areas of criminal law, the laws surrounding insanity have been shaped and reshaped by sensational cases and public reaction to those cases.

As early as the Roman Empire, the law dictated that people found to be *non compos mentis*—without mastery of mind—should not be held blameworthy for their crimes. The modern form of "mastery of mind" is *mens rea,* or the "guilty mind" that must accompany wrongful behavior. Legal proceedings against a criminal defendant begin with the presumption that the defendant was sane and therefore responsible for his or her criminal acts. To be found guilty of murder, a killer must have been aware of the wrongfulness of the criminal behavior. Sometimes, a defendant's lack of awareness of "wrongfulness" is uncontroversial. For example, when a six-year-old finds his father's gun and shoots and kills a playmate, we recognize that he could not have fully understood the consequences of his actions. But other times—as in the case of Andrea

Yates—there may be considerable dispute about the defendant's state of mind at the time of the crime.

From the fourteenth through sixteenth centuries in England, a religiously inspired "good from evil" test was used. To be found guilty, the defendant had to understand the difference between good and evil. Because the capacity to freely choose evil behavior was "restrained in children, in fools, and in the witless who do not have reason whereby they can choose the good from the evil," the "witless" were sometimes found to be guiltless (Platt & Diamond, 1966). A significant shift took place in 1724. In the case of *Rex v. Arnold,* jurors were instructed to acquit the defendant (who had wounded a British lord in an assassination attempt) if they found him to be "totally deprived of his understanding and memory, and doth not know what he is doing, no more than a brute or a wild beast." This revised instruction meant that insanity had become less a moral failing (good versus evil) and more a cognitive failing—that is, a mental deficiency involving "understanding and memory." More than a century later, the case of *Regina v. Oxford* (in 1840) shifted the standard even further. In that case, it was held that, because of a "diseased mind," the defendant was "quite unaware of the nature, character, and consequences of the act he was committing" (p. 525).

THREE IMPORTANT CASES AND THEIR CONSEQUENCES

Most attempts to tinker with the insanity defense have occurred in a politically charged atmosphere. The three cases described below sparked important reforms in insanity law.

The McNaughton Case.   Daniel McNaughton (sometimes spelled "M'Naghten") was tormented by paranoid delusions. He believed that people in the government were plotting to kill him. In 1843, he set out to kill the Prime Minister of England (Robert Peel) because he believed Mr. Peel was part of a conspiracy against him. By mistake, he shot and killed the Prime Minister's Secretary, Edward Drummond. At trial, nine medical experts testified that McNaughton was insane, and the jury found him not guilty by reason of insanity (NGRI) even though they were told that he would be sent to a psychiatric hospital instead of prison. He spent the rest of his life in Broadmoor insane asylum.

Queen Victoria was incensed by the sentence in the McNaughton case. She demanded that the House of Lords pass new laws to protect the public from "the wrath of madmen who could now kill with impunity" (Eule, 1978). The public was similarly displeased. Fifteen high court judges were directed to establish a new standard of legal insanity. The new rule—which came to be known as the McNaughton Rule—consisted of three components: (1) a presumption that defendants are sane and responsible for their crime; (2) a requirement that, at the moment of the crime, the accused must have been laboring "under a defect of reason" or "from disease of the mind;" and (3) a requirement that the defendant "did not know the nature and quality of the act he was doing, or if he did know it, that he did not know what he was doing was wrong." The McNaughton Rule was eventually imported from English law into American law. It is sometimes referred to as a "cognitive test" of insanity because it empha- sizes knowing and understanding whether an action is right or wrong.

But as many critics noted in the decades after the McNaughton Rule was established, cognition is only part of "insanity" and maybe not even the most important part. In an effort to capture the volitional aspect of insanity, some states added the term "irresistible impulse" to their defini- tions of insanity. Under this revised rule, a defendant could be acquitted if "his reasoning powers were so far dethroned by his diseased mental con- dition as to deprive him of willpower to resist the insane impulse to perpe- trate the deed, though knowing it to be wrong" (*Smith v. United States*, 1929). Put differently, a mental disorder could produce an uncontrollable impulse to commit the offense, even if the defendant remained able to understand the nature of the offense and its wrongfulness. But the "voli- tional" amendment to the definition of insanity had a short life. The prob- lem was that it was too hard to tell when an impulse was irresistible. That is, how could a jury decide whether the defendant *couldn't* resist the impulse or simply *didn't* resist the impulse? One attempt to clarify the revised definition was the "policeman at the elbow" test. It was suggested that the impulse had to be so overwhelming that the criminal would have committed the act even if a policeman stood beside him or her at the time of the crime. After much debate, the irresistible impulse standard fell away, leaving the McNaughton Rule largely intact.

The Durham Case.   The second case to reshape the definition of insanity was not as sensational. It did not involve murder or a famous victim. Monte Durham was released from the U.S. Navy in 1945 because a psychiatric examination found him unfit to continue military service. After a suicide attempt two years later, he was committed to a psychiatric hospital where he remained for two months. His already disordered mental condition appeared to deteriorate even further during a prison sentence he served for car theft and writing bad checks. In 1951, he was arrested for breaking and entering an apartment. Despite being diagnosed several times as mentally ill, the trial judge refused to let Durham plead insanity. Durham was found guilty at trial but the U.S. Court of Appeals overturned his conviction in 1954.

Durham's initial conviction generated little controversy, but his appeal prompted a prominent judge to re-examine and reformulate the McNaughton Rule. Judge David Bazelon of the U.S. Court of Appeals reviewed previous court decisions, as well as the opinions of scientific experts. He concluded that the prevailing standard of legal insanity was obsolete and misguided. Judge Bazelon threw out Durham's conviction and ordered a new trial where a new standard of insanity would be used. According to this new rule—called the Durham standard—"an accused is not criminally responsible if his unlawful act was the product of mental disease or mental defect" (*Durham v. United States,* 1954). The more modern terms "mental disease or defect" inserted the notion of mental illness as a possible cause of criminal behavior. However, though most psychologists and psychiatrists welcomed the new standard, courts responded with suspicion or even hostility. Lawyers and judges feared that it shifted the balance too far—that it might lead jurors to attach too much weight to the testimony of mental health professionals. Verdicts might turn solely on expert testimony about whether or not the defendant suffered from a "mental disease."

In response to dissatisfaction with both the Durham and McNaughton rules, the American Law Institute (ALI), a committee of prominent legal scholars, proposed a revised standard: "A person is not responsible for criminal conduct if at the time of such conduct, as a result of mental disease or defect, he lacks substantial capacity either to appreciate the criminality [wrongfulness] of his conduct or to conform his conduct to the requirements of the law" (Model Penal Code, 1985). The ALI standard attempted to satisfy everyone—it included a McNaughton-like cognitive prong (inability to appreciate wrongfulness) and an irresistible impulse-like volitional prong (unable to conform his conduct). Much was made of other subtle changes in wording. The term "substantial capacity" was thought to allow greater flexibility in judging defendants, and "appreciate" was thought to be better than the words "know" or "understand." The ALI standard enjoyed great success, being adopted by 26 states following the 1972 case of *United States v. Brawner*. A modified version was used in the federal courts.

The Hinckley Case.   It was the ALI instruction that was read to the jury in the trial of John Hinckley—the third major case to reshape the insanity defense. John Hinckley, Jr. was a loner. In 1976, he dropped out of college at Texas Tech and set out for Hollywood in the hope of making it big in the music industry. During his time in California he became obsessed with the film *Taxi Driver* and one of the movie's stars, Jodie Foster. He traveled to Yale University, where Ms. Foster was a student. In a delusional attempt to reenact a scene from *Taxi Driver* and win the love of Ms. Foster, Hinckley attempted to assassinate then President Ronald Reagan. He shot and wounded four people, including the President. A videotape of the shootings was played and replayed on national television just after the assassination attempt and during Hinckley's 1983 trial. At trial, four psychological experts testified that Hinckley suffered from severe psychological disturbance. Psychologists testifying for the prosecution disputed these claims. A jury found Hinckley not guilty by reason of insanity.

For many Americans, the NGRI verdict in the Hinckley case seemed to epitomize all that was wrong with the insanity defense: Here was an obviously guilty (albeit disturbed) man whose crime was recorded on videotape. He had the presence of mind to stalk the President, purchase a handgun, and plan out the murder attempt. Yet he was able to avoid being held accountable for his actions because his wealthy parents bought him a high-priced lawyer and several psychological experts to testify on his behalf. At least that seems to be how the public saw it at the time. Of course, the real story was a bit more complicated. Even the prosecution experts had testified that Hinckley was plagued by a mental disorder of some kind. But the most important factor in Hinckley's acquittal was probably the judge's decision to use the federal standard of proof in the case. Instead of requiring the *defense* to prove that the defendant was insane at the time of the crime, the burden of proof was placed on the *prosecution* to prove (beyond a reasonable doubt) that the defendant was sane. This shift in the burden of proof probably had more to do with the NGRI verdict than the skill of Hinckley's lawyers or experts (Caplan, 1984).

Public outrage over the Hinckley verdict quickly translated into legislative action. The Insanity Defense Reform Act of 1984 turned back the clock on the insanity defense. The ALI standard was largely abandoned in response to changes in the law made in the aftermath of the Hinckley case. The Insanity Defense Reform Act required that there be a presumption of sanity and that defendants prove "by clear and convincing evidence" that they were insane at the time of the crime. In addition, the volitional prong was erased from the definition of insanity and experts were barred from giving "ultimate issue testimony" (also called "ultimate opinion testimony") about sanity. That is, although experts were still permitted to testify about a defendant's mental state, they would not be permitted to explicitly state their opinion about whether a defendant was sane at the time of the crime. The question of whether a defendant was legally insane at the time of the crime would be left to juries (Perlin, 1990). After months of hearings and tinkering by lawmakers, the insanity law that survived was little more than a slightly retooled version of the 160-year-old McNaughton Rule.

The matter of "ultimate issue" expert testimony remains controversial. It is worth noting that attempts to prevent psychological experts from offering ultimate opinion testimony may not be entirely practical. Several scholars have pointed out that, to be useful, experts must provide opinions that are relevant to the legal definition of insanity (Ogloff, Roberts, & Roesch, 1993). While an expert might be forbidden from using the words "sane" or "insane," lawyers will ask that same expert questions about the defendant's understanding of his or her crimes. Although the expert might avoid saying the forbidden words, any meaningful expert testimony is almost certain to reveal the expert's opinion on the issue of insanity. Indeed, in an experiment examining this issue, researchers found that even when experts avoided offering a conclusion about whether the defendant was insane, mock jurors mistakenly remembered that a conclusion had been offered (Fulero & Finkel, 1991). A potential solution to this dilemma, used in some states, is to permit experts to offer ultimate issue testimony, but to clearly instruct jurors that they may give such testimony as much weight or as little weight as they deem appropriate. This instruction makes explicit the role of jurors as the triers of fact.

There have also been attempts to "fix" the insanity defense by giving jurors alternatives to the NGRI verdict. The "guilty but mentally ill" (GBMI) verdict and the "diminished capacity" defense are attempts to bypass the definitional morass of insanity. The GBMI verdict is permitted in 12 states, and is usually an additional alternative verdict to the three more standard options of guilty, not guilty, and NGRI. People who are found to be GBMI are sent to a mental hospital until judged to be sane, and are then transferred to prison to serve out the remainder of their sentence. However, a verdict of GBMI offers no guarantee that offenders will receive effective treatment for their mental disorders. The "diminished capacity" defense is also an attempt to circumvent legal definitions of insanity. A few states allow a defendant to plead diminished capacity if he or she lacks the capacity to "meaningfully premeditate the crime." Milder than insanity, diminished capacity might stem from a temporary mental condition that prevented a defendant from clearly considering his or her actions.

Like the insanity defense, the diminished capacity defense has been shaped by sensational trials. In 1978, Dan White, a former police officer and city supervisor, loaded his handgun and climbed through a window at San Francisco City Hall. He shot Mayor George Moscone several times, reloaded, and then killed Harvey Milk, his former colleague on the board of supervisors. Part of White's defense at trial was that his mental state was badly impaired by a deep depression exacerbated by his heavy intake of junk food. The press dubbed this the "Twinkie defense." The jury accepted White's diminished capacity defense and found him guilty of manslaughter instead of murder. His trial led to a ballot proposition in California to abolish the diminished capacity defense. That proposition passed by a wide margin in 1982. Dan White spent less than five years in prison, but killed himself in 1985.

TESTS AND TECHNIQUES FOR ASSESSING INSANITY

Several specialized tests have been developed to help clinicians assess whether offenders were aware of and responsible for their crimes. One such test, the Mental Screening Evaluation (MSE), attempts to screen out defendants whose crimes were not influenced by a significant mental disorder (Slobogin, Melton, & Showalter, 1984). If the MSE detects the presence of a mental abnormality that *may* have contributed to the crime, the defendant is referred for a full evaluation. The MSE requires that examiners gather and evaluate information about the defendant's history of mental disorders, the offense itself, and the defendant's current mental state. While the MSE forces the examiner to focus on issues that are relevant to an insanity or diminished capacity defense, it has been criticized for lacking a clear scoring system and strict procedures for administering the test (Nicholson, 1999).

A more widely used alternative is called the Rogers Criminal Responsibility Assessment Scales (R-CRAS). The R-CRAS attempts to translate the legal standards of insanity into components such as the ability to control one's thoughts and the ability to control one's behavior. There are a total of 25 items, and each item is rated on a numerical scale. For example, one item directs the examiner to indicate whether the defendant was suffering from "delusions at the time of the alleged crime." The six possible responses are: (0) no information, (1) delusions absent, (2) suspected delusions (e.g., supported only by questionable self-report), (3) definite delusions that contributed to, but were not the predominant force in, the commission of the alleged crime, and (4) definite controlling delusions, on the basis of which the alleged crime was committed" (Rogers & Ewing, 1992). Judgments on each of the 25 items are based on an in-depth interview with the defendant, as well as a review of relevant documents such as mental health records and police reports. A clear advantage of the R-CRAS is that it guides and organizes clinical judgments about whether a defendant is criminally responsible for his or her crimes. It forces evaluators to make their judgments explicit and to attend to several aspects of the defendant's behavior before making a global decision. Although research supporting use of the R-CRAS is not yet persuasive, the test does appear to be a significant improvement over unstructured clinical interviews (Nicholson, 1999).

HOW JURORS DEFINE INSANITY

Although legal scholars and legislators have agonized about the difference between words such as "know," "understand," or "appreciate," and have argued long and vigorously about whether insanity should be defined as an irresistible impulse or the ability to distinguish between right and wrong, the important question is how actual juries interpret these definitions to reach a verdict. We can look at each new and presumably improved definition of insanity as a loose hypothesis. When lawyers and legislators attempt to craft new definitions of insanity, they are predicting that changing a few words or a key phrase will cause jurors to consider different factors and reach "better" decisions. Although these loose hypotheses are seldom tested, they are testable. As noted above, most revisions in the definitions of insanity were intended to reduce the number of NGRI verdicts.

Rita Simon (1967) was one of the first researchers to investigate how jurors interpret different definitions of insanity. Using the same case, she had 10 juries deliberate using the McNaughton instructions and another 10 juries deliberate using the Durham instructions. Her findings were straightforward: The two instructions made no significant difference in verdicts. That is, the two instructions that legal scholars had regarded as dramatically different had no impact on verdicts. But why? Simon's main conclusion, based on her analysis of the audiotaped deliberations, was that jurors took the formal language presented in the insanity instructions and translated that language into concepts and meanings that were consistent with their own understanding of insanity and its effects. One of the jurors in the study explained the defendant's behavior this way: "He knew what he was doing in the sense that he knew how to get into the house, where to find the bedroom, what articles he wanted to take, but he still didn't know the full significance of what he was doing" (Simon, 1967).

In a more recent series of experiments designed to explore how jurors interpret the insanity defense, Norman Finkel and his colleagues presented groups of mock jurors with the full range of insanity instructions—including the McNaughton test, the irresistible impulse test, the Durham test, the ALI test, and even no test at all (jurors were instructed to simply use their own best judgment). Their findings echoed earlier findings: The content of the insanity instructions didn't seem to matter. The researchers reached the following conclusion:

> Tests with markedly different criteria failed to produce discriminably different verdicts, and failed to produce verdicts discriminably different from those produced by a no-test condition . . . jurors do not ignore instructions but they construe instructions, employing their constructs of "sane" or "insane" to determine their verdict, despite the working of the legal test given to them (Finkel, 1995, p. 282).

In explaining the ineffectiveness of insanity instructions as a means of guiding jury verdicts, Finkel does not lay the blame on jurors. It is not that jurors are too dense to understand legal subtleties, or that they are careless, or that they are intent on ignoring instructions. Indeed, mock jurors made many distinctions. They made distinctions about the types of affliction the defendant was suffering from (e.g., epilepsy or stress disorder or schizophrenia), about issues of negligence (e.g., whether a defendant should be held accountable for deciding to stop taking the medication that reduced her paranoia), and about the sort of punishment that defendants should receive (i.e., hospitalization or prison). Jurors simply failed to respond in the ways that judges and legislators had predicted that they would respond. Instead of interpreting different instructions differently, Finkel argues that jurors use their preexisting commonsense notions of insanity to inform and interpret their judgments of a defendant's responsibility and intentions. Consequently, their reasoning about the mental condition of the defendant is not constrained by the narrow bounds of legal definitions. Their reasoning is more complex and contextual than the reasoning embodied in the insanity instructions. Jurors look beyond limited notions such as "irresistible impulse" or the capacity to "distinguish right from wrong" to ". . . an essence that lies in the defendant's capacity to make responsible choices. They also consider and weigh a dimension akin to negligence or recklessness that has been notably absent or conflated in insanity law: culpability for bringing about one's disability of mind" (Finkel, 1995, p. 297).

Based on this research, Finkel has developed an alternative test of insanity that takes into account how jurors actually make decisions. This alternative test requires juries to answer a series of questions about behavior, state of mind, and culpability. First, jurors are asked to decide whether the defendant's actions caused the harm. Next, they must determine whether the defendant was "at the moment of the act, suffering from a disability of mind that played a significant role in the defendant's criminal behavior." If the defendant's mental disability is judged to have played a significant role, jurors are then asked to decide if the disability was partial or total, and whether the defendant was "culpable to some degree for bringing about the disability." Finally, the culpability is rated as partial or total. Using this more systematic scheme, a NGRI verdict is only possible if the defendant is judged to have a total disability of mind and is not culpable for creating that disability (Finkel, 1995).

THE LARGER CONTEXT OF INSANITY LAWS

Debate about the insanity defense often occurs in the overheated atmosphere created by a sensational case like McNaughton or Hinckley. During such times, politicians have denounced the insanity defense in colorful terms. It has been called "a rich man's defense" that "pampers criminals" and a means of providing a "safe harbor for criminals who bamboozle a jury." Further, it has been claimed that trials involving the insanity defense are often "protracted testimonial extravaganzas pitting high-priced prosecution experts against equally high-priced defense experts" (Perlin, 1994, p.16). Former Attorneys General have said that "there must be an end to the doctrine that allows so many persons to commit crimes of violence, to use confusing procedures to their own advantage, and then have the door opened for them to return to the society they victimized." It has also been argued that abolishing the insanity defense will "rid the streets of some of the most dangerous people that are out there, that are committing a disproportionate number of crimes" (Perlin, 1994, p. 20). The gist of these declarations by politicians is clear: Unscrupulous lawyers are frequently using the insanity defense as a convenient loophole to help violent criminals escape their rightful punishment. Furthermore, gullible, unsophisticated juries can be easily convinced to find a defendant NGRI through the use of "hired gun" psychologists. Many of these beliefs are shared by the public at large.

Scholars have noted that much of what the public believes about the use of the insanity defense is simply mistaken. These scholars have described several myths surrounding the insanity defense. One myth is that the insanity defense is overused. In fact, the best available data suggest that it is used in fewer than 1% of all felony cases, and that, when it is used, it fails 74% of the time (Silver, Cirincione, & Steadman, 1994). Also, although surveys indicate that the public believes that NGRI is most commonly used in murder cases, less than a third of insanity pleas involve the death of a victim. Further, an insanity defense is no more likely to be successful in a murder case than in any other kind of criminal case. Contrary to prevailing views, insanity is not a low-risk strategy that can be easily employed to avoid guilt and gain a lighter sentence. Indeed, when defendants who plead NGRI are found guilty, they end up serving *longer* sentences than people convicted of similar crimes who do not use the insanity defense (Perlin, 1996). When defendants are found NGRI, they end up spending nearly twice as much time in custody as defendants found guilty of the same type of crime. The difference is that for defendants found NGRI, the time is usually served in locked psychiatric hospitals instead of prisons.

Other false beliefs concern the psychological experts who must assess and testify about insanity. It is often asserted that these experts can't agree on whether a particular defendant qualifies as insane. However, in a study of defendants found NGRI over an eight-year period, there was agreement among psychological experts that the defendant was schizophrenic in 92% of cases. Indeed, most of the defendants found NGRI have a significant history of hospitalization in psychiatric facilities. Studies conducted in several states reveal that prosecutors agreed to an insanity verdict in 70% to 80% of cases in which the issue was raised (Perlin, 1996).

IN CONCLUSION

Jurors who must decide insanity cases and psychological experts who testify in such cases are asked to make an all-or-nothing, black-or-white judgment: Was the defendant legally insane or not? But jurors, like experts, want to make broader, more differentiated judgments about a defendant's mental condition and to think about degrees of impairment and degrees of responsibility. In the trial of Andrea Yates, jurors were asked to reach their verdict based on a narrow cognitive-prong-only definition of insanity. The only question was whether Yates knew the difference between right and wrong at the time she murdered her children. The prosecutor argued that, "She knew this was an illegal thing. . . . It was a sin. She knew it was wrong" (Associated Press, 2002). A psychiatrist testifying for the defense said that Mrs. Yates did not know the difference between right and wrong and that she felt she was helping her children by killing them. He testified that Yates believed she was possessed by Satan and that, "She believed that, by killing her children, she not only sent them to heaven, but saved them from an eternity in the fires of hell" (CNN, 2002).

The Yates trial highlighted three issues that continue to animate the debate over the insanity defense. The first is the conflict between the legal system's use of the old-fashioned term "insanity" with its pinched meaning and scientific psychology's use of the modern term "mental illness" with its more capacious meaning. The limited definition of insanity favored by the legal system survives, in part, because it restricts the possibility of a not-guilty verdict. A second issue concerns public uncertainty about what happens to insane defendants after trial. In the mind of the public, a central problem with use of the insanity defense is what to do with a defendant who is found NGRI. Until the myth that people found NGRI will go free or "get off easy" is dispelled, it may be difficult to move too far beyond the 160-year-old McNaughton Rule. Third, continuing tension between the desire to provide treatment for people who are mentally disturbed and the desire to punish those same people when they commit terrible crimes will continue to shape debate about the insanity defense.

Readings to Supplement This Chapter

Articles

Skeem, J. L., & Golding, S. L. (2001). Describing jurors' personal conceptions of insanity and their relationship to case judgments. *Psychology, Public Policy, and Law, 7,* 561–621.

Silver, E., Cirincione, C., & Steadman, H. J. (1994). Demythologizing inaccurate perceptions of the insanity defense. *Law and Human Behavior, 18,* 63–70.

Slobogin, C. (2000). An end to insanity: Recasting the role of mental illness in criminal cases. *Virginia Law Review, 86,* 1199–1223.

Zapf, P., & Roesch, R. (1997). Assessing fitness to stand trial: A comparison of institution-based evaluations and a brief screening interview. *Canadian Journal of Community Mental Health, 16,* 53–66.

Books

Perlin, M. L. (2000). The hidden prejudice: Mental disability on trial. Washington, DC: American Psychological Association.

Sales, B. D., & Shuman, D. W. (Eds.). (1996). *Law, mental health, and mental disorder.* Pacific Grove: Brooks-Cole.

5

Juries and Judges

Chapter Outline

● ●

Assembling a Jury: Pools, Venires, and Voir Dire
    From Jury Pool to Venire
    Voir Dire
    Cognizable Groups
Using Stereotypes and Science to Select Jurors
    Scientific Jury Selection
    The Use of Trial Consultants
    Does Trial Consulting Work?
Juror Characteristics and Attitudes as Predictors of Verdict
    General Personality Tendencies
    Attitudes about the Legal System
    Defendant-Juror Similarity
Basic Trial Procedure
Jurors as (Biased) Information Processors
    Pretrial Publicity
    Defendant Characteristics
    Inadmissible and Complex Evidence
    The Judge's Instructions as a Source of Confusion
    Models of Juror Decision Making
The Group Dynamics of Jury Deliberations
    Strong Jurors and the Power of the Majority
    Stages in the Deliberation Process
    The Size of the Jury
    Decision Rules (Unanimous or Majority Rule)
    Jury Nullification
Jury Reform
    Allowing Jury Discussion During Trial: The Arizona Project
Judges Compared to Juries
    Agreement between Juries and Judges
In Conclusion

Imagine that you've been selected as a juror. You are plucked from your normal routine and asked to listen for days, weeks, or months to lawyers, witnesses, and a judge. You may hear about specialized but slippery legal concepts—burden of proof, preponderance of evidence, proximate cause, reasonable doubt, mitigation, aggravation, negligence. You may hear about hideous crimes or terrible tragedies. Perhaps someone has been raped or murdered, perhaps faulty construction has caused a building to collapse, perhaps a shoddy medical procedure has resulted in brain damage or death. You may see photographs of dead bodies, you may hear heart-wrenching testimony from surviving victims or the loved ones of dead victims. You will almost certainly hear from competing expert witnesses who interpret the evidence in very different ways. Your job will be to make sense of it all, to interpret the law, to decide what is fair and just. The decision your jury makes will probably change lives: Large sums of money might be paid; a defendant might be released, sent to prison, or even sentenced to death.

The experience of being a juror is unnatural in several ways. First, jurors are expected to be passive spectators of the courtroom proceedings. They are expected to absorb information, to efficiently store it up for later use in the deliberation room, and to suspend final judgment until after all the evidence has been presented. Second, they are not allowed to talk with lawyers or witnesses, and they are not permitted to discuss the impending decision with friends or families until a verdict has been rendered. They are not even allowed to discuss the case with their fellow jurors until official deliberations commence. Finally, juries consist of people who may have little in common and no established relationships. It is likely that the people who serve on a particular jury have never met before the trial and, after the verdict, they may never see each other again.

Juries—these unusual groups regulated by unusual rules—are controversial. They have been praised as the best, most democratic aspect of our legal system and condemned as the worst, most biased aspect of our system. This chapter explores how juries are assembled, how they make decisions, and how the legal system can help juries do their important work. Because the main alternative to trial by jury is trial by judge, research on judges is also described.

ASSEMBLING A JURY: POOLS, VENIRES, AND VOIR DIRE

Early juries were not designed to be neutral and unbiased. They consisted of a defendant's neighbors and acquaintances. The logic was that previous dealings with the defendant and prior knowledge of his or her reputation would be useful in assessing the defendant's credibility. An understanding of the defendant would help jurors reach a just verdict (Abramson, 1995). In contrast, modern juries are intended to be impartial. The Sixth Amendment guarantees the right to a trial by an "impartial" jury in criminal cases and the Seventh Amendment guarantees the right to a trial by jury in civil cases.

But how can we achieve an impartial jury? According to the Jury Selection and Service Act of 1968 and the U.S. Supreme Court in *Taylor v. Louisiana* (1975), federal and state courts must assemble juries that constitute a "fair cross-section of the community." Some reformers have suggested that the ideal way to assemble juries would be to simply require every adult citizen to register for jury service. Then, for each jury trial, 12 people could be randomly selected from a master list and required to serve. For a variety of reasons, the actual selection procedure is far more complicated. We depart from this inclusive, perfectly random procedure for reasons of necessity and in an effort to seat a fair, impartial jury. What is usually referred to as jury selection is actually a process of deselection. At every step in the long process of assembling a jury, some potential jurors are dismissed or excluded. Every jury consists of the people who remain at the end of this long process of deselection.

From Jury Pool to Venire. To set the process in motion, a local jury commissioner needs a list of the names and addresses of citizens in a particular geographical area who speak English, are over the age of 18, are mentally competent, and have never been convicted of a felony. Unfortunately, no such list exists. Even if such a list did exist, it would need to be continually updated as people died, moved away from or into the area, turned 18 years of age, became mentally incompetent, or became convicted felons. So, jury commissioners must use the best information at their disposal. And, according to the Jury Selection and Service Act of 1968, the "primary source" for identifying eligible jurors is voter registration lists. Many states add lists of licensed drivers and telephone directories to the juror pool. Some states add other government lists, for example, tax rolls and people receiving unemployment benefits or food stamps. But the laws in most states do not require that officials go beyond voter lists. The inability (compounded by a lack of effort in some states) to obtain a full accounting of eligible potential jurors introduces the first layer of bias. The list used by jury commissioners often underrepresents poor people, African Americans, Hispanics, people who move frequently, and people who recently turned 18 (Abramson, 1995).

Next, a random sample of jurors is drawn from the jury pool, and everyone in this sample of potential jurors is sent a summons to appear in a particular courthouse at an assigned date and time. The group of prospective jurors that shows up is called the *venire* (from the Latin meaning "cause to come" or "come when called"). Unfortunately, approximately 20% to 25% of the people summoned for jury duty simply fail to show up (Dauner, 1996). In many places, these no-shows are not aggressively pursued as long as enough people do show up. There are large variations in the size of the venire (also called a panel) depending on where the case is being tried, the rulings of the presiding judge, and the characteristics of the case. For a relatively routine case with a strict judge in a small town, lawyers may begin with a 30-person venire. In a serious, high profile case that has received a lot of pretrial publicity, the venire may consist of more than 100 people. The highest-profile case in recent memory—the double murder trial of O. J. Simpson in 1995—began with a panel of 304.

No-shows shrink the size of the venire a bit; exemptions and exclusions shrink the venire even further. People who are summoned are asked to indicate on a questionnaire whether they fit into a category that may be legally exempt from jury service (e.g., non English speakers, people who are legally blind, police officers). Some jurors are lost at this stage, although in recent years the number of automatic exemptions has been reduced and continues to be reduced even further. More potential jurors are lost because of special pleas that jury service would cause them "undue hardship or extreme inconvenience." This vague category can be used to accommodate a vast number of excuses for avoiding jury service. One potential juror may have primary responsibility for the care of a young child, another might suffer from a serious medical condition, and another might have nonrefundable plane tickets to Bali. A juror might also be excused because jury service would cause hardship to the local community—he or she might be the only physician or mortician—in a small rural town. During the past decade, the "one day/one trial" method of jury service has been widely adopted to reduce the number of "hardship" exemptions and to make jury service less burdensome. Under this system, potential jurors make themselves available for one day. If they are selected to serve on a jury, they are done when that trial is over. If they are not selected (most people who show up are not selected), they are done with jury duty at the end of the day. Although some trials go on for months, most trials only last about a week (Abramson, 2002).

Voir Dire.   The final stage in the process is *voir dire* (French for "to see and tell"). During this stage, attorneys and the judge ask potential jurors a series of questions to determine who will serve on the jury (an unusual aspect of federal courts is that judges tend to conduct voir dire). Voir dire is a sort of pretrial interview, usually held in open court. It is during voir dire that lawyers (sometimes assisted by consultants) get their chance to remove or "challenge" potential jurors. Lawyers have two types of challenges at their disposal: challenges for cause and peremptory challenges. When a lawyer challenges a would-be juror for cause, he or she is claiming that because of bias or prejudice, it is unlikely that the juror will be able to render an impartial verdict based only on evidence and law. For example, a plaintiff's attorney may not want a physician serving on a medical malpractice case and, in a criminal trial, a defense attorney may not want a retired police officer on a drug possession trial. A juror can also be challenged if he or she is unable to be fair and impartial or is unable to follow the law (e.g., a juror might say that she would hold it against a defendant if he chose not to testify on his own behalf). In theory, there is no limit to the number of challenges for cause, although the judge must agree to dismiss the juror, and the patience of judges is limited.

If a judge refuses to dismiss a potential juror for cause, the lawyer must decide whether or not to use a peremptory challenge. Using this more powerful type of challenge, an attorney can dismiss a juror without giving a reason and without approval from the judge. Each attorney is allotted a small number of peremptory challenges—the number varies depending on where the trial is held and on the type and seriousness of the charge against the defendant. In a routine civil trial, each side may be given as few as three, but in a capital murder trial each side may get as many as 25. In federal felony cases, the prosecution usually gets six peremptory challenges while the defense usually gets 10. Defense attorneys usually get more peremptory challenges because their clients have more at stake—there is almost always the possibility that a criminal defendant will be sent to prison or that a civil defendant will be ordered to pay damages.

Many critics of the jury system have argued that lawyers use their challenges to "stack" juries. This is true in the sense that lawyers are hoping to remove jurors who might be unsympathetic to their client's case. In an adversarial system, lawyers don't want neutral jurors; they want jurors who will favor their side of the case. However, the underlying purpose of voir dire is to create a fair and impartial jury by allowing both sides to eliminate people who, because of their occupation, life experiences, or attitudes, might be unable to reach a verdict in an unbiased way. Voir dire is also used to educate jurors about issues relevant to the upcoming trial, and to get jurors to make commitments about how they will evaluate the evidence. For example, a defense attorney might ask if a juror supports the rule that allows criminal defendants not to testify at their own trial. This line of questioning allows the attorney to emphasize to all potential jurors that the defendant in the case won't be testifying and that this fact cannot be held against the defendant.

In sum, jury selection is a long winnowing process. Some people are excluded because their names don't appear on available lists, more people are excluded because they don't show up when summoned, a few people are legally exempt, some manage to get out of jury service because of real or claimed hardship, and some are dismissed by the prosecution or defense during voir dire. It is the people who remain who comprise a particular jury.

Cognizable Groups.   In addition to limits on the number of challenges, there are a few other broad restraints on the ability of lawyers to remove people from the jury panel. Because the goal is to empanel an unbiased, representative jury, the law forbids the intentional exclusion of specific racial groups. Such groups are "cognizable" in the sense that the group is recognized as being within the jurisdiction of the court and is also recognized as having shared interests that ought to be represented on juries. In *Batson v. Kentucky* (1986), the Supreme Court ruled that James Batson—a black man convicted of burglary by an all-white jury—had been denied his Fourteenth Amendment right to equal protection. Prosecutors had used their peremptory challenges to exclude every potential black juror in the venire. The protection provided by *Batson* was extended to the category of gender in 1994 (*J.E.B. ex rel. T.B.*, 1994). That is, women or men cannot be excluded during voir dire because of their gender.

In practice, if a lawyer uses a peremptory challenge against a black juror, the judge is likely to ask the lawyer for an explanation. That lawyer will then offer a race-neutral explanation for the challenge (e.g., the juror is married to a police officer). That explanation needs to be seen as credible by the judge. Since 1995, courts have been asked to prevent the exclusion of potential jurors who are short or obese or Italian American or Irish American. But, so far, the courts have been unwilling to extend protection beyond race and gender.

Two final points on the meaning of representativeness. First, from a statistical perspective, it is unrealistic to imagine that any group of 12 (or fewer) jurors can be fully representative of a much larger community. The sample size is simply too small. In contrast, when survey researchers attempt to predict the narrow behavior of how people will vote in an upcoming election, they generally sample 1,500 to 3,000 people in an effort to get a representative sample of the population. Although it is usually possible to find an impartial group of 12 people, achieving statistical representativeness is much more difficult. Second, while a particular jury may include a diverse assortment of people, no one is expected to represent the views of a particular constituency. A 25-year-old white female is not expected to try to represent the views of all other white females in their 20s, and a 42-year-old Asian male is not expected to try to represent the views of all other Asian males in their 40s. The best we can hope for is diversity in age, ethnicity, experience, and opinion. Such diversity is likely to reduce the expression of various forms of prejudice (e.g., racism or sexism), promote fuller discussion, and lead to better fact-finding (Abramson, 2002). Also, as discussed in Chapter 1, the legal system must have legitimacy in the eyes of the public. If juries systematically exclude women or particular racial groups, the perceived (as well as the actual) legitimacy of the legal system is damaged.

USING STEREOTYPES AND SCIENCE TO SELECT JURORS

Lawyers who are about to try a case before a jury must attempt to figure out which potential jurors will be least favorable to their side of the case. They don't have much to go on. Some juror characteristics are easy to see—female or male, old or young, thin or heavy, tall or short. Perhaps some of the men have beards. Perhaps some of the women wear a lot of makeup. Maybe some of the potential jurors wear expensive jewelry or have visible tattoos or body piercings. In addition, there may be information from a written questionnaire asking a broad range of questions about likes and dislikes, religious and political attitudes, hobbies and interests. Finally, there are the answers to the questions attorneys ask jurors during voir dire and behavior during voir dire. Do potential jurors seem honest or deceptive? Are they well-spoken or fumbling? Do they seem arrogant or humble? Do they seem interested in what the attorneys, the judge, and the other potential jurors have to say?

The problem is that no matter what attorneys are able to find out by looking and listening, they can't possibly know in advance how a particular juror will respond to the evidence in the case about to be tried, and they can't know how that juror will influence and be influenced by other jurors in the deliberation room. This lack of certainty, coupled with the high-stakes consequences of the trial, has led many attorneys to search out any information that might give them and their clients an advantage in trying to evaluate jurors. At one extreme are some anxious lawyers who, in a misguided attempt to know the unknowable, have paid for the services of handwriting analysts, astrologers, and physiognomists (consultants who make inferences about personality based on facial features such as a high forehead, a strong chin, or thin lips). At the other extreme are a few attorneys who forego voir dire and declare that they will accept the first group of jurors called. Usually this bold declaration is accompanied by a statement that the lawyer believes that every person called is fair, thoughtful, and honest, and that the facts of the case will lead each of them to the correct verdict. Of course, this strategy is intended to convey to jurors that the lawyer is highly confident about the merits of the case and to depict opposing counsel as overly concerned with trying to select a favorable jury.

To guide their decision making, some lawyers have developed crude shortcuts for selecting jurors. Manuals for trial attorneys are full of advice on how to pick jurors. Much of this advice relies on simplistic stereotypes about ethnic and occupational groups. Here is a sampling:

> Women are more punitive than men by a score of about five to one. There's a reason for that: Women always had to toe the line. Women are splendid jurors for the prosecution in rape cases, baby cases. . . .Yuppies are the worst jurors: They fear crime, love property, and haven't suffered enough to be sympathetic (Spence, cited in Adler, 1994, p. 55).

> Never take a wealthy man on a jury. He will convict, unless the defendant is accused of violating the anti-trust law, selling worthless stocks or bonds, or something of that kind. Next to the Board of Trade, for him, the penitentiary is the most important of all public buildings (Darrow, 1936, p. 37).

> The rule of thumb here: artists, writers, musicians, actors and public figures generally make good plaintiff jurors on the civil side, and good defendant's jurors in the criminal case. As plaintiff's counsel and a criminal defendant's lawyer, I love this type of juror (Belli, 1982, p. 170).

Though there may be a kernel of truth in a few of these stereotypes, they are obviously exaggerated and superficial. But are there any personal characteristics that make a juror more or less likely to convict?

Scientific Jury Selection.   Famed defense attorney Clarence Darrow said, "Never forget, almost every case has been won or lost when the jury is sworn" (Kressel & Kressel, 2002, p. 8). Darrow seems to have overstated the case for the importance of jury selection, but there is no doubt that the process of picking jurors can have important effects.

Most attorneys spend considerable time and effort using their challenges to get rid of jurors who they think will be unsympathetic to their client's case. But is this time and effort well spent? A few researchers have attempted to answer this question. In an elegant early study of this issue, Hans Zeisel and Shari Seidman Diamond (1978) examined juror votes in 12 criminal trials. To find out if jurors who were dismissed through peremptories were any more or less likely to convict than jurors who were not challenged, the researchers persuaded the stricken jurors to stay in the courtroom and listen to the case. The votes of this shadow jury were then compared with the votes of the actual jury. Making use of interviews with the shadow jurors and post-trial interviews with the real jurors, the researchers were able to reconstruct how the jury would have decided the case if there had been no peremptory challenges. Did the attorneys' use of challenges tilt the balance in favor of their clients? Not much, if at all. On a scale where zero means that an attorney made as many good challenges as bad challenges and 100 means that an attorney managed to bump every juror who would have sided against her, prosecutors' average score was near zero (.5). Defenders did better, but not by much—their average score was 17. This is not to say that all attorneys were ineffective. Despite these unimpressive average performances, there were some attorneys who did very well in specific cases (the highest score was 62). This means that if a skilled attorney is matched against one who is unskilled, the impact of voir dire on jury composition could be decisive for the case. Effective use of peremptory challenges appeared to influence verdicts in three of the 12 cases studied. In a more recent study, the jury selection strategies of seasoned lawyers were compared to those of college students and law school students (Olczak, Kaplan, & Penrod, 1991). The lawyers were no better than the students at judging the personalities of mock jurors or picking favorable jurors. When lawyers were asked to watch a videotaped voir dire and then indicate who they might strike, they were unable to perform better than chance in detecting bias. Also, in a study of four criminal trials, the juries eventually selected were, on average, no better for the prosecution or the defense than the first 12 jurors who were questioned or a randomly selected group of prospective jurors (Johnson & Haney, 1994).

If the average performance of lawyers is underwhelming, maybe selection could be improved through the systematic application of social scientific expertise. That is, maybe psychologists and other social scientists can do better than lawyers. Whereas lawyers rely on their experience and intuition, social scientists rely on data collection.

The first attempt at so-called "scientific jury selection" was in 1972 during the "Harrisburg Seven" case. In that case, a team of social scientists led by Jay Schulman, Richard Christie, and Philip Shaver worked to help attorneys defend seven Catholic anti-Vietnam War activists who were accused of pouring blood on draft records, conspiring to blow up underground electrical systems in Washington, DC, and plotting to kidnap the secretary of state. Schulman and his colleagues interviewed more than 800 residents of Harrisburg, Pennsylvania, the site of the trial. The researchers gathered demographic information (e.g., race, gender, age, education, income, political orientation, religious affiliation) and measured attitudes relevant to the trial (e.g., attitudes toward the war in Vietnam, the rights of political dissenters, trust in the federal government). Next, researchers examined the correlations between the measured characteristics and attitudes toward the defendants. These correlations were then used to construct profiles of jurors who were likely to be pro-defense or pro-prosecution. The data indicated that the ideal prosecution juror would be a Republican businessman who identified himself as a Presbyterian, Methodist, or fundamentalist Christian and who belonged to a local civic organization. The ideal defense juror was identified as "a female Democrat with no religious preference and a white-collar or skilled blue-collar job" (Schulman et al., 1973). Jury selection by the defense team was guided by the data-based profiles. During voir dire, researchers rated every one of the 46 potential jurors on a five-point scale ranging from "very undesirable for the defense" to "very good for the defense." Did these techniques work? We can't say for sure, but the trial ended in a hung jury—10 jurors voted to acquit and two voted to convict. A mistrial was declared and the government chose not to retry the case. Given prevailing public opinion and the strong evidence against the defendants, the outcome was widely regarded as a triumph of scientific jury selection.

Another high-profile case that has been regarded as a triumph of jury selection was the 1995 murder trial of O. J. Simpson. Mr. Simpson—a famous football player, minor celebrity and sometimes actor—stood trial for the brutal stabbing murders of his former wife and her friend. The defense team hired a jury consultant (Jo-Ellan Dimitrius) who was involved in every stage of the case from pretrial planning to verdict. In contrast, the prosecutors dismissed their jury consultant (Don Vinson) on the second day of jury selection and disregarded his advice, preferring to rely on their own intuition (Toobin, 1996). The prosecutor did not even use all of her peremptory challenges.

Jury consultants on both sides of the Simpson case looked closely at data from individual and group interviews. They concluded that African American women would be the group least likely to convict Simpson. Indeed, black women were more than three times as likely as black men to believe that Simpson was innocent (Kressel & Kressel, 2002). This finding was in direct conflict with the prosecutor's intuition that because of Simpson's history of wife battering, women would be much more likely to convict. Interviews with prospective jurors conducted by the jury consultants uncovered other important findings: According to the research, black females were much more likely to excuse and forgive Simpson's physical abuse of his ex-wife and were likely to view the lead prosecutor in the case (Marcia Clark) as a pushy, "castrating bitch" (Bugliosi, 1996). In addition, both male and female black jurors were found to be much more receptive to a key theme in the defense case—that corrupt, racist police officers planted evidence to frame O. J. Simpson. Finally, pretrial research showed well-educated jurors were much more inclined to trust the key incriminating evidence for the prosecution—DNA evidence. The jury that eventually heard the case included eight black women, two white women, one black man, and one Latino man. Only two of the jurors were college graduates and five had reported that they had personally had negative experiences with police officers (Toobin, 1996). The DNA evidence was unconvincing to jurors. In a post-trial interview, one of the jurors put it this way, "I didn't understand the DNA stuff at all. To me, it was just a waste of time. It was way out there and carried absolutely no weight with me" (Bugliosi, 1996, p. 68). After listening to evidence and testimony for eight months, it took the jury less than four hours to reach a verdict of "not guilty" on all charges.

Do these two high-profile cases mean that jury consultants can "rig" or "stack" juries? Probably not. An alternative explanation for the outcomes in these cases is that the lawyers in these cases were especially skilled. In general, it may be that attorneys who seek out trial consultants are also more conscientious in preparing their cases, more thorough in questioning witness, and more effective in presenting their cases. This conscientiousness and effectiveness may be what leads to success. A second alternative explanation is that although scientific jury selection doesn't make a big difference in most trials, it may make a difference in a subset of cases where juror characteristics strongly influence the interpretation of ambiguous evidence. The two trials described above may have been part of that subset.

The Use of Trial Consultants.

Trial consultants are usually hired by companies who are being sued for large sums of money. Often, the trial involves an allegedly defective product that may have caused severe injuries or even death. In these civil cases, trial consultants might employ a data-driven approach both before and during trial. First, a large group (typically 20 to 50) of eligible jurors from the community where the case will be tried are recruited and asked to fill out an extensive questionnaire about their attitudes, habits, and personal characteristics. This group then serves as a mock jury. The mock jurors then hear a condensed version of the trial and are questioned about their reactions to the case. Sometimes the mock juries deliberate as the consultant watches via video or a two-way mirror. The reactions and interpretations of the mock jurors are analyzed to provide insight into both jurors and arguments. One goal is to discover consistent relationships between juror characteristics and responses to the evidence in a particular case. The resulting profiles of favorable or unfavorable jurors then guide the use of peremptory challenges. If a case goes to trial, consultants often design and analyze supplemental juror questionnaires (questionnaires submitted by attorneys and approved by the judge) that prospective jurors fill out before voir dire. Questions might include information about personal experiences (have you ever been misdiagnosed by a physician?), beliefs (would you describe yourself as a religious person?), and affiliations (do you donate time or money to any groups, clubs, or organizations?).

Second, and probably more important, by asking mock jurors about their reactions, consultants get a clearer sense of the strengths and weaknesses of a case. Based on such analyses, litigants may decide to settle instead of going to trial, or they may be able to abandon their weak arguments and focus only on their strong arguments. Most consultants have expanded beyond jury selection to the development of trial presentation and strategy. They assist attorneys in crafting arguments that will be optimally persuasive. In high-stakes trials, consultants sometimes construct a "shadow jury"—a group of 10 to 12 people who are selected to match the demographics of the actual jury. The shadow jury may sit in the courtroom during trial, or hear a condensed version of the testimony presented in court each day, or even watch a videotape of courtroom proceedings if one is available. Because the shadow jury hears the same evidence and testimony as the actual jury, they can be questioned throughout the trial about their reactions to the evidence. Feedback from the shadow jury can then be used by attorneys to make adjustments in strategy during trial.

Does Trial Consulting Work?   It is difficult to say whether or not trial consultants are effective in helping attorneys select more favorable jurors (Strier, 1999). As noted above, one complication is that attorneys differ dramatically in their ability to select jurors who will be favorable to their case. If an attorney is already doing a good job, there may be little a trial consultant can do to help. But if an attorney is doing a lousy job, a skilled consultant might be able to significantly improve the attorney's performance. Also, in a close case, where the evidence does not clearly favor one side or the other, careful jury selection might tilt the case in one direction or the other. Although, on balance, the evidence of the effectiveness of trial consulting is equivocal, there is some support for the proposition that jury selection can be modestly improved by measuring case-specific attitudes (Moran, Cutler, & DeLisa, 1994).

Perhaps the most important question about trial consulting is ethical rather than scientific: Does it promote justice or impair justice? Just because we can use scientific methods to help select jurors or fine-tune the presentations of attorneys, should we? Jury consultants emphasize that they are merely using more systematic, sophisticated techniques to do what attorneys have always done—getting rid of jurors who might be unsympathetic to their case and identifying the most powerful arguments to use at trial. It could be argued that when consultants help a weak attorney do a better job of representing a client they may be improving the adversarial system and serving the interests of justice. But the most basic problem is that consultants usually work for wealthy business interests who are willing and able to pay the fees of consultants. This means that the scales of justice are tilted in favor of the rich. Because wealthy defendants usually have the advantage of being able to buy the best lawyers, jury consultants often amplify the advantages of rich clients. Like law firms, many trial consultants provide *pro bono* (free of charge) services to clients who can't afford to pay. But (also like law firms) these services are only a small fraction of the cases taken on by consultants. Of course, the fact that rich defendants can afford more justice cannot be blamed on trial consultants. In an adversarial system, lawyers representing the two sides of a case should ideally be equally matched. Unfortunately, there is often a mismatch, and the advantage usually goes to the wealthy (Kressel & Kressel, 2002).

JUROR CHARACTERISTICS AND ATTITUDES AS PREDICTORS OF VERDICT

When lawyers and trial consultants attempt to select a favorable jury, they try to predict how potential jurors might respond to the evidence that will later be presented at trial. Those predictions are based on the characteristics and attitudes of potential jurors. But to what extent does the verdict depend on the type of jurors selected?

Overall, the persuasiveness of the evidence presented at trial is the best predictor of whether or not a defendant is convicted or acquitted (Saks & Kidd, 1986; Visher, 1987). That is how it should be. However, if evidence alone was the only factor that determined verdict, we might expect every jury to begin deliberations in complete agreement. This seldom happens. Although every person on a given jury has been exposed to the same evidence and arguments, jurors evaluate and interpret that evidence differently. These differences in how evidence is weighed and understood must be due to differences in jurors' experience, values, and personalities. But the search for juror characteristics that predict verdict has not yielded much. Standard demographic characteristics such as age, education, and income don't provide many clues about what verdict a person will favor (Hans, 1992).

In an effort to understand the relationship between juror characteristics and verdicts, Steven Penrod (1990) examined 21 juror attitudes and characteristics as predictors in four types of simulated trials—murder, rape, robbery, and civil negligence. The study made use of multiple regression—a technique that statistically combines a large group of variables to predict an outcome variable (verdict, in this study). Taken together, the 21 predictor variables only accounted for between 5% and 14% of the variance in verdicts, depending on the type of case.

In general, the relationships between juror characteristics and verdict are modest or unreliable. Take gender. Some studies have found that, compared to males, female jurors are slightly more likely to treat accused rapists and child molesters more harshly (Ellsworth & Mauro, 1998). But this finding is not consistent. Also, women tend to be more sympathetic to plaintiffs alleging sexual harassment (see Chapter 8 for a full discussion of this finding). Here the difference is consistent but not large. A more consistent gender difference has to do with jury process rather than outcome—men talk more than women during deliberation. A related finding is that men are more likely to be elected as "foreperson." This seems to happen because men are more likely to be of high occupational status, are more likely to sit at the head of the table (the natural spot for group leaders), and are more likely to speak first (Strodtbeck & Lipinski, 1985).

General Personality Tendencies.   A few broad personality tendencies do seem to be associated with verdicts. Early research identified three general traits—locus of control, belief in a just world, and authoritarianism—that have a modest effect on how jurors interpret evidence and decide on a verdict. However, such traits appear to exert an influence on juror decisions only in cases where the evidence in favor of conviction is ambiguous or less than compelling.

Locus of control refers to how people tend to explain what happens to them. Do you believe that what you get in life—both your misfortunes and your rewards—are usually the result of your own behavior? Or, do you believe that your circumstances are largely due to forces outside your control? People with an internal locus of control tend to see their outcomes in life as due to their own abilities or effort. People with an external locus of control tend to see their outcomes as due to forces outside them, such as luck or other people with more power. There is some evidence that people's perspective on evidence presented at trial is influenced by their locus of control (Phares, 1976). Consider a sexual harassment case involving a romantic relationship between an upper-level male manager and a female middle manager. The relationship turns sour and the female breaks it off. Later she sues the company for sexual harassment. An "internal" juror might be more likely to blame the woman for her difficulties and be less likely to convict. An "external" juror may be more likely to hold the company responsible and decide in favor of the woman.

A separate but related personality characteristic—belief in a just world—seems to bear a logical relationship to verdicts and sentencing. People can be differentiated by how strongly they believe that people "get what they deserve and deserve what they get" in life, that is, by how strongly they believe that the world is just. Those people who believe in a just world have a tendency to derogate victims—to believe, for example, that women who have been raped may have done something to "bring it on themselves" (Lerner, 1980). The underlying psychological mechanism seems to be that if we can find a valid—or even an invalid—reason why someone became a victim, we can reduce our own anxiety about becoming a victim. If she hadn't been out alone at night, or hadn't drunk too much, or had dressed differently, or had stayed away from the bad part of town, maybe she would not have been raped. And, therefore, if we avoid those behaviors, we and the people we love will be safe from harm. It is simply too psychologically threatening to believe that sometimes terrible things happen to people for no good reason.

A third personality trait—authoritarianism—may also come into play when jurors are deciding cases. People with "authoritarian personalities" have the following characteristics: They tend to have conventional values, their beliefs tend to be rigid, they are intolerant of weakness, they tend to identify with and submit to authority figures, and they are suspicious of and punitive towards those who violate established norms and rules. For example, one of the items on the F-scale (the test designed to measure authoritarianism) is, "Sex crimes such as rape and attacks on children deserve more than mere imprisonment; such criminals ought to be publicly whipped or worse" (Dillehay, 1999). Those who score high on authoritarianism are more likely to convict and to hand down longer prison sentences. However, if the defendant is a police officer (an authority figure) accused of excessive use of force, authoritarians are much less likely to convict (Narby, Cutler, & Moran, 1993).

Attitudes about the Legal System.   Some researchers have argued that it is unrealistic to expect general attitudes or personality tendencies to predict verdicts, but that case-specific attitudes may be moderately predictive of verdicts. There is some evidence to support this view (Moran et al., 1994: Ajzen & Fishbein, 1980). A few scales have been specifically developed to assess attitudes that might be related to verdicts in criminal trials. For example, the Revised Legal Attitudes Questionnaire (RLAQ) consists of 30 statements, such as the following:

> Too many obviously guilty persons escape punishment because of legal technicalities.
>
> Evidence illegally obtained should be admissible in court if such evidence is the only way of obtaining a conviction.
>
> In the long run, liberty is more important than order.
>
> There is just about no such thing as an honest cop (Kravitz, Cutler, & Brock, 1993).

People filling out the questionnaire indicate their level of agreement on a scale ranging from "strongly disagree" to "strongly agree" (called a Likert format scale).

A second scale designed for use with jurors is called the Juror Bias Scale (Kassin & Wrightsman, 1983). It also uses a Likert format and contains statements such as the following:

> Too many innocent people are wrongfully imprisoned.
>
> Too often jurors hesitate to convict someone who is guilty out of pure sympathy.

These and the other 15 items in the scale attempt to isolate juror's beliefs about how likely it is that someone who is on trial for a crime actually committed that crime, and how certain a juror needs to be before convicting a defendant (i.e., how they define "reasonable doubt"). The scale also seems to measure general cynicism about the legal system. In mock jury studies, these more specialized questionnaires slightly improve the ability to predict how a juror will eventually vote (Myers & Lecci, 1998).

A few scales have been specifically developed for use in civil trials. The Civil Trial Bias Scale consists of 16 items designed to measure attitudes about the appropriate role of government regulation of business, appropriate standards for workplace and product safety, and whether or not most civil suits are justified (Hans & Lofquist, 1994). In civil trials, a plaintiff sues a defendant for an alleged harm. If the defendant is found liable (responsible for the alleged harm), monetary damages are typically awarded. That is, the defendant is usually ordered to pay the plaintiff for the harm. In addition to compensatory damages (meant to compensate the plaintiff for losses), there may also be punitive damages (meant to punish the defendant for irresponsible or malicious conduct and to discourage others from behaving similarly). Among the attitudes that appear to be related to verdicts in civil trials include the belief that there is a "litigation crisis" fueled by people filing frivolous lawsuits in an attempt to make money. The opposite belief is that corporations often engage in dangerous or irresponsible behavior that endangers consumers and that businesses need to be held accountable for that misconduct. Researchers have found modest relationships between "litigation crisis" attitudes and damage awards. Specifically, people who believe that there are too many frivolous lawsuits, and people who favor tort reform (placing caps on the size of damage awards), also tend to minimize the blameworthiness of civil defendants and to favor low damage awards (Hans, 2000).

Defendant-Juror Similarity.   Sometimes the characteristics of the defendant and the characteristics of jurors interact in ways that influence verdicts. The similarity-leniency hypothesis predicts that jurors who are similar to the defendant will empathize and identify with the defendant. Consequently, they will be less likely to convict. This hypothesis is widely held by attorneys and has great intuitive appeal. The hypothesis also seems plausible from a research perspective because there is considerable research showing that similarity promotes interpersonal attraction (Aronson, 1998). Still, many questions remain: If similarity makes a juror better able to empathize with a defendant, does that empathy then translate into leniency? Do all types of similarity (e.g., race or religion, occupation or gender) lead to leniency? Can similarity sometimes cause jurors to be more harsh instead of less harsh?

Norbert Kerr and his colleagues conducted two studies to investigate the similarity-leniency hypothesis (Kerr, Hymes, Anderson, & Weathers, 1995). They varied racial similarity between the defendant and jurors as well as the strength of the evidence against the defendant. Black and white mock jurors judged both black and white defendants. When the evidence against the defendant was weak or only moderately convincing, jurors who were racially similar to the defendant were more likely to reach a "not guilty" verdict. It seems that when evidence is inconclusive, we tend to give similar defendants the benefit of the doubt. But sometimes there was a boomerang effect—similar jurors were occasionally harsher on defendants than dissimilar jurors. For example, if the evidence against an African American defendant was strong, and African American jurors were in the minority on the jury, those jurors judged the defendant as guiltier than did European American jurors. The same relationships held for European Americans. If the evidence was strong and whites were in the minority on the jury, they were harsher with white defendants. It seems that if jurors are outnumbered by members of another racial group, they may feel compelled to treat a racially similar (but probably guilty) defendant more harshly. By doing so, they emphasize their condemnation of the defendant, they disassociate and distance themselves from the defendant, and they are able to maintain a favorable view of their own group.

In other research relevant to this hypothesis, researchers found that it was not race per se that led jurors to sympathize with O. J. Simpson in his double-murder trial. That is, it was not merely that black jurors were less likely to convict. Instead, it was prior experience with and beliefs about race discrimination that made jurors more likely to be receptive to the version of events presented by defense attorneys (Mendoza-Dinton, Ayduk, Shoda, & Mischel, 1997; Newman et al., 1997). Race was correlated with verdict, but not determinative of verdict. Similarly, in research looking at cases where a man was accused of sexually harassing a woman, it was not gender per se that was predictive of verdicts. Instead, it was receptiveness to elements of a plaintiff-oriented account of events (e.g., the sexual attention was unwelcome, management tolerated the harassment) or a defense-oriented account (e.g., the woman encouraged the harassment, she is suing the company to retaliate for being fired) (Huntley & Costanzo, 2003). Females are more likely to be receptive to a plaintiff-oriented account of events, but gender does not determine verdict.

Given the paucity of research on the similarity-leniency hypothesis, the conclusions above are still somewhat tentative. However, it appears that sometimes similarity does increase leniency, probably because jurors similar to the defendant are more likely to accept the defense account of events. The effect seems to depend on how strong the evidence is and how many "similar" people are members of the jury. It appears that similarity produces leniency only when the evidence against the defendant is inconclusive and when similar jurors outnumber dissimilar jurors. Sometimes similarity causes jurors to be more, rather than less, harsh in their judgments of a defendant. Further, only race and gender similarity have been investigated. We don't yet know if other types of similarity influence verdicts. The lesson here is the same as in most other areas of psychology and law: Simple explanations are appealing but often wrong. Relationships are complex and variables often combine and interact in ways that produce unexpected effects.

BASIC TRIAL PROCEDURE

Before discussing how jurors use information presented at trial, it is worth reviewing what happens during a trial. Trials begin with opening statements by the opposing attorneys. These statements are not considered evidence. Instead, they are meant to highlight the issues at stake and to provide jurors with an overview of evidence that will be heard. In criminal trials, the prosecution usually goes first and in civil trials (in which one party sues another), the plaintiff goes first. Although the defense usually makes an opening statement right after the prosecutor or plaintiff's attorney, defense lawyers have the option of postponing their statement until it is their turn to present evidence. The reason prosecutors and plaintiffs go first is that they "bear the burden of proof" and they are the ones alleging that the defendant broke the law. In criminal cases, a defendant must be judged guilty "beyond a reasonable doubt," while in civil cases the standard of proof for being held liable (responsible for causing the alleged harm) is usually "preponderance of the evidence." The law does not supply clear definitions of these burdens of proof, but, "beyond a reasonable doubt" is clearly the higher standard. Sometimes the "preponderance of the evidence" standard is interpreted as meaning more than 50% of the evidence favors one side, and sometimes "beyond a reasonable doubt" is interpreted as meaning that jurors must be more than 90% certain that the defendant is guilty. Reasonable doubt is sometimes defined as a doubt for which someone can give a reason (presumably a good reason).

Following opening statements, the prosecutor or plaintiff's attorney calls witnesses to testify. After a witness has been questioned by the prosecutor or plaintiff's attorney, the defense lawyer may cross-examine (that is, ask questions of) that witness. Next, the attorney who called the witness has an opportunity to question the witness yet again in a process called "redirect" examination. The last opportunity for questioning the witness is given to the defense attorney in "recross" examination. The procedure switches when the defense presents its case: The defense lawyer questions the witness first, followed by cross-examination by the prosecutor or plaintiff's lawyer, followed by redirect and recross. In this way, the two attorneys take turns questioning each witness until both sides have finished presenting their case. After all the evidence has been presented, each attorney makes a closing argument (also referred to as a "summation"). Like opening statements, closing arguments are not evidence. They are attempts to persuade jurors that one interpretation of the evidence is the correct one. The prosecution or plaintiff goes first, then the defense, and then the prosecution or plaintiff has an opportunity to give a rebuttal. Therefore, the prosecutor or plaintiff's lawyer has both the first and last word at trial.

JURORS AS (BIASED) INFORMATION PROCESSORS

The legal system expects a lot from jurors—to put aside their prejudices and preconceptions, to attend fully to the copious and often complex information presented at trial, to withhold final judgment, to refrain from asking other people about the evidence, to quickly understand the meaning of the law, and to understand how the law applies to the case they are hearing. Are these expectations reasonable?

Pretrial Publicity.   As you might suspect, research suggests that jurors don't magically shed their prejudices and preconceptions when they walk through the courthouse door. One source of possibly prejudicial information is pretrial publicity. In high-profile cases—for example, the murder of a famous person—there is likely to be substantial coverage on TV and in local newspapers before a trial ever begins and before a jury is ever impaneled. There tends to be a pro-prosecution slant to this coverage. News reports are typically based on information received from police departments and from the district attorney's office. These reports tend to focus on details of the crime, police investigation of the crime, effects of the crime on victims or their families, and incriminating evidence against the defendant. Pretrial publicity often contains information that is not admissible as evidence during trial. Several studies show that people exposed to more news coverage of a crime are significantly more likely to presume that the defendant is guilty (Kovera, 2002; Otto, Penrod, & Dexter, 1994). Unfortunately, a recent review of studies testing the effectiveness of judge's instructions to disregard pretrial publicity found that such instructions had no remedial effect (Kerr, 1994). This biasing effect of pretrial publicity is especially strong when news coverage is emotionally arousing (e.g., focusing on the brutal nature of a murder) and when television (as opposed to newspapers) is the source of the information (Ogloff & Vidmar, 1994).

In a careful study conducted by Geoffrey Kramer and his associates, 791 mock jurors were exposed to either factual publicity that described a crime but did not incriminate the defendant, or emotional publicity intended to arouse negative feelings (e.g., information about a 7-year-old girl who had been the victim of a hit-and-run accident and a plea for help from her big sister). The defendant was then tried in a mock trial. A brief, 12-day delay between exposure to news reports and the mock trial *did* eliminate the bias created by factual publicity but *did not* eliminate the bias created by emotional publicity (Kramer, Kerr, & Carroll, 1990). In addition, the pro-prosecution bias created by pretrial publicity was actually magnified by the process of deliberation—mock jurors were more inclined to convict after deliberation. Postponing a trial may be an effective remedy to some of the problems created by pretrial publicity. However, the most effective remedy appears to be a change of venue: moving the trial to a community that has not been exposed to pretrial publicity and its biasing effects.

Defendant Characteristics.   The wealth, social status, and gender of defendants don't appear to influence verdicts in any simple or straightforward way (Huss, 2002). The physical attractiveness of a defendant doesn't seem to matter much either. Although there is some evidence that jurors treat good-looking defendants more leniently and judge ugly defendants more harshly, the effect is weak (Dane & Wrightsman, 1982). However, if a very attractive defendant uses his or her attractiveness to commit a crime—for example, if a handsome young man seduces rich older women to steal their fortunes—jurors do take attractiveness into account and hand down more severe sentences. Jurors also appear to take the moral character of the defendant into account by comparing his or her character to that of the victim. If the moral character of the victim is significantly superior to that of the defendant, jurors tend to judge the defendant more harshly (Devine et al., 2001). For example, if a drug addict assaults and robs another drug addict outside a house where drugs are sold, he is likely to be treated less harshly than if he assaults and robs a school teacher outside her home. Interestingly, jurors also seem to take into account how much the defendant has already suffered for his crimes. If the defendant is badly injured during the commission of a crime, jurors are more lenient (Ellsworth & Mauro, 1998).

In civil trials, individuals who are sued tend to be ordered to pay lower monetary damage awards than corporations who are sued for similar bad acts. Many have attributed this finding to the fact that corporations have more money—"deeper pockets" as it is commonly expressed. But researchers have found that the more important reason is that corporations are expected to be more accountable for their actions than are individuals. An individual may have a lapse in judgment and harm others. But the groups of individuals who make decisions for corporations are expected to be well trained and to have checks and balances in place to guard against bad group judgment. Consequently, jurors hold them more accountable for the consequences of their decisions (Hans, 2000; MacCoun, 1993).

Inadmissible and Complex Evidence.   Jurors are not only told to ignore pretrial publicity about a crime, they are also told to ignore other types of inadmissible evidence (e.g., information that might be prejudicial). Inadmissible information may come from witnesses or attorneys.

When one attorney calls out "objection" in response to a question or statement made by the opposing counsel or a witness, the judge must either sustain or overrule the objection. If the judge sustains the objection, he or she will tell the jury to "disregard" the inadmissible statement (e.g., that a criminal defendant has a prior criminal record or that a civil defendant has a large insurance policy). In other words, the jury is supposed to forget they ever heard it and not let it influence them. Most attorneys are skeptical about whether jurors can disregard inadmissible statements made during trial. As many attorneys say, "You can't unring a bell."

Research suggests that the intuition of attorneys is usually right—that you can't unring a bell or force jurors to forget what they just heard. Indeed, the judge's admonition may sometimes have the opposite of its intended effect—telling jurors to disregard a statement may cause jurors to give that statement extra weight (Lieberman & Arndt, 2000). But why? One explanation is based on what have been called "ironic processes." When we make an effort not to think about something, it often dominates our thoughts, especially when we are under stress and much of our mental capacity is already in use (Wegner, 1994). Anyone who has suffered from obsessive thoughts has experienced this effect. Another explanation is suggested by what is known as reactance theory. According to this theory, people are motivated to maintain their freedom (Brehm & Brehm, 1981). The judge's admonition may be perceived as a threat to jurors' freedom to make a decision based on all the available evidence. Jurors may react to that threat by giving the inadmissible evidence greater weight than it would have otherwise. Third, as discussed in the last chapter, jurors tend to rely on broad commonsense notions of justice. Even if a piece of information is legally inadmissible, if jurors believe that information will help them to reach the right decision, they are likely to use it (Finkel, 2002).

In a study of jurors' ability to disregard inadmissible testimony, Kerri Pickel (1995) asked mock jurors to decide a case where a man who had been recently fired from his job was accused of stealing $5,000 from his former boss. When questioned by the prosecution, one of the defendant's former coworkers made a hearsay statement: He reported that someone had told him that the defendant said his boss would "be sorry" and that he "could walk in and get the cash without being seen." In another condition, when questioned by the prosecution, the coworker made a statement about the defendant's prior conviction ("he had to serve a few days in jail for a perjury conviction"). The defense attorney objected to these statements, and in response to that objection, the judge either ruled the evidence admissible, ruled the evidence inadmissible, or ruled it inadmissible and explained the legal basis for the ruling. Results showed that the judge's instruction to disregard the inadmissible evidence was effective for hearsay evidence but backfired for prior conviction evidence. In this and other studies, whether or not jurors make use of inadmissible evidence seems to depend not on legal considerations, but on whether or not jurors believe it is fair to consider the evidence. As Pickel notes, if jurors conclude, ". . . based on their sense of what is just, that it would be unfair to use evidence to determine guilt, then they will disregard the evidence. Alternatively, if they decide that it is not necessarily unfair to consider the evidence, then they probably will be unwilling to ignore it completely, thus producing the backfire effect" (p. 422).

The available research clearly indicates that jurors don't simply purge inadmissible evidence from their memories and that a judge's admonition sometimes highlights the legally improper evidence. A related problem concerns the use of impeachment evidence—evidence meant to damage the credibility of a witness's statements. Here, a defendant may sometimes be asked about prior dishonest conduct for the purpose of establishing the honesty of his or her current testimony. But, instead of using this information in the legally specified manner, research indicates that jurors use it to draw broader conclusions. They are likely to see past dishonest behavior as symptomatic of an enduring predisposition toward dishonest behavior (Wissler & Saks, 1985). In this area, as in other areas, jurors use a broader conception of justice. In life outside the courtroom, knowledge of a person's past behavior is a key determinant of how we interpret their current behavior. It is unrealistic to expect jurors not to consider past convictions, especially if these convictions were for crimes similar to the one being considered at trial (Finkel, 2002).

Sometimes jurors are told not to consider evidence, and sometimes they are unable to fully understand evidence. Jurors are often exposed to complex scientific and technical evidence, and that evidence is usually presented via expert testimony. Expert witnesses offer testimony based on specialized knowledge, training, or experience. For example, experts may testify about the meaning of DNA evidence based on the chemical analysis of blood, semen, or saliva. There may be fingerprint analysis or ballistics tests or testimony about medical procedures or building construction or the causes of disease. Although most jurors have limited knowledge in these specialized areas, they must strive to understand expert testimony. In a study of the impact of complex medical testimony, Joel Cooper, Elizabeth Bennett, and Holly Sukel (1996) varied both the complexity of expert testimony, as well as the credentials of the prosecution expert. The case involved a worker who alleged that he developed liver cancer and an immune system disorder because of exposure to polychlorinated biphenyls in his workplace. When the expert (a professor of biochemistry) offered complex testimony full of specialized jargon, he was persuasive only if his credentials were very strong—that is, when his degrees were from prestigious universities, when he taught at a prestigious university, and when he had published widely. When the testimony was less complex, the strength of the expert's credentials was not important. The jurors were able to make sense of the testimony and draw conclusions on the basis of the content of the testimony. These findings suggest that if the content of the expert's message is difficult to comprehend, jurors may weight the testimony based on more peripheral cues like the apparent credibility of the expert.

More generally, research on the impact of expert testimony has found that if an expert is effectively cross-examined, or if an expert's testimony is contradicted by the testimony of another expert, the impact of the testimony is weakened (Greene, Downey, & Goodman-Delahunty, 1999). In addition, testimony that is clear, specific to the issues in the case, and somewhat repetitive appears to be most persuasive (Kovera et al., 1997). However, expert testimony is not accepted uncritically by jurors and does not appear to have an overpowering impact on verdicts. Indeed, in some cases, jurors regard it with special skepticism because they may perceive experts as "hired guns" (Sunby, 1997).

The Judge's Instructions as a Source of Confusion.   After all the evidence has been presented and all the testimony has been heard, the attorneys deliver their closing arguments and the trial ends. Typically, the judge reads instructions to the jury after closing arguments. These instructions contain information about the available verdict categories (e.g., manslaughter versus second-degree murder), and the standard of proof to be used ("reasonable doubt" or a "preponderance of evidence" or "clear and convincing evidence"). Although these instructions are intended to be helpful, research has consistently demonstrated that jurors have great difficulty understanding them. This lack of comprehensibility is due to both the vagueness of the legal concepts and the poor quality of the writing. The instructions are packed with legal terminology and are written in a complex, convoluted style. As one scholar put it, ". . . typical pattern instructions drafted in an effort to be legally precise, are incomprehensible to jurors" (Tanford, 1990, p. 73).

The judge usually reads instructions to the jury without providing examples and without attempting to apply the legal categories to the case at hand. Moreover, judges almost never attempt to clarify instructions because they fear that any such attempt will provide grounds for an appeal. To illustrate the problem, consider the following instruction used to define negligence in civil cases:

> One test that is helpful in determining whether or not a person was negligent is to ask and answer whether or not, if a person of ordinary prudence had been in the same situation and possessed of the same knowledge, he would have foreseen or anticipated that someone might have been injured as a result of his action or inaction. If such a result from certain conduct would be foreseeable by a person of ordinary prudence with like knowledge and in like situation, and if the conduct reasonably could be avoided, then not to avoid it would be negligence.

A linguist and a lawyer rewrote these instructions to improve clarity while preserving the accuracy of legal concepts. They shortened the sentences, cut out unusual or abstract words and phrases ("ordinary prudence"), reduced redundancy ("foreseen or anticipated") and avoided negatives. Here are the simplified instructions:

> In order to decide whether or not the defendant was negligent, there is a test you can use. Consider how a reasonably careful person would have acted in the same situation. Specifically, in order to find the defendant negligent, you would have to answer "yes" to the following two questions:
>
> 1) Would a reasonably careful person have realized in advance that someone might be injured as a result of the defendant's conduct?
> And,
> 2) Could a reasonably careful person have avoided behaving as the defendant did?
>
> If your answer to both questions is "yes," then the defendant is negligent (Charrow & Charrow, 1979).

These clearer instructions led to clearer understanding among jurors. In studies comparing conventional legalistic instructions to simpler, rewritten instructions, the clearer instructions lead to significantly better understanding of crucial legal concepts. But, although the simpler, clearer instructions improve juror comprehension and simplify the task of the jury, they do not solve the problem completely. The abstract nature of legal concepts and the inherent ambiguities in those concepts may mean that understanding can never be perfect. As one scholar concluded, "it is the law itself that is incomprehensible" (Tanford, 1990, p. 110).

It is not only the content of instructions that matters, timing also matters. Typically, jurors are not provided with instructions until the trial is over. One helpful innovation is to read instructions to jurors before the trial begins. The value of this procedure is that it allows jurors to evaluate the legal relevance of the evidence as they hear it. "Pre-instructions" (read to jurors before the trial begins) appear to provide a schema that helps jurors organize information presented at trial. In one study, two groups of mock jurors watched an auto theft trial and reached verdicts based on the evidence (Smith, 1991). But one group did not receive the instruction about presumed innocence until *after* the trial was over. The conviction rate for that group was 59%. The other group of mock jurors received the instruction *before* evidence was presented. For that group, the conviction rate dropped to 37%. It appears that pretrial instructions create a mindset among jurors that causes them to evaluate evidence differently. Waiting to tell jurors to presume innocence until after they have heard all the evidence may simply be too little too late. They may have already formed a strong opinion about the defendant's guilt.

In a study of jury trials in Wisconsin, 33 juries were given instructions only after the trial had ended, while another 34 juries received both pre-instructions and post-instructions (Heuer & Penrod, 1989). The juries were randomly assigned to the two conditions. As compared to post-instructed-only jurors, the pre- and-post-instructed jurors were more satisfied with their trial experience, and felt they had a clearer understanding of how to apply the relevant law to the evidence presented at trial. Unfortunately, only one state (Arizona) requires judges to pre-instruct. In many other states, the decision about whether to give pre-instructions is left to the discretion of the individual judge.

Models of Juror Decision Making.   One useful way of describing the decision-making processes of jurors is through the use of mathematical models. In many such models, jurors are assumed to use a sort of "mental meter" that moves towards either a "guilty" or "not guilty" verdict based on the weight of the evidence. Pieces of evidence presented at trial are represented as numerical weights that shift the mental meter in one direction or the other. Over the course of the trial, jurors continually update their judgments, although a particular piece of evidence—for example, a persuasive eyewitness—may be so heavily weighted that the meter becomes "frozen" and further evidence does little to change the juror's overall judgment (Hastie, 1993).

A prominent alternative to mathematical models is the story model of juror decision making developed by Nancy Pennington and Reid Hastie (1993). Instead of representing decision making as the process of mathematically combining numerical weights, the story model proposes that jurors create stories to make sense of evidence presented at trial. A story is defined as a causal chain of events. That is, initiating events cause characters to have psychological responses and to form goals that motivate actions, and then these actions lead to consequences. For example, in a case used in some studies of the story model, a man named Johnson stabs and kills a man named Caldwell and is put on trial for first-degree murder. The undisputed events are that one afternoon, the two men had an argument at a bar and Caldwell threatened Johnson with a razor blade. Johnson left the bar but returned late in the evening. He and Caldwell got into a fight outside the bar. Johnson pulled a knife and stabbed Caldwell, who died from the wound. Jurors must decide whether Johnson acted in self-defense or whether it was premeditated murder. In research investigating the story model, jurors who reached a self-defense verdict inferred that Johnson was afraid and that he pulled his knife to prevent Caldwell from killing him. Jurors reaching a first-degree murder verdict inferred that Johnson felt angry and humiliated by the afternoon quarrel, went home to get his knife, and returned to the bar with the intention of killing Caldwell. In this case and most cases, the inferences necessary to complete the story—for example, whether Johnson was motivated by anger or fear—are informed by a juror's past experience and preexisting knowledge of similar events.

According to the story model, jurors construct their stories while hearing the evidence at trial. Next, they learn about possible verdicts (usually at the end of the trial when the judge reads instructions to jurors), and, finally, they select the verdict that best fits with the story they have constructed to make sense of the evidence. The story model has proven to be a useful way of describing juror decision processes in several types of trials, including murder, rape, and sexual harassment (Pennington & Hastie, 1993; Huntley & Costanzo, 2003; Olsen-Fulero & Fulero, 1997). However, we don't yet know how the differing stories of individual jurors become reconciled during jury deliberation.

THE GROUP DYNAMICS OF JURY DELIBERATIONS

Most of the research summarized in this chapter has to do with jurors rather than juries, individuals rather than groups. It makes sense to study jurors because it is individual jurors who must listen to and make sense of the evidence. But the important outcome—the verdict—is decided by the jury as a group. How does the group affect the decision-making process?

The most direct way of understanding the dynamics of juries would be to observe a large number of actual juries to see if there are recurring patterns in how groups of jurors pool their collective wisdom to arrive at a final verdict. Unfortunately for researchers, the law (with very few exceptions) precludes this direct approach. It was first tried 50 years ago. As part of the groundbreaking University of Chicago Jury Project of the 1950s, the deliberations of five juries in civil cases in Wichita, Kansas were tape-recorded. Although presiding judges and lawyers had approved these recordings, jurors were not told they were being audio-taped. When the media became aware of these tape recordings, a national scandal ensued. Newspaper editorials denounced this violation of the privacy rights of juries and a U.S. Senate subcommittee held hearings about the scandal. There was even an attempt to portray the research as part of a subversive communist plot. In their defense, the researchers (Harry Kalven, Hans Zeisel, Rita James Simon, Edward Levi, and Fred Strodtbeck) argued that attempts to improve the jury system should be based on full and accurate data about how juries actually make decisions. Apparently, this argument did little to reassure policy makers. The tape recordings were never analyzed and the controversy led to the enactment of statutes banning the observation or recording of jury deliberations (Kalven & Zeisel, 1966). Because of this ban, nearly all of the research on jury deliberations comes out of observations of mock juries or from real jurors who are interviewed after their jury service has been completed.

Strong Jurors and the Power of the Majority.   Lawyers attempt to predict the group dynamics of a jury during voir dire. They talk about some potential jurors as "strong jurors," "key jurors," or "jury leaders"—those who seem likely to have a disproportionate influence on the deliberation process. Potential jurors judged to be "strong" are often well educated, articulate, and have high occupational status (relative to other potential jurors). A powerful fictional portrayal of a strong juror can be found in the classic film *Twelve Angry Men*. In that film, a lone juror played by Henry Fonda holds steady in his belief that a defendant should be acquitted. Through logic and heroic perseverance in the face of group pressure, he persuades the other 11 jurors to change their mistaken guilty votes. Unfortunately, the available research indicates that, in reality, such jurors are quite rare. There are two basic reasons for this: First, majorities tend to prevail. If a jury begins deliberations with an eight to four majority, there is a strong probability that the majority will persuade or pressure the minority to change their votes. In Kalven and Zeisel's classic study, 215 juries began with a clear majority. Of those 215, 209 juries reached the verdict favored by the initial majority. Their conclusion was that, ". . . the deliberation process might well be likened to what the developer does for exposed film; it brings out the picture, but the outcome is predetermined" (p. 488). Second, majorities tend to have more persuasive arguments at their disposal, and they can bring strong social pressure to bear on jurors holding the minority opinion.

In an official sense, the foreperson is the leader of the jury. But the juror who is selected as foreperson does not necessarily exert disproportionate influence on the verdict decision. In fact, the foreperson may contribute less to the discussion of the evidence and the verdict decision because he or she is preoccupied with procedural issues such as tabulating votes or making sure that everyone else has an opportunity to express his or her views. The role is more that of moderator and organizer than leader and controller (Kerr, Niedermeier, & Kaplan, 1999; Strodtbeck & Hook, 1961). Any special influence the foreperson does possess is likely to stem from his or her ability to determine the order in which other jurors speak, and the amount of time each juror is allowed to speak (Manzo, 1996). Perhaps because the role of foreperson is temporary and the main job of juries is to reach a verdict, the selection of a foreperson is likely to be quick and informal. Indeed, jurors may rely on fairly superficial characteristics when choosing a foreperson. Research has revealed several factors that increase the odds of being chosen as foreperson: speaking first, being a male, having served as a juror on a prior case, having high job status, sitting at the head of the table, and asking the question, "Should we elect a foreperson?" (Hastie, 1993).

Although majorities usually prevail, what has been called the "leniency bias" is also at work in criminal trials. That is, in evenly split juries, or almost evenly split juries, where roughly half the jurors favor "guilty" on the initial vote and the other half favor "not guilty," it is much more likely that the final verdict will be "not guilty" (MacCoun & Kerr, 1988). The process of deliberation and the high standard of "reasonable doubt" seem to favor acquittal. In the deliberation room, jurors who favor ac-quittal need only to create reasonable doubt, while jurors favoring con-viction must find a way to remove nearly all doubt. Looking across several studies, Dennis Devine and his colleagues came to the following conclusion about 12-person juries in criminal cases:

> . . . if 7 or fewer jurors favor conviction at the beginning of deliberation, the jury will probably acquit, and if 10 or more jurors believe the defen-dant is guilty, the jury will probably convict. With 8 or 9 jurors initially favoring conviction, the final verdict is basically a toss-up" (Devine, Clayton, Dunford, Seying, & Pryce, 2001, p. 722).

Stages in the Deliberation Process.   The dynamics of juries differ depending on the characteristics of the case being decided and the people who make up the jury. But, based on observations of mock juries and post-verdict interviews with actual jurors, many juries appear to move through a three-stage process (Stasser, 1992). During the first phase—orientation—juries elect a foreperson, discuss procedures, and raise general issues. At the outset of deliberation, jurors tend to be con-fused about how to proceed. Some juries take a vote immediately to get a sense of where people stand, other juries postpone voting and begin by discussing the issues to be decided, and other juries begin by dis-cussing each witness who testified at trial. Observations of the delibera-tion process suggest that about 30% of juries take a vote shortly after they begin deliberations and then orient their subsequent discussions around the verdict options. This "verdict-driven" style of structuring the deliberation process leads jurors to sort the evidence into categories supporting conviction or acquittal. Other juries adopt an "evidence-driven" style, where the first vote is postponed until after there has been careful, systematic discussion of the evidence (Hastie, Penrod, & Pennington, 1983; Sandys & Dillehay, 1995). Postponing a vote until after the evidence is discussed appears to produce richer, more probing discussions. Once a vote has been taken, there is a tendency for jurors to focus on defending their position.

During the second phase—open conflict—differences in opinion among members of the jury become apparent and coalitions form among members of the group. Often, the tone of the discussion becomes contentious, with each faction challenging how others interpret the evidence. Some jurors may even attack the character or integrity of jurors who disagree with them. The process of reaching a verdict through group deliberation is essentially a process of persuasion. Either all jurors (if the verdict must be unanimous) or a majority of jurors (if only a majority is required) must be persuaded to join with others. Sometimes jurors are swayed through a process of *informational influence*: They change their opinions because other jurors make compelling arguments. At other times, jurors don't really change their private views, but they do change their votes in response to *normative influence* (Kaplan & Miller, 1987). That is, they give in to group pressure. When a strong majority is trying to persuade one or two "holdouts" to reach a unanimous verdict, group pressure can be intense (Costanzo and Costanzo, 1994). Research on civil trials suggests a difference in the type of influence used during culpability and penalty decisions. Mock juries asked to make a more fact-based decision—whether or not a defendant should be held liable—tended to rely on informational influence in the form of factual arguments. In contrast, mock juries asked to make a more subjective, value-laden decision—the amount of punitive damages—tended to rely on normative influence (Hans, 1992). Morality-based decisions must rely on appeals to basic fairness and group values, whereas fact-based decisions can follow from logical analysis of evidence (Costanzo & Costanzo, 1992).

As jurors work toward a common understanding and agreement, or as one faction simply capitulates, the jury enters the third and final— reconciliation—phase. During this final phase, attempts are made to soothe hurt feelings and make everyone feel satisfied with the verdict. Of course, hung juries never make it to the reconciliation phase.

Just like in other groups, a few people tend to dominate discussions during jury deliberations. In 12-person juries, the three people who are most vocal use up about 50% of the deliberation time and the three least vocal people contribute very little. Roughly 70% to 75% of the deliberation time is devoted to discussions of evidence, with about 20% of the time devoted to the law and the judge's instructions (Ellsworth, 1989). Although some attorneys believe that jurors are preoccupied with irrelevant and superficial characteristics of the attorneys or witnesses (e.g., their clothes, hairstyle, or speaking style), research suggests that juries spend very little time on irrelevant or trivial details. Jurors appear to take their job very seriously and they make a sincere effort to follow the rules as they understand them. Fortunately, group deliberation does create a fuller, more accurate view of the evidence. But, unfortunately, it does not appear to improve understanding of the law (Hans, 1992). As discussed above, this is probably because the law is not communicated clearly by the judge's instructions.

Recently, a team of researchers was permitted to observe the discussions and deliberations of 50 actual civil juries in Arizona (Diamond, Vidmar, Rose, Ellis, & Murphy, 2002). This groundbreaking study is described in a later section of this chapter. However, at this point, it is worth noting the Arizona researchers found it useful to compare jury discussions to another familiar type of group: "Jury discussions are, in effect, committee meetings similar to committee meetings that occur in a wide range of non-trial venues" (p.47). Like a long committee meeting, jury discussions can be focused and highly structured at times but wandering and "nonlinear" at other times. Topics may be introduced without being pursued, brief side conversations may emerge between two or more people. Some issues are raised, then dropped, only to be raised again at a later time. Like all other human decision-making groups, juries are not paragons of efficiency.

One other finding of the Arizona group is worth noting here—juries tend to make a sincere effort to take the views of every member of the group seriously. Reassuringly, researchers found that ". . . there is a strong overlay of equality displayed in juror interactions, regardless of the socioeconomic status of the members" (p. 47).

The Size of the Jury.   One of the main determinants of group dynamics is group size. For centuries, English law dictated a 12-person jury. It is not entirely clear why lawmakers settled on 12 people per jury instead of 10 or 15 or some other number. Some say it is due to the influence of Christianity (Christ had 12 apostles); some say it is simply another example of the English affinity for the number 12 (12 inches to a foot, 12 pence to a shilling, 12 of anything equals a dozen). At any rate, the American colonies inherited the 12-person jury. And 12 remained the standard jury size until the mid-1900s. Then, in *Williams v. Florida* (1970), the Supreme Court reviewed the case of a man who had been convicted of armed robbery by a six-person jury. The Court decided that it was constitutionally permissible to reduce the size of juries to six in noncapital cases (any case where there is no possibility of the death penalty). In *Ballew v. Georgia* (1978), the Court clarified the size requirement, ruling that five-person juries are too small and six-person juries are the constitutional minimum.

In permitting these radical departures from past practice, the Court appeared to rely on social scientific evidence. With respect to jury size, they cited six "research findings" indicating that there was "no discernible difference" between the verdicts reached by six- or twelve-person juries. But the Court got the science wrong. In 1977, Michael Saks reviewed the existing research on jury size and jury decision rules (unanimous or majority rule). He noted that most of the six "experiments" referred to by the Court did not qualify as systematic research studies at all: Some were casual observations, one was an account of a case that used a six-person jury, and one was a description of how smaller juries might save money. The one true experiment cited by the justices was misinterpreted. The justices reached a conclusion opposite from the conclusion reached by the researcher.

Based on his own extensive research and the research of other social scientists, Saks reached the conclusion that, as compared to smaller juries, large juries deliberate longer, recall evidence more accurately, generate more arguments, agree more on their ratings of jury performance, are more representative of the community, and produce more consistent verdicts (Saks, 1977). Larger juries are more representative in a few ways—there is broader representation of demographic groups (e.g., gender, racial and ethnic minorities), there are more people in opinion minorities, and there is a greater range of juror opinions and expertise (Roper, 1980). Jury size seems to have more influence on process than on outcomes. On average, the verdicts of 6- and 12-person juries don't differ significantly, but six-person juries are less predictable. Put differently, if 100 six-person juries and 100 12-person juries all decide the same case, there will be a more even split on verdict among the six-person juries. Also, the verdicts of larger juries are more likely to match the opinions of the larger community (Saks, 1996). This is important because juries are intended to represent the conscience of the community.

Decision Rules (Unanimous or Majority Rule). A second crucial requirement of the jury system—the decision rule requiring a unanimous verdict—was established during the fourteenth century. The American colonies inherited both 12-person juries and unanimous verdicts. But during the same time that the Court was making changes in jury size, they began to allow for nonunanimous verdicts. In 1972, the Supreme Court (*Apodaca, Cooper, & Madden v. Oregon,* 1972; *Johnson v. Louisiana,* 1972) ruled that nonunanimous decisions (with splits as large as nine to three) were constitutional. The 1979 decision in *Burch v. Louisiana,* held that if a six-person jury is used, verdicts must be unanimous. Only 27 states now require unanimity in misdemeanor verdicts, although 44 states require it in criminal felony trials, and unanimity is always required in capital murder trials.

Michael Saks also investigated decision rules and found that juries required to reach unanimity deliberated longer than majority-rule juries and were more likely to hang (Saks & Marti, 1997). Perhaps fewer hung juries and quicker decisions are good news, but there was a problem in majority-rule juries: Deliberations tended to come to a halt as soon as the requisite majority was reached (e.g., 10 out of 12). Further, Saks found that the requirement of unanimity empowers the minority: ". . . only in unanimous juries could the minority effectively alter the course set by the majority" (1977, p. 105).

In 1983, Reid Hastie, Steven Penrod, and Nancy Pennington examined the effects of three decision rules on 69 mock juries. After watching a realistic 2½ hour videotape of a murder trial, the juries were told to deliberate until they reached a unanimous verdict, or until they reached a verdict by either a 10 to 2 or an 8 to 4 majority. The majority-rule juries were dramatically different in process than the unanimous verdicts. They took votes earlier and spent significantly more time voting. This meant that they spent less time discussing the evidence. These juries were more likely to exert direct (normative) pressure on others to change their votes and, once the requisite number of votes was reached (either 10 or 8), further discussion shut down. Because of this vote-oriented, quicker, more socially intimidating atmosphere, members of majority-rule juries were left feeling less informed, less certain about their verdicts, and with fewer positive feelings about their fellow jurors. Also, jurors holding the minority opinion participated more when unanimity was required, and they were perceived as more influential by other jurors. The evidence seems to indicate that nonunanimous juries do save time, but at the cost of less thorough evaluation of the evidence. Since thorough evaluation of evidence is the primary function of the jury, this is a critical problem. Research findings validate the conclusions of the Supreme Court's minority opinion in *Johnson*:

> The collective effort to piece together the puzzle . . . is cut short as soon as the requisite majority is reached . . . polite and academic conversation is no substitute for the earnest and robust argument necessary to reach unanimity.

Many jurists and politicians have argued for nonunanimous juries because of a particular perceived benefit: a reduction in the number of "hung" juries—those who cannot reach a unanimous verdict. It is true that unanimous juries "hang" about twice as often as majority-rule juries. However, as some scholars have noted, hung juries have ". . . traditionally been taken as a sign that the jury system is operating as it should, without majorities prevailing by brute force" (Ellsworth & Mauro, 1998, p. 693). Kalven and Zeisel in 1966 found that only 3.1% of majority-rule juries hung and only 5.6% of unanimous juries hung. Although the frequency of hung juries is somewhat higher in a few urban centers with more diverse populations (e.g., New York, Los Angeles, Chicago), the rate is only about 6% nationally (Abramson, 1995). It is estimated that small and large juries reach different verdicts in only about 14% of all cases (Lempert, 1975). These tend to be cases where the evidence is inconclusive and where differing perspectives are reasonable and therefore difficult to resolve. The strength of the evidence, the effectiveness of the arguments, the clarity of the law, and community sentiment also influence the rate of hung juries.

A final note about hung juries: sometimes a jury will pass a note to the judge saying that after hours or days of arduous deliberations they still can't reach a verdict—they are hopelessly deadlocked. If the judge accepts the jury's judgment, a mistrial must be declared. But in most jurisdictions, the judge has the option of using "the dynamite charge." This charge to the jury (also called the "Allen charge" or "shotgun instruction") is an effort to break the deadlock. The judge asks the jury "to reexamine your views and to seriously consider each other's arguments with a disposition to be convinced." As we might expect, such an instruction appears to shift the balance toward normative influence and against the minority who is holding out against a strong majority. Research suggests that this instruction causes jurors to feel coerced and may even mislead jurors into thinking that a hung jury is not a viable option (Kassin, Smith, & Tulloch, 1990).

Jury Nullification.   Juries deliberate in private and are not required to justify or explain the reasoning behind their verdicts. They have the power to reject or "nullify" the law. That is, juries may base their verdicts on reasoning that ignores, disregards, or goes beyond the law. In part, this is permitted because juries are expected to represent the moral conscience of the community. That moral conscience may lead them to a different conclusion than the law prescribes. Even if a defendant is technically guilty in the eyes of the law, he or she may be morally right. Prior to the American revolution, jury nullification provided a means of resisting oppressive laws put in place by the British Crown. For example, during the colonial era, a printer named John Peter Zenger was put on trial for seditious libel because he printed articles mocking the royal governor. The trial judge forbade the defense from presenting witnesses to testify that Zenger's claims were true. In an impassioned closing argument, Zenger's defense attorney implored the jury to look beyond the law to find justice:

> It is not the cause of a poor printer, nor of New York alone, which you are now trying. No! It may in its consequence affect every freeman that lives under a British government on the main of America. It is the best cause. It is the cause of liberty (King, 2000, p. 104).

The jury was persuaded. They ignored the law and acquitted Zenger. But jury nullification is a two-edged sword. It has sometimes enabled jurors to find a just verdict in defiance of the law. At other times, it has enabled jurors to ignore just laws in favor of prejudice. Prior to the Civil War, many juries refused to enforce the 1850 Fugitive Slave Law and acquitted defendants who helped slaves escape to freedom in the North. However, following the Civil War, some Southern juries ignored the law and refused to convict whites accused of beating blacks. More modern examples of nullification include Mormon juries in Utah who have refused to convict bigamists or polygamists, and juries who acquitted draft resisters and antiwar activists during the Vietnam War.

During the 1990s, a Michigan physician named Jack Kevorkian was put on trial four times for breaking the law prohibiting doctors from helping their patients commit suicide. There was no question that Kevorkian was guilty of killing his patients. But, every one of the patients he killed was suffering from a terminal disease, all were in excruciating pain, and all had asked for Dr. Kevorkian's assistance in ending their lives. In the first three trials, juries refused to convict Kevorkian, apparently believing that the law was unjust and that Kevorkian was acting to end the terrible suffering of his patients. In a final effort to push his challenge of the laws against euthanasia, Dr. Kevorkian made a videotape showing himself giving a terminally ill man a lethal injection. In his fourth trial, he was found guilty of second-degree murder and sentenced to prison.

Despite periodic attempts to restrict or eliminate the power of juries to nullify, nullification remains intact. However, jurors are almost never told by a judge that they can disregard the law and follow their conscience when deciding on a verdict. This "don't tell" policy may be a reasonable compromise. In one of the few experimental investigations of the effect of informing jurors of their nullification powers, Irwin Horowitz compared juries exposed to several types of cases (Horowitz, 1988). In some conditions either the judge or the defense attorney informed the jury that it could ignore the law if following the law would lead to an injustice. When juries were explicitly informed about their nullification powers, they were more lenient toward defendants in a case where a nurse helped a cancer patient commit suicide and in a case where a mentally impaired man illegally purchased a handgun. However, these same instructions *increased* the likelihood of conviction in a drunk driving case where a pedestrian had been killed. The nullification instructions appeared to give jurors permission to treat sympathetic defendants more leniently and unsympathetic defendants more harshly.

One final point about nullification—sometimes what appears to be disregard for the law may actually be the result of an inability to understand the law. As noted earlier, jurors do an admirable job of assimilating evidence and remembering it during deliberation. However, they don't understand judge's instructions very well and deliberation with other jurors doesn't seem to improve their comprehension. The occasional jury decision that seems irrational can often be traced to the inadequacies of lawyers or witnesses and the confusing instructions provided by the court.

JURY REFORM

As Phoebe Ellsworth and Robert Mauro point out, criticism of juries is not new.

> For centuries the same concerns have been expressed: Jurors are ignorant and lazy, governed by passion rather than reason, incapable of understanding the applicable law, their decisions turning on all manner of legally impermissible considerations. The critics claim dangerous trends in the pattern of legal outcomes; the "evidence" however, is typically a short list of highly visible cases (1998, p. 698).

Despite a few well-publicized cases where juries have awarded plaintiffs huge amounts of money, there is no evidence that these sensationalized cases indicate a larger trend. Researchers who have analyzed patterns of jury verdicts over time have concluded that, in criminal cases, there has been no increase in verdicts favoring defendants. In civil cases, there is no evidence of a trend favoring plaintiffs or dramatic increases in median compensatory damage awards (MacCoun, 1993).

One case that received national media attention and, for many Americans, came to symbolize the irrationality of juries involved a 79-year-old woman named Stella Liebeck. Ms. Liebeck bought a cup of coffee at the drive-through window at a McDonald's restaurant in Albuquerque. As she sat in her car, she held the cup of coffee between her thighs and took off the lid to add cream and sugar. The coffee spilled and Ms. Liebeck was burned. She sued McDonald's, alleging that the coffee was too hot. A jury agreed and awarded her $2.7 million in damages. Those are the bare facts of the case. However, there were other facts that the jury took into account. First, Liebeck had to stay in the hospital for a week receiving treatment for third-degree burns. Several skin grafts were needed. McDonald's coffee was served at a temperature 20 degrees hotter than coffee from other fast food restaurants. There had been more than 700 previous complaints about the dangerously hot temperature of the coffee and McDonald's had settled many of the complaints by paying out about $500,000. Despite hundreds of complaints and the half-million dollar payout, McDonald's had not lowered the temperature of its coffee. Company officials admitted at trial that they knew their coffee was served too hot to drink and that it could cause serious burns. The jury settled on damages of $2.7 million because that was roughly equal to McDonald's coffee sales for a two-day period. The jury award did not stand for long. The trial judge reduced the award to $480,000 and Ms. Liebeck settled for an even lower amount. As for McDonald's, the corporation responded to the settlement and the publicity by finally lowering the temperature of its coffee. Other fast food chains took the step of lowering the temperature of their hot chocolate—a favorite drink among young children.

Although there have been a handful of huge, well-publicized awards, the median amount of compensatory damages against corporate defendants is $24,500 (Hans, 2000). Punitive damages are still rare and, when they are awarded, the amount of these payments is usually reduced on appeal (MacCoun, 1993; Hans, 2000). An analysis of verdicts in medical malpractice cases where patients suffered harm at the hands of physicians found that most patients end up not filing claims at all. And, even when claims are filed, most claims don't result in a payment to plaintiffs. Payments tend to be made only when injuries are severe, and usually they do not cover the losses experienced by the plaintiff (Daniels & Martin, 1997). Finally, based on post-verdict interviews with jurors in civil cases, Valerie Hans concluded that jurors are generally very suspicious of individuals who sue corporations for damages (Hans, 1996). Preexisting biases may work against plaintiffs.

Calls for jury reform come from two very different groups. Moderate reformers seem to believe we have a good system that could be made better. This group tends to focus on ways of helping jurors do their job well. Suggestions include allowing jurors to take notes during trials (some jurisdictions don't allow note taking), paying jurors more money for their time, rewriting jury instructions to improve comprehension, making jurors more comfortable while they wait for voir dire (e.g., by providing Internet access in the jury assembly room), and allowing jurors to ask questions of witnesses by handing written questions to the judge (who then decides if the questions are admissible). In contrast, radical reformers seem to believe that jurors are incapable of doing the job well and that the jury system should be overhauled or even abandoned. Those who believe the system is badly broken have called for the elimination of peremptory challenges, strict limits on the size of monetary awards, a further move away from unanimous decisions to majority rule decisions, eliminating the use of juries in complex or technical cases, and simply replacing juries with judges or panels of judges.

Allowing Jury Discussion During Trial: The Arizona Project.
One of the more controversial changes proposed by advocates of jury reform is to allow juries to discuss evidence among themselves while the trial is in progress. Advocates of this change have argued that being able to talk about evidence during breaks should help jurors correct mis-understandings prior to formal deliberations, improve later recall of information, and make deliberations more efficient. Opponents of this reform have argued that early discussion of evidence would close off full debate and lead jurors to reach premature verdicts. In the late 1990s, the state of Arizona tried out this controversial reform and allowed researchers to evaluate it. Specifically, Arizona permitted jurors to discuss the trial evidence and testimony among themselves, but only ". . . in the jury room during trial recesses as long as all jurors are present; the jurors are admonished to reserve judgment about the outcome of the case until they begin deliberations" (Diamond et al., 2002, p. iii).

In 2002, a report on this groundbreaking research was completed. The report—authored by Shari Seidman Diamond, Neil Vidmar, Mary Rose, Leslie Ellis, and Beth Murphy—described a multiyear experiment involving 50 actual civil juries in the state of Arizona. Discussions during trial as well as verdict deliberations were videotaped and analyzed. The researchers also analyzed trial materials (transcripts, exhibits, instructions, verdict sheets) and questionnaires filled out by lawyers, jurors, and judges. The 50 juries were randomly assigned to two groups: One group was permitted to discuss evidence during trial recesses in accordance with the rule quoted above, and the second group was required to forego discussion of evidence until final jury deliberations.

The results of the study provide some support for the value of the innovation. For example, jurors used recesses to gather information from one another, to help each other remember details of testimony, to seek clarification, to talk about the meaning of the facts presented, and to talk about what evidence they would like to hear to help them with their decision. Here is an example of a predeliberation discussion about medical testimony:

Juror 2:   When did the independent medical exam occur?
Juror 7:   July 1998.
Juror 2:   Right.
[All jurors talking at once]
Juror 3:   And [plaintiff] had all of those prior injuries he didn't disclose.

Juror 2:	I thought that was weird. It wasn't like they had to go to different doctors. It was all in one file.
Juror 5:	It's not unusual for doctors to disagree.
Juror 7:	His [treating doctor's] ability to treat patients seems to be just prescribe more drugs.
Juror 2:	It is just my opinion but [the plaintiff's] doctor wasn't very good, and at least this witness today knew . . .
Juror 6:	I would like to see [the exhibit about his medication] again. I just want to see what happened after the accident (p. 53).

Unfortunately, the effects of the rule were not entirely positive. Sometimes jurors in both groups violated the rules given by the court. In the discuss group, jurors often discussed the case even though not all jurors were present. And, in the no-discuss group, some juries (less than half) made multiple comments about the case before deliberations. However, these comments were "almost always brief and perfunctory" (p. 103). While none of the juries in the discuss group reached a verdict decision prior to deliberation, several jurors did indicate how they were leaning on verdict before the trial had ended. Overall, such statements did not tend to disproportionately favor either the plaintiff or the defendant. And, fortunately, these statements did not predict the positions jurors actually took during deliberations—that is, predeliberation statements about verdict did not seem to change the outcome of the trial.

Predeliberation discussions were longer and more numerous when the trial was long and complex than when it was briefer and simpler. The major benefit in the discuss group was improved recall and understanding of trial evidence. This benefit was apparently achieved without tilting juries toward one side or the other—plaintiffs were equally likely to win in discuss or no-discuss groups and damage awards did not differ significantly. Both groups of jurors deliberated about the same amount of time and both groups took about the same amount of time before taking the first vote. However, discuss jurors rated their juries as more thorough and open-minded than no-discuss juries.

Accurate recall of testimony for use during deliberation is essential if juries are to reach verdicts based on the evidence. Allowing jurors to discuss evidence during trial appears to boost such recall, so it may be worth spreading this innovation to other courtrooms. But the negative effects of the innovation—jurors who discuss evidence without all other jurors present, and jurors who prematurely express verdict preferences—need to be weighed against the benefit of improved recall of evidence. The researchers speculate that the negative effects might be reduced or even eliminated by some small changes. Specifically, they suggest that every juror be given a written copy of the rules of discussion, that a written copy be prominently posted in the jury room, and that the judge give a brief verbal reminder of the admonition (no discussion without all jurors present, and no opinions about verdict) before every recess. Finally, the researchers suggest that if judges are given the power to assign a temporary predeliberation presiding juror, that juror might be able to take responsibility for making sure discussion rules are followed.

The Arizona researchers were given unprecedented access to jurors. Their findings provide valuable insights into the functioning of real juries. However, it is unclear whether other researchers will be given such access in the future. That is unfortunate. Controlled access to real juries would give us a deeper understanding of how juries behave in other types of trials (e.g., criminal trials). Every year, juries make tens of thousands of important decisions. If we hope to improve the jury system, any change ought to be based on accurate data about how juries actually make decisions. The best way to collect such data is to try out small changes using controlled experiments and to carefully evaluate the effects of those changes.

JUDGES COMPARED TO JURIES

If juries were eliminated or used much less often, what would we put in their place? We cannot feed the facts of a case into a computer and have the computer spit out a well-considered, impartial verdict. Because the main alternative to trial by jury is trial by judge, it is important to look at how judges make decisions, as well as how often and why their decisions differ from those of juries.

One lofty view of judges emphasizes their impartiality and their immunity to the biases and errors of thinking that supposedly infect the thinking of jurors. One judge put it this way:

> Impartiality is a capacity of mind—a learned ability to recognize and compartmentalize the relevant from the irrelevant and to detach one's emotions from one's rational facilities. Only because we trust judges to be able

to satisfy these obligations do we permit them to exercise power and oversight (Peckam, 1985, p. 262).

This flattering assessment of the cognitive abilities of judges does not seem to be supported by the available data. To test the presumed impartiality and emotional detachment of judges, Stephan Landsman and Richard Rakos (1994) asked 88 judges and 104 jurors to evaluate a product liability case. The plaintiff alleged that because a gasoline container had no "flame arrester," the container exploded, burning him severely over much of his body. The decisions of judges and jurors were compared to see if judges were less affected by biasing information—for example, information that the makers of the gasoline containers had previously issued a warning about a risk of "flame flashbacks" from its gasoline containers. Interestingly, judges were no better at ignoring this inadmissible evidence than were jurors. Yet, even though both groups were equally influenced by biasing information, both judges and jurors *believed* that judges would be better able to disregard inadmissible evidence. In another study, different researchers found that a group of 167 federal judges were vulnerable to most of the cognitive biases that affect lay decision makers when judging legal materials (Guthrie, Rachlinski, & Wistrich, 2001).

Judges, like jurors, are biased. Biases based on attitudes, life experiences, and basic values are an inescapable part of human decision making. There are safeguards in place to neutralize the biases of jurors but few comparable safeguards to deal with the biases of judges. The legal system assumes that many jurors are likely to be biased. That is why attorneys are given challenges for cause as well as peremptory challenges during voir dire. Although it is possible for a judge to be removed from a case (e.g., if he or she has a direct personal or financial interest in a case), it rarely happens. Another check against the biases of jurors is that every jury contains several people with somewhat different biases. Because juries must reach a group verdict, there is only a slight chance that a lone biased juror will sway the rest of the jury. No comparable safeguard is in place to protect against biased judges. An individual judge who makes a decision in isolation from others does not have his or her biases challenged by others. Finally, judges are systematically exposed to potentially biasing information that jurors never see. Pretrial motions made to the judge usually contain information that will not be presented at trial but that may influence a judge's verdict. In contrast, juries are systematically shielded from pretrial information (Landsman & Rakos, 1994).

Agreement between Juries and Judges. As part of their classic study of the American jury, Kalven and Zeisel gathered data from more than 500 judges about the verdicts they would have reached in cases that were actually decided by juries. Analyzing data from approximately 3,500 cases, Kalven and Zeisel found that judges and juries agreed on verdicts in 74% of criminal cases and in 78% of civil cases. When juries and judges disagreed, there was a tendency for juries to be somewhat more lenient—in 16% of those cases, juries acquitted when the judge would have convicted. Other data supports these conclusions. Nearly 30 years later, in an analysis of 77 criminal trials, Larry Heuer and Steven Penrod (1994) found a jury/judge agreement rate of 74%. Here again, there was a tendency for juries to be more lenient—this time in 20% of the cases. A third study conducted in England found a jury/judge agreement rate of 82%, with a tendency for juries to be more lenient in 6% of the cases studied (Baldwin & McConville, 1979).

The high agreement rates are comforting in that both juries and judges appear to be evaluating the evidence in similar ways and reaching similar conclusions. But what about the disagreement rate? Does it mean that judges reached the wrong decision about 25% of the time? Or does it mean that juries reached the wrong decision about 25% of the time? Or, does it simply mean that judges and juries sometimes weigh the evidence differently and reach their decisions in different ways? The Kalven and Zeisel study did collect some information on the nature of the cases where disagreement occurred. They asked judges to rate the evidence in each case as being either easy or difficult, and as clearly favoring one side or as being a close call. Rates of disagreement were *not* higher in cases that judges rated as "difficult," but disagreement rates *were* higher in cases judges rated as "close." These findings suggest that jury/judge disparities are likely due to reasonable differences of opinion in cases where the evidence does not clearly favor one side. Further, disagreements cannot be easily attributed to jurors' inability to understand complex evidence (as some radical reformers have suggested). Although judges clearly understand the law better than lay jurors, there is no evidence that judges understand specialized technical or expert testimony better than jurors (Lempert, 1993). And, if 6 or 12 heads are better than one, we might expect a jury to understand complex testimony better than a judge.

Perhaps another explanation for the disparity between judges and jurors is prior experience. In research comparing more than 200 juries over more than two years, juries containing one or more members with prior jury experience were more likely to convict than juries with only first-time jurors (Dillehay & Nietzel, 1999). Put differently, experienced jurors tend to be more conviction prone. Perhaps experience has a similar effect on judges. It could be that because judges see people accused of terrible crimes day after day, they become increasingly jaded and less likely to sympathize with defendants.

Juries tend to be more lenient than judges in less serious cases involving crimes such as possession of a small amount of marijuana, gambling, or shoplifting inexpensive items. In serious cases involving crimes such as rape or murder, juries are not more lenient (Diamond, 2001). Judges may give more weight to legal considerations, while juries may focus more on broader conceptions of justice. After all, juries are meant to represent the conscience of the community. It is appropriate for judges and juries to reach decisions differently and it would not be desirable if they were always in agreement. In civil cases, the rate of juror/judge agreement seems to be even higher than in criminal cases (Vidmar, 1998). Indeed, judges are more likely than juries to rule in favor of plaintiffs who have been injured by medical procedures. In experimental studies where judges and arbitrators evaluate the same civil cases as mock jurors, there is either no significant difference in the amount of damage awards, or judges and arbitrators give somewhat higher awards (Vidmar & Rice, 1993).

One leading scholar on juries and judges—Shari Seidman Diamond—has described several advantages of using juries instead of judges. First, she notes that the jury lends legitimacy to unpopular decisions and ". . . acts as a lightning rod . . . absorbing the criticism and the second-guessing that may follow an unpopular verdict" (2001, p.7). In contrast, when a judge—a professional representative of the legal system— reaches an unpopular decision, that decision indicts the fairness of the whole system. Second, juries can allow community standards to dictate their verdicts in ways that judges cannot. Judges are more tightly bound by the law. Diamond cites the case of a mentally retarded man who was acquitted by a jury on the charge of possessing a gun. The man wanted to be a police detective and had bought the gun because a magazine article said it was required in order to train for becoming a detective. If the judge had acquitted the defendant, a precedent would have been established that would weaken the gun possession law. Diamond notes that jurors can ". . . temper the harshness of the law without introducing a change in precedent" (p. 10).

IN CONCLUSION

For many Americans, serving on a jury is one of a few direct ways of participating in government. Citizens who serve as jurors receive an education about the inner workings of the justice system. In addition, juries serve as a counterbalance to the sometimes arbitrary decisions of judges. The jury system restrains the power of government by putting decisions directly in the hands of the people. Quite simply, juries are the most direct means of making the legal system reflect the views and values of the community.

Readings to Supplement This Chapter

Articles

Bornstein, B. H. (1999). The ecological validity of jury simulations: Is the verdict still out? *Law and Human Behavior, 23,* 75–92.

Ellsworth, P. C., & Reifman, A. (2000). Juror comprehension and public policy: Perceived problems and proposed solutions. *Psychology, Public Policy, and Law, 6,* 788–821.

Lieberman, J. D., & Arndt, J. (2000). Understanding the limits of limiting instructions: Social psychological explanations for the failures of instructions to disregard pretrial publicity and other inadmissible evidence. *Psychology, Public Policy, and Law, 6,* 677–711.

Mott, N. L., Hans, V. P., & Simpson, L. (2000). What's half a lung worth? Civil jurors' accounts of their award decision making. *Law and Human Behavior, 24,* 401–420.

Sommers, S. R., & Ellsworth, P. C. (2001). White juror bias: An investigation of prejudice against black defendants in the American courtroom. *Psychology, Public Policy, and Law, 7,* 201–229.

Strier, F., & Shestowshy, D. (1999). Profiling the profilers: A study of the trial consulting profession, its impact on trial justice and what, if anything, to do about it. *Wisconsin Law Review, 51,* 441–499.

Books

Hans, V. P. (2000). *Business on Trial.* New Haven: Yale University Press.

Kressel, N. J., & Kressel, D. F. (2002). *Stack and sway: The new science of jury consulting.* Colorado: Westview Press.

6

Memory as Evidence: Eyewitness Testimony and Child Sexual Abuse

Chapter Outline

● ●

The Impact of Eyewitness Testimony
The Legal System's View of Eyewitness Testimony
    Exposing Eyewitness Bias at Trial
The Construction and Reconstruction of Eyewitness Memories
    Cross—Racial Identifications
    Weapons Focus
    Unconscious Transference
    Leading or Suggestive Comments
    Preexisting Expectations
    Witness Confidence
    When the Eyewitness is a Child
Using Research Findings to Improve Eyewitness Accuracy
    Rule 1: Blind Lineup Administrators
    Rule 2: Instructions to Eyewitnesses
    Rule 3: Unbiased Lineups
    Rule 4: Confidence Ratings
    Costs and Consequences of Following the Four Rules
Three More Eyewitness Safeguards
    Sequential Lineups
    Videotaping
    Expert Testimony
Techniques for Refreshing the Memories of Witnesses
    Hypnosis
    The Cognitive Interview

MEMORIES OF CHILD SEXUAL ABUSE

The Memories of Young Children
    The Day Care Center Cases
    Testimony by Children at Trial
Recovered Memories of Sexual Abuse
    The Ingram Case
    Were the Memories Created or Recovered?
    Research on Implanting False Memories
In Conclusion

Jennifer Thompson was a 22-year-old college student living in North Carolina. At about 3:00 AM one night, a man broke into her apartment, held a knife to her throat, and raped her. During her long ordeal, the rapist allowed her to get up. When she went to the bathroom she turned on the light and used the opportunity to get a good look at her attacker. She also managed to briefly turn on a lamp in the bedroom and get another good look at him before he turned the lamp off. When the rapist turned on the stereo, his face was illuminated by the faint light from the stereo equipment. Despite her terror, Jennifer forced herself to study his face. She told the rapist that she was thirsty and he let her to go to the kitchen to get a drink. The kitchen door—where the rapist had broken into her apartment—was still open. She ran from her apartment to a neighbor's house. The rapist did not follow. But later that night, less than a mile from Jennifer's apartment, he broke into another apartment and raped another woman.

At the police station, Jennifer looked through sketches of different types of noses, different types of eyes, different mouths. With Jennifer's direction, a police sketch artist created a composite drawing of the rapist. He was an African American man, in his 20s or 30s, with short hair and a thin mustache. The composite drawing was widely circulated and the police received several calls from people claiming to recognize the suspect. Based on those calls, police put together a photo lineup of six pictures. Jennifer looked at the photo spread for a few minutes and identified Ronald Cotton, a man who worked at a local seafood restaurant. The detective seemed relieved when she made her identification. "We thought this might be the one," he told her.

When Ronald Cotton heard the police were looking for him, he knew there had been a mistake, so he went to the police station to "straighten the whole thing out." He was arrested for both rapes and placed in a lineup with six other men. Jennifer had little difficulty identifying him. But the victim of the second rape identified a different man, one who the police knew to be innocent. Ronald Cotton was put on trial for the rape of Jennifer Thompson.

No solid physical evidence was presented at trial—no fingerprints, no hairs from the rapist, nothing conclusive from the semen analysis. At the crime scene, police found a small piece of foam that might have come from an athletic shoe owned by Ronald Cotton. There was evidence that Cotton owned a flashlight similar to the one used by the rapist. And there was a solid eyewitness identification. As the prosecutor said after the trial, Jennifer Thompson was a "terrific witness." She had made an effort to memorize the face of her rapist and she had identified him twice—once in the photo spread, and later in the lineup. During the trial, she pointed out Ronald Cotton as her assailant and told the jurors she was certain that he was the man who raped her. The jurors were convinced and Cotton was sentenced to life in prison.

Two years into his prison sentence, Cotton was told by another inmate that a third inmate—a man named Bobby Poole—had said that he knew Cotton was innocent. Bobby Poole said he knew this because he was the one who had raped the two women more than two years earlier. Cotton was eventually granted a second trial. At the second trial, Poole testified but denied any involvement in the two rapes. There was another witness who had not testified at the first trial: the second rape victim. Although she identified the wrong man in a lineup two years earlier, she testified that she was now certain that Ronald Cotton was the man who raped her. At the second trial, Cotton was convicted of both rapes and sent back to prison.

For eight more years, Cotton spent most of his time in prison writing letters to anyone who might be able to help him overturn his convictions. He probably would have died in prison if he had not been able to convince a law professor and attorney named Richard Rosen to look more closely at his case. Rosen did some investigation and found that the biological evidence in Cotton's case (a semen sample) was still well preserved in a police storage facility. In the 10 years that had passed since the first trial, DNA testing had developed to the point that it could positively identify any offender who left behind biological evidence. The semen sample was subjected to DNA analysis and Cotton was excluded. The sample was then compared to a blood sample from Bobby Poole. It was a match. Ronald Cotton was released from prison and Bobby Poole was charged with both rapes. Although Jennifer Thompson now knows that she identified the wrong man, the image in her mind hasn't changed. "It's still Ronald Cotton's face I see. . . . Even today, when I have nightmares about the rape, I still don't see Bobby Poole" (Thompson, 1999).

There are several tragedies associated with this case. There is the rape and its aftermath—Thompson still has nightmares and still feels afraid when she opens her door at night. There is the tragedy of Ronald Cotton, who spent 11 agonizing years in prison for a crime he didn't commit. And there is the tragedy of several more rapes that could have been prevented if Bobby Poole had been captured and convicted after the rape of Jennifer Thompson. This case illustrates some of the problems associated with eyewitness identification and some of the tragic consequences of mistaken identification.

THE IMPACT OF EYEWITNESS TESTIMONY

As in the case of Ronald Cotton, there are many cases in which the testimony of an eyewitness makes the difference between conviction and acquittal. Such testimony is crucial to the criminal justice system because it is often the most compelling evidence presented in court. One study examined 347 cases where the only evidence was eyewitness testimony. In 74% of these cases, the defendant was convicted. In 49% of the cases where the defendant was convicted, there was only one eyewitness (Loftus, 1984).

The persuasiveness of eyewitness testimony is only a problem if the witness is mistaken. Unfortunately, research suggests that eyewitnesses are far more fallible than is commonly supposed. It is estimated that each year more than 77,000 people become criminal defendants because an eyewitness has identified them. Although only a fraction of these cases are successfully prosecuted, the best available data indicates that each year approximately 4,500 wrongful convictions are based on mistaken eyewitness identification (Penrod & Cutler, 1999). Even more disturbing, research on people who have been convicted of crimes but are later proven innocent has revealed that mistaken eyewitness identification leads to more wrongful convictions than all other causes put together (Wells et al., 1998). In fact, mistaken identifications played a role in 65% of the cases where wrongly convicted persons were released from prison because DNA testing later proved their innocence (Wells, 2001).

But why do eyewitnesses identify the wrong person? During the past two decades, social scientists have assessed eyewitness accuracy using a variety of techniques. Researchers have staged crimes and people who have witnessed these staged crimes have been asked to identify the mock criminals. Convenience store clerks and bank tellers have been questioned about customers who engaged them in business transactions for a few minutes. Descriptions of criminals given by eyewitnesses have been compared to the actual appearance of criminals who have been identified by DNA evidence. Averaging across studies, the overall rate of correct identification is 41.8% and the rate of false identification is 35.8%. However, the figure for correct identification is probably a bit inflated because it is based on relatively brief delays between viewing and recall (usually a few hours), good opportunities to observe, and a lack of danger (Penrod & Cutler, 1999).

THE LEGAL SYSTEM'S VIEW OF EYEWITNESS TESTIMONY

In two key cases—*Neil v. Biggers* (1972) and *Manson v. Braithwaite* (1977)—the courts have emphasized five factors that should be taken into account when evaluating the accuracy of an eyewitness's identification: (1) the witness's opportunity to observe the perpetrator, (2) the witness's level of attention, (3) the accuracy of the witness's previous description of the offender, (4) the degree of certainty displayed by the witness, and (5) the amount of time between witnessing the crime and making the identification. Although these criteria seem logical, most are difficult to apply to actual crimes, and one (degree of certainty) is contrary to research findings.

With few exceptions (e.g., a hostage situation that lasts for hours), it is difficult to evaluate a witness's opportunity to observe and it is difficult to evaluate his or her level of attention. Usually, we must rely on witnesses to tell us what kind of opportunity they had to observe the suspect, and we must rely on witnesses to tell us whether they paid close attention to the crime. And, of course, there is no precise measure of attention. Was the witness "mildly attentive," "moderately attentive," or "intensely attentive"?

There is also the issue of time—how long was the witness able to look at the culprit? As you might expect, the evidence suggests that accuracy improves if witnesses look at the face of the criminal longer. But in most cases we can't know how long the witness was able to study the face of the perpetrator. People consistently overestimate the duration of a brief event, especially if the event is stressful. Consequently, time moves slowly for a frightened eyewitness. Estimates of time during a stressful event are generally three to four times the actual time length of the event (Penrod & Cutler, 1999). This means that a witness who estimates seeing a criminal for two minutes may actually have seen the criminal for only 30 seconds. Amount of elapsed time between witnessing a crime and identifying the criminal in a lineup may be a useful indicator of accuracy at the extremes—an identification minutes after the crime should be more reliable than one that occurs a month later—but it is difficult to know the effects of the passage of time in the intermediate ranges of days or weeks. In addition, as discussed later in this chapter, eyewitness certainty is an unreliable indicator of accuracy. Certainty is only weakly related to accuracy, and accuracy of description is a poor predictor of accurate identification. Especially troubling is the finding that biased questioning and lineup procedures can inflate a witness's certainty and can lead witnesses to overestimate how clear a view they had of the perpetrator (Wells et al., 1998).

Exposing Eyewitness Bias at Trial.   At every stage in the process that begins with seeing a crime and ends with testimony in court, there are possibilities for error. First, there is the ability of the witness to observe. Clearly, if the crime occurs at night, or if lighting is poor, or if the witness sees the crime from a distance, the ability to identify the criminal is impaired. Perhaps the witness's eyesight was poor; maybe the perpetrator was looking away from the witness or was only briefly in view. Luckily, any good defense attorney will expose such obvious weaknesses during cross-examination. It may even be possible to check some aspects of the witness's description—the level of ambient light at a specific time of night could be measured by an investigator with the right equipment; distances between where the witness stood and where the crime occurred can be assessed with a tape measure. But we almost always have to rely on the word of the witness about some aspects of the crime.

The legal system has a few time-honored techniques for revealing truth. These techniques include voir dire (the questioning of potential jurors during jury selection), cross-examination, and jury deliberation. But as Douglas Narby and Brian Cutler (1994) have pointed out, these techniques are not terribly effective tools for exposing mistaken identifications. Voir dire is intended to expose potentially biased jurors so that attorneys can get rid of them. But there is no set of questions that will reveal whether potential jurors will or will not view eyewitness testimony with appropriate skepticism. Even cross-examination, an extremely useful tool for bringing out weakness and deceptions in testimony, is quite limited as a means of exposing mistaken eyewitness identifications. Attorneys, judges, and jurors tend not to ask the right questions, and information about the crime scene and the lineup procedures almost always come from the eyewitness and the police (both of whom are testifying in support of the prosecution). Most important, it is impossible to expose a mistaken eyewitness as a liar because they are not lying. They believe what they are saying, but they are wrong. A final safeguard, jury deliberation, places fact-finding in the hands of a group of citizens. Unfortunately, research shows that prospective jurors place undue faith in the reliability of eyewitnesses, place too much weight on eyewitness confidence, and are not very good at distinguishing between accurate and inaccurate eyewitnesses.

THE CONSTRUCTION AND RECONSTRUCTION OF EYEWITNESS MEMORIES

When eyewitnesses describe a criminal or pick a suspect out of a lineup, they are relying on memory. So, to understand the process of eyewitness identification, it is essential to understand the basics of how memory works. Psychologists who study memory have found it useful to distinguish between three component processes—encoding, storage, and retrieval. Encoding involves gathering information and putting it in a form that can be held in memory, storage refers to holding the encoded information in the brain over time, and retrieval refers to accessing and pulling out the stored information at a later time. It is tempting to think of these memory processes as similar to videotaping. Encoding might seem like recording an event on videotape. Storage is like putting the tape aside for later use, and retrieval is like popping the tape into a VCR and pressing the play button. Unfortunately, this appealing metaphor vastly understates the subtlety and complexity of human memory.

Errors in memory can occur at each stage of the process. Information might not be well encoded. Information streams by us each day and we attend to and encode only a small fraction of that information. Even when we do make an effort to pay attention, our attention sometimes lapses and crucial information doesn't get stored. Encoding is imperfect. What we do store in memory is a selective, inexact replica of what we actually heard or saw. Second, there are imperfections in the process of storage. Our memory trace—the biochemical representation of our experience in the brain—appears to deteriorate with time. Not only do we tend to forget as time passes, but our memories become more vulnerable to revision and corruption (Flin, Boone, Knox, & Bull, 1992). Finally, even if the memory trace is perfectly preserved in the brain, distortion can occur during the process of retrieval. We may not have the necessary cues to locate and reinstate the stored memory (Hunt & Ellis, 2002).

When we encode an event, we select some aspects and ignore others. The images and sounds we store may decay over time, and the process of retrieval includes some reconstruction. Memory isn't perfect under the best of circumstances. And most crimes don't happen under the best of circumstances. Crimes often happen at night and the perpetrators are usually in a hurry. Criminals may try to alter their appearance—they wear hats, sunglasses, or even masks. They often wait until no witnesses are around. Witnesses to crimes and victims of crimes are often terrified and more concerned with their own safety than with getting a good look at the criminal. Beyond these general concerns, researchers have discovered a variety of specific biases that influence the reliability of eyewitness reports.

Cross-Racial Identifications.   In 1999, Emilio Meza was arrested for robbing Sung Woo at gunpoint in the parking lot of a Los Angeles supermarket. Mr. Woo had identified Mr. Meza first in a photo spread and later in a real lineup. At trial, when questioned by the defense attorney, Mr. Woo said that, "Sometimes if a Hispanic wears a mustache, it's very tough for me to tell . . . there are too many look-alikes." The defense attorney probed deeper: "There's a saying, sometimes said in jest, 'they all look alike to me' is that what you're saying?" "Yes sir," Mr. Woo replied.

Mr. Meza, who turned out to be innocent, was eventually released (Hubler, 1999). Although Mr. Woo may have been unusually candid about his limitations as an eyewitness, research shows that he is not alone in having difficulty identifying people from racial groups other than his own. Although there is no evidence suggesting that members of any one racial group are any more accurate as eyewitnesses than members of any other racial group, there is an interaction between the race of the witness and the race of the person being identified: Cross-race accuracy is worse than within-race accuracy. That is, it is harder for people to recognize the faces of people outside their racial group than it is for people to recognize the faces of people within their racial group. This is sometimes referred to as the "own-race bias." Race may have played a role in the case of Ronald Cotton—he was black and Jennifer Thompson was white. In a recent metanalysis of 39 studies, Christian Meissner and John Brigham (2001) found that own-race identifications were significantly more likely to be correct than cross-race identifications, and that the number of misidentifications (false alarms) was significantly higher when they were cross-racial. The own-race bias is not large but it is consequential for the legal system. Many eyewitness identifications involve witnesses of one race trying to identify suspects from another race.

The reasons for the cross-race effect are not clear. Some researchers have suggested that when we observe someone of our own race, we tend to classify their facial features in greater detail. In contrast, we may encode the features of people from other races more superficially, paying less attention to facial characteristics such as shape of face, skin tone, size of features, and hair texture (Fiske & Taylor, 1991). A related explanation is that because most of us have substantial experience with people of our own race (e.g., members of our own family), we develop better rules for making useful distinctions among faces. Those rules may not be as useful when applied to members of other racial groups. Evidence suggests that our ability to recognize faces from other racial groups improves as we gain more contact with members of that group (Brigham & Malpass, 1985; Meissner & Brigham, 2001).

Weapons Focus.   Many people believe that heightened arousal enhances memory. Perhaps family members or friends have told you that they have vivid (and presumably accurate) memories of important events in their lives—a graduation, a wedding, the birth of a child, the death of a loved one. Arousing events may lead to vivid memories, but the details of these memories may be no more accurate than memories of mundane events. In January 1986, NASA launched the space shuttle Challenger. The shuttle exploded 73 seconds after liftoff, killing all seven passengers. This tragic and surprising event was witnessed by millions and was highly emotional for many Americans. Ulric Neisser and his coworkers interviewed people one day after the explosion and then again 32 months later. They asked people about several aspects of the event, including who they were with, how they heard the news, and what they were doing when they heard about the explosion. After 32 months, only 31% of the answers were correct. Twenty-seven percent were partially correct and 42% were completely incorrect (Neisser & Harsch, 1992).

Watching a crime in progress certainly triggers arousal. But the effect of this arousal on the encoding of information is uncertain, partly because the arousal frequently includes fear for one's own physical safety. One well-established finding related to arousal has been termed the "weapon focus" effect. If eyewitnesses see the perpetrator holding a gun or a knife, their ability to recognize the assailant is impaired (Steblay, 1992). In such situations, witnesses understandably tend to focus their attention on the weapon. Consequently, there is less attention paid to other important details of the crime, like the face of the criminal.

Unconscious Transference.   When witnesses identify the wrong person, it is usually a meaningful misidentification: Sometimes the person wrongly identified closely resembles the real perpetrator. This is what happened when Jennifer Thompson identified Ronald Cotton as the man who raped her. Ronald Cotton and Bobby Poole were both African American men in their 30s with mustaches and short hair. Other times, the person wrongly identified was someone seen at or near the scene of the crime. This situation is called unconscious transference. A face familiar from one context is transferred to another context—the scene of a crime. Robert Buckhout, one of the first psychologists to conduct systematic research on eyewitnesses, staged a series of thefts and assaults in his classroom. Of the students who witnessed the mock crime, 39% showed the unconscious transference effect. These witnesses incorrectly identified a person who had been in the classroom the day of the crime (Buckhout, 1974).

In an incident that illustrates this effect, a rape victim identified psychologist Donald Thompson as her rapist. The woman gave a vivid, detailed recollection of his face. The only problem was that, at the time of the rape, Thompson was in a television studio giving an interview about the fallibility of memory. The rape victim had seen part of that television interview and unknowingly transferred her memory of Thompson's face onto the rapist (Schacter, 1996).

Leading or Suggestive Comments.

In a series of classic experiments, Elizabeth Loftus and her colleagues demonstrated how eyewitness recall could be altered by seemingly trivial changes in the wording of questions. Several groups of participants in her experiments viewed films of a car crash. Half the participants were asked to estimate the speed of the car when it "turned right" and the other half were asked to estimate the speed of the car when it "ran the stop sign." Later, when the participants were asked whether they had seen a stop sign, 35% of the first group reported seeing one, while 53% of the second group reported seeing the sign. When a statement about a barn was included in the questioning process, 17% of the participants remembered seeing a barn even though none appeared in the film. When participants were asked, "Did you see *the* broken headlight?" they were more than twice as likely to recall seeing a broken headlight than participants who were asked, "Did you see *a* broken headlight?" Estimates of the speed of the cars also varied as a function of question wording. Some participants were asked, "About how fast were the two cars going when they *contacted* each other?" In other versions of the question the words *hit, bumped,* and *smashed* were substituted for *contacted.* Cars *contacting* each other yielded an estimate of 31 miles per hour while cars *smashing* into each other yielded an estimate of 40.8 miles per hour (Loftus & Palmer, 1974). Loftus used only subtle variations in wording, but these tiny variations produced substantial changes in memory.

Recall of a crime scene may also be altered depending on how the eyewitness is initially questioned. In one laboratory study, people looked at slides of a student dorm room that had been burglarized. Experimenters later used selective questioning when asking about details of the crime scene (Koutstaal, Schacter, Johnson, & Galluccio, 1999).

Although there were many textbooks in the picture of the room (apparently thieves aren't interested in textbooks), experimenters asked only about particular types of sweatshirts. When questioned at a later time about what they saw, people tended to have good recall of the sweatshirts but poor recall of other objects like textbooks. Retrieving memories of sweatshirts made it more difficult to recall aspects of the scene (or event) about which no questions were initially asked. Selectively retrieving only some aspects of a scene "inhibits" recall of other aspects. This phenomenon is referred to as "retrieval inhibition."

Preexisting Expectations.   What we expect to see influences what we see and how we remember what we see. One form of expectations is what social scientists call scripts. Scripts are widely held beliefs about sequences of actions that typically occur in particular situations. You may, for example, have a script for the first day of a college class. You sit at a desk or table, the professor takes roll, the professor hands out a course syllabus and reviews the course requirements, etc. We appear to have preexisting scripts for many common situations. Scripts enable us to process information efficiently. Because we know what to expect, we don't have to treat each situation as completely new or unique. But scripts can also lead to error. If information is lacking or insufficiently encoded, we often rely on scripts to fill in gaps in our memory.

Consider the implications for eyewitnesses. In an interesting study of this issue, Valerie Holst and Kathy Pezdek (1992) first questioned people to determine if there were widely shared scripts for three types of crimes: a convenience store robbery, a bank robbery, and a mugging. They were able to uncover widely shared scripts for all three crimes. The convenience store script contained the following sequence of actions—robber cases the store, makes a plan, enters the store, looks around once in the store, acts like a shopper, waits for an opportunity, goes to the cash register, pulls out a gun, demands money, exits the store, drives away in a getaway car. In a follow-up study, research participants heard a mock trial of a defendant accused of a convenience store robbery. Most elements of the typical script were included in the evidence presentations. However, key elements of the script (e.g., casing the store, pulling out a gun, and taking the money) were not part of the evidence presented. As predicted, these excluded elements found their way into the mock jurors' memories of the crime. The lesson of this study and many others is that memory does not begin as a blank videotape. Prior knowledge and beliefs intrude on and get mixed in with observed events.

Witness Confidence.   If you were serving on a jury and an eyewitness identified the defendant as the person who committed the crime, how would you know whether that witness was right? Being a reasonable person, you would probably take into consideration viewing conditions: whether the crime scene was well lit, how long the witnesses had to observe the criminal, how far away the criminal was, the witness's eyesight. And, if you're like most other jurors, you would also take into account how certain the witness is. When a witness who has sworn to "tell the truth, the whole truth, and nothing but the truth" points to a defendant in open court and says something like, "I'm sure that's him, I'll never forget that face," jurors and judges tend to be persuaded. And that's a problem. Research indicates that highly confident eyewitnesses tend to persuade jurors. But although eyewitness confidence is strongly correlated with persuasiveness, it is only weakly correlated with accuracy. A witness's confidence can be a moderately good indicator of accuracy under favorable circumstances (e.g., when viewing conditions are good, lineups are well constructed, and investigators do not ask leading questions), but it may be a meaningless or even misleading indicator of accuracy under less favorable circumstances (Sporer, Penrod, Read, & Cutler, 1995).

One of the reasons that confidence is not a good indicator of accuracy is that confidence is likely to increase over time. First, the witness usually gives a verbal description of the suspect to the police. Unless the suspect has bright red hair or a tattoo on his face, it is likely that this description matches thousands of people. Next, the witness may look through a thick book of photographs to see if she can find a photo of the defendant. A vague description has now become a specific face. The witness will have plenty of time to study this face and to memorize its features. Police officers may even say that they already suspected that the identified person committed the crime. For example, when Jennifer Thompson somewhat hesitantly identified Ronald Cotton as the man who raped her, the police officer administering the photo lineup said, "We thought this might be the one." Later, the witness may be asked to identify the suspect in a lineup. If the witness has already picked out someone in a photograph, he or she may now simply be picking the person who most resembles the person in that photograph.

Finally, the witness may identify the defendant in court. At each stage, the witness gets more specific. Details get filled in, sketchy memories become more complete. And, at each step, the witness becomes more personally invested in the correctness of the identification. The witness who began by giving a tentative, indefinite description of the criminal may appear on the witness stand as confident and emphatic, free of all doubt.

Gary Wells and Amy Bradfield (1998) conducted a revealing study of how eyewitness confidence can be manipulated. Hundreds of witnesses viewed a security video in which a man entered a Target store. The witnesses were told that just after entering the store, the man murdered a security guard. Later, they were asked to identify the gunman from a photo lineup. The 352 witnesses who identified the wrong person were randomly assigned one of three conditions: confirming feedback, contradictory feedback, and no feedback. At the time of their initial identifications, the three groups were equally confident about their identifications. The first group was then told, "Good, you identified the actual suspect in the case," the second group was told, "Oh, that is not the suspect, the suspect in the case is actually number ____ ," and the third group received no feedback. Those who heard confirming feedback later remembered being very certain at the time of the identification, while those receiving disconfirming feedback later recalled being uncertain at the time. Those who were told that they fingered the right man also remembered having a better view of the criminal, having made the identification more easily, and having paid more attention to the crime. Interestingly, witnesses were not aware that they had been swayed by the feedback. Like memory itself, confidence appears to be malleable.

The post-identification boost in confidence might be predicted by the theory of cognitive dissonance (Aronson, 1998). Dissonance theory predicts that once you commit yourself to a particular course of action, you will become motivated to justify that course of action. In the case of eyewitness identification, once you have identified someone as the criminal, that action will be dissonant (inconsistent) with the knowledge that you were uncertain about your identification. That inconsistency will be uncomfortable. It is very difficult to admit that you identified the wrong person, so the most expedient means of reducing dissonance will be to increase your level of certainty. Once you have committed yourself to a particular identification, you become increasingly certain that you picked the right person.

When the Eyewitness is a Child.   As compared to adults, children provide less information and somewhat less accurate information when responding to interview questions about what they witnessed (Wells, Wright, & Bradfield, 1999). Children are about as accurate as adults when presented with lineups or photo spreads, but only if the true perpetrator is present in the lineup. If the true perpetrator is absent from the lineup, children do more poorly. Some researchers have noted that this weakness may be attributable to the greater suggestibility of children (Beale, Schmitt, & Dekle, 1995). It is possible that simply being asked to look at a lineup implies to children that the adult conducting the lineup wants them to find the criminal among the photos or members of the lineup. Comments from police officers such as "We thought this might be the one" are especially likely to influence children. The special problems of relying on child witnesses are discussed more fully later in this chapter.

USING RESEARCH FINDINGS TO IMPROVE EYEWITNESS ACCURACY

At this point, you may be thinking that psychologists are great critics, but they aren't much good at suggesting practical solutions. If eyewitnesses are so fallible, what can be done to reduce the possibility that the wrong person will be convicted? There are several options.

Gary Wells has argued that social scientists interested in eyewitness identification ought to focus on "system variables"—those factors that are under the control of the justice system (Wells, 1978). For example, the justice system cannot control who witnesses a crime, or how carefully that person observes the crime, or whether the race of the victim is different from the race of the criminal. However, the legal system can control how a witness is questioned and how lineups are constructed. Modifications in the type and order of questions asked by police can and should be made if such changes can improve the accuracy of identification.

In 1998, the American Psychology-Law Society (AP-LS) appointed a committee to review more than a quarter century of research on eyewitness testimony, with the goal of developing guidelines for gathering evidence from eyewitnesses. The committee report—authored by Gary Wells, Mark Small, Steven Penrod, Roy Malpass, Solomon Fulero, and C. A. E. Brimacombe—proposed four simple rules that would dramatically reduce the number of mistaken identifications *without* reducing the number of correct identifications. These four modifications concern who administers the lineup or photo spread, the instructions given to witnesses viewing lineups or photo spreads, who appears in the lineup alongside the suspect, and obtaining information about eyewitness confidence (Wells et al., 1998).

Rule 1: Blind Lineup Administrators.

The first rule is that, "The person who conducts the lineup or photo spread should not be aware of which member of the lineup or photo spread is the suspect" (p. 627). This recommendation may seem obvious and uncontroversial. However, it is almost always violated. One of the detectives investigating the case nearly always directs the lineup. These detectives often have strong suspicions about who committed the crime, and these suspicions are often communicated (intentionally or unintentionally) to the eyewitness.

There is a large body of evidence demonstrating how the beliefs and expectations of one person can subtly shape the responses of another person. For example, early studies of teacher-student interactions found that if teachers were told to expect particular children to experience intellectual gains, the teacher conveyed these expectations to students through a variety of subtle cues—encouraging words, positive facial expressions, smiles, tone of voice, and eye contact (Rosenthal & Jacobson, 1968). Similarly, experimenters may unintentionally communicate their expectations to people participating in their experiments. That is why whenever the effectiveness of a new medical drug is being tested, the person administering the new drug or the placebo is "blind" to which is the real drug being tested. When we test new drugs, we follow careful procedures and take great care to ensure reliable findings. We do this because the potential consequences of an error—putting an ineffective or dangerous drug on the market—are very serious. We should exercise the same care in gathering eyewitness evidence, because the potential consequences of a mistake—accusing and convicting an innocent person—are also very serious.

Rule 2: Instructions to Eyewitnesses.   The second rule is to tell eyewitnesses that the true criminal "might not be in the lineup or photo spread." This information removes the presumption that the witness is obliged to choose someone from the available options. In addition, witnesses should be told that "the person administering the lineup does not know which person is the suspect in the case" (p. 629). This information discourages the witness from looking to others in the room for clues about who is the "right" person to identify. It forces witnesses to rely solely on their own memory.

Witnesses tend to assume that the person who committed the crime is included in the lineup. After all, police have gone to the trouble of assembling a lineup and bringing the witness to the police station. They must think they know who committed the crime. In a standard lineup, where the "might not be in the lineup" instructions are absent, witnesses tend to pick whichever person looks the most like the person they remember (Wells, 2001). The recommended instruction removes the assumption that the real criminal must be in the lineup and lifts the pressure to identify someone.

Rule 3: Unbiased Lineups.   In an old comedy sketch from the TV show *Saturday Night Live,* police are trying to find a black man who committed a crime. They suspect that Richard Pryor (an African American comedian) is their man. In the first lineup, Pryor is standing with six white men. But the witness isn't sure he's the culprit. So the police try again. In the next lineup, Pryor is standing with six elderly white women. Still, no identification. In the final lineup, Pryor is standing with six household appliances including a washing machine and a refrigerator. "That's him!" cries the eyewitness, pointing to Pryor. This sketch illustrates the reasoning behind the third recommendation: Lineups and photo spreads must be constructed so that the actual suspect does not "stand out" from the alternative suspects (sometimes referred to as "distractors"). That is, all of the people in the photos or in the lineup should resemble each other and all should match the witness's verbal description of the offender. Nothing about the procedure should draw extra attention to the actual suspect. This may seem obvious, but there have been many cases where lineups have been rigged to encourage an eyewitness to select the suspect that police believed to be guilty.

To test whether a lineup is biased, a "mock witness" procedure can be used. Mock witnesses are people who did not see the crime. Each mock witness is given the eyewitness's verbal description of the culprit. For a six-person lineup, if more than two out of 12 mock witnesses can pick out the suspect, the lineup is probably biased. If, for example, five out of 12 mock witnesses identify the suspect, it means that identification is not a result of true recognition, but of mere similarity to the verbal description (Malpass & Devine, 1981).

Rule 4: Confidence Ratings.   To illustrate the importance of Rule 4, here are two quotes, taken several weeks apart, from one eyewitness in a Missouri case:

> *Eyewitness when viewing a four-person lineup to identify her attacker:*
> "Oh, my God. . . I don't know. . . . It's one of those two . . . but I don't know. . . . Oh, man . . . the guy a little bit taller than number two. . . . It's one of those two, but I don't know. . . . I don't know . . . number two?"
>
> *At trial, when asked if she was positive that her attacker was number two in the lineup, if it wasn't a "maybe":*
> "There was no maybe about it . . . I was absolutely positive"
> (Wells & Bradfield, 1998).

Because confidence is likely to change between the time of the lineup and the time of the trial, the fourth recommendation is to obtain a clear statement about how confident the witness is that the person identified is the right person. This statement must be taken immediately after the culprit is identified and *before* any feedback is given to the witness. As noted earlier, confidence tends to increase in the period between the initial identification and testimony in court. Several factors may boost confidence once the person has been identified. The police may tell you that they believe you identified the right person or they may say that other witnesses described the same person. In the quote from the Missouri case above, the lineup administrator simply said "okay" when the eyewitness identified the suspect by saying "number two?"

Costs and Consequences of Following the Four Rules.   None of the proposed changes in the questioning and lineup procedures are particularly costly. Indeed, these procedures could be computerized (e.g., photos and questions could appear on a computer screen) and they may actually be cheaper than current practices. More important, any financial expense must be weighed against the considerable human costs of false identifications: Lives of the wrongly identified are disrupted or even shattered, eyewitnesses who later discover their mistakes must live with the knowledge that they were responsible for the prosecution of an innocent person, and real criminals remain free to commit more crimes.

The AP-LS committee points out that the failure of police departments to follow these four simple rules,

> . . . invites participation by credible eyewitness experts in the case for the defense, places the prosecutor in the difficult position of having to defend the absence of good procedures, routinely elicits motions to suppress the identification evidence, and risks the jury acquitting the defendant because there is another explanation (the suggestive procedures) as to why the suspect was identified by the eyewitness (p. 638).

THREE MORE EYEWITNESS SAFEGUARDS

The AP-LS committee limited the number of rules because they did not want to overburden police departments and create resistance among the very people who are responsible for obtaining eyewitness identifications. In addition, if the four rules summarized above are carefully followed, they eliminate the great majority of problems with current eyewitness identification practices. Still, it is worth noting that other researchers have made additional recommendations. Three other safeguards against eyewitness mistakes have been supported by research.

Sequential Lineups. Sequential lineups (as opposed to the more common simultaneous lineups) could be used. In sequential lineups, the witness sees one person at a time, decides whether that person is the perpetrator, and then sees the next person. There is ample evidence to suggest that this procedure reduces the number of mistaken identifications (Steblay, Dysart, Fulero, & Lindsay, 2001; Lindsay & Wells, 1985). The underlying logic for a sequential procedure is the same as the logic behind Rule 3 (making sure the suspect does not "stand out"). Eyewitnesses tend to rely on relative judgments. In the typical simultaneous lineup, several people are standing side by side. Under such conditions, witnesses tend to compare the people in the lineup with one another and then identify the person who looks the most like their mental image of the criminal. Sequential lineups reduce people's ability to compare one candidate with another. The identification becomes absolute rather than relative.

Videotaping.   A second additional safeguard would make use of video cameras. Although it will never be possible to videotape all crimes as they occur, it might be possible to require that all identification procedures be videotaped. Ideally, a videotape of the lineup identification would serve as a lasting, objective, audiovisual record of what transpired during the identification process. Attorneys, judges, and juries could see and hear for themselves what instructions were given to witnesses, whether members of the lineup resembled one another, what feedback was given to the witness immediately after identification, how confident the witness appeared during the lineup, what sort of comments were made by police or witnesses, and how long the entire process took. Indeed, the arguments in favor of videotaping have led at least one researcher to argue that videotaping of identification procedures should be given the status of a "fifth rule" alongside the four rules listed above (Kassin, 1998). This is an area where a technological fix may actually be possible. As video recording technology improves (and becomes cheaper), cameras will be able to take in information from a larger area and recordings will become clearer. Unfortunately, it will never be possible to fully prevent a determined investigator from subverting the intention of videotaping by making sure that any biasing behavior takes place outside the view of the video camera.

Expert Testimony.   A final safeguard is to have an expert on eyewitness identification testify in court. When testifying in this capacity, psychologists summarize research findings on the conditions under which eyewitnesses are likely to be correct or incorrect in their identifications. Although expert testimony on eyewitness identification is now frequently admitted at trial, some judges have been reluctant to admit such experts because they fear that expert testimony might persuade jurors to dismiss or undervalue all eyewitness identification, even if the identification is accurate.

Brian Cutler, Steven Penrod, and Hedy Dexter (1990) conducted a series of experiments to gauge the impact of being exposed to psychological testimony on the limitations of eyewitnesses. These studies used realistic trial simulations and varied several factors: the conditions under which the eyewitness viewed the crime, whether the identification procedures were impartial or biased, the confidence of the eyewitness, and whether expert testimony about eyewitness identification was present or absent. Experts were subjected to tough cross-examination, just as they would be in a real trial. The expert testimony had the desired effect: It sensitized jurors to the importance of viewing and lineup conditions that compromise or enhance accuracy, and it caused jurors to put less credence in witness confidence as an indicator of accuracy. The mock jurors who did not hear expert testimony overestimated the accuracy of eyewitnesses, did not take into account factors known to reduce accuracy, and placed substantial weight on eyewitness confidence as an indicator of accuracy. It appears that when expert testimony is provided to jurors, they are able to make appropriate use of the information provided by experts.

TECHNIQUES FOR REFRESHING THE MEMORIES OF WITNESSES

Sometimes witnesses to crimes can't remember critical details of what they saw. Because the memories of witnesses are so crucial, various methods have been tried to "refresh" those memories.

Hypnosis.   Hypnosis has a long history. Its use began with the French physician Franz Anton Mesmer (the word "mesmerized" is a variant of his name). Mesmer believed that he could induce hypnotic states through the use of his "animal magnetism." His ideas were controversial. A scientific committee chaired by Benjamin Franklin investigated his claims and concluded that hypnosis was induced through the power of suggestion (Gauld, 1992). An English physician named James Braid originated the term "hypnosis" after Hypnos, the Greek god of sleep. Hypnosis has been used during psychotherapy, as a technique for improving athletic performance, and as a substitute for light anesthesia during medical procedures. In the legal system, its main application has been as a tool for enhancing the memories of crime victims and witnesses to crimes. There is a long-standing debate about whether hypnosis is a unique trancelike state or whether it is simply an ability to suspend critical thinking and play the role of hypnotized subject (Bowers, 1993). What is clear, however, is that a successfully hypnotized subject enters a relaxed, focused state where he or she is highly receptive and responsive to suggestions made by a hypnotist.

Once hypnotized, eyewitnesses are usually instructed to go back in time and "re-witness" the event as if they were watching a documentary of the crime on television. They might be asked to "zoom in" on important details (e.g., a getaway car or license plate or face) or to "replay" critical parts of the event. People usually recall more information when they are hypnotized than when they are not hypnotized. This phenomenon is called hypnotic hypernesia (the opposite of amnesia). But more information is not necessarily better information. The problem is that memories refreshed through the use of hypnosis may contain a large dose of fantasy and imaginative elaboration. A fragmented eyewitness memory may become fuller and more vivid during hypnosis not because the true memory has been restored, but because gaps in memory have been filled in with plausible but fictional details. Indeed, research shows that hypnosis does not increase the recall of *accurate* information (Steblay & Bothwell, 1994). A final problem is that once an event is vividly imagined under hypnosis, a witness may become confident that the memory is true.

It is clear that skilled hypnotists have sometimes helped to uncover useful information. In 1976, in Chowchilla, California, three masked kidnappers hijacked a school bus carrying 26 children. The children and bus driver were taken to a quarry and buried in a chamber six feet underground. All of them miraculously escaped, but there were few useful leads until the bus driver was hypnotized. Under hypnosis, he was asked to recount the kidnapping from beginning to end as though he were narrating a documentary film. When asked to describe the vehicle used by the kidnappers he was able to remember all but one number of the license plate. That license plate number, which the driver did not recall until he was hypnotized, was the clue police needed to find and arrest the kidnappers. The Chowchilla case illustrates an important and productive use of hypnosis in the legal system: to uncover or develop information that can facilitate investigation of a crime. When there is little physical evidence to point investigators in the right direction, it is sometimes useful to hypnotize a witness to see if new information can be uncovered. For example, if a license plate is recalled under hypnosis, it may lead to the discovery of more reliable physical evidence (e.g., drops of blood inside a car). If the hypnotically recovered memory is mistaken, little is lost.

Some advocates of hypnosis note that it may sometimes serve as a "face-saving" device. Witnesses who are reluctant or afraid or embarrassed to tell what they know may feel freer to provide information if hypnotized. For example, if a witness who is afraid of reprisal initially says that she can't remember details of the crime, she may be reluctant to disclose information later because she would have to admit she was lying earlier. By allowing herself to be hypnotized, she can tell the police what she knows but claim that she only remembered it while hypnotized (Kebbell & Wagstaff, 1998).

The law appears to share psychology's skepticism about hypnosis. Although the law is unsettled about the admissibility of hypnotically enhanced memories, the courts have typically imposed fairly severe restrictions on testimony from hypnotized witnesses. For example, in 1980 (*Minnesota v. Mack*), a Minnesota court of appeals decided that an assault victim could not testify about information she remembered only after being hypnotized and, in 1982 (*People v. Shirley*), the California Supreme Court excluded all testimony about memories that emerged through the use of hypnosis. However, in 1987 (*Rock v. Arkansas*), the U.S. Supreme Court struck down an Arkansas law that banned all hypnotically refreshed testimony. In *Rock,* a woman who had killed her husband remembered under hypnosis that the gun had misfired during a struggle with her husband. Because the trial judge had refused to let jurors hear what the woman remembered under hypnosis, the woman was granted a new trial. The Supreme Court was careful to note that the basis for its decision was the right of Ms. Rock to testify on her own behalf. Their underlying skepticism about the reliability of hypnotically refreshed memories was unchanged. What all this means is that information recalled under hypnosis is not automatically excluded at trial. Whether or not it is admitted depends on the specific characteristics of the case—for example, whose memory has been refreshed (the defendant, the victim, or an eyewitness)—and how carefully the hypnosis sessions were conducted.

The appeal of hypnosis was based on the hope that it would provide access to memories not available during normal consciousness. Unfortunately, memory distortions sometimes created by the process of hypnosis have made the technique much less useful than its proponents had hoped. Hypnosis can elicit false memories, amplify the effects of suggestive questioning, and bolster the confidence of eyewitnesses. What is needed is an alternative technique that might boost recall without promoting false or embellished recollections.

The Cognitive Interview.   One promising alternative has been developed and refined by Ron Fisher and Edward Geiselman (1992). This technique—called the cognitive interview—involves a subtle step-by-step procedure designed to relax the witness and to mentally reinstate the context surrounding the crime. The goal is to improve the retrieval of accurate information while avoiding the increased suggestibility of hypnosis.

An interviewer using this technique gently guides the witness through several stages. During Step 1, the interviewer attempts to reduce the witness's anxiety, develop rapport, and help the witness concentrate. The witness is asked to report what happened without interference, thereby avoiding suggestive questioning from the interviewer. During Step 2, the witness closes his or her eyes and attempts to mentally reinstate the context of the crime. He or she mentally pictures the setting of the crime and the surrounding sights, sounds, and feelings. Step 3 involves probing the images and actions reported by the witness. The purpose is to make sure all relevant information is brought out. Then, events are recalled in different orders—moving forward in time from beginning to end, then backwards from end to beginning. Step 4 entails taking different perspectives on the crime, such as mentally viewing the event from the perspective of the criminal and the victim. These recollections are recorded by the interviewer and then read back to the witness to uncover errors or omissions. Finally, during Step 5, background information is collected, and it is emphasized that the witness should call if he or she thinks of new information. Overall, the technique involves relaxing the witness, providing multiple opportunities to report everything he or she saw, and avoiding coercive or leading questions (Fisher, 1995).

Unfortunately, skillful use of the cognitive interview requires police to adopt an interviewing style quite different from their usual style. Police officers are accustomed to interrogating criminal suspects. As described in Chapter 2, they receive extensive training on how to extract incriminating information from these reluctant "interviewees." As Fisher and Geiselman point out, it is difficult for police officers to switch from a coercive, leading interrogation style when interviewing witnesses instead of suspects. Based on research showing that the cognitive interview improves recall of accurate information without increasing witness suggestibility, police forces in England and Wales now receive training in the technique. Police in the United States do not routinely use the cognitive interview.

Eyewitness reports rely on memory. Under some circumstances, psychologists and attorneys are especially skeptical of the memories of eyewitnesses. When charges of criminal behavior are based on the memories of very young children, or when charges are based on memories that were inaccessible for years or even decades, it is reasonable to scrutinize these memories closely.

MEMORIES OF CHILD SEXUAL ABUSE

Child sexual abuse is an especially disturbing crime because it victimizes the most innocent and defenseless members of society. It is also a disturbingly underreported crime. Very young victims are not able to talk yet so they are incapable of reporting the abuse. Young children may not interpret sexual exploitation as abuse, particularly if the abuser is a parent or trusted caregiver. Children of any age may fear retaliation and sexual abusers may explicitly threaten children with retaliation if they tell anyone about the crime. For all these reasons, most child sexual abuse is hidden from the criminal justice system. Estimates of the prevalence of child sexual abuse vary from less than 1% to as much as 12% of all children, though the true prevalence could be even higher (Barkan, 1997).

Psychologists have been at the forefront of efforts to prevent child sexual abuse, as well as efforts to develop effective treatments for victims of abuse. Psychologists have also taken the lead in examining the validity of unusual claims of sexual abuse. The late 1980s and much of the 1990s were marked by an extraordinary outbreak of reports of sexual abuse. Scores of young children in day care centers reported bizarre incidents of alleged sexual abuse at the hands of their preschool teachers. Some adults began to remember long-forgotten episodes of being sexually abused as children. This outbreak of sexual abuse allegations ignited a heated debate among psychologists about the accuracy of such memories.

THE MEMORIES OF YOUNG CHILDREN

My youngest daughter just turned three. During the past few months, she was abducted by a group of aliens who took her for a ride in their spaceship. She saw an animal that was half elephant and half monkey, and she swam across the ocean to Catalina Island (about 26 miles from the beach near our house). At least that's what she told me. I'm pretty sure that none of these events really happened. It's not that she's lying, it's just that her capacity to distinguish between fact and fantasy is not yet fully developed. Indeed, there is considerable research showing that young children (especially those under the age of about five, but also those as old as six) have difficulty distinguishing imagined events from real events (Ceci & Bruck, 1995). Because of children's less developed abilities to encode, store, and retrieve information, the problems surrounding eyewitness testimony are significantly amplified when the witness is a child.

The Day Care Center Cases.   During the late 1980s and into the 1990s, workers in several day care centers across the United States were accused of sexually abusing children in their care. Here are the allegations in three of the most notorious cases.

- In 1985, Kelly Michaels of the Wee Care Nursery School in New Jersey was accused of sexually abusing 20 three- to five-year-old children. According to allegations, Michaels played the piano naked, licked peanut butter off children's genitals, forced children to drink her urine and eat her feces, and raped children with knives, forks, spoons, and Lego blocks.
- In 1987, Ray Buckey and Peggy McMartin Buckey of the McMartin Preschool in California were charged with 207 counts of child molestation. The accusations included sodomy, taking pornographic photographs of children engaged in sex acts, tunneling underground to rob graves, hacking up corpses in front of children, and sexually molesting children while flying in a hot air balloon.
- During 1989, seven adults who worked at the Little Rascals Day Care Center in North Carolina were accused of sexually molesting 90 children who attended the center. The allegations were wide-ranging and bizarre—children reported that they had been raped

and sodomized, forced to have oral sex while being photographed, tied up and hung upside down from trees, set on fire, and thrown from a boat into shark-infested waters. Some children accused the adults of murdering babies.

What made these allegations especially shocking was not only the bizarre character of the sexual abuse, but the number of children victimized, and the apparent ability of the abusers to keep their sordid activities secret for long periods of time. Surprisingly, in all these cases there was no physical or medical evidence to support the claims. Also, no parents of the children or other teachers working at the schools ever noticed anything alarming during the many months the abuse allegedly took place.

The Wee Care case contains elements common to many other cases, so it is useful to examine how the allegations developed. Four days after Kelly Michaels left her job at Wee Care Nursery School, a four-year-old former student was having his temperature taken rectally at his pediatrician's office. "That's what my teacher does to me at school," he told the nurse. When asked what he meant, he replied, "Her takes my temperature." That afternoon, the child's mother notified New Jersey's child protective services agency. Two days later, the boy was interviewed by a state prosecutor. During the interview, the boy inserted his finger into the anus of an anatomical doll and told the prosecutor that two other boys at school had also had their temperatures taken. (Anatomical dolls have male or female genitalia. They have been used to help reluctant children show investigators what type of sexual abuse may have been perpetrated against them.)

The two other boys were then questioned. Neither seemed to know anything about having their temperature taken, but one boy said Kelly Michaels had touched his penis. The mother of the first child told a parent member of the school board what the children had said. He questioned his own son, who told him that Kelly Michaels had touched his penis with a spoon. When Wee Care school was made aware of these allegations, they sent out a letter to all parents "regarding serious allegations made by a child." A social worker who directed a hospital sexual assault unit was invited to make a presentation to parents. At that presentation, she asserted that a third of all children would be victims of an "inappropriate sexual experience" by the time they reached 18. She encouraged parents to look for telltale signs that their children may have been abused: nightmares, genital soreness, masturbation, bed-wetting, or noticeable changes in behavior.

Over a period of six months, several professionals interviewed children and their families to determine the extent of the sexual abuse. Many of the children were interviewed on several occasions. A psychotherapist who treated 13 of the children held five group therapy sessions where children discussed how they had been sexually abused. Prosecutors and their experts also interviewed the children on multiple occasions. In 1988, Kelly Michaels was convicted of 115 counts of child sexual abuse based on the testimony of 19 children. Michaels was sentenced to 47 years but served only five. In 1994, prosecutors dropped all charges against her.

When the details of the case became public, it was clear that children from Wee Care school had been subjected to coercive questioning from adults. Children under the age of five are acutely sensitive to such questioning. For example, in a study of two- to five-year-old children who had just visited the emergency room, children were asked about their interactions with medical personnel during the visit. When asked open-ended questions such as "What happened?" children provided reasonably accurate reports of their experience. However, when asked specific questions such as "Where did the doctor touch you?" the number of errors shot up from 9% to 49% (Peterson & Bell, 1996).

There were several varieties of coercive questioning used in the sexual abuse cases described above. The least coercive form was simply repeating the question several times until the child gave the desired response. Here is an excerpt from an interview in the Wee Care case:

Interviewer:	When Kelly kissed you, did she ever put her tongue in your mouth?
Child:	No.
Interviewer:	Did she ever make you put your tongue in her mouth?
Child:	No.
Interviewer:	Did you ever have to kiss her vagina?
Child:	No.
Interviewer:	Which of the kids had to kiss her vagina?
Child:	What's this? [child points to tape recorder]
Interviewer:	No, that's my toy, my radio box. . . . Which kids had to kiss her vagina?
Child:	Me. (Ceci & Bruck, 1995, p. 122).

To explore the effect of asking the same question more than once, Stephen Ceci and Maggie Bruck (1996) repeatedly asked children about events that their parents said had never occurred (e.g., getting their finger caught in a mousetrap). After repeated questioning, 58% of preschool-aged children were able to give detailed descriptions of at least one event they initially said had never happened. Twenty-five percent of the preschoolers managed to create false memories for the majority of fictitious events. Information provided by an adult interviewer who asks a question several times is likely to be incorporated into the child's description of an event. Also, by simply repeating the question, the interviewer may signal to the young child that denial of the event is unacceptable to the adult.

In 1998, researchers at the University of Texas at El Paso analyzed transcripts of interviews with children who had claimed to be sexually molested at the McMartin and Wee Care preschools (Garven, Wood, Malpass, & Shaw, 1998). Transcripts clearly revealed that the interviewers used a variety of techniques designed to elicit the responses desired by interviewers: repeated questioning, questions suggesting that particular events occurred, offering praise or rewards for the desired answers, criticizing or disagreeing with children who gave unwanted answers, and inviting children to speculate or imagine what might have happened. There is now substantial research indicating that interviewers in many of the preschool cases began with the strong belief that children had been sexually abused. This belief led investigators to question children in ways that made it likely that their preexisting suspicions would be confirmed.

Based on their analysis of transcripts, the University of Texas researchers designed an experiment that made use of the techniques employed by interviewers in the preschool abuse cases. Three- to six-year-old children were invited to listen to a man who came to their classroom to tell the story of the Hunchback of Notre Dame. After telling the story, he handed out cupcakes and napkins, said goodbye, and left the room. One week later, the children were asked about things the storyteller had done (taking off his hat, giving out cupcakes, etc.) as well as things the storyteller had not done (putting a sticker on a child's knee, throwing a crayon at a child who was talking). In a control condition where neutral, noncoercive questions were used, four- to six-year-olds said "yes" to fewer than 10% of the questions about events that never happened. Three-year-olds said "yes" to 31% of such questions. In the conditions that made use of techniques from the McMartin transcripts, four- to six-year-olds answered "yes" to 50% of the misleading questions while three-year-olds answered "yes" to 81% of the misleading questions (Garven et al., 1998).

The techniques used in the research studies probably underestimate the effects of the techniques used in the actual cases. Keep in mind that the questioning techniques used by interviewers in the real sexual abuse cases were much more forceful and intimidating than those used by researchers. Also, in the real cases, children were questioned several times by different interviewers. In some cases, children shared information in "group therapy" sessions. Interviewers shared information with parents and parents shared information with one another. These conditions raised the level of anxiety and suspicion, and probably served to make the claims of abuse increasingly extreme.

Testimony by Children at Trial.   It appears that jurors tend to believe the testimony of children in sexual abuse cases. Interestingly, younger children who testify that they were abused are more likely to be believed than adolescents. This is apparently because younger children are seen as too unsophisticated about sexual matters to create false allegations (Bottoms & Goodman, 1994). Of course, this willingness to believe young children probably does not extend to the more fantastic claims of sexual abuse (involving underground tunnels, spaceships, and hot air balloons) that were made in some of the preschool sexual abuse cases described earlier.

Child testimony poses a difficult dilemma for the legal system. Although defendants are generally entitled to confront their accusers face-to-face in court, it is usually unrealistic to expect children to speak freely in the presence of someone who has harmed them. In addition, the sterility, formality, and strangeness of the courtroom make it an especially inhospitable and intimidating setting for a young child. To spare young children the frightening and sometimes traumatizing experience of testifying in court, all but nine states allow an exception to the hearsay rule when a child is the alleged victim in a crime. Hearsay testimony—testifying about what someone else said outside of court—is usually inadmissible. The reasoning is that the person who made the remarks cannot be cross-examined, and his or her truthfulness cannot be assessed by the jury. However, when a child is the victim, a teacher, parent, physician, or other adult is often permitted to stand in for the child and testify about what the child said.

But how do jurors respond to such evidence? In an important study of this issue, John Myers and his coworkers questioned 248 jurors from 42 different trials (Myers, Redlich, Goodman, Prizmich, & Imwindel-ried, 1999). In each of the trials, there was child testimony as well as adult hearsay testimony on behalf of the child. They found that the testimony of adult hearsay witnesses was seen as more consistent, credible, complete, and accurate than the testimony of child witnesses. Perhaps it is not surprising that adult testimony was viewed as more consistent and complete than child testimony. Adults tend to be more confident and to give more thorough, detailed responses to questions. Another clue as to why adults were perceived as more accurate has to do with the attentiveness of jurors. Jurors carefully scrutinized the demeanor of the child victims in a search for clues to deception. They looked carefully at the children's facial expressions, eye contact, pauses, hesitations, gestures, speech errors, and overall nervousness. They may have interpreted some of these signs of nervousness as uncertainty or even lying by children.

An alternative method for presenting the testimony of children is the use of closed-circuit television (CCTV). In the case of *Maryland v. Craig* (1990), the U.S. Supreme Court held that if a child victim was likely to experience significant emotional trauma by being in the presence of the defendant, the child's testimony could be presented via CCTV. A large television in the courtroom enables the defendant, judge, and jury to see the testimony, but the child and the defense and prosecuting attorneys are in another room. The *Craig* decision was a significant departure from the Court's prior rulings on this issue. In effect, the Court held that a defendant's right to confront his or her accuser was outweighed by the need to protect child victims from emotional harm. The *Craig* decision was also based on the reasoning that the truth-finding function of the trial was sometimes best served by allowing children to testify by means of CCTV. That is, allowing children to testify outside the courtroom serves the goal of obtaining full and truthful testimony from children.

In a carefully conducted study of child testimony and the use of CCTV, Gail Goodman and her colleagues (1998) had five- to six-year-olds and eight- to nine-year-olds participate in a play session with a male confederate who either placed stickers on their exposed body parts (e.g., toes, arms, belly buttons) or placed stickers on their clothing. About two weeks later, the children testified about the play session in a real courtroom via live testimony or CCTV. Mock jurors recruited from the community then viewed a simulated trial containing the child testimony. The researchers found that the use of CCTV reduced the amount of emotional distress experienced by children and enabled children to give more accurate testimony. These benefits were achieved without any lowering of the conviction rate. Thirty-three states now permit the use of CCTV for testimony by children.

RECOVERED MEMORIES OF SEXUAL ABUSE

By the early 1990s, sensational claims of sexual abuse at preschools had dropped sharply. But claims of a different type of child sexual abuse shot up dramatically. This newer type of claim involved adults who began to remember that they had been sexually abused years or even decades earlier. As the 1990s progressed, these reports began to accumulate at an alarming pace.

The controversy over the authenticity of what came to be known as "recovered memories" highlights important aspects of psychology and law. First, attempts by scientists to evaluate the accuracy of recovered memories took place in a politically charged atmosphere—those who disputed claims of recovered memories were often accused of being on the side of child molesters and of encouraging the denial of sexual abuse. Those who believed in the validity of recovered memories were sometimes accused of supporting witch hunts that led to the criminal prosecution of innocent people. The controversy also deepened the split between psychological scientists (who tended to be highly skeptical of recovered memories) and psychotherapists (who tended to view recovered memories as credible) (Alpert et al., 1998).

The Ingram Case.   In one extraordinary case, a man recovered memories not of having been abused, but of having been a sexual abuser. The strange case of Paul Ingram illustrates some of the processes involved in the creation of a false memory.

Paul Ingram was a pillar of his community. He was a sheriff's deputy in the city of Olympia, Washington, he was deeply religious, and active in his local church. For most of his life, he was also considered a good father. Then, something terrible happened. One of his daughters accused him of sexually abusing her years earlier. Although Ingram strenuously denied these charges, local police were not convinced by his denials. Over the course of five months, they repeatedly questioned Ingram about the details of this alleged sexual abuse. They assisted his recall by telling him, over and over again, exactly how he had abused his children. Mr. Ingram prayed and asked the Lord to restore his memories of these horrible crimes. Investigators hypnotized him to dredge up old memories. And, eventually, Ingram confessed to gang-raping his own daughter, repeated violent assaults, animal sacrifices, and being a leader in a satanic cult that killed 25 babies. If the confessions were true, the police had successfully exposed a prolific child abuser, rapist, and serial killer.

The story began to unravel when Richard Ofshe—a leading researcher of false confessions—joined the investigation. To test Ingram's suggestibility, Ofshe created a false accusation to see if Ingram would construct a memory of the false event. The false event (which was not one of the actual allegations in the case) was that Ingram had forced his daughter and son to have sex with each other while he watched. At first, Ingram had no recollections of this sordid event. But after thinking and praying for guidance, he started to recall the details of the event. One day later, he confessed to committing the false crime. His account of what happened was strikingly vivid and detailed. He remembered the time of day, the day of the week, the room where the act had occurred, exactly what sex acts he told his children to perform, his thoughts during the event, and the reactions of his son and daughter.

Based on this and other evidence, Ofshe argued that Ingram was an exceptionally suggestible and imaginative person whose intense praying induced a trancelike state. After imagining acts of sexual abuse while in this state, the imagined events became difficult to distinguish from authentic memories (Ofshe & Watters, 1994). Despite a massive police investigation—which included digging up several sites where bodies were allegedly buried—no physical evidence was ever found to link Ingram to the crimes or even to suggest that the alleged crimes had ever happened. Nevertheless, Ingram was convicted and sent to prison.

The Ingram case is unusual because it involves recovered memories of being the *perpetrator* of sexual abuse. Recovered memories of being the *victim* of sexual abuse are far more common. But many of the elements of the Ingram case—a vulnerable and suggestible person, an interviewer who strongly suspected that sexual abuse occurred, and the use of hypnosis or other trancelike states—are at play in more typical cases of recovered memories.

Were the Memories Created or Recovered?   In examining the accumulating cases of recovered memories during the 1990s, several researchers began to discern common patterns. These patterns suggested to many psychologists that some memories of sexual abuse were not recovered but implanted (Loftus & Ketcham, 1994).

The typical series of events leading to the discovery of a long-forgotten memory of being sexually abused usually began with an adult woman who sought out psychotherapy for help in dealing with emotional or interpersonal problems. Often, the therapist fixed on the client's childhood experiences and began to strongly suspect sexual abuse. Based on these suspicions, the client might be encouraged to be receptive to vague inklings of abuse as the return of repressed memories. Some therapists encouraged their clients to read books or watch videos suggesting that victims of child sexual abuse show symptoms similar to the ones being experienced by the client herself (e.g., depression). Over the course of weeks or months, the therapist might try hypnosis, guided imagery, or dream interpretation to assist the client in trying to recover her presumably repressed memories. Under hypnosis or a similarly relaxed and suggestible state, episodes of sexual abuse would be vividly imagined. Finally, a client might be encouraged to join therapy groups whose members included others who had recovered memories of being abused.

Some researchers argued that, through the process described above, false memories were implanted during therapy. Over time, as the false memories became more vivid and elaborate, they took on the appearance of authentic memories. But many psychotherapists had a simpler explanation: The memories of abuse had been repressed and later recovered during therapy. The concept of repression (popularized by Sigmund Freud) holds that painful, threatening, or traumatic memories can be pushed out of conscious awareness (Holmes, 1990). This repression of traumatic memories was thought to occur unconsciously and involuntarily. According to the repression hypothesis, traumatic memories could remain intact but locked away in the unconscious for years or even decades. To unearth these deeply buried memories, it might be necessary to use relaxation and visualization techniques.

Although research psychologists have carefully documented the process of forgetting, they point out that there is little evidence for the concept of repression. David Holmes, a researcher at the University of Kansas put it forcefully,

> Despite over sixty years of research involving numerous approaches by many thoughtful and clever investigators, at the present time there is no controlled laboratory evidence supporting the concept of repression. It is interesting to note that even most of the proponents of repression agree with that conclusion. However, they attempt to salvage the concept of repression by derogating the laboratory research, arguing that it is contrived, artificial, sterile and irrelevant to the "dynamic processes" that occur in the "real world" (p. 96).

But even outside the rarified world of the research laboratory, there is little evidence of repression. Indeed, there is considerable evidence that most people have vivid memories of traumatic events. For example, a study of five- to ten-year-old children who had witnessed the murder of one or both parents found no evidence that these children repressed their traumatic memories (Malmquist, 1986). Although they tried to keep these terrifying images of violence out of their minds, they could not. Like other victims of traumatic events, their problem was not repression but intrusion—despite their attempts to suppress the memory, the memory intruded into consciousness. Soldiers who have experienced massacres on the battlefield are often tormented by unwelcome flashbacks, rape victims are often haunted by memories of the rape that intrude into their consciousness, and people who have been tortured have great difficulty putting memories of that torture out of their minds. This is not to say that some disturbing memories cannot be forgotten. However, it is important to note that the most common response to a traumatic experience is not forgetting but uncontrolled remembering (Loftus & Ketcham, 1994). Because of the vividness and persistence of most traumatic memories, it is difficult to accept that some traumatic memories could vanish from conscious awareness for years or even decades.

Even the strongest evidence of repression is ambiguous. In a widely cited study, Linda Williams (1994) used hospital records to identify 129 adult women who had been victims of sexual abuse as children. She found that 38% of these women said they didn't remember the event *or* chose not to tell an interviewer about it. Is this evidence of repression? Perhaps, but there are many other possible explanations: Some of the milder forms of abuse (such as inappropriate touching) may not have been experienced by the children as sexual abuse; the hospital records may not have been accurate (e.g., the examining physician may have been mistaken about whether abuse actually occurred); the women may have forgotten that the abuse occurred because it happened during very early childhood (i.e., under the age of five); or the women may simply have been unwilling to admit to a stranger that they had been abused. Also, the study tells us nothing about whether or not the apparently forgotten memories could be recovered.

Research on Implanting False Memories.   During the peak of the recovered memory debate, psychologists who believed in repression correctly pointed out that there was no research showing that false memories could be implanted and mistaken for real memories of actual events. So, in the mid-1990s, Elizabeth Loftus, a leading researcher in the area of eyewitness identification and a leading authority on memory, set out to test the proposition that false memories could be implanted. Of course, it would be cruel and unethical to intentionally implant a traumatic memory of sexual abuse. As an alternative, Loftus set out to create a memory of being "lost at the mall." Twenty-four people, ranging in age from 18 to 53, were asked to tell what they remembered about four childhood events. Three of the four events had actually happened—they were experiences reported by parents or other close relatives. But the fourth event had never happened. That event involved being lost in a mall (or another public place) around age five, crying, being rescued by an elderly woman, and then being reunited with the family. Participants were asked about the four events twice. After two interviews conducted over a period of weeks, 25% of the people came to remember most or all of the implanted "lost in the mall" event (Loftus, 1997).

A series of follow-up studies by Ira Hyman and his colleagues attempted to create memories of other, more unusual false events. Using the same basic procedures as the earlier "lost in the mall" studies, participants in the study were told, "When you were five you were at the wedding reception of some friends of the family and you were running around with some other kids, when you bumped into the table and spilled the punch bowl on the parents of the bride." At first, none of the participants could remember the punch bowl event. However, 27% eventually came to accept the event as real. Some of the false recollections were quite vivid. For example, one participant described the father of the bride as:

> A heavyset man, not like fat, but like tall and big beer belly, and I picture him having a dark gray suit . . . grayish dark hair and balding on top . . . with a wide square face, and I picture him getting up and being kind of irritated or mad (Hyman, Husband, & Billings, 1995, p. 194).

These studies not only showed that false memories could be implanted with relatively little effort, they highlighted the crucial importance of visual imagery in creating false memories. In the punch bowl studies, people who scored higher on scales measuring the vividness of visual imagery also tended to develop the most detailed and elaborate false memories. In addition, people who were instructed to relax and imagine an event they could not initially recall were much more likely to develop a false memory of the event. Later research suggested that memories of mildly traumatic events—being attacked by an animal, a serious outdoor accident, or being hurt by another child—can be implanted in about a third of the people tested (Porter, Yuille, & Lehman, 1999).

Several conclusions can be drawn from research on implanted memories. First, false memories can't be successfully implanted in everyone. In the research summarized above, only one-quarter to one-third of people came to accept a false memory as real. Second, it appears that some techniques routinely used in therapy to search out childhood memories—hypnosis, dream interpretation, guided imagery—facilitate the production of detailed visual images that can later be mistaken for real memories. Third, expectancies seem to play a crucial role. For example, one study found that people who were told that it is possible to remember whether a colored mobile dangled above their crib the day after their birth are more likely to remember seeing one (Spanos, Burgess, Samuels, & Blois, 1999). Similarly, people who believe that they have lived before often remember events from their "past lives" while under hypnosis. Finally, the relative success of experiments designed to implant false memories is surprising because the techniques used by experimenters were relatively weak. In real cases, the people who recovered memories of sexual abuse were subjected to much greater pressure over a much longer period of time.

The controversy over recovered memories has cooled during the past few years, although some residual bitterness remains. Although most claims of recovered memories appear to have been implanted through the use of highly suggestive therapy techniques, there also appear to be a few documented cases where forgotten episodes of actual abuse are suddenly recalled. For example, in one well-documented case, a 30-year-old man became anxious and agitated while watching a movie where the main character dealt with traumatic recollections of being sexually abused as a child. After the movie had ended, the man experienced a flood of vivid memories. The memories involved being sexually abused by a priest during a camping trip 18 years earlier (Schooler, 1994). The reemergence of this traumatic memory occurred without psychotherapy. It also occurred in 1986, before widespread public awareness of the recovered memory debate.

Several explanations for the forgetting and remembering of sexual abuse have been proposed. The simplest explanation is the transience of memory, forgetting that occurs with the passage of time (Schacter, 2001). But transience is only a small part of the story because most memories of important events deteriorate gradually, they don't simply vanish without a trace. Another potential explanation follows from the finding that people who say they were sexually abused as children are more likely to temporarily forget the abuse if the abuser is a family member or trusted caretaker. Michael Anderson has suggested that this may be because the child is physically and emotionally dependent on that family member (Anderson, 2001). Memories of the abuse would damage the essential relationship between caregiver and child by creating fear and distrust. To prevent this damage, and to maintain an adaptive relationship with the caregiver, a child might selectively recall positive memories. By repeatedly, selectively retrieving positive memories, retrieval of negative memories becomes increasingly difficult. This is a variant of the phenomenon of "retrieval inhibition" mentioned earlier. The negative memory may only enter awareness when exposure to powerful cues (such as watching a movie about child sexual abuse) allows the memory to be retrieved.

Individual differences may also be part of the story. Some people may simply be better at keeping unpleasant experiences out of their minds. Lynn Myers and Chris Brewin (1998) have identified people who appear to be especially good at denying their emotional responses. When physiological measures (like blood pressure and heart rate) indicate they are experiencing high levels of stress and anxiety, they report that they are feeling relaxed and free of stress. Such people are less able to remember negative events from their past and are less able to remember details of the negative events they do recall.

In short, there appear to be many cases where people have constructed false memories of sexual abuse. There also seem to be a few cases where memories of sexual abuse have resurfaced after having been forgotten for years. How can we know which memories were created and which were recovered? Based on their careful review of the scientific literature on recovered memories, Stephen Lindsay and Don Read (1994) conclude that we should consider five criteria when evaluating claims of recovered memories of abuse. Specifically, we should be especially skeptical of allegedly recovered memories that: (1) were recovered over a period of time using suggestive or coercive techniques; (2) began as vague images or feelings instead of clear, detailed recollections; (3) involve repeated abuse that extended into adolescence (such abuse is unlikely to be forgotten); (4) involve abuse that occurred before the age of three or in early childhood (before enduring memories can be formed); and (5) involve extremely rare forms of abuse (e.g., sexual abuse as part of a satanic ritual).

By the year 2000, claims of recovered memories had plummeted. There were good reasons for the sharp decline. Many people who once claimed that they had recovered memories of sexual abuse later retracted those claims. Some of those people (and the people they had accused of being abusers) brought successful lawsuits against psychotherapists who had created false memories. As a consequence, many therapists switched to less suggestive approaches.

IN CONCLUSION
• •

Good detectives understand the critical importance of keeping a crime scene uncontaminated. If someone has been murdered, investigators photograph the scene from multiple angles. The position of the body, the pattern of spattered blood, and the nature of the wounds are all carefully noted before anything is disturbed. Evidence is preserved and carefully transported so that it can be tested for fingerprints or other trace evidence. If blood is found at the scene of the crime, strict testing procedures are followed to prevent contamination of the DNA sample.

In many cases, the crucial evidence is not physical but psychological: It is the memory of a victim or other eyewitness. Like blood and fingerprints, human memory can be easily contaminated and distorted. Psychologists have now revealed the kinds of questioning and investigative procedures that are likely to corrupt existing memories or even create false ones. If a police laboratory uses sloppy procedures, a DNA analysis can be challenged and discredited. If suggestive or coercive procedures are used to gather information from witnesses, the recollections of witnesses can be challenged and discredited. The reason for handling both physical and psychological evidence carefully is the same: to make sure the right person is arrested and convicted.

Readings to Supplement This Chapter

Articles

Behrman, B. W., & Davey, S. L. (2001). Eyewitness identification in actual criminal cases: An archival analysis. *Law and Human Behavior, 25,* 475–492.

Clark, S. E., & Tunnicliff, J. L. (2001). Selecting lineup foils in eyewitness identification experiments: Experimental control and real-world simulation. *Law and Human Behavior, 25,* 199–216.

Goodman, G. S., Bottoms, B. L., Rudy, L., Davis, S. L., & Schwartz-Kenney, B. M. (2001). Effects of past abuse experiences on children's eyewitness memory. *Law and Human Behavior, 25,* 269–298.

Hunt, J. S., & Borgida, E. (2001). Is that what I said?: Witnesses' responses to interviewer modifications. *Law and Human Behavior, 25,* 583–603.

Orcutt, H. K., Goodman, G. S., Tobey, A. E., Batterman-Faunce, J. M., & Thomas, S. (2001). Detecting deception in children's testimony: Factfinders' abilities to reach the truth in open court and closed circuit trials. *Law and Human Behavior, 25,* 339–372.

Porter, S., Birt, A. R., Yuille, J. C., & Lehman, D. R. (2000). Negotiating false memories: Interviewer and rememberer characteristics relate to memory distortion. *Psychological Science, 11,* 507–510.

Wells, G. L. (2001). Police lineups: Data, theory, and policy. *Psychology, Public Policy, and Law, 7,* 791–801.

Books

Ceci, S. J., & Bruck, M. (1995). *Jeopardy in the courtroom: A scientific analysis of children's testimony.* Washington, DC: American Psychological Association.

Loftus, E., & Ketcham, K. (1991). *Witness for the defense.* New York: St. Martin's Press.

7

Predicting Behavior: Risk Assessment and Child Custody Decisions

Chapter Outline

• •

ASSESSING THE RISK OF FUTURE VIOLENCE

The Evolution of Research on Risk Assessment
The List of Risk Factors
 Historical Markers
 Dynamic Markers
 Risk Management Markers
 Helping Clinicians Use the Markers
Jurors' Reactions to Risk Assessment Evidence
Treatment to Reduce the Risk of Violence

CHILD CUSTODY AND PARENTAL COMPETENCE

The Evolution of Child Custody Standards
Research on Children's Responses to Divorce
The Psychologist's Contribution to Custody Decisions
Custody Mediation as an Alternative to Litigation
In Conclusion

$\mathcal{S}$ometimes the legal system asks psychologists to predict the future. There are two types of predictions psychologists are often asked to make: (1) whether someone poses a risk of behaving violently sometime in the future, and (2) following a divorce, which type of child custody arrangement will best promote the future development and well-being of a child. In many ways, assessing the risk of violence and creating the right child custody arrangement are very different kinds of tasks. But, in both types of predictions, psychologists attempt to evaluate past and current circumstances as a means of estimating future outcomes.

ASSESSING THE RISK
OF FUTURE VIOLENCE

The 1976 case of *Tarasoff v. Regents of the University of California* changed the way mental health professionals dealt with clients who appear to pose a risk of violent behavior. The case involved Prosenjit Poddar, a graduate student from India who was studying engineering at the University of California at Berkeley. Poddar was receiving psychotherapy at the university health center. During a therapy session, he expressed his desire to kill Tanya Tarasoff, a young woman who had rejected his romantic advances. The psychotherapist was understandably alarmed by this confession and alerted campus police that Poddar had made a death threat. The police interviewed Poddar but decided that he was not dangerous. About two months later, Poddar stabbed Tanya Tarasoff to death in her home.

Tarasoff's parents sued the university for negligence, charging that university employees should have told Tanya that Poddar had threatened her, and that they should have confined Poddar to protect their daughter. The parents won their lawsuit, and the California Supreme Court held that psychotherapists had a "duty to protect" potential victims of violence. Because of the *Tarasoff* decision, when a patient poses a serious risk of violence, therapists are obliged to take "reasonable care" to protect the intended victim (e.g, by notifying the police and the potential victim). In the years following *Tarasoff*, courts and legislatures in many states enacted "duty to protect" laws. If a client threatens violence against someone during therapy and later acts on that threat, psychotherapists can be sued even in jurisdictions where "duty to protect" laws are not in effect. In addition, several successful lawsuits have been brought against psychiatric facilities that have released patients who later harm or kill someone (Poythress & Brodsky, 1992).

The *Tarasoff* decision produced a strong reaction among psychologists. Many psychotherapists felt that the "duty to protect" requirement would undermine the effectiveness of therapy by breaking the bond of trust between therapist and client. If therapists were required to reveal what was said during a private therapy session, how could a client be expected to express his or her innermost thoughts and feelings without fear? There was also the issue of which threats were serious. Many therapists pointed out that the great majority of clients who express a desire to hurt someone (or describe violent fantasies) never act on that desire. The *Tarasoff* case not only created controversy among psychotherapists, it focused public attention on the issue of whether mental health professionals were capable of predicting which clients might become violent sometime in the future.

Around the same time as the *Tarasoff* case, the "deinstitutionalization" movement was gaining momentum. That movement involved the release of inmates from mental institutions into the community. Deinstitutionalization was made possible by the development of antipsychotic drugs that enabled some mentally ill people to take care of themselves outside the hospital (Perlin, 1996). The movement was partly motivated by a humanitarian urge to help mental patients lead fuller, more satisfying lives beyond the confines of psychiatric hospitals. The hope was that former mental patients would be reintegrated into the community and would learn to function in the world at large. But deinstitutionalization was also motivated by the less-than-humanitarian desire to cut back on the cost of hospitalization for mentally ill patients. Though there were many causes of deinstitutionalization, one clear consequence was a dramatic increase in the number of mentally ill homeless people (Lamb & Weinberger, 2001). The fearful response of the public to the sometimes bizarre behavior of these homeless people raised public anxiety about the link between mental illness and violence, and helped spur interest in predicting which people might become dangerous.

The issue of future dangerousness is important in many other contexts. As a practical matter, parole boards or prison release review boards must decide if an inmate being considered for parole is likely to commit acts of violence if released into the community. In the workplace, managers must try to screen out job applicants who show a propensity towards violence. Human resource managers may even be asked to decide whether an employee who is acting strangely is likely to become violent on the job. School psychologists may be held accountable if they failed to notice warning signs before a student smuggles a gun into school and opens fire in the cafeteria. Police must decide if a homeless person who is screaming on a public street should be forcibly taken to a mental institution. "Dangerousness towards others" is a key consideration when deciding if someone can be placed in a psychiatric facility against his or her will (this is known as "involuntary commitment"). Finally, in a few states, jurors are asked to consider whether a murderer will be dangerous in the future when deciding between a sentence of life in prison or the death penalty. In each of these contexts, the challenge is to achieve an optimal balance between the need to protect society and the rights of a *possibly* dangerous individual.

Society has a legitimate interest in being protected from violent individuals. But those individuals have a right to be protected from harassment by authorities and from arbitrary arrest and detention based on mere suspicion. Many scholars have argued that preventative detention—holding someone in a jail or hospital because he or she *might* become violent—is ethically problematic (Ogloff, 1998). Others have argued that mental health professionals should simply refuse to make predictions about future dangerousness because the accuracy of such predictions has not yet been clearly demonstrated (Grisso & Appelbaum, 1992). However, it is important to compare the accuracy of predictions based on different methods. An essential question is whether the use of a particular method *improves* decision making by courts (Heilbrun, 1997). Research shows that scientific approaches to risk assessment do not produce infallible predictions. Nonetheless, scientific approaches do produce more accurate predictions than those based on the subjective judgments of psychotherapists, judges, jurors, and prison administrators.

The traditional way of discussing and presenting research findings in the area of prediction is by referring to a two-by-two contingency table like the one that follows.

OUTCOME: Did the person later become violent?

		YES	NO
PREDICTION:			
Did we predict that the person would become violent?	YES	True Positive	False Positive
	NO	False Negative	True Negative

The two rows of the table concern the prediction: Will the patient become violent or not? The two columns of the table concern the actual outcome: Did the person actually commit an act of violence at some later time? Of course, researchers have to wait to find out the answer to this question. If we cross the prediction with the outcome, there are four possibilities, two accurate and two inaccurate. If it was predicted that a person would become violent, and then that person does become violent, it is called a "true positive." A "true negative" occurs when a person who was predicted not to become violent turns out not to be violent. The two forms of error are called either "false positives" (predictions of violence that don't come true) or "false negatives" (people predicted to be nonviolent who later become violent). True predictions are sometimes called "hits" and false predictions are sometimes called "misses."

Most efforts to improve prediction have involved measuring a variety of factors known to be or suspected to be associated with individual violence. These factors are then correlated with actual violence in institutions (usually psychiatric hospitals or prisons) or in the community. The goal is to identify those factors that reliably predict later violence.

THE EVOLUTION OF RESEARCH ON RISK ASSESSMENT

The most important reason for trying to predict future violence is the obvious one: If we can predict who will become violent, perhaps we can prevent him or her from becoming violent. But requiring mental health professionals or others to predict who is likely to become violent skips over the more basic issue: Are they able to do it well? During the 1970s and early 1980s, the answer to that question was a resounding "no."

Two major studies published during the 1970s illustrate the difficulty of predicting violence. In the case of *Baxstrom v. Herold* (1966), the U.S. Supreme Court ordered the release of inmates from Dannemora State Hospital for the criminally insane. Henry Steadman and Joseph Cocozza (1974) followed 98 patients for four years following their release into the community. Although all 98 of the released inmates were considered dangerous, only 20 were ever arrested and only seven of those 20 were arrested for a violent crime. That is, only 7.14% of the total sample later became violent. That's a staggering false positive rate of 92.8%. A few years later, as a result of *Dixon v. Attorney General of the Commonwealth of Pennsylvania* (1971), more than 400 purportedly dangerous mentally ill offenders were released from a prison hospital. Terence Thornberry and Joseph Jacoby (1979) were able to follow the released offenders. Three years after their release, only 14.5% had been arrested or hospitalized for violent behavior. The surprising news from these and other studies was that so few people considered dangerous by the criminal justice system actually ended up committing violent crimes when set free in the community.

In 1981, a leading scholar in the field—John Monahan—published a major review of research on predicting violent behavior. Monahan found that the most striking problem in the field was the overprediction of violence. That is, in virtually all of the studies, errors in predicting violence were in the same direction: A large percentage of the people predicted to become violent did not become violent. A second major conclusion was that actuarial prediction was substantially more accurate than clinical prediction. Actuarial prediction involves mechanically feeding relevant data into a statistical equation to calculate an estimate of future violence. The statistical equation is built on prior research identifying which characteristics are reliably associated with later violent behavior. Factors that are more strongly correlated with future violence are weighted more heavily in the equation. It is a nomothetic, quantitative approach—that is, it is based on characteristics identified in research on large groups of people, and it relies on statistics. In comparison, clinical prediction is an ideographic, qualitative approach. It focuses on a specific individual and it relies on subjective judgments made by a clinical psychologist. Actuarial predictions are built on past research and clinical predictions are built on the past professional experience of the clinician.

One reason for the relative weakness of clinical prediction is lack of feedback about success or failure. When clinical psychologists make predictions about whether or not an individual client will later become violent, they seldom find out whether the client actually becomes violent at some later time. It is impossible to improve predictions without reliable information about which predictions later prove to be correct and which predictions turn out to be wrong. In contrast, actuarial predictions are explicitly based on data showing who actually ends up becoming violent. A second problem is that a prediction made by a particular clinician might be based on flawed information: a plausible but untested theory, mere intuition, or even prejudice. Actuarial prediction is based on purely statistical relationships between variables.[1]

A final point about clinical versus actuarial prediction can be illustrated by comparing the process of predicting violence to the process of predicting the weather (Monahan & Steadman, 1996). A local weather forecaster, relying on extensive actuarial data from the National Weather Service, may be ready to predict a warm, sunny day. But if she looks out the window and sees dark storm clouds rolling in, she may want to raise her estimate of the chance for rain. Similarly, if the best actuarial methods suggest that a particular person is very unlikely to become violent but, while talking to a clinical psychologist, that person threatens violence against someone else, the psychologist should adjust the risk estimate upward (Quinsey, Harris, Rice, & Cormier, 1998). The point is that, on rare occasions, it may be helpful to use clinical judgment to temper or augment actuarial predictions.

In a series of books and articles, Monahan and his frequent collaborator Henry Steadman identified several flaws in research studies and proposed a series of methodological and statistical reforms that might

....

[1] Although a sizeable majority of researchers who have studied risk assessment agree with the conclusion that actuarial methods produce much more accurate predictions than clinical judgments, some controversy persists. For example, in a recent review, Thomas Litwack has argued that it is premature to conclude that clinical judgment is unreliable. He argues that current research is too limited and the populations studied have been too restricted to allow for strong conclusions. See Litwack, T. R. (2001). Actuarial versus clinical assessments of dangerousness. Psychology, Public Policy, and Law, 7, 409–443.

improve the accuracy of predictions. A key consideration was the information used to predict violence. Monahan and Steadman (1994) urged researchers to gather more data and more forms of data. They called for researchers to gather information about physiological factors, psychological factors, and personal history, as well as information about the situations the person might face after release from an institution. Just as predictors needed to be expanded and refined, so did measures of outcome. Measures of violent behavior needed to be more sensitive and inclusive. Researchers were urged to distinguish between types of violence (e.g., shoving, punching, stabbing, or shooting), targets of violence (e.g., spouse, child, or stranger), and contexts in which violence occurs (e.g., at home or in public). Using only arrest records—as some early studies did—led to an underestimation of violent behavior because much violence is unreported or not noticed by police. Also, because even a violent crime can be prosecuted as a lesser nonviolent crime through plea bargaining, some truly violent behavior never even showed up in police reports or court records. Additional data needed to be gathered from interviews with the people being studied and the people with whom they interact. In a recent study, estimates of violent behavior rose from 4.5% to 27.5% when such additional measures of violent behavior were added to the analysis (Steadman et al., 1998).

Finally, predictions needed to move beyond simplistic either/or judgments—either "yes this person will become violent" or "no, this person will not become violent." Instead, predictions needed to be expressed in terms of probability statements. For example, the likelihood that someone will become violent can be expressed as a percentage. Although the legal system often prefers a simple yes or no answer to squishier statements about the likelihood of future violence, probability statements more clearly express the uncertain nature of forecasts. As an alternative to yes-or-no predictions, Edward Mulvey and Charles Lidz (1995) have advocated the use of "conditional prediction." That is, predictions might take the form of "under this set of conditions, this person's risk of violence will increase by ___%." Or, more specifically, "if this person stops taking medication and is not able to work, then the probability of violence will increase by ___%."

It is important to keep in mind that predicting future behavior of any sort (not just violence) is enormously difficult. Human behavior is influenced by a vast array of variables. Characteristics of the person (e.g., personality and physiology), as well as characteristics of the social situation (e.g., support from friends and family, perceived threats from others in the environment) influence behavior (Ross & Nisbett, 1991). It is impossible to carefully measure every characteristic of the person and the environment that *might* contribute to violent behavior sometime in the future. In addition, people change over time and their circumstances change over time. We can never know in advance what situations people will eventually find themselves in. It is audacious to think that we can predict what a person will do one year or 10 years from the time a prediction is made. Although the accumulation of findings and advancements in measurement will continue to boost the accuracy of prediction, predictions will never be perfect.

Another difficulty in prediction arises from the low base rate of violence. "Base rate" refers to the overall likelihood of an event in a population of interest, in this case, the number of people in a particular population who actually become violent. If a psychologist (or parole board or judge) is asked to predict how many people out of 100 are likely to become violent, and only five later become violent, it will be exceedingly difficult to predict which five people will later become violent. If the base rate is low—that is, if the behavior is very infrequent— our ability to predict that behavior will be very limited (Grove & Meehl, 1996).

From a research perspective, there is yet another problem that limits our ability to predict violence: It is rare to be able to study the full range of potentially violent offenders. Some people serving time in prisons and hospitals are consistently violent. For obvious reasons, these are exactly the people who tend not to be released into the community. Consequently, it is usually the people who are less likely to be violent who are released and then studied by researchers. Put differently, the people whose violence is easiest to predict are generally not included in research studies. We simply don't want to risk releasing them into the community.

The realistic goal of prediction is to use the best data available to arrive at a probability estimate of the likelihood of future violence. That estimate should typically be accompanied by recommendations on how to reduce the risk of violence (Webster, 1998). Such recommendations help to shift the focus from prediction of violence to prevention of violence.

THE LIST OF RISK FACTORS

Despite the inherent difficulty of predicting violence, the enterprise has seen significant advances during the past three decades. If you think for a few minutes, you can probably generate a fairly long list of factors that might plausibly be related to future violent behavior. During the past few decades, researchers have sifted through data to find the best predictors of violence. Several useful predictors have been identified. In one recent review, Kevin Douglas and Christopher Webster distinguished between three broad categories of risk factors ("markers") associated with violent behavior: historical markers, dynamic markers, and risk management markers (Douglas & Webster, 1999).

Historical Markers.   Most of the useful predictors are historical in nature. Such predictors are static in the sense that they don't change. They are part of the person's history or they can't be changed through intervention. Douglas and Webster place several factors in this category: past violent behavior, young age, instability in social relationships, job instability, abuse of alcohol and/or other drugs, major mental disorder, psychopathy, early maladjustment at home or school, attempted or actual escapes from psychiatric facilities, and personality disorder.

Past behavior is often one of the strongest predictors of future behavior, so it is not surprising that past violence helps to predict future violence. Being young (generally classified as under the age of 30) is associated with violent behavior. Especially at risk are people whose first act of violence was committed at a young age. Consistent conflict or disturbance in personal relationships—for example, being abusive towards a spouse, or an inability to maintain lasting relationships—turns up as a solid correlate of later violence. The next predictor is childhood maladjustment. Such maladjustment encompasses disturbed family relationships, such as being removed from parental care before age 16, being subjected to cruelty or physical abuse from caregivers, and failing at school or being expelled from school because of behavior problems. Reliance on drugs may be associated with violence because distressed people may use drugs to relieve their own suffering and drug use may lower inhibitions against violence (Douglas & Webster, 1999).

The remaining factors in the "historical" category—personality disorder, major mental disorder, and psychopathy—all indicate impaired psychological functioning. Personality disorders include antisocial traits (being manipulative, irresponsible, and exploitive of others) while major disorders involve schizophrenics who suffer from paranoid delusions that others are conspiring to do them harm. Finally, psychopathy is a distinctive, extreme form of antisocial disorder characterized by a lack of empathy for others and a lack of remorse for cruel or violent behavior. Although psychopaths tend to be glib and superficially charming, they also tend to be dishonest, manipulative, and unwilling to accept responsibility for their antisocial behavior (Hare, 1996). Psychopaths are especially difficult to treat. Indeed, some forms of therapy actually appear to make things worse by allowing psychopaths to hone their skills of manipulating others (Hart, 1998).

Dynamic Markers.   Dynamic predictors fluctuate over time. Moods, attitudes, and thought processes don't remain fixed over time and can be responsive to treatment. A major dynamic factor is lack of insight into oneself or others. People who become violent tend to have less awareness of their mental disorder and tend to lack awareness into the motives and behaviors of others. They also tend not to recognize their need for treatment. In an interesting series of studies illustrating one aspect of this lack of insight, Ken Dodge and his colleagues studied violent adolescents (Dodge, Price, Bachorowski, & Newman, 1990). As compared to typical adolescents, violent adolescents were much more likely to attribute hostile intent to others. Behaviors (facial expressions, statements, gestures) that most people interpreted as neutral and nonthreatening were viewed as hostile and provocative by violent adolescents. Other researchers have found that to justify their actions, violent youths often report that their victims "brought it on themselves," or deserved to be the targets of violence, or did not suffer greatly from being attacked (Henderson & Hewstone, 1984). Not surprisingly, persistent strong feelings of anger and hostility are consistently related to violent behavior. People who are physically aggressive tend to have more intense feelings of anger and hostility and tend to act impulsively on those feelings (Novaco, 1994).

What is called "psychiatric symptomatology" is also a dynamic factor. Sometimes psychiatric symptoms are "active" in the sense that they are readily apparent in a person's thoughts and behavior. At other times, symptoms may be dormant. Symptoms can sometimes be quieted by medication and some types of symptoms follow a cyclical pattern, waxing and waning over time. Especially important are what have been called threat/control-override (TCO) symptoms (Link & Stueve, 1994). TCO symptoms refer to beliefs—common in schizophrenics—that other people or forces are controlling one's thoughts or implanting thoughts in one's mind. Paranoids believe that other people want to do them harm. This perceived threat from others overrides self-control. When someone who is already suspicious and fearful of others starts to hear voices commanding him or her to act violently, violent behavior is likely to follow. Other symptoms such as sadistic fantasies, intrusive homicidal thoughts, self-injury, and suicide attempts are also associated with violence (Bonta, Law, & Hanson, 1998).

Impulsivity is the inability to exert control over one's emotions, thoughts, and behaviors. Particularly when it is expressed as a lack of control over anger, impulsivity can lead directly to violence (Barratt, 1994). A final marker in this category is lack of responsiveness to treatment. Some psychiatric patients may lack the ability to benefit from treatment, others may not be motivated to change, and some may deteriorate after release from an institution. Many people who are released from psychiatric institutions simply stop taking their medication.

Risk Management Markers.   Violence is also a function of how well the adjustment of a potentially violent person is managed after that person leaves a treatment facility. The general finding here is simple and logical: Stable, supportive post-release environments lower the risk of violence. To the degree that the person has adequate housing and is capable of managing basic necessities like food and finances, the risk of violence is reduced. Post-release treatment is also critical. Those at highest risk for violence require more intensive post-release supervision and treatment. James Ogloff and Kevin Douglas (1995) point out that treatment plans after release must address the specific needs of each person. Release into an environment that includes easy access to guns or drugs lowers the barriers against violence.

The social environment can either encourage or discourage violence. Antisocial peers may entice a released patient into violent behavior, while a supportive network of friends and relatives may keep violent tendencies in check. What appears to be key is not the size of the social network, but whether the people in that network are kind, sympathetic, and skilled at dealing with the person at risk (Estroff & Zimmer, 1994).

The social network can harm as well as help—disappointment with family members or frequent arguments may elevate the risk of violence. The general level of stress created by less-than-optimal living situations increases the likelihood of violence. So does failure to continue taking medication or failure to continue therapy. Finally, lack of availability of follow-up care in the community contributes strongly to all of these problems.

Helping Clinicians Use the Markers. Several techniques have been devised to help psychologists and others make the prediction process more systematic and reliable. For example, the Historical, Clinical, and Risk Management-20 (HCR-20), the Violence Risk Appraisal Guide (VRAG), and the Violence Prediction Scheme (VPS) are attempts to improve predictions by helping decision makers identify and combine factors known to be associated with later violence (Douglas & Webster, 1999). The VRAG asks clinicians to assess people at risk for violence in 12 different areas (e.g., diagnosis of schizophrenia, history of property crimes, psychopathy, alcohol abuse) and using the HCR-20 requires rating the person on 20 scales. These risk assessment schemes improve predictions by forcing clinical psychologists to attend to characteristics that are reliably associated with violence. Once a person has been evaluated using these assessment tools, numerical ratings for each risk factor are mathematically combined to generate a prediction.

In 2001, a prominent team of researchers funded by the MacArthur Foundation published a book describing a massive study of the relationship between mental disorder and violence. In summarizing the ability of clinicians to make accurate predictions, the researchers reached the following conclusion:

> It is no longer reasonable to expect clinicians unaided to be able to identify the variables that may be influential for a particular person, integrate that information, and arrive at a valid estimate of the person's risk for violence. . . . At best, predictions will involve approximations of the degree of risk presented by a person, presented as a range rather than a single number, with the recognition that not every person thus classified, even one accurately determined to be in a high risk group, will commit a violent act (Monahan et al., 2001, p. 143).

JURORS' REACTIONS TO
RISK ASSESSMENT EVIDENCE

• •

This chapter began with a description of the *Tarasoff* case. When therapists or psychiatric hospital administrators are sued for releasing someone who later becomes violent, an important issue involves how a jury will respond to such a case. Will they conclude that the therapist should have known that the patient would become violent? In an interesting study of this issue, mock jurors read descriptions of a *Tarasoff*-like case where a potentially violent patient made a threat during therapy. The therapist took the threats seriously and took appropriate steps to prevent the threatened violence. But the main determinant of whether or not the therapist was judged to be negligent by mock jurors was not what the therapist did, but what the patient did—whether or not he carried out his threat of violence. When the case description did not say whether or not the patient later became violent, only 9% of mock jurors judged the therapist to be negligent. If the patient did not become violent, the therapist was found negligent by only 6% of mock jurors. However, when the patient did become violent, 24% of mock jurors found the therapist negligent (LaBine & LaBine, 1996). Even though the therapist's behavior was identical in the three case descriptions, the ratings of negligence varied dramatically. When the patient later became violent, the actions of the therapist were rated as less reasonable, and the violence was rated as more foreseeable. It appears that the mock jurors in this study reasoned backward. That is, because they already knew the outcome (that the patient did, in fact, act on his threats), jurors believed that the outcome should have been foreseeable. This is an illustration of a general tendency known as the "hindsight bias" (Fischoff, 1975). After an event has happened, people tend to overestimate how easy it would have been to anticipate that event. In retrospect, what actually happened seems unsurprising and predictable. This is problematic in cases involving the prediction of dangerousness, because a judge or jury only hears about a case after a great harm has been done.

As noted earlier, actuarial methods (informed by research and using statistical techniques) produce more accurate predictions than clinical judgments based on intuition and professional experience. However, the ideographic, individualized nature of a clinical prediction may be more appealing to jurors and judges. Daniel Krauss and Bruce Sales (2001) conducted an experiment to see how mock jurors responded to expert testimony about dangerousness in the context of a realistic sentencing trial. In some conditions, an expert testified about the future dangerousness of a defendant based on clinical methods, and in other conditions an expert testified about dangerousness based on actuarial methods. Expert testimony based on each method was then challenged in one of four ways: ineffective cross-examination, effective cross-examination, a competing expert who used the same prediction method but reached the opposite conclusion, or a competing expert who used the alternative prediction method and reached the opposite conclusion. Results indicated that clinical testimony had a significantly greater impact on jurors' ratings of dangerousness than did actuarial testimony. Mock jurors rated clinical testimony as more influential and persuasive. They also rated it as just as scientific and credible as actuarial testimony. Cross-examination or a competing expert did undercut the persuasiveness of both types of testimony. However, clinical testimony withstood such attacks better—jurors' faith in the clinical prediction was less shaken by cross-examination or by competing expert testimony.

Although actuarial methods produce better predictions, a clinical psychologist who testifies in great detail about a particular defendant and then makes a prediction based on professional experience and judgment is more likely to be believed by jurors. Clinical testimony seems more specific, is easier to understand, and appears to be more directly relevant to the defendant on trial. In comparison, actuarial testimony may seem more abstract, harder to understand, and less directly relevant to the particular defendant jurors are being asked to judge.

TREATMENT TO REDUCE THE RISK OF VIOLENCE

Some scholars have argued that, instead of focusing our efforts on trying to predict violence, it might be more productive to focus on preventing and managing the risk of violence in the community. Several researchers have investigated what can be done to help mentally disordered criminals adapt successfully to the inevitable stressors of life outside an institution. In a review of treatment programs, Grant Harris and Marnie Rice (1997) found that effective treatment—that is, treatment that promotes better adjustment and improves public safety—tends to be comprehensive. The best programs are assertive about assisting offenders in several domains of life. Some programs provide help with housing and getting a job, and also provide training and advising for family members. Comprehensive programs help to improve social skills and impulse control of offenders and also offer services to prevent social isolation. All treatment must be tailored to the legal status of the client. Offenders who are hospitalized because they have been deemed to be incompetent to stand trial should be given shorter hospital stays and more focused treatment designed to restore competence. In contrast, offenders who have been found NGRI need longer-term treatment that will equip them for eventual release into the community (Heilbrun & Griffin, 1999).

Communication is a key component of all post-release treatment programs. People running the programs are obliged to communicate with legal officials about behaviors that may violate conditions of release or threaten public safety (e.g., contact with a former victim). Clear communication with the client is also essential. Kirk Heilbrun and Patricia Griffin (1999) emphasize that there ought to be a specific contract with the client. That contract should list required behaviors and specify the consequences of failing to comply with the contract. Required behaviors might include taking medications, showing up for scheduled sessions with therapists, not taking illegal drugs, and not possessing a weapon. An offender might also be required to find employment and housing. Once offenders demonstrate that they can function well under restrictive conditions after release, they can gradually be given more freedom. For example, they may first be held in a restrictive hospital, later in a hospital that allows occasional travel from the institution, still later at a supervised community home or "halfway house," and, finally, they will be permitted to live in the community but still be required to visit local treatment centers regularly.

Kirk Heilbrun and his associates have also emphasized the importance of risk management. If the goal is effective risk management, ongoing monitoring of the client is essential. The client must be frequently reassessed to determine if the risk of violence has changed. Further, the focus must be on dynamic risk factors that might be changed through treatment, and there must be interventions available for lowering risk if it becomes high (Heilbrun, Nezu, Keeney, Chung, & Wasserman, 1998).

CHILD CUSTODY AND PARENTAL COMPETENCE
• •

Sometimes psychologists are asked to make predictions about what kind of child custody arrangement will be best for children whose parents are going through a divorce. If one of the parents is mentally ill, physically or emotionally abusive, or otherwise incompetent to raise children, the task of deciding custody is greatly simplified—the children go with the fit parent. But far more frequently, courts must try to structure a fair custody arrangement that takes into account the needs of the children, as well as the desires of two parents who may despise one another but love their children. The "best" arrangement for a particular child is the one that will promote happiness and healthy development many years into the future.

First, a basic distinction: Courts distinguish between legal custody and physical custody. Legal custody concerns the rights and responsibilities of parents. For example, a parent with legal custody has the authority to decide which school a child should attend and, if necessary, what sort of medical treatment a child should receive. Such decisions must be negotiated if parents share legal custody. Physical custody refers to how much time a child spends with each parent. If parents share physical custody, the child lives with each parent some of the time. For example, an eight-year-old may live with his mother most of the time but stay with his father every Wednesday, every other weekend, and most of the summer. The basic alternative to joint (or shared) custody is sole custody. In sole custody, one parent has legal and physical custody while the other is generally given some rights to visit the child at regular intervals.

In theory, it may seem ideal to have a child spend the same amount of time with each parent, but this arrangement is often difficult from a practical standpoint. It can be hard on a child to spend alternate weeks with each parent if one of the parents lives far from the child's school and friends. Still, joint custody is increasingly common. Its primary advantage is that it ensures that both parents remain closely involved in raising the child. This may be psychologically beneficial to both children and parents. A secondary benefit of joint custody is that financial support of the child is more stable than it would be in a sole custody arrangement where the custodial parent may have to continually seek child support payments from an embittered parent who does not have custody rights. Researchers have found that mothers, fathers, and children usually prefer joint to sole custody, and joint custody tends to improve family adjustment and cohesiveness (Kelly, 1993). However, despite these considerable benefits, joint custody is not always the best arrangement. A significant disadvantage is that it requires communication, cooperation, and coordination between two parents who may dislike one another.

Sole custody is preferred when one parent is clearly incompetent, addicted to drugs, or physically or psychologically abusive toward the children. However, even in cases where both parents are competent and caring, it is sometimes argued that sole custody is in a child's best interest. A child with a strong need for stability may benefit by continuing to live in the family home with one custodial parent. Also, a sensitive child may be shielded from the conflicts that often arise if two hostile parents who share custody must continue to interact with one another to arrange visits and make decisions about the child. Indeed, there is evidence that hostile, conflict-ridden relationships between parents are associated with emotional disruption for the child and poorer long-term adjustment (Hetherington, Bridges, & Insabella, 1998). Consequently, neither joint custody nor sole custody is best in all situations.

Most custody decisions are made without resorting to litigation. If the divorcing parents both agree to a particular custody arrangement (on their own or with the help of a mediator), a judge will almost always endorse that arrangement. Non-litigated decisions typically involve some form of joint custody. Child custody disputes occur in only about 10% of divorces. Among divorcing families who turn to the courts to decide child custody, about a third of those families can be described as engaging in extreme levels of conflict (Pruett & Hoganbruen, 1998). The intensity of negative feelings in these relatively rare cases puts children at acute risk for emotional damage.

THE EVOLUTION OF CHILD CUSTODY STANDARDS

Determining child custody used to be simple. Under English common law, children were considered property and women were not permitted to own property. Consequently, fathers were automatically entitled to custody of their children (Bratt, 1979). By the 1800s, the idea of children as mere property had been replaced by the idea that childhood was an important stage of life that contributed to the development of the adult person. By the end of the nineteenth century, the "tender years" doctrine had become the prevailing standard for deciding child custody. The doctrine was articulated in 1899 in the case of *People v. Hickey*:

> . . . an infant of tender years will generally be left with the mother, where no objection is shown to exist as to her, even if the father be without blame, because of the father's inability to bestow on it that tender care which nature requires, and which it is the peculiar province of the mother to supply; and this rule will apply with much force in case of female children of a more advanced age (Einhorn, 1986, p. 121).

Though the doctrine now seems sexist, it seemed perfectly natural and self-evident at the time it was written. It was not until the middle of the twentieth century that "tender years" was seriously challenged on the grounds that it violated the Fourteenth Amendment's guarantee of equal protection under the law. Fathers began to assert their rights to custody and to challenge the sexually stereotyped view of parent-child relations implied by the old doctrine. Although the tender years doctrine has been abandoned, the tendency to award custody to the mother persists.

Current law in most states now asks that child custody arrangements serve "the best interests of the child." In some ways, this is a laudable and elegant standard—there is no presumption that either the father or the mother is entitled to custody, and the needs of parents and other interested parties are secondary to what is best for the children. The overriding goal is to place the child in the most favorable environment, the environment that will promote healthy development. But there are at least three problems with the "best interests" standard. The first is vagueness. Here, as in other areas of law, vagueness places discretion in the hands of judges who must make the final custody decision. And, if judges strongly favor maternal custody, the vague "best interests" standard may not be a great step forward from the tender years doctrine. The second problem is that the best interests standard may unintentionally escalate conflicts between parents. A divorcing parent who is seeking custody of a child gains an advantage by exaggerating every fault and failing of the other parent. If, for example, the father portrays the mother as irresponsible or immoral, he might be more likely to win custody of the child. The lingering anger and distrust created by such allegations can disrupt the child's post-divorce adjustment. A third problem with the best interests standard is that it asks courts to predict the future. Judges must imagine what form of custody will promote healthy development of the child years or even decades after the decision is made.

To assist judges and to reduce the vagueness of the best interests standard, many states have adopted what are called preferred custody arrangements. This means that a particular type of custody—usually either joint custody or primary caretaker custody—should be ordered *unless* it can be shown that this preferred arrangement is not in the child's best interest. Preferred arrangements may have the benefit of discouraging litigation because parents and their lawyers know in advance how custody disputes are likely to be resolved (Cochran, 1991).

The primary caretaker preference suggests that courts should award primary custody to the parent who has been primarily responsible for raising the child prior to the divorce. Courts have held that "continuity of care" and the "warmth, consistency, and continuity of the primary relationship" is critical to the well-being of the child (Cochran, 1991). In assessing who is the primary caretaker, courts look at which parent buys and washes the child's clothes, who bathes and grooms the child, who disciplines the child, who prepares meals for and feeds the child, who helps with homework, who puts the child to bed at night and wakes him or her up in the morning, who cares for the child when ill and takes the child to the physician, and who arranges for the child to spend time with friends. Because women still tend to assume the primary caretaker role more often than men, states that favor the primary caretaker standard tend to award custody to mothers in 84% of cases (Hetherington, Bridges, & Insabella, 1998).

In reaching decisions about which parent should be awarded custody, the values and the biases of the judge sometimes intrude on the custody decision. For example, in the case of *Palmore v. Sidoti* (1984), a judge took custody of a white girl away from her mother and granted custody to the father because the mother had married a black man. The judge's decision was based on his belief that the girl would suffer from "social stigmatization" as a consequence of living in a mixed-race household. Although the ruling was upheld by a Florida appeals court, the U.S. Supreme Court eventually overturned the decision, holding that "custody decisions cannot turn on racial considerations."

In the past, sexual orientation was an explicit consideration in child custody decisions. Gay parents were disfavored, and homosexuality was viewed as an indication of a lack of moral fitness. These views have changed and, currently, 12 states have laws that homosexuality per se should *not* be considered a factor in custody decisions. In the 1994 case of *Bottoms v. Bottoms,* a Virginia court ordered Sharon Bottoms to relinquish custody of her two-year-old son. Sharon's mother, the boy's grandmother, had filed to gain custody, claiming that Sharon's lesbian relationship made her an unfit mother. A Virginia appellate court later overturned the decision and returned the child to Sharon Bottoms. The appellate court cited an *amicus curiae* brief submitted by APA and other professional organizations. That brief summarized research findings indicating that children raised by homosexual parents are no more likely than other children to become homosexual, are no different in their social relationships, and are no more likely to be stigmatized or harassed because of their parent's homosexuality. Many states currently allow sexual orientation to be considered if it is linked to a claim of emotional harm to the child.

RESEARCH ON CHILDREN'S RESPONSES TO DIVORCE

For a variety of reasons, it is difficult to conduct research on how divorce affects the development of children. First, a full understanding of the adjustment process requires "longitudinal" research that tracks the development of children over time. It is very difficult to collect data from parents and children over a period of years. Second, it is hard to distinguish between psychological problems that predate the divorce and problems that were caused by the divorce. For example, written records may indicate that a child was having disciplinary problems at school prior to the divorce. But it is hard to know whether those problems were caused by conflict in the home or difficulties at school. Finally, the outcome of interest—healthy adjustment—is difficult to measure. The multifaceted concept of "adjustment" may include satisfying social relationships, self-esteem, feelings of contentment, and school achievement, as well as the relative absence of psychological problems such as depression and aggressive behavior. Since no one measure can capture every facet of adjustment, researchers usually try to use batteries of psychological tests, as well as in-depth interviews.

Despite the formidable obstacles to research on the effects of divorce, there are now several longitudinal studies and many comparisons of same-age children from divorced and intact families. The positive news from this research is that the great majority of children whose parents divorce manage to adapt and to grow into psychologically healthy adults. Of course, this is not to diminish the psychological, social, emotional, and even financial disruptions often produced by divorce. Problems appear to be especially intense during the year following divorce, when feelings of loss, separation, anger, and depression may be exacerbated by dealing with the logistics of setting up separate households and shuttling the child between parents (Kelly, 1993). Sometimes serious problems persist. A major review of research found that about 20% to 25% of children of divorced parents experienced significant ongoing emotional, social, and behavioral problems. In comparison, only about 10% of children from intact families showed similar levels of distress (Hetherington, Bridges, & Insabella, 1998). Later, as children pass through adolescence and become young adults, children of divorce are somewhat more likely to feel dissatisfied with their lives. Some research suggests that they are less trusting of others and feel increased anxiety about the possibility of abandonment and betrayal (Wallerstein & Blakeslee, 1989). Compared to children of non-divorced parents, children of divorced parents who grow up and marry are more likely to divorce. Finally, it should be mentioned that divorce can occasionally be positive. For a minority of children, divorce brings a welcome relief from serious interpersonal conflict and emotional turbulence (Leupnitz, 1982).

It is important to ask whether research can tell us what type of custody will serve the children's "best interests." Clearly, the ideal custody arrangement is one where both parents are strongly committed to their children, and where each parent is also committed to helping the children maintain healthy relationships with the other parent. That ideal is often difficult to achieve. But psychological research does give us some clues about how to promote healthy adjustment.

In a recent review, Marsha Liss and Marcia McKinley-Pace (1999) summarize research findings that should be considered when courts decide on custody arrangements. That research indicates that the strength and stability of personal relationships is the factor that most clearly affects adjustment during childhood. There is ample research attesting to the benefits of stability and continuity in relationships with parents, siblings, and members of an extended family. A core developmental task during early childhood is the construction of strong emotional ties with other people. Studies of children who do not develop secure attachments to a parent show that such children suffer from increased anxiety, weaker relationships with peers, decreased self-confidence, poorer social skills, less exploration of their environments, and more difficulties in adjusting to school (Ellis, 2000). Further, these problems are not easily corrected in later childhood. Research also indicates that relationship disruptions following divorce often decrease a child's motivation and achievement in school, promote earlier sexual activity, and are associated with earlier marriage and increased probability of divorce. Divorce also leads to relationship disruptions indirectly by increasing the probability of changes in school, and increasing the amount of time young children spend in day care (Kelly, 1993).

One line of research suggests that maintaining contact with an extended family can help to buffer children against the negative effects of divorce. If a child has strong relationships with several adults, that child is able to turn to those adults for support before, during, and after divorce. Relationships with grandparents or other members of the extended family may also play an important role in a child's adjustment after divorce. There is considerable variation in the importance of bonds with the extended family. If pre-divorce contact with grandparents has been frequent and satisfying to the child, then it may be appropriate for a judge to consider how that bond can be preserved following the divorce (Liss & McKinley-Pace, 1999). There is even research suggesting that sibling relationships ought to be given some weight in custody decisions. If children feel isolated from friends following a divorce, they often rely on brothers or sisters for emotional support. More generally, siblings help each other develop social skills and problem-solving skills. Of course, discussion of these family relationships begs the question of what constitutes a family. Research indicates that children tend to define family in terms of emotional ties rather than biological relationships. It may be the "psychological family" that is particularly important to preserve in the wake of divorce (Gindes, 1995).

The role of the child's personality also plays a role in adaptation after divorce. Our personalities shape our social relationships and our close relationships shape our personalities. Some researchers have identified a cluster of personality traits termed "resilience" that may be related to adaptation to divorce. In a large longitudinal study of every child born on the Hawaiian island of Kauai in 1955, 201 children were identified as being at risk because of exposure to poverty and severe family discord. Yet, despite being at high risk, about a third of these children grew up without significant psychological problems (Werner, 1993). Such "resilient" children may be able to thrive during and after divorce because of their abilities to elicit positive interactions from others, to maintain or expand relationships with supportive adults, and to find caretakers who nurture their self-esteem and feelings of competence. These findings underscore the importance of making case-by-case determinations of child custody. Judges and evaluators need to take into account the individual personality of each child and to craft custody arrangements that preserve supportive relationships with adults.

THE PSYCHOLOGIST'S CONTRIBUTION TO CUSTODY DECISIONS

The Uniform Marriage and Divorce Act of 1976 proposed five criteria to be used for determining custody: (1) the wishes of the child's parents, (2) the wishes of the child, (3) the relationships between the child, his parents, siblings, and any other person who significantly affects the child's best interests, (4) the child's adjustment to home, school, and community and (5) the physical and mental health of everyone involved with the child. Of course, these criteria are inescapably psychological. They concern assessments of the quality of interpersonal relationships, emotional attachments between parent and child, coping ability, and consistency and stability of relationships over time. Courts must address psychological issues with or without the assistance of psychological experts. Although the opinions of psychological experts are likely to be much less precise than we would like, they probably improve the quality of custody decisions by adding information to the decision-making process.

Sometimes a clinical psychologist acts as an adviser to the court, and sometimes psychologists who have different views of what is best for a particular child will offer opposing testimony in support of the father or the mother. Often, judges appoint their own psychological expert to conduct a custody evaluation on behalf of the court. It is also possible for each side to hire its own expert or for both sides to contribute money to hire a shared, independent expert (Weissman, 1991). In their thorough analysis of how mental health experts are used in child custody disputes, Gary Melton, John Petrila, Norman Poythress, and Christopher Slobogin (1997) argue that such experts simply do not possess enough scientifically valid evidence to make useful recommendations about many issues surrounding custody. However, they also argue that mental health professionals can make productive use of their expertise in dealing with people during times of emotional stress. That expertise can be put to work gathering information from parents and children in the midst of a family trauma. Psychologists working for the court can be called upon to investigate family relationships and to identify the strengths and weaknesses of each parent.

Psychologists who are asked to conduct an assessment should rely on multiple sources of information. American Psychological Association Guidelines suggest that custody evaluators gather information relevant to three issues: (1) the psychological needs and development of the child, (2) the strengths and weaknesses of each parent, and (3) the interactions and relationships between every member of the family (APA, 1994). A well-conducted evaluation might begin with an interview with each parent and each child. To further assess the relationships between parent and child, the evaluator will usually set up a situation where each parent can be observed interacting with each child (e.g., a parent and child might be asked to plan a vacation together). To supplement information gathered from interviews and direct observation, written records relevant to the custody decision are then reviewed. Relevant documents might include children's school records (e.g., report cards, attendance records, disciplinary reports), records of medical treatment for physical or mental health problems, and letters or other written communication submitted in the case. Sometimes there are also interviews with people who may have observed or interacted with the family over time: grandparents, aunts and uncles, nannies, teachers, and the family physician. Finally, the psychologist is likely to administer standardized psychological tests designed to assess the mental health of the parents and children. On average, evaluators spend 26.4 hours on each evaluation (Ackerman & Ackerman, 1997).

Most psychologists who conduct custody evaluations use general tests of psychological functioning, with the MMPI or the revised MMPI-2 being the most frequently used scales (LaFortune & Carpenter, 1998). However, this reliance on general psychological tests may be changing. A few scales have now been specifically developed for the task of custody evaluations. The two most prominent are the Bricklin Perceptual Scales (BPS) and the Ackerman-Schoendorf Scales for Parent Evaluation of Custody (ASPECT).

The BPS has the ambitious but ambiguous goal of evaluating the child's ". . . gut-level, unconscious perceptions of parental behavior" (Bricklin, 1984). The child is asked 32 questions about each parent. The questions attempt to tap into the child's perceptions of each parent's supportiveness, competence, consistency, and possession of desirable traits. An additional measure developed by Bricklin—the Perception of Relationships Test, or PORT—attempts to measure how strongly the child seeks emotional closeness and positive interactions with each parent. Clearly, it is important to assess parenting ability and emotional attachment between parent and child when trying to decide custody arrangements. However, serious questions have been raised about the scientific validity and reliability of both the BPS and the PORT. Until much additional data has been collected and analyzed, it will not be clear how much confidence should be placed in the Bricklin measures (Nicholson, 1999).

The ASPECT consists of 56 items designed to detect negative indicators such as parental drug abuse and physical or sexual abuse, as well as positive indicators such as involvement with the child and good social judgment. The psychologist rates each parent on each of the 56 items. Those ratings are based on information gathered through interviews, observations, answers on a questionnaire, and a battery of psychological tests administered to children or parents. The evaluator combines the ratings to yield an overall index of each parent's effectiveness. Although the structured approach offered by the ASPECT may eventually improve the usefulness of custody recommendations, the validity and reliability of the ASPECT have not yet been convincingly demonstrated. Several thoughtful reviews of these measures caution psychologists that results should be viewed with some skepticism (Arditti, 1995). Although both the BPS and the ASPECT provide a structure for gathering and distilling relevant information, neither test has yet been shown to have impressive validity or reliability (Nicholson, 1999).

When a psychologist writes a child custody evaluation report for the judge, he or she must strive for scientific objectivity and try to remain neutral (Stahl, 1994). The goal should not be to provide ultimate opinion testimony about the best custody arrangement, but to clearly and fully describe the character of the family relationships. However, as in other areas, this ideal is often difficult to achieve because many judges want psychologists to simply recommend the best custody arrangement.

Occasionally, after going through the process of assessment, couples decide to opt out of litigation and resolve the custody dispute themselves.

CUSTODY MEDIATION AS AN ALTERNATIVE TO LITIGATION

Fights for child custody create emotional trauma that entangles children as well as parents. In an effort to contain the damage caused by bitter, protracted court battles, many states have enacted "mandatory mediation" laws. These laws require couples seeking a divorce to first attempt to reach a settlement with the help of a mediator. Mediation has the added benefit of lowering court costs and generally eliminates the need for a full psychological assessment. In many cases, mediation helps to de-escalate family conflict and clear the way for a custody agreement.

A mediator is a neutral third party who brings the couple together in a nonadversarial setting. Mediators may be psychologists, social workers, lawyers, or specially trained laypersons. The aim is to create a divorce settlement and custody arrangement that both parents can endorse. The mediator does not impose an agreement, but tries to create an environment where the parents can craft their own agreement. Compared to a courtroom proceeding, mediation is much less structured and formal. In court, elaborate rules of evidence dictate what information can be considered. Two or more attorneys compete to win the type of custody that favors their client. In contrast, during mediation, any information that might be useful can be considered. Mediation sessions include a single mediator and the two parents. Sometimes lawyers for each parent are also present. What transpires during mediation is confidential, and parents are free to generate a variety of creative custody options.

The goal of mediation is to get parents to rise above their differences and to focus on the needs of their children. The hope is that the private, less adversarial, less formal process of mediation will enable parents to work through differences. When it works well, mediation can begin the process of creating a new, more constructive working relationship between the parents. If the couple cannot reach an agreement through mediation, the case is then referred to a judge who decides on a custody arrangement, as well as division of property and child support payments. Just over half the custody cases referred to mediation are settled through mediation. The most common outcome is the same in mediation and litigation—joint legal custody, with the mother getting physical custody (Pearson & Thoennes, 1990).

Although advocates of mediation have claimed that the technique produces a variety of benefits, there is relatively little systematic research on the topic. In a series of well-conducted studies of mediation, Robert Emery and his colleagues arranged to have divorcing couples randomly assigned to either mediation or litigation. Overall, the researchers found that mediation led to custody agreements more quickly and in fewer sessions. Couples who went through mediation were generally more satisfied with the custody settlement, although there was a gender difference: Fathers who used mediation expressed more satisfaction than fathers who litigated, but mothers expressed roughly equal satisfaction with mediation or litigation. Mothers felt that the mediation process was better for the children, but also felt they might have done better in litigation (Emery, Matthews, & Kitzmann, 1994; Emery, Matthews, & Wyer, 1991). This finding and other findings suggest that preexisting power inequalities may resurface in the mediation setting and lead to unfair outcomes. A skilled mediator may be able to neutralize these power disparities, but not all mediators are highly skilled. In contrast, although not all lawyers are highly skilled, litigation at least provides both fathers and mothers with their own advocates.

Sometimes mediation should be avoided. In cases where there has been wife abuse, mediation may lead to harm by providing the abuser with continued access to his victim. Also, in cases where the wife or the husband is not fully competent—one or the other is severely depressed, mentally ill, mentally retarded, or under the influence of drugs—it is unlikely that the impaired parent will be able to effectively represent him or herself during mediation.

Looking across the few studies that have evaluated the effectiveness of mediation, we can draw a few tentative conclusions. Compared to litigation, child custody mediation saves time and money, leads to greater satisfaction with the divorce process, and results in more awards of joint custody (as compared to sole custody) and more reliable child support payments (Liss & McKinley-Pace, 1999). Some scholars have hypothesized that, as a consequence of increased satisfaction, joint custody, and reliable support, there may be greater parental involvement and improved child adjustment following divorce (Beck & Sales, 2000). Also, because mediation is faster than litigation, it may shorten the period of intense conflict between parents. Mediation may also resolve uncertainty about living arrangements more quickly, which may be a relief to children. However, as one recent review points out, as yet there is little data to support the claim that mediation leads to improved emotional and psychological health in children (Emery, 1994).

IN CONCLUSION

Although it is impossible to predict the future, the legal system is sometimes required to try. With or without the help of psychologists and other social scientists, the legal system will continue to make predictions about whether people are likely to become dangerous in the future, and about which custody arrangement will promote the well-being of children for years to come. These consequential predictions ought to be based on the best information currently available. The research summarized above will not enable courts to make perfect predictions. However, knowledge accumulated through research will continue to inform and improve those predictions.

Readings to Supplement This Chapter

Articles

Beck, C. J. A., & Sales, B. D. (2000). A critical reappraisal of divorce mediation research and policy. *Psychology, Public Policy, and Law, 6,* 989–1056.

Edens, J. F., Petrila, J., & Buffington-Vollum, J. K. (2001). Psychopathy and the death penalty: Can the psychopathy checklist-revised identify offenders who represent "a continuing threat to society?" *Journal of Psychiatry and Law, 29,* 433–481.

Gale, J., Mowery, R. L., Herrman, M. S., & Hollett, N. L. (2002). Considering effective divorce mediation: Three potential factors. *Conflict Resolution Quarterly, 19,* 389–420.

Krauss, D. A., & Sales, B. D. (2000). Legal standards, expertise, and experts in the resolution of contested child custody cases. *Psychology, Public Policy, and Law, 6,* 843–879.

Kropp, P. R., Hart, S. D., & Lyon, D. R. (2002). Risk assessment of stalkers: Some problems and some solutions. *Criminal Justice and Behavior, 29,* 590–616.

Books

Monahan, J., Steadman, H. J., Silver, E., Appelbaum, P. S., Robbins, P. C., Mulvey, E. P., Roth, L. H., Grisso, T., & Banks, S. (2001). *Rethinking risk assessment: The MacArthur study of mental disorder and violence.* Oxford University Press.

Beck, C. J. A., & Sales, B. D. (2001). *Family mediation: Facts, myths and future prospects.* Washington, DC: American Psychological Association.

8

Workplace Law: Harassment, Discrimination, and Fairness

Chapter Outline
● ●

The Evolution of Sexual Discrimination Law
Sexual Harassment: Prevalence and Perceptions
The Legal Boundaries of Sexual Harassment
Current Status of Harassment Law
    Sexual Harassment Lawsuits
The Psychology of Sexual Harassment
    Some Causes
    Some Effects
    Prevention
A Broader Look at Workplace Discrimination
    Racial Discrimination in the Workplace
The Psychology of Perceived Fairness
    Three Models for Allocating Rewards
    Research on Perceptions of Fairness
In Conclusion

It was a sort of love letter, though less romantic and gushy than most. The man, an executive at a large company, sent the letter to his beloved—a junior vice president at the same company. He wrote,

> I know this may seem silly or unnecessary to you, but I really want you to give very serious consideration to the matter as it is very important to me. I want to assure you that under no circumstances will I allow our relationship or, should it happen, the end of our relationship, to impact on your job or our working relationship.

Attached to the letter was a copy of the company's sexual harassment policy.

The woman's response was similar in tone:

> My relationship with you has been (and is) voluntary, consensual, and welcome. I also understand that I am free to end this relationship at any time and, in doing so, it will not adversely impact on my job (Hansen, 1998).

The letters—which were suggested by the company's lawyer—were written as part of a "consensual relationship agreement." The hope is that such agreements will help shield companies from sexual harassment lawsuits when a love affair at work ends badly. Their use reflects a growing awareness of the legal risks associated with some types of interactions in the workplace. This chapter explores how the law attempts to regulate decisions and social interactions in the workplace.

THE EVOLUTION OF SEXUAL DISCRIMINATION LAW

Sexual discrimination law was created by a political miscalculation. During congressional debate over the Civil Rights Act of 1964 (known as Title VII), a conservative U.S. Representative named Howard Smith attached an amendment. His amendment added a ban on gender discrimination to Title VII's ban on racial discrimination in employment. Smith hoped that adding sexual discrimination to Title VII would cause the entire bill to go down in defeat. During debate he mockingly suggested that his amendment would "protect our spinster friends." To Smith's surprise, the Civil Rights Act, and his amendment to it, passed. Discrimination based on race and gender became illegal.

In 1979, Yale Law Professor Catharine MacKinnon published her influential book, *Sexual Harassment of Working Women.* Her argument—radical at the time—was that sexual harassment was a form of discrimination. She defined two types of sexual harassment: "quid pro quo" and "hostile environment." Quid pro quo harassment involves a "more or less explicit exchange: the woman must comply sexually or forfeit an employment benefit" (p. 48). For example, a woman might be told that if she fails to submit to a sexual request, she will not be given a coveted job or promotion. The second form of harassment—hostile environment—describes a situation where life is made so difficult for the victim that she can't carry out her job responsibilities. MacKinnon described it this way. "Less clear, and undoubtedly more pervasive, is the situation in which sexual harassment simply makes the work environment unbearable" (p. 49). The two basic forms of sexual harassment identified by MacKinnon are now enshrined in law.

By 1980, the Equal Employment Opportunity Commission (EEOC)—the government agency created to enforce Title VII—issued the first federal guidelines on gender discrimination. Sexual harassment was defined as "unwelcome sexual advances, requests for sexual favors, and other verbal or physical conduct of a sexual nature." "Hostile environment" exists where an employee is subjected to unwelcome sexual conduct that interferes with the performance of work activities or creates an intimidating, hostile, abusive, or offensive work environment. "Quid pro quo" is a stronger form of harassment because it involves direct sexual barter or coercion. An employee is told that in exchange for sexual favors, she will receive a benefit—for example, a bonus, salary increase, promotion, desirable job assignment, or favorable performance evaluation. Alternatively, an employee might be told that she will experience negative consequences if she refuses to submit sexually. These sorts of crude attempts at sexual bargaining are quite rare compared to hostile environment harassment.

EEOC guidelines state that employers have an obligation (an "affirmative duty" in the words of the guidelines) to maintain a workplace free from harassment, intimidation, or insult. Further, employers must act to eliminate harassing practices and to correct the damaging effects of such practices (*EEOC v. Murphy Motor Freight Lines, Inc.,* 1980). Plaintiffs in harassment cases must show that unwelcome verbal and physical behaviors created an intimidating or offensive environment that unreasonably interfered with job performance or restricted employment opportunities. In addition, it must usually be shown that the employer knew or should have known about the harassing conduct but failed to take prompt and appropriate action to remedy the situation (*Burlington Industries v. Ellerth,* 1998; *Faragher v. Boca Raton, Fla.,* 1998).

SEXUAL HARASSMENT: PREVALENCE AND PERCEPTIONS

A precise accounting of how much sexual harassment occurs on the job is difficult for several reasons: Not all studies have asked about the same types of harassment or used the same checklists of harassing behaviors. Also, people are often asked about events dating back several years. Such retrospective reports of harassment may be biased because of distorted memories. Finally, rates of harassment vary across work settings. Some settings are relatively free of harassing behavior, while others are rife with harassment. Despite these difficulties, several clear patterns emerge from the available data. First, virtually every study has found that females are far more likely than males to be the victims of sexual harassment. Overall, women experience harassment at a rate three to four times the rate for men. In large-scale surveys of federal employees in 1981, 1987, and 1994, about 42% of women and 15% of men claimed to have experienced sexual harassment at work during the past two years (U.S. Merit Systems Protection Board, 1995). Similarly, 43% of women lawyers working in large law firms reported being pinched, touched, or cornered in a sexually harassing way by a partner in their firm (Slade, 1994). A 1996 survey of more than 45,000 members of the armed forces found significantly higher rates of reported harassment among military personnel—64% for females and 17% for males during the preceding year (Bastian, Lancaster, & Reyst, 1996). Looking across several studies, Barbara Gutek (1993) estimated that approximately 53% of working women had been sexually harassed by men at some time during their careers and about 9% of working men had been sexually harassed by women at some time during their careers. The most likely targets of harassment are young unmarried women.

A second interesting finding concerns the ratio of men to women in the work setting. Women working in jobs dominated by men (e.g., engineering, truck driving, surgery, construction) are more likely to experience sexual harassment. Work settings where women are a distinct minority tend to be more sexualized than settings where males and females are roughly equal in number. The more sexualized culture of workplaces where men greatly outnumber women is sometimes manifested in the display of posters and calendars depicting women in suggestive dress or poses, sexual jokes, sexual terms and metaphors, and obscene language. Also, men appear to overinterpret sexual behavior. Compared to women, men are more likely to say they have been touched by a coworker in a sexual way, and are more likely to mistake friendly behavior for sexual seduction (Gutek, 1993; Goodman-Delahunty, 1999).

A third conclusion is that when males are victims of harassment, the harassment is slightly more likely to come from another male than from a female. That is, just over half the time, males are harassed by other males. In contrast, when women are the victims, their harassers are other women only about 2% of the time (Waldo, Berdahl, & Fitzgerald, 1998). Male-male harassment appears to have a different character than cross-gender harassment. Male perpetrators tend to harass other men through the use of lewd and obscene comments and through "enforcement of the male gender role" (Foote & Goodman-Delahunty, 1999), that is, by suggesting that another male performs unmanly activities or behaves in an effeminate way. Just over half the time, harassment of men by men involves coworkers rather than a supervisor and subordinate. When men are harassed by women, the harassment generally involves either unwanted sexual attention, or disparaging gender-related comments such as "men only have one thing on their mind," or "men are too clueless and insensitive to make good managers" (Waldo, Berdahl, & Fitzgerald, 1998).

But which behaviors do people label as sexual harassing? At the extremes, there is widespread agreement: Less than 10% of males and females classify flirting, occasional use of coarse language, or nonsexual touching as harassment. But 99% of males and females view sexual bribery (requiring sexual favors in exchange for job benefits) as harassment (Frazier, Cochran, & Olson, 1995). Also, people are more likely to view harassment as serious if the harasser is the victim's boss or someone else who potentially has power over her pay, promotion, or work assignments. There is also widespread agreement that aggressive, unwelcome physical contact—grabbing, groping, sexual touching—

should be defined as illegal harassment. But even though there is near consensus about extreme behaviors, there is considerable disagreement about more ambiguous behaviors—for example, staring, repeated requests for dates, sexual jokes, public displays of calendars depicting swimsuit models, or frequent crude language. These more ambiguous behaviors are perceived somewhat differently by men and women. In a 1998 metanalysis of 111 studies involving more than 34,000 participants, Jeremy Blumenthal found that, across cultures, age groups, and research techniques, women rated ambiguous behaviors as more offensive than did men. But this gender difference is relatively small. In studies using mock jurors, about 10% of the variance in judgments about hostile environment was accounted for by juror gender (Wiener, Watts, Goldkamp, & Gasper, 1995). Again, this small gender difference only emerges in the ambiguous midrange of harassing behavior—If the harassment is severe, both men and women will condemn the behavior and if the harassment is mild, men and women will generally agree that it does not qualify as harassment (Gutek & O'Connor, 1995).

THE LEGAL BOUNDARIES OF SEXUAL HARASSMENT

Just as it is sometimes difficult for the public to agree on which behaviors constitute sexual harassment, it has been difficult for the courts to provide a clear, precise definition of hostile environment harassment. When does boorish, crude, or inappropriate behavior cross a legal line and become illegal sexual harassment? Does telling dirty jokes or repeatedly asking a woman at work for a date constitute harassment? What if a man asks a woman for a date a third time after she has politely declined twice?

Because there is no precise list of sexually harassing behaviors, most courts have relied on a "reasonable person" standard. And because concepts such as "offensive" are inherently subjective, a judgment must be made as to whether other similar people would have experienced the work environment as offensive or hostile. Consequently, a woman alleging sexual harassment must establish that a reasonable person would have found the behavior in question severe enough and pervasive enough to create an abusive working environment (*Harris v. Forklift Systems, Inc.,* 1993; *Oncale v. Sundowner Offshore Services, Inc.,* 1998). By focusing on the reasonable similar person, the law attempts to prevent claims based on trivial or mildly offensive conduct and claims by unusually sensitive employees. Some courts have instructed jurors to interpret evidence from the perspective of a "reasonable woman." This standard was first proposed in 1991, in the case of *Ellison v. Brady.* In that case, the Ninth Circuit Court of Appeals adopted the standard partly in response to research suggesting that males and females have different views of sexual conduct in the workplace. In that case, Kerry Ellison had been harassed by a coworker who wrote her a series of love letters. The court reasoned that women would be more likely than men to view the letters as menacing and disturbing.

Many social scientists have objected to the creation of a "reasonable woman" standard. Barbara Gutek and Maureen O'Connor (1995) have raised several concerns. First, research finds only small differences in how males and females define harassment. Those differences are usually only evident when the incidents are much less severe than those that typically end up in court. Second, the reasonable woman standard is inconsistent with legal standards in other areas of law. For example, courts would be unlikely to consider analogous separate standards for reasonable religious persons or reasonable nonreligious persons. Third, instead of creating a separate standard, it would be more productive to create a consensus about what constitutes sexual harassment. Fourth, it may make more sense to focus on power differences instead of gender differences and to create a "reasonable victim" standard. Gutek and O'Connor argue that the reasonable woman standard inappropriately shifts the focus away from the behavior of the perpetrator toward the behavior of the victim and that distinguishing a reasonable woman from a reasonable person may contribute to sexist attitudes by suggesting that we need to treat women as weak, fragile, oversensitive, and in need of special protection.

At least for now, the Supreme Court has held that a reasonable person would need to find the environment hostile and that the environment must be "both objectively and subjectively offensive" (*Faragher v. Boca Raton, Fla.,* 1998; *Harris v. Forklift Systems, Inc.,* 1993).

CURRENT STATUS OF HARASSMENT LAW

Sexual harassment is still a relatively new and unsettled area of law, but recent court decisions have drawn clearer boundaries. The case of *Harris v. Forklift Systems, Inc.* (1993), marked a turning point in sexual harassment law. Theresa Harris had been the rentals manager at Forklift Systems in Nashville, Tennessee. The company president had made several sexually suggestive and demeaning remarks to her over the course of nearly two years (e.g., asking her in public whether she had had sex with clients to get their accounts). For a while, she simply tried to ignore his comments. Eventually she confronted him and he promised to stop. When he continued to make sexually suggestive comments, she quit. She appealed her case all the way to the U.S. Supreme Court.

The Supreme Court agreed to hear Harris's case because lower courts seemed to be using different standards in deciding such cases. One point of disagreement concerned impact. Some courts seemed to require that the victim experience psychological injury while other courts seemed to require only that the harassment interfere with the performance of job duties. A second point of disagreement concerned perspective. Some courts had used a more subjective perspective—the impact of the alleged harassment on the plaintiff in the particular case. Other courts took an objective perspective—they asked whether a reasonable person would have judged the work environment as hostile and offensive. In a unanimous decision, the Court ruled in favor of Theresa Harris. The decision, written by Justice O'Connor, held that it was not necessary to demonstrate psychological injury and that a reasonable person standard should be applied.

In *Oncale v. Sundowner Offshore Services, Inc.* (1998), the Court made clear that sexual harassment law is gender blind. The *Oncale* ruling reinstated the case of Joseph Oncale, a man who had suffered harassment while working on an oil rig in the Gulf of Mexico. He claimed that, while in the shower room, his male coworkers attacked him and shoved a bar of soap between his buttocks. Also, three coworkers held him down and threatened to rape him. A lower court had held that male-on-male harassment didn't qualify as discrimination unless the harasser was gay and choosing his victim *because of* his gender. The

U.S. Supreme Court rejected that reasoning and ruled that same-sex harassment could be grounds for a lawsuit.

The Supreme Court has declared that gender-related jokes, teasing, and occasional use of abusive language do not rise to the level of illegal conduct. The Court ruled that "innocuous differences in ways men and women routinely interact with members of the same sex and of the opposite sex" do not constitute harassment and that harassment law should not be viewed as a "general civility code" (*Faragher v. Boca Raton, Fla.*, 1998). Lower courts have been instructed to apply a "totality of circumstances test" to gauge whether the conduct in question created an unlawful hostile environment. The context of the objectionable conduct, as well as its frequency and severity, must be evaluated. Courts have emphasized two responsibilities of employers: to prevent harassment by establishing clear policies and training procedures, and to correct harassment by thorough investigations of complaints and disciplinary actions against harassers. Victims are responsible for reporting harassment and taking advantage of complaint procedures (*Burlington Industries v. Ellerth*, 1998; *Faragher v. Boca Raton, Fla.*, 1998).

Sexual Harassment Lawsuits.   It is important to note that legal, permissible sexual behavior at work is far more common than illegal sexual harassment. The law does not attempt to regulate behavior that is merely inappropriate, crude, or offensive. Usually, only severe cases of harassment that result in significant injuries end up in court.

For a case to go to trial, several elements usually need to be in place: clearly harassing conduct, a plaintiff who is willing to endure the strains of litigation, a lawyer who is willing to take the case (usually on a contingency basis), witnesses who are willing to testify that harassment occurred, and an organization that failed to prevent or correct illegal conduct. At trial, a jury often must weigh conflicting stories about what really happened to decide if the alleged behavior rises (or sinks) to the level of unlawful sexual harassment. For example, if a victim experiences harassment over a significant period of time and fails to report the incidents, it may later be argued in court that the victim welcomed the attention or did not really find the behavior offensive or serious. The counterargument would be that the victim delayed reporting the incidents because she feared retaliation from the harasser or because she wanted to avoid conflict or potential loss of privacy.

It might also be argued that the upper-level management of the organization either actively or passively created an atmosphere that tolerated harassment. Generally, only egregious cases make it to court, and even among those that are litigated only about 35% are decided in favor of the plaintiff (Terpstra & Baker, 1992). The three cases below led to litigation.

Barbara Gutek, a leading researcher in the area of sexual harassment, describes a case involving Boeing Aerospace Corporation (Gutek, 1993). The plaintiff was a woman who delivered tools to several production buildings. She was fired after claiming she could not return to her job because of the stress caused by the persistent harassment she experienced at work. According to testimony presented at trial, the environment at Boeing included publicly displayed posters showing women in suggestive poses (e.g., a poster showing a dog licking a woman's genitals and a magazine advertisement for an inflatable female sex partner). There was routine use of sexual slang (e.g., referring to the women's restroom as the "beaver pond"), and several incidents of hostility against women. The plaintiff found a condom filled with hand lotion in her coat pocket and found feces smeared on her car. A male supervisor had sexually propositioned several female employees. At trial, attorneys for Boeing argued that the plaintiff encouraged sexually suggestive behavior. She was a body builder who had recently had breast implants. These facts came up at trial. For example, she had a photograph displayed on her desk at work that showed her flexing her muscles in a bikini. The plaintiff lost her case at trial.

A very different kind of sexual harassment case involved the large accounting firm of Price Waterhouse. Here the problem was not sexual hostility, but discrimination based on gender stereotypes. Ann Hopkins was not promoted to partner despite her popularity with clients, despite having brought in millions of dollars in new accounts, and despite having worked more billable hours than anyone else being considered for partner. Traits considered desirable in her male colleagues—being ambitious, aggressive, competitive, and driven—were, in her case, viewed as indicative of an "interpersonal skills problem." She was advised, in part, to be more "ladylike," to walk and talk in a more feminine way, to "wear make-up, have her hair styled, and wear jewelry," and to "take a course at charm school." Hopkins eventually won her case, even though Price Waterhouse appealed all the way to the Supreme Court (Fiske & Stevens, 1993).

Evidence of sexual harassment was clear and pervasive at Mitsubishi's massive automotive assembly plant in Normal, Illinois. Some men at the plant simulated masturbation in front of women and others exposed themselves to female coworkers. The harassment was frequently physical. Several male workers grabbed women's breasts, and some men used air guns to deliver painful blasts to women's breasts and crotches. Supervisors ignored or retaliated against women who complained. One supervisor warned a woman who complained that if she pursued the complaint, the harassers would fabricate stories about her wild sexual exploits to redirect attention toward her. Another supervisor took no action when one man threatened to rape and kill a woman coworker. In 1997, Mitsubishi Company agreed to pay $9.5 million to settle a lawsuit brought by 27 women workers. Then, in 1998, Mitsubishi abandoned a three-year fight against federal charges of sexual harassment at the plant, and agreed to pay $34 million to more than 300 female employees (Braun, 1998).

There has been relatively little research on how jurors make sense of evidence presented during sexual harassment trials. To investigate this issue, Jill Huntley and I looked at how jurors responded to evidence in eight simulated sexual harassment trials. These realistic trial simulations were conducted in cooperation with a trial consulting firm. All eight simulations involved real cases that were about to go to trial and all involved male harassers and female victims. Mock jurors were drawn from the actual trial venues and attorneys presented arguments and evidence in abbreviated form. We then looked for differences between jurors who voted to convict the company on trial and jurors who voted to acquit the company. Jurors who voted to convict believed that the victim was a good employee of good character, that the company knew about the harassment and failed to respond, that the harassment was systemic (i.e., the harasser victimized others or there were other people in the company who were also harassers), that the company retaliated against the victim for complaining about the harassment, that the victim feared she would lose her job if she reported the harassment, and that the victim suffered (psychologically and in her job) because of the harassment. In contrast, jurors who voted to acquit the company believed that the victim was oversensitive and exaggerating her claims, that the victim may have encouraged or contributed to the harassment, that the company acted to stop the harassment once they became aware of it, that the company had antiharassment policies in place, that the victim brought the lawsuit to retaliate against the company, and that the victim failed to follow proper reporting procedures. Although the two sets of jurors diverged sharply in their interpretations of evidence, all jurors focused on the victim's character, the consequences suffered by the victim, and the response (or lack of response) by the company (Huntley & Costanzo, 2003).

In an important study of what case characteristics make lawsuits successful, David Terpstra and Douglas Baker (1992) analyzed 133 sexual harassment cases. Plaintiffs won only 38% of the cases. Winning cases had five characteristics: (1) the harassment was severe; (2) there were witnesses who corroborated the plaintiff's charges; (3) there were documents supporting the claim of harassment; (4) before filing charges, the victim had told management about the harassment; and (5) the company failed to take action against the harasser. If a case had all five characteristics, the odds of winning were more than 99%. If the case had none of the five characteristics, the odds of winning were less than 1%.

THE PSYCHOLOGY OF SEXUAL HARASSMENT

Some Causes.   Sexually harassing behaviors may arise from different motives. Some problematic behavior is motivated by a man's genuine romantic interest in a woman coworker. Because of a lack of social skills or insensitivity to social cues, the man may persistently proposition the woman despite her expressions of disinterest. Unable to accept the woman's disinterest, the frustrated man may then escalate his overtures, or the experience of being rebuffed may trigger hostility toward the woman. Alternatively, the underlying motive may begin as hostility. In such cases, harassment may be manifested as attempts to intimidate, dominate, or humiliate (Pryor & Whalen, 1997).

Susan Fiske and Peter Glick (1995) point out that motive may interact with job type in ways that promote different forms of sexual harassment. The harasser's underlying motive may be a desire for intimacy or a desire to dominate or a mixture of both desires. Traditionally female "pink collar" jobs such as waitress, school teacher, secretary, or flight attendant may encourage forms of harassment rooted in men's earnest desire for intimacy with women. Because such jobs tend to emphasize the traditional female roles of nurturing and sexual attractiveness, they may elicit protectiveness and sexual attention. In contrast, jobs that have been historically held by men may encourage different forms of harassment. Because occupational status and achievement is a significant component of male identity, the job success of women in traditionally male occupations may threaten the self-esteem of some men. Those men may then engage in harassment to undermine the job performance of women. "Blue collar" jobs such as mechanic, laborer, dockworker, or construction worker emphasize traditionally masculine traits such as strength and toughness. In these work settings, women are more likely to face competitive and hostile forms of harassment that seek to dominate women and show that women don't belong. "White collar" jobs such as physician, lawyer, professor, or business executive have tended to be dominated by males and may be seen as valuing traits such as intelligence and ambition. Women in these occupational roles have more often been subject to hostile harassment in an effort to "put women in their place" (Fiske & Glick, 1995).

As noted earlier, sexual harassment of women is far more likely to occur in workplaces where men significantly outnumber women. Of course, this is often the situation when women first enter occupations traditionally held by men. Intrusions of women into such workplaces may disrupt the masculine work culture and lead to discomfort, tension, and resentment among some men. A comfortable camaraderie may be disrupted. Because the men in such settings may have no experience dealing with a female coworker, there may be a "sex role spillover": a tendency to relate to women coworkers using gender stereotypes. Violations of these stereotypes (e.g., a tough, strong woman working on a loading dock) may lead to a backlash (Goodman-Delahunty, 1998).

Some Effects.   Louise Fitzgerald and her colleagues have attempted to link the coping strategies of victims of sexual harassment to the coping strategies typically used by people to cope with stressful events. After analyzing victim responses from a large-scale study of sexual harassment, they identified two basic forms of coping: internal and external (Fitzgerald, Swan, Fischer, 1995). Internally focused coping involved attempts to manage cognitive and emotional reactions to the harassment. For example, a victim may ignore the behavior and do nothing, tell herself that the behavior is not having an effect on her, or tell herself that she simply doesn't care that much. She might also blame herself for misleading the harasser or attribute his behavior to benign causes such as loneliness or a lack of social skill. Externally focused coping involves practical efforts to manage, or alter the harassing environment. Examples of this type of coping include attempts to avoid contact with the harasser, or attempts to appease the harasser and avoid direct confrontation through the use of humor or excuses. The victim might also tell friends and coworkers about the harassment, tell the harasser to stop, notify a supervisor, bring an internal complaint, or file a formal complaint with EEOC.

Which type of coping a particular victim of harassment will use depends on how she interprets the event and perceives the consequences of a particular course of action. Specifically, the victim will evaluate the likely impact of a particular response. For example, she might consider the consequences of reporting the harassment to a supervisor on her personal and professional well-being. She will also look at the potential costs and benefits of other options that are realistically available to her. Research indicates that milder, less confrontational responses are far more common than formal complaints or lawsuits. As might be expected, researchers have found that severe (i.e., obvious and repeated) harassment is more likely to elicit formal complaints, while less explicit or transitory harassment is likely to be met with avoidance or appeasement (Fitzgerald, Swan, & Fischer, 1995).

Prevention.   When psychologists analyze and try to predict behavior, they focus on the interaction between the person and the situation. Whether and how strongly a personality trait is expressed depends on whether the situation encourages or discourages expression of the trait. For example, even if you are a boisterous, outgoing person, it is unlikely that you will be loud and loquacious at a funeral or at the library. Your natural tendencies will be inhibited by the situation. Similarly, even if a man is inclined to harass coworkers, that inclination won't be expressed if the workplace environment strongly discourages harassment. To assess whether someone is predisposed to harass others, John Pryor and his colleagues have developed a scale called the Likelihood to Sexually Harass (LSH) scale (Pryor & Whalen, 1997; Pryor, Giedd, & Williams, 1995). Men with high scores on the LSH scale tend to describe themselves in stereotypically masculine terms, have a strong need to dominate women, endorse traditional sex roles, endorse myths about rape (e.g., that women want to be sexually overpowered), and are more likely to have sexual fantasies involving themes of coercion. However, the actual behavior of these "high LSH" men is powerfully controlled by the workplace environment. In research using the LSH scale, Pryor and his colleagues found that local norms had a dramatic impact on whether or not women were harassed. Specifically, if managers were perceived as tolerant or dismissive of harassing behaviors, incidents of harassment were more frequent. If a workplace is perceived as soft on harassment, men who are predisposed to harass are likely to express their predispositions. From a legal perspective, a work environment where sexual harassment seems to be tolerated puts a company at great risk.

Based on their analysis of the psychological dynamics of sexual harassment, Susan Fiske and Peter Glick (1995) make several recommendations for reducing the incidence of harassment. These recommendations include making clear that sexual informality and sexual joking are inappropriate in a professional environment, eliminating sexually explicit materials in the workplace, and taking steps to make sure that recruiting and promotion are gender neutral. Other researchers emphasize that increasing the number of the underrepresented gender (males in nursing, females in engineering) to a critical mass of 20% or more of employees changes the climate of the workplace and removes the perception that people have been hired because of their gender (Pettigrew & Martin, 1987). Other ways of reducing harassing and discriminatory behavior are discussed more fully later in this chapter.

A BROADER LOOK AT WORKPLACE DISCRIMINATION

During the late 1800s and early 1900s, the distinctively American idea of "employment at will" was created. For employers, this principle meant that employees may be fired "at will" without cause and without notice, for good reasons or bad reasons, for moral or immoral reasons, or for no reason at all (Muhl, 2001). Conversely, it meant that people could quit their jobs at any time, without cause or notice. The presumption of "at will" employment persists in the law. Most employees can still be terminated for any reason *unless* that reason is prohibited by law. Title VII and subsequent employment laws put limits on the ability of employers to hire or fire at will.

Title VII prohibits discrimination based on race, color, national origin, religion, and gender. What is termed "discriminatory adverse action" may include discriminatory firing of an employee, failure to promote, or unfair restriction of employment opportunities. The Age Discrimination in Employment Act (ADEA) was passed in 1967, extending protection to people over the age of 40, and the Americans With Disabilities Act (ADA), which became law in 1990, prohibits discrimination based on physical and mental disabilities. The overriding purpose of these laws is to provide clear legal protection for the free expression of political and religious beliefs (as guaranteed by the Constitution and the Bill of Rights) and to prevent disparate treatment of employees on the basis of immutable personal characteristics such as race, national origin, gender, age, and disability. In the eyes of the law, these employee characteristics are legally "protected categories."

Employers can be held liable for four broad categories of discrimination: (1) hostile workplace environment, (2) disparate treatment, (3) adverse impact, and (4) failure to provide "reasonable accommodation" for someone with a disability (Goodman-Delahunty, 1999). The first category—hostile workplace environment—has already been discussed. Disparate treatment occurs when an employer treats some workers less favorably because of some personal characteristic such as race, gender, or religion. A successful claim of disparate treatment requires the employee to prove (by a preponderance of the evidence) that the employer *intended* to discriminate. Intent is difficult to prove, and generally requires evidence of comments made by management that show intent to discriminate, as well as statistical evidence that certain groups (e.g., females) were systematically excluded from benefits such as promotion. Even where such comments exist, an employer will try to prove that apparent intent did not influence actual practices in hiring, promotion, salary increases, and firing. Even if it appears that the plaintiff has been denied some employment benefit, the employer will claim that the reason behind the denial was legitimate—some deficit in the worker's skills or job performance. Frequently, claims of discriminatory treatment on the job are accompanied by other claims such as defamation (saying or writing something that damages the reputation of an employee), intentional infliction of emotional distress, or retaliation for whistle-blowing (e.g., a company firing a worker who exposes test results indicating that a product is dangerous).

Adverse impact occurs when employment practices that may not look discriminatory on the surface have the clear effect of discriminating against a particular group. Put differently, if the result of treating all employees the same is that some groups are systematically prevented from receiving some job benefit, adverse impact has occurred. In the case of *Griggs v. Duke Power Co.* (1971), African American employees successfully challenged Duke Power's practice of requiring a high school diploma and a particular score on a scholastic aptitude test to decide who was hired or promoted. Although that practice was not intended to discriminate, it resulted in fewer African Americans being hired and promoted. The Court held that the use of such tests had to be abandoned unless it could be demonstrated that test scores were clearly related to the ability to perform the job. Some adverse impact is tolerated if a practice can be "justified by business necessity." If there had been clear evidence that a high school diploma or score on the test predicted actual job performance, then the company might have been permitted to continue the practice. Adverse impact extends beyond the issue of employment testing. For example, if recruiting for job candidates is done informally through word-of-mouth, and this practice effectively excludes members of particular groups, an adverse impact claim can be made. In a series of cases refining the doctrine of adverse impact, the courts have held not only that statistically significant differences between groups must be evident but also that those differences must be caused by employment practices (*Lopez v. Laborers International Union Local 18,* 1993).

One more example: In the past, some police departments had a height requirement. People who wanted to become police officers had to be at least five feet nine inches tall. The argument was that taller officers would be better able to physically defend themselves in dangerous situations (e.g., apprehending a criminal) and that taller (presumably more physically intimidating) officers wouldn't need to defend themselves. That is, taller people would be less likely to be challenged by criminal suspects trying to escape. Because women are, on average, shorter than men, the policy resulted in far fewer women being qualified to serve as police officers. While the courts ruled that such height requirements were illegal because of their adverse impact on female applicants, other physical characteristics such as physical strength, stamina, and agility are legal and justifiable because they are clearly related to job requirements. Police officers can be required to demonstrate physical endurance, lifting strength, and running speed (Simmons, 1997).

The fourth type of claim only refers to cases involving religion or disabilities. Employees may claim that employers failed to make sufficient adjustments to allow them to participate in religious rituals or to observe religious holidays. A legal claim can also be made if an employer fails to make adequate adjustments to permit disabled employees to work effectively despite the limitations of their disabilities. Such accommodations are required unless they create an "undue hardship or burden" on the employer's business. In *Trans World Airlines, Inc. v. Hardison* (1977), the airline operated seven days a week, 24 hours per day. Mr. Hardison observed a Saturday Sabbath and refused to work Saturdays. However, because of lack of seniority, he was required to work Saturdays. His supervisors tried unsuccessfully to find someone who would voluntarily switch schedules with him, but no one with greater seniority was willing to switch. The employer refused to force another worker to switch schedules and refused to offer extra pay to entice others to work on Saturdays. The Court ruled against the employee and held that Trans World Airlines had attempted to accommodate Hardison but was not required, ". . . to carve out a special exception to its seniority system."

For a claim of discrimination based on religion, several elements have to be in place: There must be a sincerely held, *bona fide* religious belief that interferes with a job requirement; the employer must be made aware of the conflict; and the employee must suffer some adverse effects because the employer refused to reasonably accommodate the religious practices (*Anderson v. General Dynamics,* 1978).

The 1991 Civil Rights Act made compensatory damages available in cases of unlawful, intentional employment discrimination. If an organization is found guilty of discrimination, a variety of legal remedies are possible. If someone has been fired, they can be reinstated. Lost wages can be paid, retroactive promotions can be made, and retroactive pay raises can be ordered. However, to receive such damages, the plaintiff must present evidence of actual emotional or psychological harm caused by discrimination. The range of psychological harms might include anxiety-related problems such as depression, insomnia, extreme fatigue, mental anguish, or damage to one's professional reputation and social standing. Punitive damages are also possible, but only when an employer is shown to have acted with "malice or reckless indifference to the federally protected rights of an aggrieved person." This more extreme form of damages is intended to punish the employer, to deter future discrimination by that employer, and to send a message to other employers that there will be severe consequences for malicious discrimination.

Racial Discrimination in the Workplace.   During much of the twentieth century, racism against African Americans was blatant, routine, and supported by law. The law permitted segregation of whites from blacks at work and at school. The first black Americans to integrate schools and businesses faced open hostility expressed in verbal abuse, racial slurs, physical assaults, and even death threats.

But the law and public opinion have both changed dramatically. Now the law expressly prohibits intentional workplace discrimination based on race. It is illegal to hire, promote, or fire someone because of his or her race. This is a clear step forward from the times when employment decisions were made in an unapologetically racist manner. But is it sufficient to prevent racism in the workplace? Of course, it is usually very difficult to prove that an employment decision was racially motivated, because it is rare for employers to admit that they were motivated by racism. Employers can usually claim that a particular decision was not based on race, but on some aspect of merit.

Public opinion surveys spanning more than 40 years indicate a steady decline in reported prejudice towards blacks. Only a tiny percentage of white Americans now say they would object to having a black friend or coworker (Gallup, 2001). Part of the explanation for this decline is that racism is much less strong than it used to be. But another part of the explanation may be that it is simply no longer acceptable to admit to racial prejudice. Both explanations appear to have validity. Many researchers and many lines of evidence suggest a decisive shift away from blatant forms of racism toward more subtle or "modern" forms of racism. Modern racism differs from traditional racism in that it is less extreme, less conscious, and less overt. And, whereas it used to be acceptable to claim that members of a particular racial group were simply inferior, modern explanations of discriminatory conduct tend to be rationalized in more socially acceptable ways. Most people want to see themselves as fair-minded and free of racial prejudice, but they still feel some discomfort and suspicion in the presence of racially different people. This discomfort generally reveals itself in subtle but consequential behaviors that favor similar people (Pettigrew & Meertens, 1995; Dovidio & Gaertner, 1996).

In an experiment that illustrates the subtlety of prejudice, white people were shown several photographs of white and black people and asked to imagine interacting with the people in the photos. They also rated how much they would probably like the person. Overall, they reported liking the black people slightly more than the white people. But a more direct measure of liking—movements of facial muscles associated with positive or negative emotions—indicated more positive reactions to white people and more negative reactions to black people (Vanman, Paul, Kaplan, & Miller, 1990). Were the people lying about who they liked best? Not necessarily. Not wanting to feel prejudice, they may not have been fully aware of their feelings of discomfort. In studies that further underscore the automatic nature of responses to race, John Dovidio and Samuel Gaertner (1996, 1997) have made use of reaction time measures. They reasoned that it takes longer to react to stimuli that are inconsistent with attitudes than it does to process information that fits with existing attitudes. White participants pressed a button in response to word pairs that appeared on a screen. Racially charged words like "blacks" and "whites" were paired with positive words (e.g., smart) or negative words (e.g., stupid). Participants quickly rejected the negative terms for both blacks and whites, but they more quickly associated positive terms with whites than with blacks. These differences were evident in people who were not classified as racist according to standard paper and pencil tests. In a classic study of subtle differences in cross-racial interactions, Carl Word and his colleagues asked people to conduct job interviews with several equally qualified black or white job candidates. There was no evidence of overt prejudice against black candidates. However, there were subtle, measurable differences: When interviewing a black candidate, white interviewers sat farther away, made more speech errors (i.e., used more pauses and more fillers like "um" or "ah"), and held shorter interviews. In response, the black job candidates behaved in a more anxious, awkward manner (Word, Zanna, & Cooper, 1974).

People who know they are prejudiced are reluctant to admit it. And even people who sincerely believe they are not prejudiced may behave differently around people of another race than they behave around people of their own race. Subtle forms of racism are likely to leak out via subtle nonverbal cues and, consequently, create colder, more strained social interactions. These more awkward interactions are likely to lead to more negative impressions and attributions about other people's intentions and abilities. In the workplace, the effects of subtle "modern" racism may have especially strong effects when there are very few members of a minority group on the job. Thomas Pettigrew and Joanne Martin (1987) have shown that when there are only a few "token" minorities on the job, they tend to receive disproportionate praise for their achievements and disproportionate criticism for their failures. In addition, members of the majority group often doubt the competence of the first minorities to enter a work environment, believing that they were hired for the sake of minority representation, not because of their abilities.

Some researchers have observed that prejudice is similar to a bad habit. Like most habits, prejudice resists change and cannot be tamed by logic alone. Even when people make sincere efforts to be unbiased when dealing with people of different races, automatic, irrational, emotional reactions still assert themselves. Reducing prejudice is possible, but it happens slowly over time and through repeated positive contact with people from disfavored groups (Devine, 1995). In some ways, direct, overt racism is easier to deal with than indirect, covert racism. Antidiscrimination laws are powerful tools for correcting blatant discrimination. But subtle, nonconscious racism may be harder to change. Some legal scholars have argued that there is a fundamental mismatch between the forms of racial bias condemned by law, and racism as it is actually practiced in organizations (Krieger, 1995). Fortunately, research suggests that even subtly discriminatory behavior can be effectively reduced.

Some clear lessons can be drawn from the American experience of desegregation of the public schools. Much social-psychological research was prompted by the landmark Supreme Court decision *Brown v. Board of Education* in 1954 (see Chapter 1). In that decision, the Court ruled that separate schools for blacks and whites were inherently unequal and therefore unconstitutional. This led to massive desegregation of the public schools. It came as a great surprise to many that the effects of this desegregation were not entirely positive. In fact, a comprehensive review of the research on desegregation conducted by Walter Stephan in 1986 reported that 53% of the studies found that desegregation led to an increase in prejudice of whites towards blacks, 34% reported no change in prejudice, and only 13% found a decrease in prejudice.

The discouraging findings of Stephan's review prompted researchers to try to identify the conditions under which interracial contact decreases prejudice. Research conducted over the past several decades has revealed that four conditions are essential to reducing stereotypes and prejudice. First, there must be equal-status contact between groups.

Bringing in members of a disfavored group and placing them in low-status jobs or positions may only reinforce stereotypes that such people are undeserving of and unsuited for higher-status positions. Second, there must be personal interaction between members of the two groups. That is, the organization (e.g., the school or business) must promote one-on-one contact instead of permitting members of the two groups to avoid each other. Third, the environment must be structured to foster cooperation. Specifically, members of the two groups must be induced to work together in an effort to achieve goals important to both groups (so-called "superordinate goals"). For example, members of the two groups could be assembled into interdependent work teams where each member of the team has an important role to play. This ensures that people must rely on and attempt to help each other. Fourth, local social norms must favor intergroup contact and equal treatment—It must be viewed as desirable to try to work well with members of the other group. Such norms are generally created and supported by people who have authority in the work environment (Brehm, Kassin, & Fein, 1999). In addition, it is important to highlight the job qualifications of the new group, to increase the number of people from the underrepresented group in supervisory positions, for managers to monitor employee relations, and to require clear accountability for behavior (Fiske & Glick, 1995). When these conditions are in effect, racial (or gender) integration is likely to reduce prejudice and enhance the functioning of the organization.

THE PSYCHOLOGY OF PERCEIVED FAIRNESS

To understand the concept of unfair discrimination, it is necessary to consider the opposite, more fundamental concept of fairness. Fairness almost always serves as the official justification for decisions about hiring, promotion, benefits, salaries, bonuses, and firing. Claims of harassment or discrimination and lawsuits against employers are motivated by a perceived lack of fairness.

The lofty ideal of just treatment was neatly expressed by the philosopher Aristotle in the fourth century B.C.: "All virtue is summed up in dealing justly" (Tripp, 1970). In 1670, Blaise Pascal noted that what is viewed as just depends on prevailing circumstances: "We see neither justice nor injustice which does not change its nature with change in climate" (Tripp, 1970). But my favorite quote about justice came from my oldest daughter, who discovered the concept of justice when she was about three years old. Whenever she was told that she had to go to bed, take a bath, or leave a playground, she would loudly protest, "Not fair! Not fair!" After a week or two of this, I asked her what she meant by "not fair." Her answer was direct and to-the-point: "Not fair is when I don't get what I want." My daughter's insight has now been buttressed by psychological research. We are not dispassionate arbiters of fairness—our judgment that some decision or action is unfair is most often triggered by not getting what we want. And, as you probably suspect, we are far less likely to view a decision as unfair if it results in us getting more than we actually deserve.

Unlike philosophers, psychologists are more concerned with how people *actually* think and behave than with how people *ought* to think and behave. When psychologists have examined how people think about fairness, three interrelated dimensions have emerged: distributive, procedural, and interpersonal. Distributive justice refers to how available rewards are distributed or divided up among members of a group. More specifically, it concerns the relationship (or lack of relationship) between contributions and outcome. The second dimension—procedural justice—concerns the perceived fairness of the procedures and rules used to allocate the available benefits, that is, the way outcomes are decided. If people feel they have an opportunity to "state their case" and voice their concerns during the decision-making process, they are much more likely to view the procedure as fair (Finkel, 2000). Although there is a strong relationship between fair procedures and fair outcomes, fair procedures sometimes lead to unjust outcomes and unjust procedures sometimes lead to fair outcomes. The third dimension people use when deciding whether someone has been treated fairly is called interpersonal justice. Here the concern is style: Were people treated courteously and with respect? Interpersonal justice refers to the consideration and care shown by the people who have the power to allocate rewards. So, in sum, what matters is who gets what, how it is decided who gets what, and how people are treated during and after those decisions are made (Baron & Byrne, 2000).

Three Models for Allocating Rewards.   Edward Sampson analyzed the concept of distributive justice. He identified three basic schemes for dividing up resources (Sampson, 1975). The principle of "need" dictates that each person gives to the group based on his or her ability and each person gets from the group according to what he or she needs. This standard of distributive justice tends only to be used in small, intimate groups. For example, if one child in a three-child family suffers from a serious chronic illness, a family may devote most of its financial resources to medical treatment for the child. The parents, and perhaps even the siblings, will spend a disproportionate amount of time and energy caring for the sick child. Brothers and sisters will receive less— less attention, less money, less time from their parents. The sick child simply needs more, so that child gets more.

The second, and simplest, norm of justice is "equality." Using this principle, everybody gets the same rewards. Let's say a small but successful software company of 10 people has managed to budget one million dollars to distribute as salary. How much does each person get as salary? Maybe they should just divide the money equally and give everybody a salary of $100,000. Of course, some might argue that not everyone *deserves* the same salary. That may be true. But the advantage of using equality is that in groups where everyone makes a different but important contribution, and the value of each contribution is difficult to calculate, equality promotes social harmony (Lerner, 1980). At least temporarily, the small software company might want to reward all 10 workers equally in order to encourage everyone to work together as equal members of a team. Because the social functioning of the group is essential to its continued success, it might be best to postpone the potentially divisive, emotionally charged discussion of who deserves more.

The third norm of distributive justice is the most widely used. It is called "equity." The idea is that rewards ought to be distributed in proportion to each person's contributions to the group. That is, people who contribute more ought to receive more benefits. Although equity may harm group cohesiveness and social harmony, it tends to encourage people to work harder on those tasks that are well compensated. At least in the abstract, the principle of equity seems eminently reasonable. The problem is that it is usually difficult to quantify contributions, to decide on what constitutes merit. Put differently, *which* contributions should be defined as worthy of lesser or greater rewards? Take lawyers. In a big law firm, money is usually generated by billing clients for the time of attorneys. So perhaps lawyers' salaries ought to be based on who bills the most hours per year. While it is true that nearly every law firm values billable hours, it can't be the only consideration. Let's say one of the attorneys bills relatively few hours, but brings in several clients—that is, because she is smart and charming and gregarious, several people hire the firm to do legal work. Bringing in clients (which may involve playing golf and going to social events) is an important contribution, even though it may cut into billable hours. Perhaps another attorney raises the profile of the firm by serving as president of the local bar association and writing a legal column for the local newspaper. Perhaps another attends to the internal functioning of the firm by mediating disputes between coworkers or setting the agenda for meetings or developing a vision for the long-term development of the firm. Maybe another attorney isn't much good at bringing in new clients, but her thorough knowledge of the law enables her to write winning briefs. The point is that there is no single, unassailable method for determining the value of different contributions, no precise calculus for deciding the relative merit of different work activities. Fair allocation of rewards is substantially subjective. In the abstract, virtually everyone supports the appealing concepts of performance-based rewards, accountability, and merit. But, in practice, it is difficult to translate these vague, value-laden, but appealing concepts into clear measures that everyone agrees are fair.

One persistent inequality is the salary discrepancy between men and women. Women earn about 70% of what men earn, and college-educated men earn about $13,000 more annually than college-educated women (Rothenberg, 1995). During the 1980s, some states attempted to equalize salaries for jobs of "comparable worth." Attempts to assess the worth of various jobs and to base pay on job characteristics were, in part, an attempt to reduce the gender gap in salaries. Comparable-worth assessments can also be seen as an interesting approach to making "merit" or "deservingness" explicit when trying to use the norm of equity. For example, many efforts to quantify the worth or value of particular jobs have scored each job type (e.g., physician, teacher, lawyer, warehouse worker, architect) on several categories. Here are some of the categories that have been used in efforts to calculate the "worth" of a job: level of education required, years of experience needed, initiative and ingenuity required, need for independent judgment, physical demand, mental demand, responsibility for equipment and materials, responsibility for safety of others, responsibility for work of others, unpleasantness of working conditions, personal risk or exposure to hazards, and hours per week spent working (Lowe & Wittig, 1989). A point value (e.g., between one and 10) is assigned for each category and each category may be weighted differently. The result is then mathematically combined to give a numerical indication of worth.

Sometimes a direct evaluation of job characteristics leads to a reduction in the salary gender gap. Using a numerical assessment of comparable worth, the state of Washington found that the female-dominated job category of clerk-typist deserved the same salary as the male-dominated category of warehouse worker. Prior to the assessment, clerk-typists were paid 25% less than warehouse workers (Lowe & Wittig, 1989).

Research on Perceptions of Fairness.

For decades, psychologists have studied how individuals and groups distribute rewards. Several laboratory studies have involved bringing people together in small or large groups to perform a task or solve a problem. Sometimes the tasks are mathematical or verbal and other times the tasks involve simulated business decisions (e.g., deciding how to allocate a hypothetical budget). Once the task is complete, participants (and often outside observers) are asked to distribute the available rewards (usually money). Other types of studies have used interviews and surveys of working people (Bruce & Blackburn, 1992). Typically, people are asked about fairness of the salary structure at work and other job benefits.

Several conclusions can be drawn from this body of research. First, judgments of fairness tend to be self-serving. Although we tend to feel distressed about not getting as much as we feel we deserve, we tend not to be as bothered by getting more than we deserve (Diekmann, Samuels, Ross, & Bazerman, 1997). (For example, college students tend to complain to professors when they receive a course grade that is lower than they expected, but tend not to complain when they are given a grade higher than they expected.) Another aspect of this self-serving tendency is that people tend to rate their own contributions somewhat higher than outside observers rate their contributions. A second conclusion is that males and females seem to differ in how they apply principles of fairness. As compared to men, women tend to undervalue their contributions. For example, in laboratory studies where both men and women are asked to work as long as they think is fair for a specific sum of money, women tend to work about 20% to 25% longer. Also, when asked to divide rewards fairly between themselves and a coworker, men take more of the reward for themselves and give correspondingly less to a coworker. Women tend to divide the money more equally (Major, 1993). Also, in surveys of workers, women tend to value salary somewhat less than men. As compared to men, women workers seem to place more value on good coworkers, control over schedules, sense of accomplishment, and good working conditions (Jackson, 1989). A third conclusion is that, in deciding whether they are fairly rewarded, people compare their inputs and outcomes to the inputs and outcomes of similar others. People try to assess whether they are being treated the same as similar coworkers doing similar jobs (Locke & Latham, 1990). Although these comparisons may be influenced by self-serving biases, they help anchor judgments in the reality of the workplace. A final conclusion is that because no distribution of rewards is entirely equitable for everyone, people's satisfaction with their outcomes often depends heavily on procedural and interpersonal considerations (Cropanzano, Byrne, Bobecel, & Rupp, 2001). If employees feel that the procedures used to decide outcomes are reasonable and communicated clearly and courteously, the outcomes are more likely to be accepted. Mysterious, biased, or poorly communicated procedures can create dissatisfaction even when they result in equitable allocations. Open, fair, clearly communicated procedures can dampen dissatisfaction even when allocations are inequitable.

People often feel that their employer has treated them unfairly. These perceived inequities have consequences for employers. Jerald Greenberg conducted a study at three manufacturing plants owned by the same parent company. To reduce expenses, salaries were temporarily cut. Greenberg arranged to vary conditions so that at the first plant, no salary cuts were made. At the second plant, workers were told that to cut expenses, 15% salary cuts would be made for 10 weeks. At the third plant, workers were given the same salary cut but with an explanation of why the cuts were necessary and an expression of regret from management. As predicted, company inventories of supplies revealed that there was a dramatic rise in employee theft at plant two, the plant where management provided no reasonable explanation for the salary cut (Greenberg & Alge, 2000).

There is now a large body of evidence showing that if employees feel they have been treated unfairly (in terms of distributive, procedural, or interpersonal justice), they often act to restore a sense of equity. They may try to "get even." They may spend fewer hours at work, they may not work as hard while on the job, they may spread rumors about or form coalitions against the people who treated them unfairly, they may steal from the employer, they may sabotage the initiatives of management, they may quit, and, of course, they may file lawsuits.

IN CONCLUSION

Virtually all employment litigation is an attempt to restore perceived fairness and to punish perceived injustice. Employment law has done a lot to reduce harassment and discrimination in the workplace. Unfortunately, current law is a weak tool for creating full justice in the workplace. Jane Goodman-Delahunty, a former judge and leading scholar in the area of psychology and civil law has called attention to the divergence between what people expect on the job and what the law requires. She writes,

> Anti discrimination legislation and laws provide no guarantee of fair or equal treatment. They simply outlaw adverse or inequitable treatment motivated by illegal bias or prejudice based on race, color, national origin, gender, religion, age, disability, or reprisal. . . . Many employees are disappointed to learn that there is no constitutional right to merit-based decisions in the workplace, and that anti-discrimination laws do not mandate fair or equitable treatment. Numerous cases arise because what occurred is manifestly unfair, evincing poor judgment, sloppy management, administrative or judgmental errors, rudeness, favoritism, nepotism and so on, but the conduct, although unpleasant, does not amount to unlawful discrimination (1999, p. 298).

Employment law lays down boundaries that cannot be crossed, but for employees who want to create a truly fair workplace, following the law is only a start.

Readings to Supplement This Chapter

Articles

Elkins, T. J., Phillips, J. S., & Konopaske, R. (2002). Gender-related biases in evaluations of sex discrimination allegations: Is perceived threat the key? *Journal of Applied Psychology, 87,* 280–292.

Finkel, N. J. (2000). But it's not fair! Commonsense notions of unfairness. *Psychology, Public Policy, and Law, 6,* 898–952.

Goodman-Delahunty, J. (1999). Pragmatic support for the reasonable victim standard in hostile workplace sexual harassment cases. *Psychology, Public Policy, and Law, 5,* 519–555.

Huntley, J. E., & Costanzo, M. (2003). Sexual harassment stories: Testing a story-mediated model of juror decision-making in civil litigation. *Law and Human Behavior, 27,* 29–51.

Shestowsky, D. (1999). Where is the common knowledge? Empirical support for requiring expert testimony in sexual harassment trials. *Stanford Law Review, 51,* 367–381.

Wiener, R. L., Hackney, A., Kadela, K., Rauch, S., Seib, H., Warren, L., & Hurt, L. E. (2002). The fit and implementation of sexual harassment law to workplace evaluations. *Journal of Applied Psychology, 87,* 747–764.

9
Sentencing, Imprisonment, and the Death Penalty

Chapter Outline

• •

SENTENCING DECISIONS

Disparities and Guidelines

IMPRISONMENT

The Goals of Imprisonment
The Evolution of the American Prison
    The 1800s
    The 1900s
Prisoner Rights and the Role of the Courts
Some Statistics on Prisons and Prisoners
    Who Goes to Prison?
    Gender
    Race
The Distinctive Culture of Prison
    The Power of the Prison Situation
    The Harsh Realities of Prison Life
    Violence and Threats of Violence
    Gangs
    Drugs
Does Prison Work?
Alternatives to Prison

THE DEATH PENALTY

Supreme Court Decisions
    Research on Capital Murder Trials and the Court's Response
    Jury Decision Making in the Penalty Phase
Racial Disparities and the Death Penalty
The Death Penalty as a Deterrent to Murder
Errors and Mistakes in Death Penalty Cases
In Conclusion

Prison is the centerpiece of our system of punishment. For more than three decades, the U.S. prison system has continued to expand whether the crime rate rises or falls (Clear & Cole, 2000). Steven Donziger, the former head of the National Criminal Justice Commission, summed up the circular rationale for prison construction in the following way: "If crime is going up, then we need to build more prisons to hold more criminals; and if crime is going down, it's because we built more prisons—and building even more prisons will therefore drive down crime even lower" (Schlosser, 1999, p. 52).

Most prisons no longer look like the huge stone fortresses featured in Hollywood movies. Though many still have gun towers and high walls or fences topped with coils of razor wire, new features have been added to improve security. For example, New Folsom prison in California is encircled by a "death wire" fence that sends a lethal jolt of electricity into anyone who touches it. The federal super maximum-security prison in Florence, Colorado, uses 168 video cameras to continuously monitor the activities of inmates. Inside the cells, there is no moveable furniture, and there are no detachable objects (such as toilet handles or soap dishes) that might be converted into weapons. Every prisoner experiences something close to perpetual solitary confinement—the cells are built at angles so that prisoners are not able to see or talk to each other (Federal Bureau of Prisons, 1996).

At some points in our history, prisons have been optimistically viewed as great social laboratories for reforming the lives and habits of people who have gone astray. At other times, they have been pessimistically viewed as little more than vast warehouses for vile criminals who can never be reformed. This final chapter examines what happens after a defendant is found guilty: how the legal system decides on appropriate sentences for convicted criminals; the role of prisons and the psychological effects of imprisonment; and use of the death penalty.

SENTENCING DECISIONS

After conviction and before punishment, the criminal must be sentenced. How judges, jurors, and the public decide on the appropriate punishment for a particular crime depends not only on the seriousness of the crime, but also on attributions about the criminal. When people attempt to explain the behavior of others, they distinguish between internal causes (such as personality or free choice) and external causes (such as powerful situational forces). Researchers who study attributions also refer to two other dimensions of perceived cause: controllability and stability. *Controllability* refers to whether or not a person could have controlled their behavior, and *stability* refers to whether the cause appears to be temporary or permanent. Criminal behaviors that are attributed to internal, controllable, stable causes evoke the strongest punitive responses. Crimes attributed to external, less controllable, unstable causes may elicit empathy and more lenient sentences (Weiner, Graham, & Reyna, 1997). Consider the case of a man who robs a convenience store. We would be more inclined to lean toward minimal punishment or rehabilitation if he has no criminal record (his behavior does not appear to be stable), if he is mentally deficient (his behavior was less controllable), and his friends persuaded him to do it (his actions were the result of external causes). In contrast, an armed robber who has a prior criminal record, is of normal intelligence, and who acted on his own is likely to provoke anger rather than compassion or mercy.

DISPARITIES AND GUIDELINES

Two people who commit the same crime do not necessarily receive the same punishment. Sentencing disparities are sometimes the logical result of differences in the details of seemingly similar crimes. But, too often, disparities arise from the biased discretion of judges. In a study conducted when judges had considerable discretion, researchers asked 50 federal judges to evaluate 20 case files and recommend sentences for each defendant. There were dramatic differences across judges. For example, in a tax evasion and credit fraud case, the sentences ranged from a three-year prison term with no fine, to a 20-year prison term combined with a $65,000 fine (Partridge & Eldridge, 1974). In another study, researchers found that general attitudes of the judges, as well as the race and gender of the defendant, were significant predictors of sentence—African Americans were treated more harshly and women were treated more leniently (Tonry, 1996). And, finally, an analysis of more than 10,000 felony cases found that although men and women were convicted at the same rates for similar crimes, male judges gave women significantly lighter sentences (Associated Press, 1984).

Partly in an effort to reduce such troubling inequities in sentencing, many states and the federal government constructed elaborate sentencing guidelines to help judges decide on appropriate sentences. Guidelines generally list factors that ought to be considered when determining a sentence—for example, type of crime, viciousness of crime, defendant's prior criminal record, circumstances of the current offense, and the average sentence given in the past for similar crimes. However, in many jurisdictions, although judges must consult the guidelines, they are not required to hand down the recommended sentence. In these jurisdictions, judges must usually declare that they considered the guidelines and provide some written justification for deviating from the guidelines (Tonry, 1996).

A more radical approach involves "determinate sentencing" (sometimes called mandatory sentencing). Determinate sentencing requires judges to hand down a sentence that falls within a prespecified range if a defendant is found guilty of a particular crime. Concern over sentencing disparity, a widespread public perception that judges were too lenient, and the desire of elected officials to appear "tough on crime" led to passage of the Sentencing Reform Act of 1984. As a result of this act, a commission of judges, lawyers, and legislators was established to develop sentencing guidelines. The federal guidelines devised by the commission may be the most elaborate sentencing system ever developed.

The guidelines require judges to refer to a "grid" (a table with rows and columns). The 43 rows of the grid are intended to indicate the severity of the offense, and the six columns of the grid represent six levels of prior criminal history. The rows are further subdivided into four "zones" and the columns are further subdivided by "criminal history points" that range from "0" to "13 or more." The body of the table lists specific sentence ranges expressed in months. The lowest sentence range for a level 1 offense with no prior criminal history is zero to six months, and the highest range is 360 months to life. At roughly the midpoint of the grid (level 21, category 4), the range is 57 to 71 months in prison. Robbery is a level 20 offense, but that level can be adjusted upward if there are aggravating circumstances (e.g., a gun was used, the victim was seriously injured), or adjusted downward if there are mitigating circumstances (e.g., the defendant accepts personal responsibility for his crime, his accomplice was more responsible for the crime). Aside from the personal characteristic of prior criminal history, characteristics of the defendant such as age, intelligence, education, family relationships, drug addiction, and employment stability are usually not part of the sentencing calculation at the federal level (Ruback & Wroblewski, 2001). The inability of judges to take the personal characteristics into account required one federal judge to sentence a quadraplegic man to 10 years in prison for selling LSD (*United States v. Goff*, 1993).

Many critics have argued that the guidelines are unnecessarily complex and undesirably rigid. Some social scientists have reached the conclusion that the guidelines have created a mere "facade of precision" and needlessly require "judges to consider and give specific weight to an ever-growing number of inappropriately detailed sentencing factors" (Ruback & Wroblewski, 2001, p. 742). Judges have also been critical of the guidelines. The guidelines usurp the ability of judges to take into account the individual circumstances of the crime and the criminal. Judges generally prefer to have such discretion. However, as noted above, giving judges full discretion leads to troubling disparities in sentencing. Also, as described in Chapter 5, judges seem to overestimate their ability to take multiple factors into account and to ignore biasing information. There is even evidence that judges don't have much awareness of their own decision-making processes.

In a classic study of sentencing decisions conducted at a time when judges still had considerable discretion, Vladimir Konecni and Ebbe Ebbesen (1982) analyzed more than 400 sentencing hearings. Prior to each hearing, judges received a file containing information about the offender's personal history and prior convictions, as well as a report written by a probation officer. During each sentencing hearing, judges heard sentencing recommendations from prosecutors and defenders and listened to any statement the offender made on his own behalf. When asked about how they made sentencing decisions, judges reported that they carefully weighed multiple subtle characteristics of the crime and the criminal (e.g., family situation, drug/alcohol addiction, prior record, severity of the crime, mental status of the offender, probability of rehabilitation, expressed remorse of defendant). However, the data contradicted the judges' account. Researchers found that judges merely accepted the recommendation of the parole officer in 84% of the cases (in the remaining cases, judges were more lenient 10% of the time, and more severe 6% of the time). When the researchers looked at how the parole officers reached their recommendations, they found that those recommendations were almost fully determined by three factors: the severity of the crime, the offender's prior criminal record, and jail/bail status (whether the defendant was held in jail or released on bail between arrest and conviction). In Konecni and Ebbesen's view, the sentencing hearings were merely expensive "legal rituals" that "presented a false impression of the functioning of the criminal justice system" (p. 326).

Justice dictates that people convicted of similar crimes should receive similar sentences. It is also important for judges to be able to take unusual circumstances of an individual criminal or crime into account when deciding on a sentence. The challenge is to find the optimal blend of sentencing consistency and judicial discretion. Recently, two social scientists—Barry Ruback and Jonathan Wroblewski—have proposed an alternative sentencing scheme that attempts to balance consistency and discretion. They propose a two-stage sentencing process. In the first stage, judges would refer to a simplified sentencing grid with about a dozen offense categories (instead of the current 43 categories). Then, in the second stage, both aggravating factors (circumstances that increase the severity of the crime or the guilt of the defendant) and mitigating factors (circumstances that lessen the severity of the crime or the guilt of the defendant) would be considered. Judges would select the final sentence from predetermined sentence ranges for either aggravated or mitigated crimes of a particular type. This approach would constrain discretion by forcing judges to select a sentence within a predetermined range, while simultaneously allowing greater discretion to the judges "who see and hear the individuals involved in the case and who best know the context in which the crime was committed" (2001, p. 773).

The "three strikes and you're out" laws passed by voters and legislatures in many states are interesting variants of mandatory sentencing.

The state of Washington passed the first three-strikes law in 1993, and now 27 states have such laws. Generally, three-strikes laws require that criminals receive a long sentence or a life sentence when they are convicted of a third felony. Some states have narrow three-strikes laws that target only violent or sexual offenders, while other states have more broadly written laws. If the felonies involve violence like rape or murder, these laws seem reasonable and popular with the public. But many controversial cases have involved "strikes" that are nonviolent. For example, crimes such as stealing a few slices of pizza, forging a check for a few hundred dollars, and possession of marijuana for personal use have each led to a third strike conviction and a life sentence (Currie, 1998). Many criminologists have argued that the more broadly written versions of such laws are inefficient and needlessly expensive. Prison is far more expensive than any sentencing option except the death penalty.[1] Often, people are sentenced to a long prison term for a third strike at a time when they are "aging out" of violent crime. Because 65% to 70% of violent crimes are committed by males under the age of 30, three-strike laws usually incarcerate offenders near the end of their criminal careers (Greenwood et al., 1994).

IMPRISONMENT

First, a few basic distinctions. The criminal justice system can hold people in jails or prisons. Jails are distinguished from prisons by their function. Jails are short-term holding cells operated by cities or counties and administered by local authorities (usually county sheriffs or city police). Sometimes people convicted of misdemeanors (relatively minor crimes usually punishable by less than a year in prison) serve out short sentences in the local jail. Jails are also places where potentially dangerous defendants charged with serious violent crimes can be held before

---

[1] Capital murder trials are about three times more expensive than noncapital murder trials and are more costly at every step of the trial process—investigation, pretrial, jury selection, and trial. In addition, substantial costs are associated with the penalty phase, the appeals process, and the maintenance of death rows and execution chambers. For a full discussion of this issue, see Costanzo (1997).

and during trial. Nonviolent criminals (e.g., embezzlers or thieves) might be held in jail before and during trial to prevent them from fleeing to escape justice. Later, if a defendant is convicted, he or she is held in jail between conviction and sentencing, and between sentencing and transport to a prison. Jails (like prisons) are overcrowded. Several detainees might be held in a large cell and many scandals have involved assaults on nonserious offenders by violent offenders held in the same cell (Anderson, 1998).

Prisons hold convicted criminals for long periods of time, sometimes years, sometimes decades. Most prisoners will eventually be released into free society, but a small minority will live out the remainder of their natural lives behind prison walls. A tiny minority of prisoners (a fraction of 1%) will be held until they are killed in an execution chamber (Costanzo, 1997). Every state has its own prison system where it houses people convicted of felonies. There are also federal prisons for people who break federal law. Federal laws attempt to target crimes that reach beyond the borders of individual states or crimes that involve multistate conspiracies. At present, drug offenders are the largest group of inmates in federal prisons, constituting more than 60% of the total (Bureau of Justice Statistics, 2001).

State and federal prisons range from minimum security to maximum security. At one end of the continuum are the open-security federal prisons for offenders convicted of white-collar crimes such as insider trading, fraud, or embezzlement. These "Club Feds," as they are sometimes facetiously called, have no fences, guards, or cellblocks. Prisoners are held in cottages or dormitories; they interact with few restrictions and spend much of their time doing light prison labor. These institutions usually have exercise equipment, athletic fields, and, sometimes, tennis courts and softball leagues. Some medium-security "campus style" prisons feature small, scattered buildings enclosed by a tall fence (Clear & Cole, 2000).

At the other end of the continuum are "supermax" (super maximum-security) prisons reserved for people deemed to be especially serious or violent criminals. Inmates are held in small cells, interaction is tightly controlled, and educational and recreational opportunities are scarce or entirely absent. An early version of a supermax prison was built on the small island of Alcatraz in San Francisco Bay. In 1934, the escape-proof island prison became home to about 300 prisoners judged to be of "the vicious and irredeemable type" (Rotman, 1995). It is now a state park and major tourist attraction. Further up the California coast, just below the Oregon border, stands Pelican Bay Prison, a modern super-max prison that holds prisoners considered to be the worst, most incorrigible criminals. Inmates in Pelican Bay's Secure Housing Unit (known as the "SHU") spend 23 hours a day alone in their cells without counseling, vocational training, or prison jobs. During the remaining hour, prisoners are permitted to exercise (usually in shackles) in the prison "yard." According to the federal judge who heard a class-action suit alleging inhumane conditions at Pelican Bay, these conditions of extreme isolation and sensory deprivation, ". . . press the outer bounds of what most humans can psychologically tolerate" (*Madrid v. Gomez,* 1995, p. 1267). Indeed, over time, about half of the inmates exposed to such conditions develop serious mental illness, including profound depression and psychosis (Human Rights Watch, 1997).

THE GOALS OF IMPRISONMENT

Even the terms used to describe prisons reveal ambivalence. "Penal institution" implies a place of punishment; the term "penitentiary" is religious in origin and refers to a place where one can repent and atone for one's sins; and the term "correctional institution" suggests a place where the behavior of the criminal can be improved or corrected.

Prisons serve many ends. The simplest goal is *incapacitation* through containment. If a criminal is securely contained inside prison walls, he or she is unable to harm people outside the prison. The criminal is incapacitated. Society is spared the crimes that may have been committed if the prisoner were still free. Successful incapacitation requires only that prisons hold criminals securely—that they cannot escape. A second goal of prison is *deterrence*. For a particular criminal, it is hoped that the experience of suffering in prison will dissuade him from committing further crimes after he is released from prison (this is called specific deterrence). We also hope for general deterrence—that other people will choose not to commit crimes because they fear going to prison.

The third goal, *retribution,* is less practical and more emotional. Most of us feel a sense of rage and revulsion when we hear about an especially hideous crime (e.g., the murder of a child). We want to see the murderer punished. Prison is a punishing environment where the convict will suffer. Because societies are held together, in part, by a shared consensus of what constitutes immoral behavior, law-abiding members of society feel a justified sense of moral outrage when someone commits a terrible crime. The criminal who violates the moral order must be punished to restore moral balance. Retribution, it is argued, promotes moral solidarity among law-abiding citizens and educates potential criminals about which behaviors are strongly condemned (Berns, 1979). The problem with retribution is that there is no precise formula for deciding how much suffering to inflict. And there is also the question of ethics—how much pain can be ethically inflicted on criminals? Retribution is largely backward looking in that it focuses on the crime.

The final, most forward-looking goal of prisons is *rehabilitation.* Nearly all prisoners will eventually be released back into free society, so it makes sense to try to "improve" criminals during their time in prison. Although today's prison administrators seldom claim that they are in the business of rehabilitating criminals, American prisons were developed for the explicit purpose of transforming criminals into productive members of society. A core problem is that the optimistic goal of rehabilitation is in conflict with the other goals of imprisonment. Painful, unpleasant prisons are likely to make prisoners angrier and more aggressive while providing few of the skills necessary to become law-abiding citizens.

The basic justifications for punishment are even older than prisons. For example, around 300 B.C., the Greek philosopher Plato articulated the goals of rehabilitation and deterrence: ". . . the proper office of all punishment is twofold: he who is rightly punished ought either to become better and profit by it, or he ought to be made an example to his fellows, that they may see what he suffers, and fear to suffer the like, and become better" (cited in MacKenzie, 1981).

THE EVOLUTION OF THE AMERICAN PRISON

In the American colonies, lists of crimes included not only theft, assault, rape, and murder but also moral transgressions such as witchcraft, adultery, idolatry, and blasphemy. A range of punishments was available. Vagabonds who wandered into town and committed a crime could simply be banished and threatened with severe punishment if they ever returned. But locals who were judged guilty of crimes were usually subjected to public shaming. The offender might be locked into the stocks (typically a wood structure that holds the wrists and neck) or a public cage. Townspeople would be able to taunt and spit on them to show their disapproval of the crime. Some offenders were chained or tied to a post and publicly whipped. Justice was not equal. Those who were wealthy or well connected were often permitted to pay a fine as a way of avoiding the stocks or the lash. One innovation in the colonies was a graduated series of punishments for repeat offenders. The first conviction of a thief could lead to a fine or a whipping. For the second theft, the fine would be tripled, the offender would sit for an hour on the gallows with a noose around his neck, and he would then be tied to the whipping post for 30 lashes. For the third offense, the criminal was hung (Rothman, 1995). This may have been the first "three-strikes" law.

Following the Revolutionary War, Americans were eager to develop a system of criminal punishment distinct from the laws inherited from England. Reformers sought to abandon the "corrupt, barbarous, and unjust" punishments of the monarchy (Drapkin, 1989). The death penalty was greatly restricted in nearly every state and, instead of beating and killing, the new country decided to rely on incarceration. Criminals would be kept apart from the rest of society and the cruel punishments of the past would be set aside. Between 1790 and 1800, eight states built prisons (Clear & Cole, 2000).

The 1800s.   The American optimism that fueled the construction of prisons slowly eroded from 1800 through 1820. Two decades of experience with prisons led many to conclude that prisons created as many problems as they solved. Escapes, small-scale disturbances, and even large-scale riots were frequent (Spierenberg, 1995). During their time in prison, inmates freely shared their knowledge of their criminal trades and used their time to refine their criminal skills. By 1820, most public officials had come to believe that prisons spawned crime instead of suppressing it.

Disillusionment with prisons and changes in American society prompted a deeper analysis of the causes and consequences of crime. Earlier attitudes toward criminals were rooted in religious beliefs, and so no real theory of crime was necessary. If humans were born sinful, some evil deeds were simply inevitable. But as American society became more distinctive and more secular, religious explanations lost some of their resonance. During the first half of the nineteenth century, a new theory of criminal behavior began to gain prominence. Dorothea Dix, a leading social reformer of the period, neatly summed up the emerging perspective: "It is to the defects of our social organization, to the multiplied and multiplying temptations to crime that we chiefly owe the increase in evil doers" (cited in Rothman, 1995, p. 105).

This was a fundamental shift in thinking about crime. The cause for criminal behavior was no longer located only within the individual criminal. Social disorganization was also to blame. Reformers cited several societal trends that encouraged criminality: the decline of the influence of the church; the increased mobility of citizens, which led to unstable communities where neighbors no longer cared about each other; schools that failed to discipline children and teach them the difference between right and wrong; and uninvolved fathers who spent too much time at work and allowed their children to leave home at too young an age (Friedman, 1993). These new, more sociological theories of crime seemed to demand a fresh approach to dealing with criminals. Prisons were reconceived and redesigned. Rehabilitation became the new ideal. To reform criminals, prisons would have to reeducate and reshape prisoners. If families, churches, schools, and neighborhoods had failed to instill proper values and habits, prisons would do the job.

During the 1820s, prisons were established in New York and Pennsylvania with the goal of putting the new rehabilitative model into practice. The emphasis was on strict routine and social order. The Pennsylvania plan required inmates to remain in their cells for virtually their entire sentence. They ate alone in their cells, worked alone in their cells (spinning wool was the usual work), and slept alone in their cells. To enforce lack of contact between inmates, new prisoners were escorted to their cells with hoods over their heads so that they would not see or be seen by other inmates. Prisoners were not permitted to correspond with friends or family and visitors were rare. After all, outsiders were part of the unwholesome social environment that had encouraged criminal behavior. The Bible was the only reading material permitted (Friedman, 1993). The New York system was a bit more relaxed. Though prisoners spent most of their time in individual cells, they were allowed to eat and work in groups. The groups, however, were silent and noninteractive—talking was forbidden and even the exchange of glances was prohibited.

News of American prisons reached the countries of Europe and representatives were dispatched to examine these great laboratories for

human reform. In 1831, Gustave de Beaumont and Alexis de Tocqueville were sent to study the American prison and to advise the
French government on what France might borrow from the new institution. They concluded that, ". . . the habits of order to which the prisoner is subjected for several years, influence very considerably his moral
conduct after his return to society. Perhaps leaving prison he is not an
honest man, but he has contracted honest habits" (1964, p. 79).
Charles Dickens, the great English novelist and journalist, was less
impressed. He toured a Philadelphia prison in 1842 and concluded,

> Those who devised this system and those benevolent gentlemen who
> carry it into execution, do not know what they are doing. I believe that
> very few men are capable of estimating the immense amount of torture
> and agony that this dreadful punishment, prolonged for years, inflicts
> upon the sufferers. . . . Those who have undergone this punishment
> must pass into society again morally unhealthy and diseased (Dickens,
> 1850, p. 128).

Most observers seemed to agree with Dickens's assessment of the Pennsylvania system. Critics pointed out fundamental problems: It was
impractical and expensive, and the extreme isolation drove many prisoners insane. Mental breakdowns, self-mutilations, and suicides were
common (Friedman, 1993). Because of these problems, the cheaper,
less extreme New York plan eventually prevailed and became the model
adopted by other states.

Around this time, overcrowding was emerging as a major problem.
By 1866, roughly a third of all prisoners were being housed two to a cell
(McKelvey, 1977). This meant that silence and isolation—the foundation of earlier rehabilitative models—were no longer possible. Although
rehabilitation was still the official goal of prisons, the sheer size of the
inmate population and the increase in the number of serious offenders
frustrated efforts at reform. And, to preserve their precarious authority
in overcrowded prisons, officials often resorted to brutal forms of discipline. Prisoners could be locked into the yoke—a flat iron bar with wrist
manacles and a large center ring for the neck—or subjected to "buck-
ing"—tying or cuffing the wrists together, forcing the arms over the bent
knees, and inserting a bar under the knees and over the elbows. Solitary
confinement in an isolated cell, a concrete box, or even a tall, narrow
cage was widely used. Prisoners could be "thrown in the hole" for days

or even weeks with a daily food ration of as little as four ounces of bread and a quart of water (Walker, 1998).

Bigotry also contributed to the abandonment of reform. Prisons were holding a disproportionate number of new immigrants (especially Irish) and there was less sympathy for inmates. Many felt that the new immigrants were morally and intellectually inferior. When rehabilitation failed, it was usually blamed on the incorrigible nature of the inmates rather than on the failures of the prison system (Friedman, 1993).

By the beginning of the twentieth century, most reforms had been abandoned. Advocates of rehabilitation were derided as naive and idealistic. Security and maintenance of minimal order now seemed like the only achievable goals.

The 1900s. For the first half of the twentieth century, prisons felt the growing influence of medical and social science. Some criminals began to be seen as suffering from psychological dysfunctions that could benefit from therapeutic treatment. The "medical model" bolstered the commitment to indeterminate sentencing: Just as it made no sense for a physician to decide on the length of a hospital stay immediately after diagnosis, it made no sense to sentence convicts to an immutable prison term immediately after conviction. Just as patients were to be released from the hospital whenever they were cured, inmates were to be released from prison whenever they were rehabilitated. There would be periodic review of an inmate's progress. And, if there was clear evidence that the inmate was participating in constructive prison activities and showing signs of improvement, his sentence could be reduced.

Use of the medical model had other implications. In medical practice, curing an ailment requires accurate diagnosis and individualized treatment. For prisons, this meant that officials needed to develop classification schemes for differentiating one inmate from another on the basis of his or her problems. In theory, classification would dictate therapeutic approach (McKelvey, 1977). Unfortunately, given the vagueness of prisoner classification schemes of the time, there was considerable disagreement about which inmates belonged in which category. And, of course, many prisoners belonged in more than one category. In addition, well-behaved, more treatable prisoners usually failed to receive treatment or retraining, but inmates classified as incorrigible or unresponsive to treatment could be treated more harshly.

By the late 1960s, there was growing concern about the brutality and ineffectiveness of prisons. Based on a multiyear study, the President's Council on Law Enforcement and the Administration of Justice issued a report in 1966. That report painted a bleak picture of prison conditions:

> Life in many institutions is at best barren and futile, at worst unspeakably brutal and degrading. To be sure, the offenders in such institutions are incapacitated from committing further crimes while serving their sentences, but the conditions in which they live are the poorest possible preparation for their successful reentry into society, and often merely reinforce in them a pattern of manipulation and destructiveness" (cited in Rothman, 1995, p. 173).

Federal and state government commissions emphasized the need for rehabilitation, reintegration of the offender into the community after release, and alternatives to incarceration.

The tentative commitment to reform did not last. In 1974, Robert Martinson published an influential analysis of 231 prison rehabilitation programs. His conclusion was devastating for advocates of rehabilitation: "With few and isolated exceptions, the rehabilitative efforts that have been reported so far have had no appreciable effect on recidivism" (p. 22). This "nothing works" conclusion had a powerful effect on prisons beginning in the late 1970s (Martinson later became more optimistic about rehabilitation). In addition to the perceived ineffectiveness of rehabilitation, the victim's rights movement shifted the focus away from offenders. An increasing emphasis on crime victims made the public less interested in reforming criminals and more interested in making them "pay" for their crimes (Anderson, 1998). By the 1980s, many prison educational and vocational programs were dramatically scaled back or even eliminated. Sports and recreational programs were curtailed in many prisons. Indeed, nearly all programs came under attack as examples of coddling criminals and being soft on crime. It was during this time that, in many jurisdictions, flexible sentencing and time off a sentence for good behavior in prison were abandoned. During the late 1980s, state and national politicians began to compete for the label of "tough on crime." Candidates pledged to imprison more criminals for longer periods of time and to impose the death penalty more often (Ellsworth & Gross, 1994).

PRISONER RIGHTS AND
THE ROLE OF THE COURTS

Until the middle of the twentieth century, federal and state courts did not exert much control over the internal management of prisons. There were several reasons for this "hands off" doctrine: It was felt that judges lacked the expertise to intervene in prison administration, that tinkering by the courts would undermine prison discipline, that complaints from prisoners usually involved privileges rather than rights, and that societal standards favored (or at least accepted) the harshness of prisons (National Advisory Commission on Criminal Justice Standards and Goals, 1973).

Especially during the years when Earl Warren served as Chief Justice of the Supreme Court, there was a broad expansion of civil liberties for many of society's least powerful groups, including racial minorities, women, children, and prison inmates. An early victory for prisoners came in 1964, when Black Muslim inmates were permitted to receive copies of the Koran, eat meals free of pork, and hold religious meetings (*Cooper v. Pate,* 1964). In *Procunier v. Martinez* (1974), the Supreme Court approved the rights of prisoners to receive mail and to make use of law students and paralegals to investigate their cases. Through the 1960s and 1970s, the courts responded to prisoner class-action lawsuits by defining minimum health care standards and raising due-process standards for disciplinary actions against prison inmates. Courts also imposed limits on prison overcrowding.

But the Court's willingness to act on behalf of inmates did not continue into the 1980s. In 1981, the Supreme Court signaled its intention to retreat from its commitment to easing inhumane conditions in prisons. In *Rhodes v. Chapman,* the Court suggested that as long as conditions were not "grossly disproportionate to the severity of the crime" and not "totally without peneological justification," they would no longer be viewed as "cruel and unusual." Double-celling (holding two people in a six- by nine-foot cell), for example, was judged to be acceptable. In the Court's view, "To the extent that such conditions are restrictive and even harsh, they are part of the penalty that criminal offenders pay for their offenses against society." A decade later, in *Wilson v. Seiter* (1991) the Court went even further: To be judged cruel and unusual, conditions would not only have to be inhumane, but officials would need to show "deliberate indifference" to those inhumane conditions. Extending this new standard in 1994 in a case where an inmate had been raped by other inmates, the Court held that inmates would be required to prove "subjective recklessness" on the part of prison officials (*Farmer v. Brennan,* 1994).

Prison officials are still obliged to provide treatment for "serious" mental illness. But to qualify as "serious" the condition must, ". . . result in further significant injury, not routine discomfort that is part of the penalty that criminal offenders pay for their offenses against society" (*McGuckin v. Smith,* 1992). Whether or not a prisoner receives treatment is typically left to the discretion of prison wardens. If a prisoner is perceived as "faking" to get sympathy or time away from his cell, requests for help may be denied. Prisoners cannot be forced to take psychoactive medications until it has been determined that the drug is medically warranted or necessary to prevent the prisoner from doing harm to himself or others (*Washington v. Harper,* 1990).

SOME STATISTICS ON PRISONS AND PRISONERS

The United States now imprisons a larger percentage of its citizens for longer periods of time than any other industrialized democracy in the world. And, since the 1980s, the U.S. rate of incarceration has averaged about six times higher than that of other industrialized democracies (Mauer, 1999). At the beginning of 2001, the number of people imprisoned per every 100,000 people in the population was 39 in Japan, 60 in Sweden, 91 in France, 111 in Canada, 124 in Great Britain, 400 in South Africa, 644 in Russia, and 699 in the United States (Sentencing Project, 2001). Within the U.S., California, our most populous state, holds the largest number of prisoners. In fact, California now has a prison system larger than France, Germany, Great Britain, and Japan combined. But if we examine incarceration *rates* by state, California doesn't even make the top 10, which include, in order, Texas, Louisiana, Oklahoma, South Carolina, Nevada, Arizona, Alabama, Georgia, Mississippi, and Florida (Stern, 1998).

Longer sentences, mandatory sentences, three-strikes laws, reductions in the use of parole, and increased imprisonment of juveniles have all contributed to the stunning rise in the rate of imprisonment (Siegel,

1998). The prison population explosion has also been strongly fueled by the increase in the number of people imprisoned for drug offenses. Because of the so-called "war on drugs," the number of people arrested for drug crimes jumped more than 60% during the 1990s. The conviction rate for drug offenders also increased, from 39% to 52%. And the number of convicted offenders that were sent to prison increased from 41% to 48%. Federal sentencing guidelines and those of many states require long prison terms for many drug offenses (Mauer, 1999).

Who Goes to Prison?   Criminals tend not to come from privileged or stable circumstances. About 40% of prisoners have at least one other family member who has been incarcerated. About 62% are regular drug users before incarceration, and fewer than one-third have completed high school. Only 18% are married, and 53% earned less than $12,000 in the year preceding incarceration (Siegel, 1998). Though our prisons have experienced a population explosion, they are not exploding with only rapists, murderers, and other violent criminals. As of 2001, 49% of people sentenced to state prisons were convicted of violent crimes. The remaining 51% were convicted of drug, property, or "other" crimes. In federal prisons, only 14% had been convicted of violent crimes, while 58% were convicted of drug offenses (Mauer, 1999).

Gender.   Psychologists have devoted considerable attention to identifying reliable differences between the behavior of men and women. Many of the differences identified are small or subtle. But the largest gender difference is in the propensity for aggressive and violent behavior. Males are far more likely to be violent, more likely to come into contact with the criminal justice system, and more likely to end up behind prison walls for violent (and even nonviolent) offenses. Consequently, the most striking characteristic of prisoners is their gender: The male-to-female ratio of the prison population is wildly disproportionate to the general population. About 93% of the prisoners in state and federal prisons are male (The Sentencing Project, 1999).

Probably because women represent only about 7% of the adult prison population, there has been relatively little research on life inside women's prisons. Females are far more likely to be held in minimum-security prisons and dormlike rooms instead of cells. Violence is much less prevalent. Female prisoners appear to attempt self-mutilation and suicide at higher rates than male prisoners, and are more likely than men to be given psychoactive, mood-altering drugs (Morash, Harr, & Rucker, 1994). Some have argued that women are more likely to adapt to prison life by forming surrogate families with other inmates, and by adopting the roles of mother, father, and siblings (Fletcher, Shaver, & Moon, 1993).

Race.   Another startling feature of U.S. prisoners is the color of their skin. Although African American males make up just under 12% of the U.S. population, they constitute 46% of inmates in state prisons. Moreover, the rate of imprisonment of black males has risen much faster than that of white males. The bulk of this growth is due to the dramatic increase in people being sentenced for drug offenses. While the number of European Americans imprisoned for drug crimes (i.e., drugs were their only or most serious offense) rose a staggering 306% between 1985 and 1995, the number of African Americans imprisoned for drug crimes increased by an astonishing 707% during the same period. In federal prisons, 64% of male and 71% of female African Americans are incarcerated for drug crimes (Haney & Zimbardo, 1998). Although whites and blacks use drugs at about the same rate, blacks are arrested at a rate about five times that of whites (Schlosser, 1999). Further, the possession of relatively small quantities of "crack" cocaine—a drug that has been far more prevalent in black communities—carries a relatively long prison sentence.

THE DISTINCTIVE CULTURE OF PRISON

Maximum-security prison is a distinct subculture with its own rules, norms, power hierarchy, rewards, and punishments. Social scientists who have studied prisons have written about the process of *prisonization*—the assimilation of new inmates into the values, norms, and language of the prison. There also appears to be a strong component of prison culture that is imported into prison from the outside world (Jacobs, 1983). Many inmates come from a street culture where perceived disrespect and threats to honor must be answered with violence (Nisbett & Cohen, 1996). These two processes—prisonization and the importation of violent street culture—combine to produce an especially brutal environment. Within the self-contained culture of prison, some prisoners are interested in staying out of trouble so that they can finish their sentences and get out. Others see themselves as "convicts" who have no hope of ever living a productive life on the outside (Silberman, 1995).

Rewards and punishments in prison can come from prison officials or other inmates. For example, prison officials can give well-behaved prisoners better work assignments, and uncooperative inmates can be locked in their cells or put in solitary confinement. Other inmates can provide rewards in the form of comradery and protection, or punishment in the form of intimidation and violence.

The Power of the Prison Situation.   One of the great lessons of social psychology is that powerful situations can sometimes overwhelm individual differences. That is, at times, personality characteristics have much less influence on behavior than the characteristics of the situations that people find themselves in. One of the earliest and most compelling demonstrations of the power of situations was a prison simulation study conducted at Stanford University in 1971.

Each potential participant in the Stanford prison study was given an extensive battery of psychological tests, and the 20 most psychologically healthy young men were accepted for inclusion in the study. Then came the crucial event: 10 of the men were randomly assigned to the role of prison guard, and 10 were randomly assigned to the role of prisoner. A few days later, police cars with red lights flashing pulled up to the homes of the "prisoners." The young men were handcuffed and taken into custody. Next, they were arrested, booked, fingerprinted, and escorted to a simulated prison in the basement of the Stanford University psychology building. They were stripped, searched, and given a prison uniform—a loose-fitting white smock with an identification number and a pair of sandals. The "guards" wore khaki uniforms and carried handcuffs, nightsticks, keys, and whistles. Other prison-like conditions were put in place. There were routine head counts of the prisoners, supervised trips to the toilet, meals at preset times, and the prisoners remained in the mock prison 24 hours a day. With these basic conditions in place, the participants were simply allowed to interact.

After two weeks, the researchers (Craig Haney, Curtis Banks, and Phillip Zimbardo) were going to retest the participants to see if there had been subtle shifts in attitudes or self-concepts. But something unexpected and disturbing happened—the guards seemed intoxicated with their new power and became increasingly abusive. Physical abuse was not permitted, so the guards resorted to verbal harassment. They also employed more direct forms of abuse such as solitary confinement, waking up prisoners in the middle of the night for surprise head counts, withholding toilet privileges, and making the prisoners do pushups while a guard rested a heavy foot on the prisoner's back. Initially, some prisoners resisted. But after only a few days, even the rebellious prisoners became passive and demoralized. The experimenters released the first prisoner after only 36 hours because he was showing signs of severe depression, and the entire experiment had to be abruptly terminated after only six days. In the words of the researchers,

> Our planned two-week experiment had to be aborted after only six days because the experience dramatically and painfully transformed most of the participants in ways we did not anticipate, prepare for, or predict (Haney, Banks, & Zimbardo, 1973, p. 91).

So, what should be made of this famous study? Many have criticized the Stanford study as unrealistic. Perhaps the mock guards were merely reenacting roles they had seen in movies and, clearly, six days in a simulated prison cannot possibly recreate the realities experienced by actual guards and prisoners. But there are a couple of important implications of the experiment. First, if a relatively tame simulation can produce such striking effects in so little time, then the vastly more potent realities of an actual prison might be expected to produce far more extreme effects. Second, because all participants were psychologically healthy and randomly assigned to conditions, we cannot attribute the changes in the behavior of the participants to personality differences. Something intrinsic to the situation—for example, the gross disparity in power between prisoners and guards—at least temporarily transformed the attitudes and behaviors of the participants.

The Harsh Realities of Prison Life.   Because it is impossible to fully simulate the realities of prison life in the laboratory, and because it would be unethical to expose research participants to the punishing conditions of prison life, social scientists have relied on other methods to investigate prisons. Researchers have used observational methods, in-depth interviews with prisoners and prison officials, and analyses of prison records over time (e.g., number of violent incidents). Based on these data, several scholars have described the ways in which life inside prison is strikingly different from life on the outside (Toch & Adams, 1989). First, the prisoner is banished from the outside world—separated from the people and surroundings he or she cares about. Over time, most inmates lose contact with all but the most devoted friends and family members. Inmates are assigned to prisons based primarily on their crimes and the availability of space. Family members (who tend not to be rich) must often travel great distances to visit prisoners. Mail (except from the inmate's attorney) can be censored or even destroyed. Second, prisoners have no decision-making power over important aspects of their lives. Where they can go, how they spend their time, what they eat, and who they associate with are all largely decided by prison officials. Third, the physical environment is stark and oppressive. In most large maximum-security prisons, inmates spend nearly all their time in a windowless, six- by ten-foot cell. They often share this cell with one other person. Fourth, there is an extreme lack of privacy, particularly for double-celled inmates. Prisoners can be observed by prison officials at all times. Fifth, there is the threat or reality of violence—from other prisoners, from groups of prisoners, and from guards. Finally, there is enforced idleness and routine. Life in the modern American prison is characterized by relentless, deadening routine (Toch & Adams, 1989; Goffman, 1973). These conditions and their psychological effects have been described by prisoners in the following ways:

> . . . the major problem is monotony. It is the dull sameness of prison life, its idleness and boredom that grinds me down. Nothing matters; everything is inconsequential other than when you will be free and how to make time pass until then. But boredom, interrupted by occasional bursts of fear and anger, is the governing reality of life in prison (Morris, 1995, p. 205).

> . . . [the prison] is nothing but an absurd machine for breaking those men who are thrown into it. Life there is a kind of mechanized madness; everything in it seems to have been conceived in a spirit of mean calculation how best to enfeeble, stupefy and numb the prisoner and poison him with inexpressible bitterness (Serge, 1984, p. 34).

> Prison not only robs you of your freedom, it attempts to take away your identity. Everyone wears a uniform, eats the same food, follows the same schedule. It is by definition a purely authoritarian state that tolerates no independence and individuality. . . . It is dehumanizing, for it forces you to adapt by becoming more self-contained and insulated (Mandela, 1994, p. 376).

Violence and Threats of Violence.   The maximum-security prison poses great risk to both physical and psychological health. There is a lack of opportunity for physical activity as well as the possibility of being assaulted, raped, or even killed. Hans Toch (1977) points out that prisons ". . . have a climate of violence which has no free-world counterpart. Inmates are terrorized by other inmates and spend years in fear of harm" (p. 53). Threats come not only from other prisoners but also from prison guards. Psychological threats come from arbitrary enforcement of prison rules, a continuing state of fear and vigilance, and a lack of control over nearly every aspect of life. The dehumanizing conditions of many prisons create destructive rage and resentment and may produce criminals who are more likely to retaliate against society once they are released from prison (Silberman, 1995). A further source of bitterness among prisoners is what they perceive as the arbitrariness of the criminal justice system. Inmates are likely to come into contact with people who have committed similar crimes but have received very different sentences (Parisi, 1982).

Many of the cultural norms inside prison concern enforcement of rules through violence. What has been called the "convict code" emphasizes that inmates who "snitch" on other inmates should be beaten, stabbed, or even killed, and that each prisoner should show loyalty only to himself and members of his group or gang. Violence is often the most effective means of reaching goals in prison, and any attack on a member of a gang must be avenged by that gang (Silberman, 1995). One prisoner put it this way:

> It is no accident that convicts speak of penal institutions as gladiator schools. In such places, circumstances teach men how to kill one another. . . . If you are a man, you must either kill or turn the tables on anyone who propositions you with threats of force. It is the custom among prisoners. In so doing, it becomes known to all that you are a man. . . . Here in prison the most respected and honored men among us are those who have killed other men, particularly other prisoners (Abbott, 1991, p. 126).

Homosexual rape is used to demean and dominate other inmates. And, if the victim fails to fight off the rapist or to retaliate against him, he is likely to become the target of further sexual assaults (Silberman, 1995). An inmate can be placed in protective custody (away from the general prison population), but because a request to be placed in protective custody may be seen as a form of "snitching," it can put the victim in further danger. Younger, more vulnerable inmates are especially likely to be raped and some are even kept as sexual slaves who can be sold or traded to other inmates (Rideau & Wikberg, 1992).

Gangs.   Criminal behavior continues inside prison, and much of that behavior is facilitated by prison gangs. One reason gangs flourish in many U.S. prisons is that inmates vastly outnumber guards. As one prison scholar put it, "It is not always appreciated by the general public that immediate power within the prison belongs to the prisoners" (Morris, 1995, p. 221). An ironic consequence of legal rulings limiting the ability of prison officials to physically punish prisoners has been to increase the power of prison gangs. In response to such rulings, prison officials began to take a more passive approach towards prisoners. That is, officials became less likely to respond to complaints of prisoners who were physically or sexually abused by other prisoners. In effect, prisoners were told to "fend for themselves" (Johnson, 1996).

Gangs with names like the Aryan Brotherhood, the Gangsta Killer Bloods, the Mexican Mafia, and the Nazi Lowriders have a powerful influence on prison culture. Prison gangs are often subsidiaries of street gangs and the norms and leadership structures sometimes transfer from one setting to the other. Within prisons, gang members can bribe correctional officers to facilitate crimes such as extortion, homosexual prostitution, gambling, drug sales, and robbery (Johnson, 1996). According to some studies, about half of all prison violence is the result of gang activities (Barkan, 1997). The oath taken by members of the Nuestra Familia gang makes expectations of violence very clear: "If I go forward, follow me. If I hesitate, push me. If they kill me, avenge me. If I am a traitor, kill me" (Siegel, 1998, p. 540).

Drugs.   If you set out to create an environment likely to encourage the use of drugs, you would probably design something like a prison—bored, angry, frustrated, confined people longing for an escape from their miserable reality. Many criminals come to prison suffering from drug addictions. Even though possession of drugs in prison is illegal and punishable, small quantities are apparently available in most prisons. Prison guards are sometimes bribed to let visitors smuggle drugs to inmates. Several cases have been brought against correctional officers who helped prisoners run their drug-dealing businesses in prison (Valentine, 1999). According to one inmate,

Drugs, all drugs, are readily available at about twice their street price, payable inside or outside the prison. Some drugs come over prison walls; some are brought in by guards; some make their way in with visitors, despite the administration's efforts. . . ." (Morris, 1995, p. 210).

The availability of drugs in prisons is sometimes exaggerated by prisoners and minimized by administrators. Estimates of drug use can be based on random drug testing of prisoners, although this method under-estimates the use of drugs that pass out of the human body quickly (e.g., heroin). Drug tests suggest that only about 11% of prisoners are actively using illegal drugs at any given time (Stern, 1998).

Although only about 40% of prisoners incarcerated for drug offenses are receiving some form of treatment for their addictions, evaluation research shows that treatment can be effective. Prisoners who complete drug rehabilitation programs have a 20% lower rate of rearrest after release than prisoners who receive no such treatment (Currie, 1998).

DOES PRISON WORK?

Imprisonment is a public program paid for by taxpayers. The effectiveness of that program can be evaluated by researchers. Of course, prisons may achieve some goals but not others. And, in deciding whether prisons work, there needs to be a cost-benefit analysis—an assessment of whether prisons are worth the cost, and whether less expensive alternatives might work as well or better.

Of all possible responses to crime except for the death penalty, prison is by far the most expensive, costing on average over $23,000 per prisoner per year (Currie, 1998). Prison is so costly because it is so encompassing. When we put someone behind bars, we pay for their basic needs 24 hours per day, 365 days per year, year after year. Sometimes it makes sense to pay this steep price. It is imperative to take murderers out of circulation, even if it is costly. Moreover, even from a crassly financial perspective, a justification can be made for imprisoning murderers. According to some estimates, a single murder costs society more than a million dollars because of lost wages and productivity and increased public services to families of victims (Currie, 1998). However, for nonviolent offenders, it is difficult to justify imprisonment from a financial perspective. Money spent on prisons is money not spent on other public needs. From 1990 to 2000, state spending on higher education decreased by 18% but spending on prisons increased 30% (Caplow & Simon, 1999).

As prisoners age and develop health problems, it costs even more to keep them behind bars. The average cost of imprisonment for prisoners over the age of 55 is more than $60,000 per year (Coalition for Sentencing Reform, 2003). Medical care for prisoners is especially costly because prison is not an environment that promotes physical or mental health. Poor nutrition, lack of exercise, physical injuries, inadequate medical care, fear, high levels of stress, and a lack of intellectual and recreational opportunities combine with the normal aging process to produce many prisoners with serious health problems. Moreover, disease spreads quickly among prisoners. The rate of HIV/AIDS among state and federal prisoners is 13 times higher than the rate in the general population. Prisons also spawn new forms of infectious disease. In 1990, the emergence of a virulent, drug-resistant form of tuberculosis was traced to prisons in the state of New York (Mauer, 1999). Because of mandatory sentencing laws and so-called "truth in sentencing" laws that have eliminated parole for many crimes, elderly prisoners must remain in prison. Some states have established special geriatric prisons to house elderly, ailing inmates.

Another way of assessing the effectiveness of prisons is to ask how well they achieve their stated goals. Prisons do an extraordinarily good job of incapacitating criminals. Once a criminal is admitted into a maximum-security prison, the chance of escape is near zero. The individual prisoner is prevented from committing crimes in free society (though not in prison) for as long as he or she is inside the prison walls. Unfortunately, just because a particular criminal is kept away from society doesn't always mean that the crime rate will fall. This is because of what criminologists call the problem of "new recruits." For chronically violent offenders—for example, some rapists, child molesters, and murderers—further crimes are probably prevented by holding the violent offender in prison. But financially-motivated crimes, such as selling drugs, stealing cars, and fencing stolen property, seem to be organized like a labor market. If a criminal is taken off the streets, a sort of job vacancy is created that tends to be quickly filled with a new recruit (Petersilia, 1994).

If measured against the goal of retribution, prison is also a great success. Few doubt that any period of confinement in a maximum-security prison is a frightening, numbing experience marked by anxiety, frustration, unrelenting monotony, and loss of control. Although minimum-security prisons are vastly more pleasant than maximum-security prisons, even minimum security inflicts the essential pains of imprisonment: loss of autonomy, loss of power, loss of privacy, banishment from loved ones, and removal from the opportunities of free society.

When measured against the goal of rehabilitation, prisons are a failure. As noted earlier, the obvious problem with abandoning the goal of rehabilitation is that nearly all prisoners will eventually return to free society. If no attempt has been made to give them the skills and resources necessary to mend their ways, released convicts will be likely to return to a life of crime. There is ample evidence that prison does little to improve the behavior of criminals. A study conducted by the RAND Corporation compared two groups of convicts. The groups were matched on a variety of variables including age, crime, and prior criminal record. They differed only in the sentence they received: One group was sent to prison while the other group received supervised probation. After tracking the offenders for more than three years, the researchers found that the prison group did worse than the probation group. Compared to the probation group, drug offenders who had been to prison were 11% more likely to be charged with another crime, violent offenders sent to prison were 3% more likely to be charged again, and property offenders were 17% more likely to re-offend (Petersilia, Turner, & Peterson, 1986). In this study, prison time increased crime. Furthermore, the overall rate of recidivism is not encouraging. Following their release from prison, about 67% of former inmates will be rearrested for serious crimes and sent back to prison (Reiman, 1998). The punishing aspects of prison tend to work against rehabilitation.

Rehabilitation programs can take a variety of forms. But all aim to change the criminal so that he or she will be less likely to continue breaking the law after release from custody. Some programs involve group therapy intended to change the thinking and behavior of criminals. Educational and training programs are also rehabilitative in that they attempt to provide prisoners with marketable skills that may lead to productive employment after release. There have now been several large-scale analyses of what makes rehabilitation programs successful. Based on their extensive analyses of programs, Lawrence Sherman and his colleagues found that the most effective programs attempt to:

(1) correct educational and job skill deficits, (2) change attitudes and thinking patterns that promote criminal behavior, (3) improve self-awareness and self-esteem, (4) enhance interpersonal relationship skills, (5) reduce drug abuse, and (6) reduce contact with criminal peers (Sherman et al., 1997).

ALTERNATIVES TO PRISON

At the far end of the sentencing spectrum is the death penalty. The next most severe option is life in prison without the possibility of parole, followed by a long prison term. But several other alternatives are available. Perhaps the least serious sentence is to pay a fine (e.g, for a speeding ticket or other traffic violation). Forfeiture of "goods and instrumentalities" used to commit crimes is a more severe type of financial penalty. Federal law allows law enforcement to seize the property of drug traffickers, including cars and boats used to transport drugs, buildings used to store drugs, and houses paid for with profits from drug deals. Paying monetary *restitution* (e.g., a petty thief paying for stolen property) or paying restitution through labor (e.g., a teenager repainting a wall he spray-painted) is a possibility for some types of crimes. Community service is a more general form of restitution. People convicted of nonviolent crimes can be sentenced to community service and placed in a variety of settings, including hospitals, homeless shelters, schools, and nursing homes. Restitution is often used in combination with probation and has increasingly been used as a means of compensating victims, helping the community, and repairing the damage caused by minor crimes (Anderson, 1998).

Probation involves suspending a jail or prison sentence and releasing the criminal into the community under the supervision of a probation officer. The conditions of probation can be fairly strict, requiring the convict to meet weekly with a probation officer, to find and keep a job, to submit to random drug tests, and to attend therapy groups. If the offender violates the conditions of probation, he can be sent to prison. Each year about 1.5 million Americans are placed on probation and about 1.3 million complete their probationary sentence (Siegel, 1998). Unfortunately, probation has a relatively high failure rate. In a massive study of nearly 79,000 probationers in 17 states, 43% of people on probation were rearrested within three years (Langan & Cuniff, 1992). Although this recidivism rate is discouraging, it is substantially better than the recidivism rate for inmates released from prison.

A relatively recent variation on probation is *house arrest* (also called home confinement) enforced through some form of electronic monitoring. House arrest is likely to involve many of the same conditions of parole, with the additional requirement that the offender not leave his or her home or yard except to go to school or work. Electronic bracelets locked on to the ankle or wrist alert authorities when the offender leaves the house. A somewhat less high-tech version involves random, frequent, computer-generated phone calls to the offender's home. These phone calls must be answered quickly by the offender (e.g., picked up before the fourth ring). Home arrest is often a last chance—if the offender leaves the designated areas, he or she can be sent to prison.

Other alternatives to prison involve brief incarceration or what has been called *shock incarceration*. The "shock" usually consists of a brief period where young offenders are put in prison. One example is the widely publicized "scared straight" program that became popular during the 1980s. That program took juvenile offenders into maximum-security prisons where they were verbally abused by inmates serving life sentences for violent crimes. The "lifers" told the young criminals about the horrors of prison life (e.g., rape, fear, violence) in graphic, frightening detail. An extended version of shock incarceration is the "boot camp" program modeled after military basic training programs. For several weeks, nonviolent offenders are subjected to an abusive, demanding drill sergeant; tough living conditions; marching; and intense exercise. Although such programs enjoy popularity and support among prison officials and the general public, they don't seem to have beneficial effects on the juvenile offenders who go through the program. Systematic analyses of shock incarceration programs indicate that they often backfire—graduates of shock programs are somewhat more likely to become repeat offenders than offenders who are simply put on probation (Bottcher, Isorena, & Belnas, 1996; Peters, 1996). Heavy reliance on fear, disrespect, and humiliation appear to undermine the effectiveness of such programs and to create a negative response in many youthful offenders. Indeed, the shock incarceration programs that do produce benefits devote several hours a day to therapy, education, or drug treatment and provide follow-up supervision after offenders have left the program (MacKenzie, Brame, MacDowell, & Souryal, 1995; Finckenauer, Gavin, Hovland, & Storvoll, 1999).

Residential community corrections centers (better known as "halfway houses") are also used as a sentencing option for some offenders. These are places (sometimes large houses or small apartment buildings) where groups of offenders live in a communal environment and attend some form of group therapy. Offenders are usually required to find jobs and to perform household chores. Originally, these facilities were designed to ease the shock of reentry into free society. The final months of a prison sentence could be spent in a halfway house so that the ex-convict could find a job, build up cash reserves, find an apartment, and reestablish family relationships. Currently, if a judge believes that a particular offender should not be sentenced to prison but needs a more structured environment than probation, that offender can be sentenced to a residential community corrections center (Barkan, 1997).

Alternatives to prisons are essential for several reasons. First, all alternatives to prison are much cheaper than prison. Second, prison is much too severe a punishment for many crimes and may make offenders more likely to commit crimes. Third, there is simply not enough public money to build and maintain prisons to hold every criminal. Fourth, alternatives allow first-time offenders and people convicted of nonserious crimes to avoid the trauma and stigma of imprisonment.

THE DEATH PENALTY

In most Western democracies, the death penalty is viewed as a violation of basic human rights. It has been abolished in Canada and Mexico, Australia and New Zealand, and all the countries of Western Europe. South Africa made the death penalty unconstitutional in 1995, and most of the countries of Central and South America have abandoned it or reserve it only for extraordinary crimes such as treason. Many countries refuse to extradite criminals to the United States if they might be eligible for the death penalty, and some countries donate money and legal aid to their citizens who face execution in the United States. In those parts of the world where the death penalty is still used, hanging and shooting are the most widely used forms of legal execution. Beheading is also widely used. The modern technological forms of execution familiar to Americans—the electric chair, gas chamber, and lethal injection—are only used in the United States (Costanzo, 1997).

Although 38 states, the federal government, and the U.S. military authorize use of the death penalty, executions are rare. Even in years when executions are relatively frequent, less than 1% of murderers are executed. Most of the more than 3,700 prisoners currently on death row will die of natural causes before they are escorted to the execution chamber. From 1990 through 2000, 548 people were killed in U.S. execution chambers. Eighty-five people were executed in 2000, 66 in 2001, and 71 in 2002. Alaska, Maine, Minnesota, Vermont, Hawaii, Massachusetts, North Dakota, West Virginia, Iowa, Michigan, Rhode Island, Wisconsin, and the District of Columbia do not have the death penalty.

For those states that retain the death penalty, aggravated murder is the only crime punishable by death. The definition of aggravated murder varies across jurisdictions, but it generally includes murder for hire, murder of more than one person, murder of a police officer, murder of a child, and murder during the commission of another felony (e.g., robbery, rape, drug dealing). Under federal law, capital crimes include treason and espionage, murdering a government official, using a weapon of mass destruction, and sending bombs or other lethal weapons (e.g., anthrax) through the U.S. mail.

SUPREME COURT DECISIONS

Constitutional challenges to the death penalty have been based on the Eighth Amendment's prohibition against "cruel and unusual punishment" or the Fourteenth Amendment's guarantee of "equal protection" under the law. In 1972, in the case of *Furman v. Georgia,* the Supreme Court ruled in a 5 to 4 decision that capital punishment—as then administered—was unconstitutional. However, the majority was deeply divided about *why* the death penalty should be considered unconstitutional. Each of the five justices wrote a separate opinion based on somewhat different reasoning. The points on which all five justices seemed to agree were that the penalty was "wantonly and freakishly applied," that there was "no meaningful basis for distinguishing the few cases in which it is imposed from the many cases in which it is not," and that these problems were probably due to "the uncontrolled discretion of judges or juries." The *Furman* decision did not rule out use of the death penalty in principle; it only prohibited the way it was being carried out at the time.

Following the *Furman* decision, many state legislatures redesigned their death penalty sentencing procedures to address the concerns of the Court. Specifically, they tried to find ways of controlling the discretion of jurors in capital murder trials. In 1976, in *Gregg v. Georgia* and its companion cases, the Supreme Court rejected the idea of erasing all discretion by making death sentences mandatory for certain types of murder, but it approved a series of reforms designed to "guide" the discretion of jurors. Under these "guided discretion" statutes, defendants accused of capital murder are tried by juries in a two-phase (bifurcated) proceeding. Guilt is decided in the first phase. If the defendant is found guilty of capital murder, his sentence (either death by execution or life in prison without the possibility of parole) is decided in the second (penalty) phase. As a further check against the "unbridled discretion" of jurors, all death sentences are reviewed by state supreme courts. Executions resumed in 1977 when Gary Gilmore abandoned his appeals and was killed by a firing squad in Utah.

At the end of the penalty phase of a capital trial, jurors are typically instructed to "weigh" those characteristics of the murder and the murderer that support a death sentence (these are called aggravating factors) against those characteristics that support a sentence of life imprisonment (these are called mitigating factors). Several cases decided by the Supreme Court since *Gregg* have focused on what jurors can and cannot consider as they attempt to weigh aggravating against mitigating factors. The Court has held that jurors must be allowed to consider "any aspect of a defendant's character or record and any of the circumstances of the offense" that are offered as mitigation. Jurors "may determine the weight to be given to relevant mitigating evidence," but they "may not give it no weight by excluding such evidence from consideration" (*Lockett v. Ohio,* 1978). Jurors may also consider the defendant's future behavior and potential adjustment to prison, as well as how the death of the victim harmed his or her survivors.

Two recent decisions place further limits on death sentences. In 2002, in a 6 to 3 decision, the Court put an end to the execution of mentally retarded prisoners (*Atkins v. Virginia*). Writing for the majority, John Paul Stevens argued that "a national consensus has developed" against executing mentally retarded prisoners and that, "Because of their disabilities in areas of reasoning, judgment, and control of their impulses . . . they do not act with the level of moral culpability that characterizes the most serious adult criminal conduct." Less than a week later, in a 7 to 2 decision (*Ring v. Arizona*), the Court held that it is unconstitutional for judges to decide whether a convicted murderer should be sentenced to death or life imprisonment. Only a jury can make that decision.

Research on Capital Murder Trials and the Court's Response.
In addition to the bifurcated nature of death penalty trials, there is another unique aspect of capital trials—the process of "death qualification." During voir dire, potential jurors in capital murder cases are asked about their willingness to vote for the death penalty if the defendant is found guilty. In 1985, in the case of *Wainwright v. Witt,* the Supreme Court ruled that potential jurors whose beliefs "substantially impair" their ability to consider or impose a death sentence must be excused from serving on a capital jury. If a potential juror expresses a lack of willingness to seriously consider execution as a punishment, he or she is not permitted to serve on a capital jury. This typically means that between 30% and 40% of potential jurors are excluded from serving on capital juries (Thompson, 1989). Those excluded potential jurors are more likely to be female, African American, and politically liberal.

Research shows that death qualification affects both who gets on the jury and the attitudes of jurors towards the defendant. Compared to jurors who are screened out by the process, death-qualified jurors are more likely to vote to convict the defendant. Death-qualified jurors are not only more conviction prone when deciding guilt, they tend to be more receptive to aggravating factors and less receptive to mitigating factors during the penalty phase (Bowers, Sandys, & Steiner, 1998). A second, more subtle effect occurs because jurors try to make sense of the odd process of death qualification. Jurors who answer a series of questions about their willingness to vote for a death sentence during voir dire often infer that both defense attorneys and prosecutors anticipate a conviction and a death sentence (Luginbuhl & Burkhead, 1994). Why else would they be asking about a death sentence before the trial begins? This effect works against the defendant.

In the 1986 case of *Lockhart v. McCree,* the Supreme Court reviewed the research on death qualification and then dismissed it as irrelevant. In the majority decision, Justice Rehnquist wrote:

> We will assume for purposes of this opinion that the studies are both methodologically valid and adequate to establish that death-qualification in fact produces juries somewhat more "conviction-prone" than non-death-qualified juries. We hold, nonetheless, that the Constitution does not prohibit the states from death-qualifying juries in capital cases.

Although the Supreme Court did not view the research as important, many prosecutors appear to understand the biasing effects of the death-qualification process. For example, in the Andrea Yates trial (discussed in Chapter 4) some legal scholars have argued that the prosecutor's motivation for charging Ms. Yates with *capital* murder was to assemble a jury that was more likely to convict her on the murder charges (Dershowitz, 2002). Indeed, once Yates was convicted, prosecutors did not vigorously pursue a death sentence during the penalty phase. In his penalty phase summation, the prosecutor appeared to argue against execution: "If you want to sentence her to life rather than a death sentence, you will have done the right thing" (Stack, 2002, p. A14). Apparently, the goal was to use the death-qualification process to, ". . . get a pro-prosecution jury, one more likely to reject the insanity defense and return a verdict of guilt" (Dershowitz, 2002, p. A18).

Jury Decision Making in the Penalty Phase.

The penalty phase of a capital murder trial is qualitatively different from other criminal proceedings. The question posed to jurors is not "did the defendant commit the crime?" but "should the defendant be killed in the execution chamber?" That question cannot be answered by examining the facts of the case or by applying rules of logic.

To help jurors make this life-or-death decision, judges instruct jurors to weigh aggravating factors against mitigating factors. Unfortunately, those instructions appear to provide little help. Research using both trial simulations and post-verdict interviews with actual jurors demonstrates that jurors misunderstand the penalty phase instructions (Ellsworth, Haney, & Costanzo, 2001). For example, many jurors wrongly believe that they cannot take into account the full range of mitigating factors, or that if they find any aggravating factors to be present, they *must* vote for death. Many jurors also believe that unless they vote for death, the murderer will be eligible for parole (Costanzo & Costanzo, 1994; Wiener et al., 1997).

The meanings of the key terms "aggravating factors" and "mitigating factors" are unclear to jurors, and jurors are unclear about how to "weigh" the two sets of factors. Here is a quote from a juror who was interviewed after serving on a capital murder trial:

> The different verdicts that we could come up with depended on if mitigating outweighed aggravating or if aggravating outweighed mitigating, or all of that. So we wanted to make sure. I said 'I don't know that I exactly understand what it means.' And then everybody else said, 'No, neither do I,' or 'I can't give you a definition.' So we decided to ask the judge. Well, the judge wrote back and said, 'You have to glean it from the instructions' (Haney, Sontag, & Costanzo, 1994, p. 157).

If jurors are not able to rely on the court to clarify the nature of their task, they must rely on their own rough translations of the meaning of penalty phase instructions. Here's how a different juror put it:

> All that becomes very foggy and gray and just sort of burns off in the sun. . . . Did he do it? Yeah. Did he mean it? Yeah. That's what the people on the jury broke it down to (Costanzo & Costanzo, 1994, p. 161).

If instructions to jurors are difficult to understand, jurors may fall back on their own preconceptions or prejudices. In an experimental test of this proposition, Mona Lynch and Craig Haney (2000) asked 397 mock jurors to view a realistic videotaped simulation of a capital penalty trial for a defendant who had been found guilty of robbery and murder. The content of the videotape and the jury instructions were held constant for all mock jurors, but the race of the defendant and the race of the victim were varied. There were four conditions: white defendant-black victim, white defendant-white victim, black defendant-black victim, and black defendant-white victim. The findings revealed that both race and comprehension of instructions had an impact on sentencing. In the condition where the defendant was white and the victim was black, 40% of mock jurors handed down a death sentence. But in the condition where the defendant was black and the victim was white, 54% of mock jurors recommended a sentence of death. Perhaps more important, the researchers found an interaction between comprehension of instructions and race of defendant. Among jurors who understood the instructions well, the rate of death sentences did not differ as a function of race. However, among jurors with poor comprehension of instructions, the rate of death sentences for white defendants was 41% while the rate for black defendants was 60%. These findings suggest that if the instructions given to jurors fail to provide jurors with clear, comprehensible guidance about how to make the life-or-death decision, racial bias may creep into the decision-making process.

RACIAL DISPARITIES AND THE DEATH PENALTY
• •

Prior to the Civil War, the behavior of blacks in the South was regulated by a set of laws called "The Black Codes." Blacks could be executed for theft, but whites could pay a fine. The rape of a black woman was not considered a crime, but many black men were executed for allegedly raping white women. Although blacks and whites later became equal under the law, discrimination persisted. Racial discrimination in the application of the death penalty continued and was especially conspicuous in cases of rape. Between 1930 and 1967, 455 men were executed for the crime of rape. Eighty-nine percent of those men were black. In 1973, Marvin Wolfgang and Marc Riedel analyzed 361 rape convictions. After statistically controlling for many other variables, the researchers found that the best predictor of a death sentence was the race of the offender combined with the race of the victim. Black men convicted of raping white women were 18 times more likely to be sentenced to death than any other racial combination (white-black, black-black, or white-white). Use of the death penalty for the crime of rape was examined in the 1977 case of *Coker v. Georgia*. In that case, the Supreme Court held that the death penalty was disproportionately severe for the crime of rape. Surprisingly, the shocking racial disparities in the imposition of the death penalty for rape were not an explicit factor in the Court's decision. However, it may have been that research on racial disparity had an influence "behind the scenes" (Ellsworth & Mauro, 1998).

Although evidence of racial discrimination is clearest for cases involving rape, discrimination has not been limited to the crime of rape. Several analyses of death penalty cases indicate that race has an impact at several stages in the legal process. Following arrest, black defendants are more likely than white defendants to be charged with capital murder and, once charged, they are more likely to be convicted. Following conviction, blacks are more likely to be sentenced to death and, once sentenced, they are more likely to be executed (Bowers, 1984; Baldus, Woodworth, Zuckerman, Weiner, & Broffit, 1998). The race of the *victim* is especially important. If the victim is white, prosecutors are more than twice as likely to seek a death sentence than if the victim is black, and blacks who kill whites are about four times more likely to be charged with capital murder than blacks who kill blacks (Baldus et al., 1998; Paternoster & Kazyaka, 1988). In a sophisticated analysis of race and the death penalty, David Baldus, George Woodworth, and Charles Pulaski (1990) found that, even after taking over 20 relevant variables into account, prosecutors decided to seek the death penalty five times more often against killers of whites than against killers of blacks. In addition, Baldus and his colleagues analyzed 594 homicides in Georgia. They found that blacks convicted of killing whites were sentenced to death in 22% of capital cases, while whites convicted of killing blacks received a death sentence only 3% of the time. Looking more deeply at their data, the researchers took into account more than 250 characteristics of the murder, the offender, and the victim. Even after removing the influence of all these variables, the odds of receiving a death sentence were 4.3 times higher for murderers of whites than for murderers of blacks.

These findings were presented to the Supreme Court in the case of *McCleskey v. Kemp* (1987). In the view of many social scientists, the majority of the Court (it was a 5 to 4 decision) was frustratingly unreceptive to this evidence. Although the justices were unable to offer any explanation for the striking racial disparities, they were unwilling to accept the research findings. The majority decision in *McCleskey* (written by Justice Powell) held that some unfairness is tolerable and inevitable because discretion is an inescapable aspect of capital sentencing. In addition, the Court held that any discrimination in McCleskey's case was not intentional and the defendant's attorney had failed to present ". . . evidence specific to his own case that would support an inference that racial consideration played a part in his sentence." Put differently, to overturn a death sentence because of racial bias, there would need to be strong evidence that jurors acted with "discriminatory purpose." Some scholars have pointed out that this standard of proof is higher than the legal standard needed to demonstrate discrimination in housing or employment. Consequently, "[a] person denied housing or employment has more protection from racial discrimination than a person whose life is at stake" (Ellsworth & Mauro, 1998, p. 720).

More recent analyses of both state and federal court decisions indicate that discrimination in death sentences—particularly by race of victim—persists. Blacks and whites are about equally likely to become the victims of aggravated murder (the kind punishable by death). However, a black murderer whose victim is white is six times more likely to receive a death sentence than a white murderer whose victim is black (Baldus et al., 1998). At present, 41% of the prisoners on death row are African American.

THE DEATH PENALTY AS A DETERRENT TO MURDER

Largely because of a belief in deterrence, early forms of execution were gruesome, slow, and public. It was thought that more terrifying executions would be more powerful deterrents. And, if more people watched, more potential criminals would be deterred. Executions were festive public events. In Germany, prior to the 1700s, huge crowds gathered to watch criminals be broken at the wheel. On a raised stage, criminals would be tied to a large wagon wheel. The executioner would methodically smash the bones of the legs and arms with a steel bar before bringing death by a blow to the throat (Costanzo, 1997). To deter crime in England, criminals were disemboweled and decapitated after being strangled in a public ceremony. The heads of executed criminals were displayed at crossroads and on London Bridge to serve as visible warnings to other potential wrongdoers (Laurence, 1931).

The proposition that capital punishment deters homicide can be tested. If the death penalty does deter murder, states with the death penalty should have relatively low murder rates. To test this hypothesis, researchers have compared the murder rates in no-death-penalty states to murder rates in similar, geographically adjacent death-penalty states (e.g., Michigan is compared to Ohio, Rhode Island to Connecticut, North Dakota to South Dakota). Findings indicate that, overall, states with the death penalty have significantly *higher* murder rates than states without it (Sellin, 1980).

A second hypothesis derived from deterrence theory is that murder rates should rise or fall when death penalty laws change. This hypothesis can be tested by closely examining murder rates over time. Specifically, deterrence theory predicts that, if a state abolishes the death penalty (or suspends it for a period of time), the murder rate will increase because the deterrent is no longer in effect. Conversely, if a state establishes the death penalty (or reinstates it after a period of absence), murder rates should fall because the deterrent is now in effect. Like the first hypothesis, this second hypothesis has not been supported by the data (Bailey & Peterson, 1997). Multiple studies conducted in the United States and 12 other countries provide no evidence that capital punishment suppresses the murder rate (Archer & Gartner, 1984).

When comparing adjacent states or measuring changes in murder rates over time, most studies have used statistical procedures that remove the influence of other factors known to affect rates of violence (e.g., unemployment, number of young men in the population, size of police force) (Bailey & Peterson, 1997). In addition, some studies have looked only at the specific types of murder punishable by death, for example, killing of a police officer (Bailey & Peterson, 1994). Finally, many studies have looked at the effects of each actual execution rather than the effect of simply having the death penalty on the books (Bowers, 1988). Despite many decades of research by a variety of researchers using a variety of methods, there is still no credible evidence that the death penalty deters murderers. Indeed, a few researchers have come to the opposite conclusion: that executions increase murder rates. For example, William Bowers (1988) examined data from nearly 70 studies on the relationship between the death penalty and murder rates. His conclusion was that executions usually *stimulate* a small increase in murders (one to four murders) in the weeks following an execution. This "brutalization effect" is stronger for highly publicized executions. Like other forms of violence in the media, executions may weaken inhibitions against violent behavior, desensitize people to killing, and communicate the message that killing is an acceptable and justifiable response to provocation (Huesmann, Moise-Titus, Podolski, & Eron, 2003).

Deterrence is a theory about psychological processes in the mind of the murderer. It posits that potential murderers will be restrained by the knowledge that they might be executed if they act on their desire to kill—that is, their fear of execution will stop them from killing. There are several problems with this theory. First, there is no evidence that people engage in a rational weighing of costs and benefits before committing a murder. In fact, most murders are crimes of passion—the product of rage, jealousy, hatred, or fear (Costanzo, 1997). In addition, the murderer is often under the influence of drugs or alcohol. Second, most murderers believe that they will not be put to death. And, they're right. As noted earlier, the probability that they will be executed is very low. Of course, many murderers believe they won't even be caught or that, if they are caught, they won't be convicted or sentenced to death. Third, it is not clear whether the prospect of being executed elicits more or less fear than the prospect of life in prison without parole. Life in prison without hope of release may be no less frightening than the remote possibility of being executed sometime in the distant future.

ERRORS AND MISTAKES IN DEATH PENALTY CASES

One way of gauging the effectiveness of our system of capital punishment is to analyze how many death verdicts are overturned and why they are overturned. In a massive study of how capital cases move through the legal system, James Liebman and his colleagues examined every capital case in the United States from 1973 through 1995 (Liebman, Fagan, & West, 2000). They found that 68% of death sentences were reversed because of serious errors at trial. When these reversed cases were retried, 82% of the defendants were given a punishment less than death and 7% of the defendants were found "not guilty" of the crime that had sent them to death row. The most frequent causes of error included incompetent defense lawyers (37% of cases), faulty or misleading jury instructions (20% of cases), and various forms of prosecutorial misconduct, such as suppression of evidence or intimidation of witnesses (19% of cases). Although 7% of death row inmates were later found to be "not guilty," the Liebman study does not tell us how many innocent people were actually executed. Once an inmate is executed, all appeals cease.

The most troubling form of error in capital cases is the wrongful conviction, imprisonment, and execution of an innocent person. In their landmark study of wrongful convictions since 1900, Hugo Bedau and Michael Radelet identified 416 people who were wrongfully convicted of murder and sentenced to death (Radelet, Bedau, & Putnam, 1992). Their analysis suggests that, in 23 of those cases, the innocent person was executed. What makes these wrongful convictions especially disturbing is that most were caused by factors that are difficult for the legal system to detect. The main causes for these miscarriages of justice were police error (coerced or false confessions, sloppy or corrupt investigation), prosecutor error (suppression of exculpatory evidence, overzealousness) witness error (mistaken eyewitness identification, perjured testimony), as well as various other errors such as misleading circumstantial evidence, forensic science errors, incompetent defense lawyers, exculpatory evidence that is ruled inadmissible, insufficient attention to alibis, and pressure created by community outrage.

Perhaps the most important recent development in the death penalty debate has been the use of DNA evidence to prove the innocence of people on death row. In June 2002, Ray Krone became the 100th person to be released from death row because of exonerating evidence. In most of the more than 100 cases of prisoners released from death row, some form of biological trace evidence—skin under the fingernails of a victim who fought against her killer, a semen stain on the panties of a victim of rape and murder—was used to identify the real murderer and to exclude the wrongly convicted person. Although it is essential for prisoners on death row to have access to DNA testing that may exonerate them, DNA is only useful in a minority of murder cases. To make use of DNA testing to prove guilt or innocence, biological evidence (e.g., blood, semen, saliva, skin) must be available. In most murder cases, biological evidence doesn't exist—either none was left at the scene, or none was properly collected at the scene, or, if it was collected, it was not preserved by police. As recently as 2002, the Los Angeles Police Department destroyed biological evidence in more than 1,100 cases involving rape (Daunt & Berry, 2002). Some of these cases involved prisoners on death row who had been convicted of murder during the commission of a rape.

In a recent case that may have ended in the execution of an innocent man, no biological evidence was available. Gary Graham was convicted of shooting a man in a grocery store parking lot during a holdup. The sole evidence against him was the eyewitness testimony of a woman who claimed to have seen Graham through her windshield from across a parking lot. Two other eyewitnesses who were willing to testify that Graham was *not* the killer were never called to testify at trial. Later, after viewing videotaped testimony from these two uncalled witnesses, three jurors in the case signed affidavits saying that they would have acquitted Graham if they had been allowed to hear from these other two witnesses at trial. The Texas Board of Pardons found this evidence unpersuasive. In June 2000, a team of prison guards dragged Gary Graham to the execution chamber and strapped him to the lethal injection gurney. He proclaimed his innocence to the very end.

IN CONCLUSION

Prisons are an essential component of our criminal justice system, but they are expensive, frequently harmful, and other less severe sanctions often produce better results. More than a century and a half ago, de Tocqueville and de Beaumont wrote that the U.S. had been swept up into a "monomania of the penitentiary system." They criticized the American belief that prisons could be "a remedy for all the evils of society." The "monomania" of the prison is still with us today and seems to drive public policy more now than it did in de Tocqueville's time.

Social science can often provide answers to the question, "What works?" If we are interested in finding out which forms of punishment or rehabilitation are effective for which types of criminals, researchers can usually tell us. But arguments about punishment often turn on political and moral considerations. Although questions of morality are largely beyond the reach of social science, data are essential to inform moral decisions. Whether or not the severe punishment of confinement in a supermax prison is moral depends, in part, on the emotional, psychological, and societal impact of such confinement. And whether the death penalty is morally justified depends, in part, on whether it is imposed fairly and consistently, without discrimination or error. We must assess the morality of a particular punishment not by imagining how it might work in a perfect world, but by looking at how, and how well, it actually works in the real world.

Readings to Supplement This Chapter

Articles

Bedau, H. A. (2002). Causes and consequences of wrongful convictions: An essay-review. *Judicature, 86,* 115–119.

Costanzo, M., & Peterson, J. (1994). Attorney persuasion in the capital penalty phase: A content analysis of closing arguments. *Journal of Social Issues, 50,* 125–147.

Darley, J. M., Carlsmith, K. M., & Robinson, P. H. (2000). Incapacitation and just desserts as motives for punishment. *Law and Human Behavior, 24,* 659–684.

Ruback, R. B., & Wroblewski, J. (2001). The federal sentencing guidelines: Psychological and policy reasons for simplification. *Psychology, Public Policy, and Law, 7,* 739–775.

St. Amand, M. D., and Zamble, E. (2001). Impact of information about sentencing decisions on public attitudes toward the justice system. *Law and Human Behavior, 25,* 515–528.

Books

Costanzo, M. (1997). *Just revenge: Costs and consequences of the death penalty.* New York: St. Martin's Press.

Currie, E. (1998). *Crime and punishment in America.* New York: Metropolitan Books.

Glossary of Key Legal Terms

Adversarial System   System of justice in which opposing parties present competing versions of the evidence in an effort to win a favorable judgment. In the United States, a trial is an adversarial proceeding because lawyers (adversaries) compete to win a verdict in their favor. The American legal system assumes that truth will emerge through a contest between adversaries who present opposing interpretations of the evidence to a neutral fact finder (a jury or judge).

Affidavit   A written, signed statement made under oath attesting to an issue relevant to a dispute.

Affirmative Defense   A defendant offers new evidence to avoid an adverse judgment. The defendant has the burden of proving the defense.

Aggravating   Circumstances (also called factors) of the crime or criminal that increase the seriousness of the crime or the guilt of the criminal. For example, in a murder case, premeditation and the brutality of the crime are aggravating factors.

Alternative Dispute Resolution (ADR)   Alternatives to formal trials. Examples include mediation (a neutral third person helps the two opposing parties reach an agreement) and arbitration (a retired judge or other arbitrator is hired by the disputants to hear arguments and evidence and render a binding decision).

***Amicus Curiae* Brief**   "Friend of the court" briefs submitted by people or groups who are not parties to the case but who want to provide information to the court relevant to issues in the case.

Appeal   The formal process of asking a higher court to review the actions and decisions of a lower court. The appeals court is asked to decide whether the determination of the lower court should be affirmed, modified, or reversed.

Arraignment   An initial hearing before a judge in a criminal case. The defendant is advised of the charges against him or her, and enters a preliminary plea. The defendant is also informed of his or her constitutional rights (e.g., to have a jury trial, to have a defense attorney appointed, to plead not guilty). The judge must also decide whether or not the defendant is to be detained in jail while awaiting trial, or the amount of bail if not detained.

Bail   In an effort to guarantee that a defendant shows up for trial, a judge sets bail. The judge decides that a defendant can remain free until trial if he or she pays a specified amount of money (i.e., bail). If a defendant is a flight risk (i.e., he or she might flee the jurisdiction to avoid trial) or charged with a violent crime, bail might be denied.

Bench Trial   Trial held before a judge (instead of a jury). The judge hears the evidence and decides the case on both facts and law.

Beyond a Reasonable Doubt   Standard of proof used in criminal trials. To convict a criminal defendant, the jury or judge must be strongly persuaded (to have no reasonable doubt) that the defendant is guilty of the crime. The prosecution bears the burden of convincing the jury or judge of guilt beyond a reasonable doubt.

Bill of Rights   The first 10 amendments to the U.S. Constitution. The Bill of Rights guarantees basic civil rights such as freedom of speech, freedom from unreasonable search and seizure, and the right to trial by jury.

Brief   Briefs (which are seldom brief) are written documents submitted to a judge or panel of judges. Attorneys for both sides of the case submit briefs. Typically, a brief offers interpretations of relevant law and summarizes facts and arguments for a party to the dispute.

Burden of Proof   The duty of a prosecutor in a criminal case or a plaintiff in a civil case to prove the allegation of wrongdoing. The level of certainty (or lack of doubt) that needs to be established in the minds of jurors or judges.

Capital   A capital crime is potentially punishable by death—almost always murder with aggravating circumstances. A capital murder trial is a trial where, if a defendant is found guilty, death by execution is a potential punishment.

Case Law   Law drawn from decisions made by judges in previous cases. Current law is based, in part, on rulings made by judges in prior cases.

Cause of Action   The alleged act or event that entitles one party in a civil lawsuit to seek a remedy in court.

Certiorari   "To make certain." A writ or action that moves a case from an inferior court to a superior court (e.g., the U.S. Supreme Court) for review. A litigant petitions the higher court to grant a review (to grant a "writ of certiorari").

Challenge for Cause   A claim that a prospective juror should be dismissed because some bias discovered during questioning appears to make him or her unable to decide the case in a fair and impartial manner.

Change of Venue Motion   A request to the court, usually made by a defense attorney, to move a trial from one location to another. A change of venue request is typically made when there has been substantial pretrial publicity that may have created biases in the jury pool.

Civil   Law regulating disputes between private parties, including business relationships, and rights or duties between individuals and other entities. Contrasted with criminal law. Includes areas such as child custody, breach of contract, and copyright infringement.

Class Action   When a group of people brings a lawsuit on behalf of an even larger group of people who have allegedly suffered a wrong (e.g., who have been injured by a prescription drug).

Clear and Convincing Evidence   A standard of proof between the less demanding standard of "preponderance of evidence" (used in most civil cases) and the more demanding standard of "beyond a reasonable doubt" (used in criminal cases). Used only in a minority of civil cases.

Closing Argument   A final argument made by an attorney to a judge or jury at the end of a trial. In closing arguments (also called summations), lawyers summarize and interpret evidence and attempt to show why the case should be decided in their favor.

Common Law   Law based on judicial precedent instead of legislative acts. Originally derived from the unwritten laws in England. General principles derived from cases decided by judges over time.

Comparative Negligence   An attempt to apportion liability between a plaintiff and a defendant according to how much they contributed to the wrong. Generally expressed in terms of percentages. For example, one party may be judged to be 60% responsible and the other may be judged to be 40% responsible.

Compensatory Damages   A monetary award paid to a plaintiff to compensate for harm caused by a defendant.

Competence   The ability to understand legal procedures and the consequences of legal decisions.

Contributory Negligence   When the plaintiff contributes to the wrong or injury he or she suffered. A defendant in a civil case may try to demonstrate that the plaintiff failed to exercise reasonable care or caution and thereby contributed to his or her own injuries.

Crime   An act that damages the public good and that is punishable by law.

Criminal Law   The body of law concerned with the prosecution or defense of criminal acts.

Cruel and Unusual Punishment   Punishment that is viewed as shocking or disgusting by ordinary citizens (e.g., physical torture). Cruel and unusual punishment is prohibited by the Eighth Amendment, but definitions of what is cruel and unusual change as standards of decency change.

Damages   Monetary compensation awarded to a plaintiff in a civil suit. Damages are meant to compensate the plaintiff for some harm or loss suffered because of an action (or lack of action) by a defendant.

Death Qualification   A unique aspect of jury selection in a capital trial. Prior to trial, potential jurors are asked whether they would be able to vote for the death penalty if the defendant is found guilty. People who say they would be unable to consider the death penalty are not permitted to serve as jurors in capital trials.

Deposition   A pretrial interview in which a witness answers questions under oath.

Determinate Sentencing   An effort to restrict the discretion of judges when making sentencing decisions. The length of a sentence for a particular crime is determined in advance and judges are given only minimal discretion.

Directed Verdict   A ruling by a trial judge that, due to the failure of one side to present sufficient evidence in support of its position, the jury must return a certain verdict.

Discovery   A procedure for disclosing information between the parties in a lawsuit. Litigants are required to disclose documents and facts relevant to the case to the opposing counsel in accordance with established rules and procedures.

Disparate Impact   A policy or practice (e.g., a hiring or promotion procedure) that has the effect of favoring one group (e.g., males) at the expense of another group (e.g., females).

Double Jeopardy   If a person has been found "not guilty" of a particular crime, he or she cannot be tried a second time for that same crime. A provision of the Fifth Amendment to the U.S. Constitution.

Due Process of Law   The set of procedures required by law, including, for example, the requirement that a suspect be informed about the charges against him or her and be afforded a fair hearing.

Dynamite Charge   An instruction given by a judge to a hung jury. If a jury has told the judge that they are deadlocked, the judge may tell the jury to continue to deliberate with a predisposition to reach a verdict. Also called the "shotgun instruction" or the "Allen charge."

Exclusionary Rule   The rule requiring that illegally gathered evidence (e.g., drugs found in a home that was being illegally searched) cannot be used against a defendant at trial.

Exculpatory Evidence   Any evidence that tends to demonstrate that a defendant is not guilty.

Executor   The person specified in a will to carry out the terms and conditions of the will.

Federal Rules of Evidence   A uniform set of rules that governs whether evidence is admissible or inadmissible in federal courts.

Felony   A crime that is punishable by a year or more in prison or by death. A serious crime contrasted with a minor crime (called a misdemeanor).

Finder of Fact   The person (usually a judge) or the group of people (usually a jury) that is responsible for determining the facts and deciding what really happened. A jury, for example, must decide if a defendant actually committed the crime for which he or she is on trial.

Gag Order   An order by a trial judge that prohibits attorneys or witnesses from talking to the press. The purpose of such an order is to prevent publicity that might influence a verdict or sentencing decision.

Grand Jury   A group of people (usually 23 people) who are asked to decide whether there is sufficient evidence to indict (formally charge) someone for a crime. Contrasted with a petit jury—the ordinary trial jury of six to 12 people.

Grant of Certiorari   When an appeals court grants certiorari, it agrees to review a case.

Habeas Corpus Petition   A petition that requires officials to bring a prisoner to court and show that he or she is being detained legally. Habeas corpus means "you have the body."

Harmless Error   The assertion by a higher court that, although an error may have occurred at trial, that error did not influence the verdict.

Hearsay   An out-of-court statement offered for its truth. For example, if I testify in court that my friend told me that she overheard the defendant say he committed a burglary, it is hearsay. Generally, hearsay is not admissible because there was no opportunity to cross-examine the person who made the statement and the person who made the statement was not under oath. There are many exceptions to the hearsay rule.

Indictment   A formal accusation, issued by a grand jury at the request of a prosecutor, that someone has committed a specific crime.

Injunction   An order issued by a judge to perform a specific act or to refrain from performing a specific act.

Inquisitional System   The legal model used in many parts of Europe. Differs from the adversarial model in that the judge (the fact finder) takes a more active role by appointing the lawyers and questioning the witnesses.

Interrogatories   Questions submitted in writing to a witness or party in a lawsuit. These questions require written responses given under oath.

Joinder   Joining together two or more parties in a single trial.

Judicial Waiver   A judge's decision to transfer a juvenile offender from juvenile court to adult court.

Jurisprudence   The science and philosophy of law, including the study of the structure and origins of law.

Jurist   A legal scholar or judge. Someone well versed in the law.

Juvenile Court   A special court created to decide the cases of criminal defendants under the age of 18.

Law   The body of formal rules, principles, and procedures that govern behavior in a particular society.

Liability   Responsibility for conduct. A duty or obligation to do something or to not do something. To be held liable means to be held responsible for the alleged harm.

Limiting Instruction   Instructing jurors to use information presented at trial (e.g., information about a defendant's prior criminal record) only for limited purposes (e.g., for gauging the credibility of the defendant).

Malpractice   Failure of a professional to fulfill his or her duty. Malpractice lawsuits allege that a professional (e.g., a physician or accountant) caused injury by failing to perform his or her duties in accordance with professional standards.

Misdemeanor   A minor or lesser crime punishable by less than a year of confinement in jail.

Mediation   An alternative to litigation in which a neutral third party attempts to assist disputants in creating a resolution that both parties can endorse.

Mitigating   Circumstances surrounding a crime or characteristics of a criminal that lessen the degree of guilt or the severity of the crime. Youth and mental impairment are examples of mitigating factors.

Motion   A party's request to a judge for a ruling or order in his or her favor.

Motion in Limine A motion made at the outset of a trial that asks the judge to establish rules for the admissibility of evidence expected to arise at trial.

Motion to Suppress A request that some piece of evidence be ruled inadmissible at trial.

Negligence Failure to exercise reasonable care—that is, the degree of care a reasonable person would show in circumstances similar to those faced by the defendant.

Opening Statements Statements made by counsel as the trial begins. Generally, such statements provide an overview of the evidence to be presented.

Penalty Phase The second phase of a capital murder trial. During the penalty phase, jurors are asked to decide whether the defendant should be sentenced to life in prison or death by execution.

Peremptory Challenge A challenge (dismissal of a potential juror) that can be made without having to state a reason. Each side in a case is given a specified number of such challenges.

Perjury Knowingly making false statements while under oath.

Plaintiff The party who initiates a civil lawsuit because of an alleged harm. Plaintiffs bear the burden of proof (as do prosecutors in criminal cases).

Plea Bargain An agreement between a prosecutor and a defendant whereby the defendant gives up the right to a trial in exchange for being charged with a lesser crime or receiving a reduced sentence. The defendant avoids the uncertainty of a trial and the legal system saves time and resources.

Precedents Previous decisions by courts in similar cases.

Preponderance of the Evidence Standard of proof common in civil trials. Requires that a judge or jury find that the plaintiff's version of the facts is more probable than not. The weight of the evidence is greater for one side than for the other (51% or more of the weight of the evidence).

Preventative Detention Holding someone in custody not because of what he or she has already done, but because of what he or she might do in the future (usually involves a perceived threat of future violence).

Privileged Communications Statements made within a legally protected, confidential relationship (e.g., therapist-client, husband-wife, lawyer-client, physician-patient). Participants in the relationship cannot be compelled to disclose the substance of communication shared in the relationship.

Probable Cause The requirement that a police officer have information that reasonably leads to a conclusion that a crime has been committed and that the suspect was probably responsible for the crime. A requisite condition for a valid arrest or search and seizure.

Probative Evidence   Probative evidence tends to prove a proposition at issue in a case or to allow triers of fact to infer an important fact. To be admissible in court, the probative value of a piece of evidence must outweigh its prejudicial value.

Proportionality   The principle that the severity of the punishment should be commensurate with the seriousness of the crime. In sentencing, the principle that people who have committed similar crimes should receive similar sentences.

Propensity Evidence   Evidence of past illegal or immoral behavior that suggests that a defendant has a general propensity or tendency to engage in criminal conduct.

Proximate Cause   The cause that is necessary to produce the effect; the immediate cause of the injury or wrong. In a civil lawsuit, the plaintiff must prove that the defendant's action or inaction was the proximate cause of the injury.

Punitive Damages   Monetary damages awarded to a plaintiff by a judge or jury with the intent of punishing the defendant for malicious or reckless behavior. Punitive damages are also meant to send the message that there will be serious financial consequences for others who behave similarly to the defendant.

Rape Shield Laws   Laws that place limits on questioning a rape victim at trial about her prior sexual history (other than with the defendant).

Recross   To cross-examine a witness a second time.

Redirect   A second direct examination of a witness following cross-examination by the opposing attorney.

Remittitur   A decision by a judge to reduce a monetary award by a jury because the judge considers the award to be excessive.

Sequestration   Isolating jurors serving on a sensational trial so they will not be exposed to outside influences such as publicity about the case. Jurors stay in a hotel and only have access to censored news reports.

Standard of Proof   The standard a prosecutor or plaintiff must meet in order to prove their case.

Stare Decisis   Literally, "let the decision stand." Doctrine that current decisions by judges should be strongly influenced by previous decisions in similar cases. This doctrine serves the interest of stability and predictability.

Statute of Limitations   A legally specified period of time after the alleged crime or cause of action occurs. A charge or civil suit must be brought against the suspect within this period of time. There is no statute of limitations for murder.

Statutory Law   Law created by an act of a legislature.

Summary Judgment   A pretrial judgment by a court in response to a motion by a plaintiff or defendant claiming that because there is no factual dispute, a trial is unnecessary and the judgment can be based only on governing law.

Testamentary Capacity   Mental capacity required to execute a legally binding will.

Tort   A wrong. A civil injury or wrong committed between private parties where no contract is involved. In tort cases (e.g., personal injury or medical malpractice), plaintiffs seek monetary damages from a defendant for an alleged negligent or intentional act.

Trial Court   The court that first hears evidence in a case and renders a verdict.

Ultimate Issue   The issue the trier of fact (a judge or jury) must decide. For example, whether a defendant is guilty of the murder he is accused of committing.

Venire   A group or panel of prospective jurors who are questioned by judges and attorneys to determine who will serve on a jury for a particular case.

Victim Impact Statements   Statements given on behalf of victims during sentencing. For example, following a murder trial, relatives of a murder victim may testify about the impact the victim's death has had on his or her family.

Voir Dire   A process where lawyers and judges question potential jurors to uncover juror biases and to determine who will be chosen to serve on a particular jury.

Writ of Certiorari   An order issued by an appellate court in response to an appeal by a lower court. Such a writ indicates that a higher court agrees to hear an appeal.

References

Abbott, J. H. (1991). *In the belly of the beast.* New York: Vintage Books.

Abramson, J. (1995). *We, the jury.* New York: Basic Books.

Abramson, J. (2002, June). *The evolution of the jury.* Paper presented at the annual conference of the American Society of Trial Consultants, Denver, CO.

Ackerman, M. J., & Ackerman, M. C. (1997). Custody evaluation practices: A survey of experienced professionals. *Professional Psychology: Research and Practice, 28,* 137–145.

Adler, S. (1994). *The jury: Trial and error in the American courtroom.* New York: Times Books.

Age Discrimination in Employment Act, 29 U.S.C. sections 621 *et seq.* (1967).

Ajzen, I., & Fishbein, M. (1980). *Understanding attitudes and predicting social behavior.* Englewood Cliffs, NJ: Prentice-Hall.

Allison, J. A., & Wrightsman, L. (1993). *Rape: The misunderstood crime.* Thousand Oaks, CA: Sage Publications.

Alpert, J. L., Brown, L., Ceci, S. J., Coutrois, C. A., Loftus, E. F., & Ornstein, P. A. (1998). Final report of the American Psychological Association working group on investigation of memories of childhood abuse. *Psychology, Public Policy, and Law, 4,* 931–1306.

American Psychiatric Assocation. 1994. *Diagnostic and statistical manual of mental disorders.* (4th ed.). Washington, DC: Author.

American Psychological Association. (1994). Guidelines for child custody evaluations in divorce proceedings. *American Psychologist, 49,* 677–680.

Americans With Disabilities Act, 42 U.S.C. §12101 *et seq.* (1990).

Anderson v. General Dynamics, 589 F.2d 397 (9th Cir. 1978).

Anderson, D. C. (1998). *Sensible justice: Alternatives to prison.* New York: The New Press.

Anderson, M. C. (2001). Active forgetting: Evidence for functional inhibition as a source of memory failure. In J. J. Freyd & A. De Prince (Eds.), *Trauma and cognitive science: A meeting of minds, science, and human experience* (pp. 48–64). New York: Haworth Press.

Apodaca, Cooper, & Madden v. Oregon, 406 U.S. 404 (1972).

Archer, D., & Gartner, R. (1984). *Violence and crime in cross-national perspective.* New Haven, CT: Yale University Press.

Arditti, J. A. (1995). Review of the Ackerman-Schoendorf Scales for the Parental Evaluation of Custody. In J. C. Conoley & J. C. Impara (Eds.), *Twelfth mental measurements yearbook* (pp. 20–22). Lincoln: University of Nebraska Press.

Arizona v. Fulminante, 111 S. Ct. 1246 (1991).

Aronson, E. (1998). *The social animal.* New York: Worth Publishers.

Associated Press. (1984, November 24). Judicial leniency toward women found. *San Diego Tribune,* p. A12.

Associated Press. (2002). Mother faces jury for drowning five kids. Retrieved March 2, 2002, from www.courttv.com.

Atkins v. Virginia. 122 S. Ct. 2428 (2002)

Bailey, W. C., & Peterson, R. D. (1994). Murder, capital punishment, and deterrence. *Journal of Social Issues, 50,* 53–74.

Bailey, W. C., & Peterson, R. D. (1997). Murder, capital punishment and deterrence: A review of the literature. In H. A. Bedau (Ed.), *The death penalty in America: Current controversies.* New York: Oxford University Press.

Baldus, D. C., Woodworth, G., & Pulaski, C. L. (1990). *Equal justice and the death penalty: A legal and empirical analysis.* Boston: Northeastern University Press.

Baldus, D., Woodworth, G., Zuckerman, D., Weiner, N. A., & Broffit, B. (1998). Racial discrimination and the death penalty in the post-Furman era: An empirical and legal overview with recent findings from Philadelphia. *Cornell Law Review, 83,* 1630–1770.

Baldwin, J., & McConville, M. (1979). *Jury trials.* Oxford: Clarendon.

Ballew v. Georgia, 435 U.S. 223 (1978).

Barkan, S. E. (1997). *Criminology.* Upper Saddle River, NJ: Prentice-Hall.

Barland, G. H. (1988). The polygraph test in the USA and elsewhere. In A. Gale (Ed.), *The polygraph test: Lies, truth, and science.* (pp. 73–96). London: Sage Publications.

Barnard, G. W., Thompson, J. W., Freeman, W. C., Robbins, L., Gies, D., & Hankins, G. C. (1991). Competency to stand trial: Description and initial evaluation of a new computer-assisted assessment tool (CADCOMP). *Bulletin of the American Academy of Psychiatry and Law, 19,* 367–381.

Baron, R. A., & Byrne, D. (2000). *Social psychology.* Boston: Allyn & Bacon.

Barratt, E. S. (1994). Impulsiveness and aggression. In J. Monahan & H. J. Steadman (Eds.) *Violence and mental disorder: Developments in risk assessment* (pp. 61–79). Chicago: University of Chicago Press.

Barthel, J. (1976). *A death in Canaan.* New York: E. P. Dutton.

Bastian, L., Lancaster, A., & Reyst, H. (1996). *Department of Defense 1995 sexual harassment survey.* Arlington, VA: Defense Manpower Data Center.

Batson v. Kentucky, 476 U.S. 79 (1986).

Baxstrom v. Herald, 383 U.S. 107 (1966).

Beale, C. R., Schmitt, K. L., & Dekle, D. (1995). Eyewitness identification of children: Effects of absolute judgments, nonverbal response options and event encoding. *Law and Human Behavior, 19,* 197–216.

Beck, C. J. A., & Sales, B. D. (2000). A critical reappraisal of divorce mediation research and policy. *Psychology, Public Policy, and Law, 6,* 989–1056.

Beck, C. J. A., & Sales, B. D. (2001). *Family mediation: Facts, myths and future prospects.* Washington, DC: American Psychological Assocation.

Becker, J. V., Skinner, L. J., Abel, G. G., Axelrod, R., & Traecy, E. C. (1984). Depressive symptoms associated with sexual assault. *Journal of Sex and Marital Therapy, 10,* 185–192.

Bedau, H. A. (2002). Causes and consequences of wrongful convictions: An essay-review. *Judicature, 86,* 115–119.

Behrman, B. W., & Davey, S. L. (2001). Eyewitness identification in actual criminal cases: An archival analysis. *Law and Human Behavior, 25,* 475–492.

Belli, Melvin, quoted in Monahan, J., & Walker, L. (1998). *Social Science in Law.* Westbury, NY: The Foundation Press. p. 570.

Ben-Shakhar, G., & Furedy, J. (1990). *Theories and applications in the detection of deception.* New York: Springer-Verlag.

Ben-Shakhar, G., Bar-Hillel, M., & Kremnitzer, M. (2002). Trial by polygraph: Reconsidering the use of the guilty knowledge technique in court. *Law and Human Behavior, 26,* 527–541.

Berns, W. (1979). *For capital punishment.* New York: Basic Books.

Bersoff, D. N. (1999). Preparing for two cultures. In R. Roesch, S. D. Hart, & J. R. Ogloff (Eds.), *Psychology and law: The state of the discipline* (pp. 375–401). New York: Kluwer Academic/Plenum Publishers.

Bersoff, D. N., Goodman-Delahunty, J., Grisso, J. T., Hans, V., Poythress, N. G., & Roesch, R. G. (1997). Training in law and psychology. *American Psychologist, 52,* 1301–1310.

Blumenthal, J. A. (1998). The reasonable woman standard: A meta-analytic review of gender differences in perceptions of sexual harassment. *Law & Human Behavior, 22,* 33–58.

Boeschen, L. E., Sales, B. D., & Koss, M. P. (1998). Rape trauma experts in the courtroom. *Psychology, Public Policy, and Law, 4,* 414–432.

Bonnie, R. J. (1993). The competence of criminal defendants: Beyond Dusky and Drope. *University of Miami Law Review, 47,* 539–601.

Bonta, J., Law, M., & Hanson, R. K. (1998). The prediction of criminal and violent recidivism among mentally disordered offenders: A meta-analysis. *Psychological Bulletin, 123,* 124–143.

Bornstein, B. H. (1999). The ecological validity of jury simulations: Is the verdict still out? *Law and Human Behavior; 23,* 75–92.

Bottcher, J., Isorena, T., & Belnas, M. (1996). LEAD: A boot camp and intensive parole program: An impact evaluation. Sacramento, CA: State of California Department of Youth Authority.

Bottoms v. Bottoms, 444 S.E. 2d 276 (1994).

Bottoms, B., & Goodman, G. (1994). Perceptions of children's credibility in sexual assault cases, *Journal of Applied Social Psychology, 24,* 702–732.

Bowers, K. (1993). *Hypnosis for the seriously curious.* New York: W. W. Norton.

Bowers, W. J. (1984). *Legal homicide: Death as punishment in America.* Boston: Northeastern University Press.

Bowers, W. J. (1988). The effect of executions is brutalization, not deterrence. In K. C. Haas & J. A. Inciardi (Eds.), *Challenging Capital Punishment* (pp. 49–89) Newbury Park, CA: Sage.

Bowers, W. J., Sandys, M., & Steiner, B. D. (1998). Foreclosed impartiality in capital sentencing: Jurors' predispositions, guilt-trial experience, and premature decision-making. *Cornell Law Review, 83,* 1476–1556.

Bratt, C. (1979). Joint Custody. *Kentucky Law Journal, 67,* 271–308.

Braun, S. (1998). Mitsubishi to pay $34 million in sexual harassment case. *Los Angeles Times,* pp. A1, A20.

Brehm, S. S., & Brehm, J. (1981). *Psychological reactance.* New York: Academic Press.

Brehm, S. S., Kassin, S. M., & Fein, S. (1999). *Social psychology.* Boston: Houghton-Mifflin.

Bricklin, B. (1984). *Bricklin perceptual scales: Child perception of parent series.* Furlong, PA: Village Publishing.

Brigham, J. C. (1999). What is forensic psychology anyway? *Law and Human Behavior, 23,* 273–298.

Brigham, J. C., & Malpass, R. S. (1985). The role of experience and contact in the recognition of faces of own and other race persons. *Journal of Social Issues, 41,* 139–156.

Brown v. Board of Education, 347 U.S. 483 (1954).

Browne, A. (1987). *When battered women kill.* New York: Free Press.

Bruce, W. M., & Blackburn, J. W. (1992). *Balancing job satisfaction and performance.* Westport, CT: Westport.

Brussel, J. A. (1968). *Casebook of a crime psychiatrist.* New York: Bernard Geis.

Buckhout, R. (1974). Eyewitness testimony. *Scientific American, 231,* 23–31.

Bugliosi, V. (1996). *Outrage: Five reasons why O.J. Simpson got away with murder.* New York: Island Books.

Burch v. Louisiana, 441 U.S. 242 (1979)

Bureau of Justice Statistics (2002). *Profile of Federal Prisoners in 2001.* Washington, DC: U.S. Department of Justice.

Burgess, A. W., & Holmstrom, L. L. (1974). Rape Trauma Syndrome. *American Journal of Psychiatry, 131,* 981–999.

Burgess, A. W., & Holmstrom, L. L. (1979). Rape: Sexual disruption and recovery. *American Journal of Ortho Psychiatry, 49,* 648–657.

Burlington Industries, Inc. v. Ellerth, No. 97-569 (U.S. filed June 26, 1998).

Campbell, D. T. (1969). Reforms as experiments. *American Psychologist, 24,* 409–429.

Campos, P. F. (1998). *Jurismania: The madness of American law.* New York: Oxford University Press.

Cantor, N. (1930). Law and the social sciences. *American Bar Association Journal, 16,* 385–392.

Caplan, L. (1984). *The insanity defense and the trial of John Hinckley, Jr.* New York: Godine.

Caplow, T., & Simon, J. (1999). Understanding prison policy and population trends. *Crime and Justice, 26,* 63–120.

Carroll, J. S. (1980). An appetizing look at law and psychology. *Contemporary Psychology, 25,* 362–364.

Cavoukian, A. (1979, June). The effect of polygraph evidence on people's judgments of guilt. Paper presented at the meetings of the Canadian Psychological Association, Toronto, Canada.

Ceci, S. J., & Bruck, M. (1995). *Jeopardy in the courtroom: A scientific analysis of children's testimony.* Washington, DC: American Psychological Association.

Charrow, R., & Charrow, V. (1979). Making legal language understandable: A psycholinguistic study of jury instructions. *Columbia Law Review, 79,* 1306–1374.

Cimerman, A. (1981). They'll let me go tomorrow: The Fay case. *Criminal Defense, 8,* 7–10.

Clark, S. E., & Tunnicliff, J. L. (2001). Selecting lineup foils in eyewitness identification experiments: Experimental control and real-world simulation. *Law and Human Behavior, 25,* 199–216.

Clear, T. R., & Cole, G. F. (2000). *American Corrections.* Belmont, CA: West/Wadsworth.

CNN (2002, March 1). *Psychiatrist: Yates thought she was defeating Satan.* www.cnn.com. Coalition for Sentencing Reform (2000, March). *Elderly prisoner initiative.* www.sentencing.org.

Cochran, R. F. (1991). Reconciling the primary caretaker preference, the joint custody preference, and the case-by-case rule. In J. Folberg (Ed.), *Joint custody and shared parenting* (pp. 218–240). New York: Guilford Press.

Coker v. Georgia, 433 U.S. 584 (1977).

Collins v. Brierly, 492 F.2d 735 (3d Cir., 1974).

Colorado v. Connelly, 497 U.S. 157 (1986).

Committee on Ethical Guidelines for Forensic Psychologists. (1999). Specialty guildelines for forensic psychologists. In R. Roesch, S. D. Hart, & J. R. P. Ogloff (Eds.), *Psychology and law: The state of the discipline* (pp. 423–435). New York: Kluwer Academic.

Cooper v. Oklahoma, 116 S.Ct. 1373 (1996).

Cooper v. Pate, 378 U.S. 546 (1964).

Cooper, J., Bennett, E. A., & Sukel, H. L. (1996). Complex scientific testimony: How do jurors make decisions. *Law and Human Behavior, 20,* 379–394.

Costanzo, M. (1997). *Just revenge: Costs and consequences of the death penalty.* New York: St. Martin's Press.

Costanzo, M., & Peterson, J. (1994). Attorney persuasion in the capital penalty phase: A content analysis of closing arguments. *Journal of Social Issues, 50,* 125–147.

Costanzo, M., & Costanzo, S. (1992). Jury decision-making in the capital penalty phase: Legal assumptions, empirical findings, and a research agenda. *Law and Human Behavior, 16,* 185–202.

Costanzo, S., & Costanzo, M. (1994). Life or death decisions: An analysis of capital jury decision-making under the special issues sentencing framework. *Law and Human Behavior, 18,* 151–170.

Craig v. Boren, 429 U.S. 190 (1976).

Cropanzano, R., Byrne, Z. S., Bobecel, D. R., & Rupp, D. E. (2001). Moral virtue, fairness heuristics, social entities, and other denizens of organizational justice. *Journal of Vocational Behavior, 58,* 164–209.

Culombe v. Connecticut, 367 U.S. 568 (1961).

Currie, E. (1998). *Crime and punishment in America.* New York: Metropolitan Books.

Cutler, B. L., Penrod, S. D., & Dexter, H. R. (1990). Nonadversarial methods for sensitizing jurors to eyewitness evidence. *Journal of Applied Social Psychology, 20,* 1197–1207.

Dane, F., & Wrightsman, L. (1982). Effects of defendants' and victims' characteristics on jurors' verdicts. In N. L. Kerr & R. M. Bray (Eds.), *The psychology of the courtroom.* New York: Academic Press.

Daniels, S., & Martin, J. (1997). Persistence is not always a virtue: Tort reform, civil liability for healthcare, and the lack of empirical evidence. *Behavioral Sciences and the Law, 15,* 3–19.

Darley, J. M. (2001). Citizens' sense of justice and the legal system. *Current Directions in Psychological Science, 10,* 10–13.

Darley, J. M., Carlsmith, K. M., & Robinson, P. H. (2000). Incapacitation and just desserts as motives for punishment. *Law and Human Behavior, 24,* 659–684.

Darrow, C. (1936, April). Attorney for the defense. *Esquire, 5,* 36–40.

Daubert v. Merrell Dow Pharmaceuticals, Inc., 113 S. Ct. 2786 (1993).

Dauner, J. (1996, March 20). Potential jurors fail to appear. *Kansas City Star,* p. C4.

Daunt, T., & Berry, S. (2002, July 30). LAPD says evidence destroyed. *Los Angeles Times,* pp. B1, B4.

Davis v. North Carolina, 384 U.S. 737 (1966).

Davis, D., & Follette, W. (2002). Rethinking the probative value of evidence: Base rates, intuitive profiling, and the "postdiction" of behavior. *Law and Human Behavior, 26,* 133–158.

de Beaumont, G., & de Tocqueville, A. (1964, reprint). *On the penitentiary system in the United States and its application in France.* Carbondale, IL: Southern Illinois University Press.

Dershowitz, A. M. (2002, March 17). Andrea Yates' prosecutors used the death penalty as a trial tactic. www.latimes.com.

Devine, D. J., Clayton, L. D., Dunford, B. B., Seying, R., & Pryce, J. (2001). Jury decision-making: 45 years of empirical research on deliberating groups. *Psychology, Public Policy, and Law, 7,* 622–727.

Devine, P. G. (1995). Prejudice and outgroup perception. In A. Tesser (Ed.), *Advanced Social Psychology* (pp. 467–524). New York: McGraw-Hill.

Dewey, J. (1929). *The quest for certainty.* New York: Putnam's.

Diamond, S. S. (2001). Convergence and complementarity between professional judges and lay adjudicators. In P. J. Van Koppen & S. D. Penrod (Eds.), *Adversarial versus inquisitional justice.* New York: Plenum.

Diamond, S. S., Vidmar, N. Rose, M., Ellis, L., & Murphy, B. (2002). Civil juror discussions during trial: A study of Arizona's Rule 39(f) from video-taped discussions and deliberations. www.law.northwestern.edu/diamond/papers/arizona.

Dickens, C. (1850). *American Notes.* London: MacDonald and Sons.

Diekmann, K. A., Samuels, S. M., Ross, L., & Bazerman, M. H. (1997). Self-interest and fairness in problems of response allocation: Allocators versus recipients. *Journal of Personality and Social Psychology, 72,* 1061–1074.

Dillehay, R. C. (1999). Authoritarianism and jurors. In W. Abbott and J. Batt (Eds.), *A handbook of jury research* (pp. 1–18). Philadelphia: American Law Institute and American Bar Assocation.

Dillehay, R. C., & Nietzel, M. T. (1999). Prior jury experience. In W. Abbott &

J. Batt (Eds.), *Handbook of Jury Research* (pp. 127–149). Philadelphia: American Law Institute and American Bar Association.

Dixon v. Attorney General of the Commonwealth of Pennsylvania, 325 F. Supp. 966 (M.D. Pa. 1971).

Dodge, K. A., Price, J. M., Bachorowski, J., & Newman, J. P. (1990). Hostile attributional biases in severely aggressive adolescents. *Journal of Abnormal Psychology, 99,* 385–392.

Dodge, M., & Greene, E. (1991). Jurors and expert conceptions of battered women. *Violence and Victims, 6,* 271–282.

Donaldson, S. I., & Scriven, M. (Eds.). (2003). *Evaluating social programs and problems.* Mahwah, NJ: Lawrence Erlbaum.

Douglas, J., & Olshaker, M. (1997). *Journey into darkness.* New York: Pocket Books.

Douglas, K. S., & Webster, C. D. (1999). Predicting violence in mentally and personality disordered individuals. In R. Roesch, S. D. Hart, & J. R. P. Ogloff (Eds.), *Psychology and law: The state of the discipline* (pp. 175–239). New York: Kluwer/Plenum.

Dovidio, J. F., & Gaertner, S. L. (1996). Affirmative action, unintentional racial biases, and intergroup relations. *Journal of Social Issues, 52,* 51–75.

Dovidio, J. F., & Gaertner, S. L. (1997). On the nature of contemporary prejudice: The causes, consequences and challenges of aversive racism. In J. L. Eberhardt & S. T. Fiske (Eds.), *Racism: The problem and the response* (pp. 211–232). Newbury Park, CA: Sage Publications.

Drapkin, I. (1989). *Crime and punishment in the ancient world.* Lexington, MA: Lexington Books.

Durham v. United States, 362 U.S. 402 (1960).

Dusky v. United States, 362 U.S. 402 (1960).

Dutton, D. G. (1995). *The batterer: A psychological profile.* New York: Basic Books.

Dutton, D. G. (2000). *The domestic assault of women.* Vancouver: University of British Columbia Press.

Dutton, M. A. (2000). Critique of the "Battered Woman Syndrome" model. www.vaw.umn.edu.

Edens, J. F., Petrila, J., & Buffington-Vollum, J. K. (2001). Psychopathy and the death penalty: Can the psychopathy checklist-revised identify offenders who represent "a continuing threat to society?" *Journal of Psychiatry and Law, 29,* 433–481.

EEOC v. Murphy Motor Freight Lines, Inc., 488 F. Supp. 381 (D. Minn. 1980).

Einhorn, J. (1986). Child custody in historical perspective: A study of changing social perceptions of divorce and child custody in Anglo-American law. *Behavioral Sciences and the Law, 4,* 119–135.

Ekman, P. (1985). *Telling Lies.* New York: W. W. Norton.

Elaad, E., Ginton, A., & Jungman, N. (1992). Detection measures in real-life guilty knowledge tests, *Journal of Applied Psychology, 77,* 757–767.

Elkins, T. J., Phillips, J. S., & Konopaske, R. (2002). Gender-related biases in evaluations of sex discrimination allegations: Is perceived threat the key? *Journal of Applied Psychology, 87,* 280–292.

Ellis, E. M. (2000). *Divorce wars.* Washington, DC: American Psychological Assocation.

Ellison v. Brady, 924 F.2d 871 (9th Circuit, 1991)

Ellsworth, P. C. (1989). Are twelve heads better than one? *Law and Contemporary Problems, 52,* 205–224.

Ellsworth, P. C. (1991). To tell what we know or wait for Godot? *Law and Human Behavior, 15,* 77–90.

Ellsworth, P. C., & Getman, J. G. (1987). Social science in legal decision-making. In L. Lipson & S. Wheeler (Eds.), *Law and the social sciences* (pp. 26–51). New York: Russell Sage.

Ellsworth, P. C., & Gross, S. R. (1994). Hardening of the attitudes: Americans' views on the death penalty, *Journal of Social Issues, 50,* 19–52.

Ellsworth, P. C., Haney, C., & Costanzo, M. (2001). *Society for the Study of Social Issues* (SPSSI) position statement on the death penalty. www.spssi.org.

Ellsworth, P. C., & Mauro, R. (1998). Psychology and law. In D. T. Gilbert, S. T. Fiske, & G. Lindzey (Eds.), *The Handbook of Social Psychology* (pp. 684–732). Boston: McGraw-Hill.

Ellsworth, P. C., & Reifman, A. (2000). Juror comprehension and public policy: Perceived problems and proposed solutions. *Psychology, Public Policy, and Law, 6,* 788–821.

Emery, R. E. (1994). *Renegotiating family relationships: Divorce, child custody, and mediation.* New York: Guilford.

Emery, R. E., Matthews, S. G., & Kitzmann, K. M. (1994). Child custody mediation and litigation: Parents' satisfaction and functioning one year after settlement. *Journal of Consulting and Clinical Psychology, 62,* 124–129.

Emery, R. E., Matthews, S. G., & Wyer, M. M. (1991). Child custody mediation and litigation: Further evidence on the differing views of mothers and fathers. *Journal of Consulting and Clinical Psychology, 59,* 410–419.

Equal Employment Opportunity Commission. (1980). *Guidelines on discrimination on the basis of sex* (29 CFR Part 1604). Federal Register, 45(219).

Estelle v. Smith, 451 U.S. 454 (1981)

Estroff, S. E., & Zimmer, C. (1994). Social networks, social support, and violence among persons with severe, persistent mental illness. In J. Monahan & H. J. Steadman (Eds.), Violence and mental disorder: Developments in risk assessment (pp. 259–295). Chicago: University of Chicago Press.

Eule, J. (1978). The presumption of sanity: Bursting the bubble. *UCLA Law Review, 25,* 637–699.

Everington, C. T. (1990). The competence assessment for standing trial for defendants with mental retardation (CAST-MR): A validation study. *Criminal Justice and Behavior, 17,* 147–162.

Ewing, C. P. (1987). *Battered women who kill: Psychological self-defense as legal justification.* Lexington, MA: Lexington.

Faigman, D. L. (1999). *Legal alchemy: The use and misuse of science in the law.* New York: W. H. Freeman and Company.

Faigman, D. L., Kaye, D. H., Saks, M. J., & Sanders, J. (1997). *Modern scientific evidence: The law and science of expert testimony.* St. Paul, MN: West.

Faragher v. Boca Raton, Fla., No. 97–282 (U.S. filed June 26, 1998).

Faretta v. California, 422 U.S. 806 (1975).

Farmer v. Brennan, 114 S. Ct. 1970 (1994).

Federal Bureau of Prisons. (1996). *State of the Bureau, 1995.* Washington, DC: U.S. Government Printing Office.

Finckenauer, J. O., Gavin, P., Hovland, A., & Storvoll, E. (1999). *Scared straight: The panacea phenomenon revisited.* Prospect Heights, IL: Waveland Press.

Finkel, N. J. (1995). *Commonsense justice: Jurors' notions of the law.* Cambridge, MA: Harvard University Press.

Finkel, N. J. (2000). But it's not fair! Commonsense notions of unfairness. *Psychology, Public Policy, and Law, 6,* 898–952.

Finkel, N. J. (2002). *Not fair! The typology of commonsense unfairness.* Washington, DC: American Psychological Association.

Fischoff, B. (1975). Hindsight = foresight: The effect of outcome knowledge on judgment under uncertainty. *Journal of Experimental Psychology: Human Perception and Performance, 11,* 288–299.

Fisher, R. P. (1995). Interviewing victims and witnesses of crime. *Psychology, Public Policy, and Law, 1,* 732–764.

Fisher, R. P., & Geiselman, R. E. (1992). *Memory-enhancing techniques for investigative interviewing: The cognitive interview.* Springfield, IL: Charles C. Thomas.

Fiske, S. T., & Glick, P. (1995). Ambivalence and stereotypes cause sexual harassment: A theory with implications for organizational change, *Journal of Social Issues, 51,* 151–166.

Fiske, S. T., & Stevens, L. E. (1993). What's so special about sex? Gender stereotyping and discrimination. In M. Costanzo & S. Oskamp (Eds.), *Gender Issues in contemporary society.* Newbury Park, CA: Sage Publications.

Fiske, S. T., & Taylor, S. E. (1991). *Social cognition.* New York: McGraw-Hill.

Fitzgerald, L. F., Swan, S., & Fischer, K. (1995). Why didn't she just report him? The psychological and legal implications of women's responses to sexual harassment, *Journal of Social Issues, 51,* 117–138.

Fletcher, B., Shaver, L. D., & Moon, D. (1993). *Women prisoners: A forgotten population.* Westport, CT: Greenwood Press.

Flin, R., Boone, J., Knox, A., & Bull, R. (1992). The effect of a five-month delay on children's and adult's eyewitness memory. *British Journal of Psychology, 83,* 323–336.

Follingstad, D. R., Polek, D. S., Hause, E. S., Deaton, L. H., Bulger, M. W., & Conway, Z. D. (1989). Factors predicting verdicts in cases where battered women kill their husbands. *Law and Human Behavior, 13,* 253–269.

Foote, W. E., & Goodman-Delahunty, J. (1999). Same-sex harassment: Implications of the Onacle decision for forensic evaluation of plaintiffs. *Behavioral Sciences and the Law, 17,* 123–139.

Ford v. Wainwright, 477 U.S. 399 (1986).

Fox, J., & Levin, J. (1998). Multiple homicide: Patterns of serial and mass murder. *Crime and Justice, 23,* 407–456.

Frazier, P. A., & Borgida, E. (1992). Rape Trauma Syndrome: A review of case law and psychological research. *Law and Human Behavior, 16,* 293–311.

Frazier, P. A., Cochran, C. C., & Olson, A. M. (1995). Social science research on lay definitions of sexual harassment. *Journal of Social Issues, 51,* 21–39.

Frazier, P., Conlon, A., & Glaser, T. (2001). Positive and negative life changes following sexual assault. *Journal of Consulting and Clinical Psychology.*

Freud, S. (1906). Psychoanalysis and the ascertaining of truth in courts of law. In E. Jones (Ed.), *Collected papers of Sigmund Freud* (1959, Vol. 2, 13–24). New York: Basic Books.

Friedman, L. M. (1993). *Crime and punishment in American history.* New York: Basic Books.

Frontline. (1999). *What Jennifer saw.* PBS Video. Accessed at www.pbs.org.

Fulero, S. M., & Finkel, N. J. (1991). Barring ultimate issue testimony: An insane rule? *Law and Human Behavior, 15,* 495–507.

Furman v. Georgia, 408 U.S. 238 (1972).

Gale, J., Mowery, R. L., Herrman, M. S., & Hollett, N. L. (2002). Considering effective divorce mediation: Three potential factors. *Conflict Resolution Quarterly, 19,* 389–420.

Gallup Poll (2001). *Black-white relations in the United States.* www.gallup.com.

Garven, S., Wood, J. M., Malpass, R. S., & Shaw, J. S. (1998). More than suggestion: The effect of interviewing techniques from the McMartin Preschool case. *Journal of Applied Psychology, 83,* 347–359.

Gatowski, S. I., Dobbin, S. A., Richardson, J. T., Ginsburg, G. P., Merlino, M. L., & Dahir, V. (2001). Asking the gatekeepers: A national survey of judges on judging expert evidence in a post-Daubert world. *Law and Human Behavior, 25,* 433–458.

Gauld, A. (1992). *A history of hypnotism.* Cambridge: Cambridge University Press.

Gindes, M. (1995). Guidelines for child custody evaluations for psychologists: Overview and commentary. *Family Law Quarterly, 29,* 39–50.

Godinez v. Moran, 113 S. Ct. 2680 (1993).

Goffman, E. (1973). Characteristics of total institutions. In L. Orland (Ed.), *Justice, Punishment and Treatment* (pp. 153–161). New York: Free Press.

Goldberg, S. (1994). *Culture clash: Law and science in America.* New York: NYU Press.

Golding, S., & Roesch, R. (1988). Competency for adjudication: An international analysis. In D. N. Weisstub (Ed.), *Law and mental health: International perspectives* (pp. 73–109). New York: Pergamon.

Goodman, G. S., Bottoms, B. L., Rudy, L., Davis, S. L., & Schwartz-Kenney, B. M. (2001). Effects of past abuse experiences on children's eyewitness memory. *Law and Human Behavior, 25,* 269–298.

Goodman, G. S., Tobey, A., Batterman-Faunce, J., Orcutt, H., Thomas, S. Shapiro, C., & Sachsenmairer, T. (1998). Face to face confrontation effects of closed-circuit technology on children's testimony and jurors' decisions. *Law and Human Behavior, 22,* 165–202.

Goodman-Delahunty, J. (1998). Approaches to gender and the law: Research and implications. *Law and Human Behavior, 22,* 129–143.

Goodman-Delahunty, J. (1999). Civil law: Employment and discrimination. In R. Roesch, S. D. Hart, & J. R. P. Ogloff (Eds.), *Psychology and law: The state of the discipline.* New York: Kluwer Academic/Plenum Publishers.

Goodman-Delahunty, J. (1999). Pragmatic support for the reasonable victim standard in hostile workplace sexual harassment cases. *Psychology, Public Policy, and Law, 5,* 519–555.

Greenberg, J., & Alge, B. J. (2000). Aggressive reactions to workplace injustice. In R. W. Griffin, A. O'Leary-Kelly, & J. Collins (Eds.), *Dysfunctional behavior in organizations.* Greenwich, CT: JAI Press.

Greene, E., Downey, C., & Goodman-Delahunty, J. (1999). Juror decisions about damages in employment discrimination cases. *Behavioral Sciences and the Law, 17,* 107–121.

Greenwood, P., Rydell, C., Abrahamse, A., Calukins, J. P., Chiesa, J., Model, K. E., & Klien, S. P. (1994). *Three strikes and you're out.* Santa Monica, CA: RAND.

Gregg v. Georgia, 428 U.S. 153 (1976).

Griggs v. Duke Power Co., 401 U.S. 324 (1971).

Grisso, T., & Appelbaum, P. S. (1992). Is it unethical to offer predictions of future violence? *Law and Human Behavior, 16,* 621–634.

Grisso, T. (1991). A developmental history of the American Psychology-Law Society. *Law and Human Behavior, 15,* 213–232.

Grisso, T. (1997). The competence of adolescents as trial defendants. *Psychology, Public Policy, and Law, 3,* 3–34.

Grisso, T., & Saks, M. J. (1991). Psychology's influence on constitutional interpretation: A comment on how to succeed. *Law and Human Behavior, 15,* 208–398.

Grove, W. M., & Meehl, P. E. (1996). Comparative efficiency of informal (subjective, impressionistic) and formal (mechanical, algorithmic) prediction procedures: The clinical-statistical controversy. *Psychology, Public Policy and the Law, 2,* 293–323.

Gudjonsson, G. H. (1988). How to defeat the polygraph tests. In A. Gale (Ed.), *The polygraph test: Lies, truth, and science* (pp. 126–136). London: Sage Publications.

Gudjonsson, G. H. (1992). *The psychology of interrogations, confessions, and testimony.* Chichester, England: Wiley.

Gudjonsson, G. H. (1994). Investigative interviewing: Recent developments and some fundamental issues. *International Review of Psychiatry, 6,* 237–245.

Gutek, B. A., & O'Connor, M. (1995). The empirical basis for the reasonable woman standard. *Journal of Social Issues, 51,* 151–166.

Gutek, B. A. (1993). Responses to sexual harassment. In M. Costanzo & S. Oskamp (Eds.), *Gender issues in contemporary society.* Newbury Park, CA: Sage Publications.

Guthrie, C., Rachlinski, J., & Wistrich, A. (2001). Inside the judicial mind. *Cornell Law Review, 86,* 777–830.

Hafemeister, T. L., & Melton, G. B. (1987). The impact of social science research on the judiciary. In G. B. Melton (Ed.), *Reforming the law: Impact of child development research* (pp. 29–59). New York: Guilford.

Hagen, M. (1997). *Whores of the court.* New York: Harper-Collins.

Haney, C. (1981). Psychology and legal change: On the limits of a factual jurisprudence. *Law and Human Behavior, 4,* 147–199.

Haney, C. (1993). Psychology and legal change: The impact of a decade. *Law and Human Behavior, 17,* 371–398.

Haney, C., Banks, W., & Zimbardo, P. (1973). Interpersonal dynamics in a simulated prison. *International Journal of Criminology and Penology, 1,* 69–97.

Haney, C., Sontag, L., & Costanzo, S. (1994). Deciding to take a life: Capital juries, sentencing instructions and the jurisprudence of death. *Journal of Social Issues, 50,* 149–176.

Haney, C., & Zimbardo, P. (1998). The past and future of U.S. prison policy. *American Psychologist, 53,* 709–727.

Hans, V. P. (1992). Jury decision making. In D. K. Kagehiro & W. S. Laufer (Eds.), *Handbook of Psychology and Law* (pp. 56–76). New York: Springer.

Hans, V. P. (1996). The contested role of the civil jury in business litigation. *Judicature, 79,* 242–248.

Hans, V. P. (2000). *Business on trial.* New Haven: Yale University Press.

Hans, V. P., & Lofquist, W. S. (1994). Perceptions of civil justice: The litigation crisis attitudes of civil jurors. *Behavioral Sciences and the Law, 12,* 181–196.

Hans, V. P., & Vidmar, N. (1986). *Judging the jury.* New York: Plenum.

Hansen, M. (1998). Love's labor laws. *American Bar Association Journal, 84,* 78–80.

Hare, R. D. (1996). Psychopathy: A clinical construct whose time has come. *Criminal Justice and Behavior, 23,* 25–54.

Harris, G. T., & Rice, M. E. (1997). Mentally disordered offenders: What research says about effective service. In C. D. Webster & M. A. Jackson (Eds.), *Impulsive people: Approaches to assessment and treatment.* New York: Guilford.

Harris v. Forklift Systems, Inc., 114 S. Ct. 567, 510 U.S. 17 (1993).

Hart, S. (1998). The role of psychopathy in assessing risk for violence: Conceptual and methodological issues. *Legal and Criminological Psychology, 3,* 121–137.

Hastie, R. (1993). Algebraic models of juror decision processes. In R. Hastie (Ed.), *Inside the juror* (pp. 84–115). Cambridge: Cambridge University Press.

Hastie, R., Penrod, S. D., & Pennington, N. (1983). *Inside the jury.* Cambridge, MA: Harvard University Press.

Heilbrun, K. (1997). Prediction versus management models relevant to risk assessment: The importance of legal decision-making context. *Law and Human Behavior, 21,* 347–361.

Heilbrun, K., & Griffin, P. (1999). Forensic treatment: A review of programs and research. In R. Roesch, S. D. Hart, & J. R. P. Ogloff (Eds.), *Psychology and Law: The state of the discipline* (pp. 241–274). New York: Kluwer/Plenum.

Heilbrun, K., Nezu, C. M., Keeney, M., Chung, S., & Wasserman, A. L. (1998). Sexual offending: Linking assessment, intervention, and decision-making. *Psychology, Public Policy, and Law, 4,* 138–174.

Henderson, M., & Hewstone, M. (1984). Prison inmates' explanations for interpersonal violence: Accounts and attributions. *Journal of Consulting and Clinical Psychology, 52,* 789–794.

Herman, J. L. (1992). Complex PTSD: A syndrome in survivors of prolonged and repeated trauma. *Journal of Traumatic Stress, 5,* 377–390.

Hetherington, E. M., Bridges, M., & Insabella, G. M. (1998). What matters? What does not? Five perspectives on the association between marital transitions and children's adjustment. *American Psychologist, 53,* 167–184.

Heuer, L., & Penrod, S. D. (1989). Instructing jurors: A field experiment with written and preliminary instructions. *Law and Human Behavior, 13,* 409–430.

Heuer, L., & Penrod, S. D. (1994). Trial complexity: A field investigation of its meaning and effects. *Law and Human Behavior, 18,* 29–51.

Hickey, E. W. (1997). *Serial murderers and their victims* (2nd ed.). Belmont, CA: Wadsworth.

Hirst, J. (1995). The Australian experience: The convict colony. In N. Morris & D. J. Rothman (Eds.), *The Oxford history of the prison.* (pp. 235–265). New York: Oxford University Press.

Hofstede, G. (1991). *Culture and organizations.* London: McGraw-Hill.

Hoge, S. K., Bonnie, R. J., Poythress, N., Monahan, J., Eisenberg, M., & Feucht-Haviar, T. (1997). The MacArthur adjudicative competence study: Development and validation of a research instrument. *Law and Human Behavior, 21,* 141–179.

Holmes, D. (1990). The evidence for repression: An examination of sixty years of research. In J. L. Singer (Ed.), *Repression and dissociation: implications for personality theory, psychopathology, and health* (pp. 28–45). Chicago: University of Chicago Press.

Holmes, O. W. (1881). *The common law.* Boston: Little, Brown.

Holmes, O. W. (1897). The path of law. *Harvard Law Review, 10,* 457–471.

Holmes, O. W. (1954). Learning and science (speech to Harvard Law School Association, June 25, 1895). In M. Lerner (Ed.), *The mind and faith of Justice Holmes* (p. 34). New York: Modern Library.

Holmes, R. M., & DeBurger, J. (1988). *Serial murder.* Newbury Park, CA: Sage Publications.

Holst, V. F., & Pezdek, K. (1992). Scripts for typical crimes and their effects on memory for eyewitness testimony. *Applied Cognitive Psychology, 6,* 573–587.

Holtzworth-Munroe, A. (2000). A typology of men who are violent toward their female partners: Making sense of the heterogeneity in husband violence. *Current Directions in Psychological Science, 9,* 140–143.

Homant, R. J., & Kennedy, D. B. (1998). Psychological aspects of crime scene profiling. *Criminal Justice and Behavior, 25,* 319–343.

Honts, C. R. (1995). The polygraph in 1995: Progress in science and the law. *North Dakota Law Review, 17,* 987–1020.

Honts, C. R., Raskin, D., & Kircher, J. (1994). Mental and physical countermeasures reduce the accuracy of polygraph tests. *Journal of Applied Psychology, 79,* 252–259.

Horowitz, I. (1988). Jury nullification: The impact of judicial instructions, arguments, and challenges on jury decision making. *Law and Human Behavior, 12,* 439–454.

Horowitz, S., Kircher, J., Honts, C. R., & Raskin, D. (1997). The role of comparison questions in physiological detection of deception. *Psychophysiology, 34,* 108–115.

Hubler, S. (1999, May 3). When a justice system stumbles, *Los Angeles Times,* p. E1.

Huesmann, L. R., Moise-Titus, J., Podolski, C. L., Eron, L. D. (2003). Longitudinal relations between children's exposure to TV violence and their aggressive and violent behavior in young adulthood: 1977–1992. *Developmental Psychology, 39,* 201–221.

Human Rights Watch. (1997). *Cold storage: Super-maximum security confinement.* New York: Author.

Hunt, J. S., & Borgida, E. (2001). Is that what I said?: Witnesses' responses to interviewer modifications. *Law and Human Behavior, 25,* 583–603.

Hunt, R. R., & Ellis, H. C. (2002). *Fundamentals of cognitive psychology.* Boston: McGraw-Hill.

Huntley, J. E., & Costanzo, M. (2003). Sexual harassment stories: Testing a story-mediated model of juror decision-making in civil litigation. *Law and Human Behavior, 27,* 29–51.

Huss, M. T. (2002). Psychology and law, now and in the next century. In S. F. Davis and J. Halonen (Eds.), The many faces of psychological research in the twenty-first century. Retrieved from www.teachpsych. lemoyne.edu.

Hyman, I. E., Husband, T. H., & Billings, F. J. (1995). False memories of childhood experiences. *Applied Cognitive Psychology, 9,* 181–197.

Iacono, W. G., & Patrick, C. J. (1999). Polygraph (lie detector) testing: The state of the art. In A. K. Hess & I. B. Weiner (Eds.), *The Handbook of Forensic Psychology* (2nd ed., pp. 440–473). New York: John Wiley.

Inbau, F. E., Reid, J. E., Buckley, J. P., & Jayne, B. C. (2001). *Criminal interrogation and confessions.* Gaithersburg, MD: Aspen Publishers.

Irving, B., & McKenzie, I. K. (1989). *Police interrogation: The effects of the Police and Criminal Evidence Act,* 1984. London: Police Foundation.

Irwin, J. (1980). *Prisons in turmoil.* Boston: Little, Brown.

J. E. B. ex rel. T. B., 114 S. Ct. 1419 (1994).

Jackson v. Indiana, 406 U.S. 715 (1972).

Jackson v. State of Florida, 553 So.2d 719 (Fla. 4th dist. Ct. App.) (1989).

Jackson, J. L., & Bekerian, D. A. (Eds.). (1997). *Offender profiling: Theory, research and practice.* New York: Wiley.

Jackson, L. A. (1989). Relative deprivation and the gender wage gap. *Journal of Social Issues, 45,* 117–133.

Jacobs, J. B. (1983). *New perspectives on prisons and imprisonment.* New York: Cornell University Press.

James, W. (1907). *Pragmatism.* New York: Longmans-Green.

Janofsky, M. (1998, June 5). Maryland troopers stop drivers by race, suit says. *The New York Times,* p. A10.

Jobes, D. A., Casey, J. O., Berman, A. L., & Wright, M. (1991). Empirical criteria for the determination of suicide and manner of death. *Journal of Forensic Sciences, 36,* 244–256.

Johnson v. Louisiana, 406 U.S. 356 (1972).

Johnson v. Zerbst, 304 U.S. 458 (1938).

Johnson, C., & Haney, C. (1994). Felony voir dire: An exploratory study of its content and effects. *Law and Human Behavior, 18,* 487–507.

Johnson, R. (1996). *Hard time: Understanding and reforming the prison.* Belmont, CA: Wadsworth.

Kalven, H., & Zeisel, H. (1966). *The American jury.* Boston: Little, Brown.

Kaplan, M., & Miller, C. (1987). Group decision making and normative vs. informational influence. *Journal of Personality and Social Psychology, 53,* 306–313.

Kasian, M., Spanos, N. P., Terrance, C. A., & Peebles, S. (1993). Battered women who kill: Jury simulation and legal defenses. *Law and Human Behavior, 17,* 289–312.

Kassin, S. M. (1997). The psychology of confession evidence. *American Psychologist, 52,* 221–233.

Kassin, S. M. (1998). Eyewitness identification procedures: The fifth rule. *Law and Human Behavior, 22,* 649–653.

Kassin, S. M., & McNall, K. (1991). Police interrogations and confessions: Communicating promises and threats by pragmatic implication. *Law and Human Behavior, 15,* 233–251.

Kassin, S. M., & Neumann, K. (1997). On the power of confession evidence: An experimental test of the fundamental difference hypothesis. *Law and Human Behavior, 21,* 469–484.

Kassin, S. M., Smith, V. L., & Tulloch, W. F. (1990). The dynamite charge: Effects on the perception and deliberation behavior of mock jurors. *Law and Human Behavior, 14,* 537–550.

Kassin, S. M., & Sukel, H. (1997). Coerced confessions and the jury: An experimental test of the harmless error rule. *Law and Human Behavior, 21,* 27–46.

Kassin, S. M., & Wrightsman, L. S. (1983). The construction and validation of a junior bias scale. *Journal of Research in Personality, 17,* 423–442.

Kebbell, M. R., & Wagstaff, G. F. (1998). Hypnotic interviewing: The best way to interview witnesses? *Behavioral Sciences and the Law, 16,* 115–29.

Kelly, J. B. (1993). Current research on children's postdivorce adjustment. *Family and Conciliation Review, 31,* 29–49.

Kerr, N. L. (1994). The effects of pretrial publicity on jurors. *Judicature, 78,* 120–127.

Kerr, N. L., Hymes, R. W., Anderson, A. B., & Weathers, J. E. (1995). Defendant-juror similarity and mock juror judgments. *Law and Human Behavior, 19,* 545–568.

Kerr, N. L., Niedermeier, K. E., & Kaplan, M. F. (1999). Bias in jurors vs. bias in juries. *Organizational Behavior and Human Decision Processes, 80,* 70–86.

King, N. J. (2000). The American criminal jury. In N. Vidmar (Ed.), *World Jury Systems* (p. 104). Oxford, UK: Oxford University Press.

Kircher, J. C., Horowitz, S. W., & Raskin, D. C. (1988). Meta-analysis of mock crime studies of the control question polygraph technique. *Law and Human Behavior, 12,* 79–90.

Kolata, G., & Peterson, I. (2001, July 21). New way to insure eyewitnesses can ID the right bad guy. *The New York Times,* p. A1.

Konecni, V., & Ebbesen, E. B. (1982). An analysis of the sentencing decision. In V. Konecni & E. B. Ebbesen (Eds.), *The criminal justice system.* San Francisco: W. H. Freeman.

Koss, M. P., & Harvey, M. R. (1991). *The rape victim: Clinical and community interventions.* Thousand Oaks, CA: Sage Publications.

Koss, M. P., & House-Higgins, C. (2000). Women. In R. Gottesman & R. M. Brown (Eds.), *Encyclopedia of violence.* New York: Charles Scribner's Sons.

Koutstaal, W., Schacter, D. L., Johnson, M. K., & Galluccio, L. (1999). Facilitation and impairment of event memory produced by photograph review. *Memory and Cognition, 27,* 478–93.

Kovera, M. B. (2002). The effects of pretrial publicity on juror decisions: An examination of moderators and mediating mechanisms. *Law and Human Behavior, 26,* 43–72.

Kovera, M. B., Borgida, E., Gresham, A. W., Gray, E., & Regan, P. C. (1997). Does expert psychological testimony inform or influence juror decision making? A social cognitive analysis. *Journal of Applied Psychology, 82,* 178–192.

Kovera, M. B., & McAuliff, B. D. (2000). The effects of peer review and evidence quality on judge evaluations of psychological science: Are judges effective gatekeepers? *Journal of Applied Psychology, 85,* 574–586.

Kramer, G. P., Kerr, N. L., & Carroll, J. S. (1990). Pretrial publicity, judicial remedies, and jury bias. *Law and Human Behavior, 14,* 409–438.

Krauss, D. A., & Sales, B. D. (2000). Legal standards, expertise, and experts in the resolution of contested child custody cases. *Psychology, Public Policy, and Law, 6,* 843–879.

Krauss, D. A., & Sales, B. D. (2001). The effects of clinical and scientific expert testimony on juror decision making in capital sentencing. *Psychology, Public Policy, and Law, 7,* 267–310.

Kravitz, D. A., Cutler, B. L., & Brock, P. (1993). Reliability and validity of the original and revised Legal Attitudes Questionnaire. *Law and Human Behavior, 17,* 661–677.

Kressel, N. J., & Kressel, D. F. (2002). *Stack and sway.* Boulder, CO: Westview Press.

Krieger, L. H. (1995). The content of our categories: A cognitive bias approach to discrimination and equal employment opportunity. *Stanford Law Review, 47,* 1161–1248.

Kropp, P. R., Hart, S. D., & Lyon, D. R. (2002). Risk assessment of stalkers: Some problems and some solutions. *Criminal Justice and Behavior, 29,* 590–616.

Kumho Tire Co. Ltd. v. Carmichael, 526 U.S. 137 1999.

LaBine, S. J., & LaBine, G. (1996). Determinations of negligence and the hindsight bias. *Law and Human Behavior, 20,* 501–516.

LaFond, J. Q. (1996). The impact of law on the delivery of involuntary mental health services. In B. D. Sales & D. W. Shuman (Eds.), *Law, mental health, and mental disorder.* Pacific Grove, CA: Brooks-Cole.

LaFortune, K. A., & Carpenter, B. N. (1998). Custody evaluations: A survey of mental health professionals. *Behavioral Sciences and the Law, 16,* 207–224.

Lamb, R. H., & Weinberger, L. E. (2001). *Deinstitutionalization: Promise and problems.* San Francisco: Jossey-Bass.

Landsman, S., & Rakos, R. (1994). A preliminary inquiry into the effect of potentially biasing information on judges and jurors in civil litigation. *Behavioral Sciences and the Law, 12,* 113–126.

Langan, P., & Cuniff, M. (1992). *Recidivism of felons on probation.* Washington DC: Bureau of Justice Statistics.

Lassiter, G. D. (2002). Illusory causation in the courtroom. *Current Directions in Psychological Science, 11,* 204–208.

Lassiter, G. D, & Irvine, A. A. (1986). Videotaped confessions: The impact of point of view on judgments of coercion. *Journal of Applied Social Psychology, 16,* 268–276.

Lassiter, G. D., Slaw, R. D., Briggs, M. A., & Scanlan, C. R. (1992). The potential for bias in videotaped confessions. *Journal of Applied Social Psychology, 22,* 1837–1850.

Laurence, J. (1931). *A history of capital punishment.* London: Sampson, Low, Marston & Company.

Lempert, R. D. (1975). Uncovering "nondiscernable" differences: Empirical research and the jury size cases. *Michigan Law Review, 73,* 643–708.

Lempert, R. O. (1993). Civil juries and complex cases: Taking stock after twelve years. In R. E. Litan (Ed.), *Verdict: Assessing the civil jury system* (pp. 181–247). Washington, DC: The Brookings Institution.

Leo, R. A. (1992). From coercion to deception: The changing nature of police interrogation in America. *Crime, Law and Social Change, 18,* 35–59.

Leo, R. A. (1996). Miranda's revenge: Police interrogation as a confidence game. *Law and Society Review, 30,* 259–288.

Lerner, M. J. (1980). *The belief in a just world.* New York: Plenum.

Leupnitz, D. A. (1982). *Child custody.* Lexington, MA: Lexington Books.

Lieberman, J. D., & Arndt, J. (2000). Understanding the limits of limiting instructions: Social psychological explanations for the failures of instructions to disregard pretrial publicity and other inadmissible evidence. *Psychology, Public Policy, and Law, 6,* 677–711.

Liebman, J. S., Fagan, J., & West, V. (2000). Capital attrition: Error rates in capital cases, 1973–1995. *Texas Law Review, 78,* 1839–1861.

Lindsay, D. S., & Read, J. D. (1994). Psychotherapy and memories of childhood sexual abuse: A cognitive perspective. *Applied Cognitive Psychology, 8,* 281–338.

Lindsay, R. C. L., & Wells, G. L. (1985). Improving eyewitness identification from lineups: Simultaneous versus sequential lineup presentations. *Journal of Applied Psychology, 70,* 556–564.

Link, B. G., & Stueve, A. (1994). Psychotic symptoms and the violent/illegal behavior of mental patients compared to community controls. In J. Monahan & H. J. Steadman (Eds.), *Violence and mental disorder: Developments in risk assessment* (pp. 137–159). Chicago: University of Chicago Press.

Lipsitt, P. D., Lelos, D., & McGarry, A. (1971). Competency for trial: A screening instrument. *American Journal of Psychiatry, 128,* 105–109.

Liss, M. B., & McKinley-Pace, M. J. (1999). Best interests of the child: New twists on an old theme. In R. Roesch, S. D. Hart, & J. R. P. Ogloff (Eds.), *Psychology and law: The state of the discipline* (pp. 339–372). New York: Kluwer/Plenum.

Litwack, T. R. (2001). Actuarial versus clinical assessments of dangerousness. *Psychology, Public Policy, and Law, 7,* 409–443.

Llewellyn, K. N. (1931). *The bramble bush.* Dobbs Ferry, NY: Oceana Press.

Locke, E. A., & Latham, G. P. (1990). *A theory of goal setting and task performance.* Englewood Cliffs, NJ: Prentice-Hall.

Lockett v. Ohio, 438 U.S. 586 (1978).

Lockhart v. McCree, 106 S. Ct. (1986). 1764.

Loftus, E. F. (1984). Expert testimony on the eyewitness. In G. L. Wells & E. F. Loftus (Eds.), *Eyewitness testimony: Psychological perspectives* (pp. 273–283). New York: Cambridge University Press.

Loftus, E. F. (1997). Memory for a past that never was. *Current Directions in Psychological Science, 6,* 60–65.

Loftus, E. F., & Ketcham, K. (1991). *Witness for the defense.* New York: St. Martin's Press.

Loftus, E. F., & Ketcham, K. (1994). *The myth of repressed memory.* New York: St. Martin's Press.

Loftus, E. F., & Palmer, J. C. (1974). Reconstruction of automobile destruction: An example of the interaction between language and memory. *Journal of Verbal Learning and Verbal Behavior, 13,* 585–589.

Lopez v. Laborers International Union Local 18, 987 F.2nd 1210 (5th Cir., 1993).

Lowe, R. H., & Wittig, M. A. (Eds.). (1989). Approaching pay equity through comparable worth. *Journal of Social Issues, 45,* 223–246.

Luginbuhl, J., & Burkhead, M. (1994). Sources of bias and arbitrariness in the capital trial. *Journal of Social Issues, 50,* 98–108.

Lykken, D. T. (1998). *A tremor in the blood: Uses and abuses of the lie detector.* New York: Plenum Trade.

Lynch, M., & Haney, C. (2000). Discrimination and instructional comprehension: Guided discretion, racial bias, and the death penalty. *Law and Human Behavior, 24,* 337–358.

MacCoun, R. J. (1993). Inside the black box: What empirical research tells us about decision-making by civil juries. In R. E. Litan (Ed.), *Verdict: Assessing the civil jury system* (pp. 137–180). Washington, DC: The Brookings Institution.

MacCoun, R. J., & Kerr, N. L. (1988). Asymmetric influence in mock jury deliberation: Juror's bias for leniency. *Journal of Personality and Social Psychology, 54,* 21–33.

MacKenzie, D. L., Brame, R., MacDowell, D., & Souryal, C. (1995). Boot camp prisons and recidivism in eight states. *Criminology, 33,* 327–358.

MacKenzie, M. M. (1981). *Plato on punishment.* Berkeley: University of California Press.

MacKinnon, C. (1979). *Sexual harassment of working women.* New Haven, CT: Yale University Press.

Madrid v. Gomez, 889 F. Supp. 1146 (N.D. Cal. 1995).

Major, B. (1993). Gender, entitlement, and the distribution of family labor. *Journal of Social Issues, 49,* 141–159.

Malmquist, C. P. (1986). Children who witness parental murder: Post traumatic aspects. *Journal of the American Academy of Child Psychiatry, 25,* 320–325.

Malpass, R. S., & Devine, P. G. (1981). Measuring the fairness of eyewitness identification lineups. In S. M. Lloyd-Bostock & B. R. Clifford (Eds.), *Evaluating witness evidence* (pp. 81–102). London: Wiley.

Mandela, N. (1994). *Long walk to freedom.* London: Little, Brown.

Manson v. Braithwaite, 432 U.S. 98 (1977).

Manzo, J. F. (1996). Taking turns and taking sides: Opening scenes from two jury deliberations. *Social Psychology Quarterly, 59,* 107–125.

Marston, W. M. (1938). *The lie detector test.* New York: Smith.

Martinson, R. (1974). What works? Questions and answers about prison reform. *Public Interest, 35,* 1–24.

Maryland v. Craig, 110 S. Ct. 3157 (1990).

Matsumoto, D. (1997). *Culture and Modern Life.* Pacific Grove, CA: Brooks-Cole.

Mauer, M. (1999). *Race to incarcerate.* New York: The New Press.

McCleskey v. Kemp, 107 S. Ct. 1756 (1987).

McConville, M. (1992). Videotaping Interrogations. *New Law Journal, 10,* 960–962.

McGarry, A. L. (1971). The fate of psychiatric offenders returned for trial. *American Journal of Psychiatry, 127,* 1181–1184.

McGrath, M. (2001). Academy of Behavioral Profiling: A letter from the president. www.profiling.org.

McGuckin v. Smith, 974 F. 2d 1050 (9th Cir.), 1992.

McKelvey, B. (1977). *American prisons: A history of good intentions.* Montclair, NJ: Patterson-Smith.

Medina v. California, 112 S. Ct. 2572 (1992).

Meissner, C. A., & Brigham, J. C. (2001). Thirty years of investigating the own-race bias in memory for faces: A meta-analytic review. *Psychology, Public Policy, and Law, 7,* 3–35.

Meissner, C. A., & Kassin, S. M. (2002). He's guilty!: Investigator bias in judgments of truth and deception. *Law and Human Behavior, 26,* 469–480.

Melton, G. B. (1987). Bringing psychology to the legal system: Opportunities, obstacles, and efficacy. *American Psychologist, 42,* 488–495.

Melton, G. B., Monahan, J., Saks, M. J. (1987). Psychologists as law professors. *American Psychologist, 42,* 502–509.

Melton, G. B., Petrila, J., Poythress, N. G., & Slobogin, C. (1997). *Psychological evaluations for the courts: A handbook for mental health professionals* (2nd Ed.). New York: Guilford.

Melton, G. B., & Saks, M. J. (1990). AP-LS's pro bono amicus brief project. *American Psychology-Law Society News, 10,* 5.

Mendoza-Dinton, R., Ayduk, O. N., Shoda, Y., & Mischel, W. (1997). Cognitive-affective processing system analysis of reactions to the O.J. Simpson criminal trial. *Journal of Social Issues, 53,* 563–581.

Menninger, K. (1966). *The crime of punishment.* New York: Viking.

Miller, G. A. (1969). Psychology as a means of promoting human welfare. *American Psychologist, 24,* 1063–1075.

Minnesota v. Mack, 292 N.W.2d 764 (Minn. 1980).

Miranda v. Arizona, 384 U.S. 486 (1966).

Model Penal Code 4.01(1) (1985).

Monahan, J. (1981). *Predicting violent behavior: An assessment of clinical techniques.* Beverly Hills, CA: Sage Publications.

Monahan, J., & Steadman, H. J. (1994). Toward a rejuvenation of risk assessment research. In J. Monahan & H. J. Steadman (Eds.), *Violence and mental disorder: Developments in risk assessment* (pp. 1–17). Chicago: University of Chicago Press.

Monahan, J., & Steadman, H. J. (1996). Violent storms and violent people: How meteorology can inform risk communication in mental health law. *American Psychologist, 51,* 931–938.

Monahan, J., Steadman, H. J., Silver, E., Appelbaum, P. S., Robbins, P. C., Mulvey, E. P., Roth, L. H., Grisso, T., & Banks, S. (2001). *Rethinking risk assessment: The MacArthur Study of Mental Disorder and Violence.* Oxford, UK: Oxford University Press.

Monahan, J., & Walker, L. (1998). *Social science in law: Cases and materials.* Westbury, NY: The Foundation Press, Inc.

Moran, G., Cutler, B. L., & DeLisa, A. (1994). Attitudes toward tort reform, scientific jury selection, and juror bias. *Law and Psychology Review, 18,* 309–328.

Morash, M., Harr, R., & Rucker, L. (1994). A comparison of programming for women and men in U.S. prison in the 1980s. *Crime and Delinquency, 40,* 197–221.

Morris, N. (1995). The contemporary prison. In N. Morris & D. J. Rothman (Eds.), *The Oxford history of the prison* (pp. 203–231). New York: Oxford University Press.

Morrow v. Maryland, 433 A. 2nd. 108 (Md. 1982).

Moston, S., Stephenson, G., & Williamson, T. M. (1992). The effects of case characteristics on suspect behavior during police questioning. *British Journal of Criminology, 32,* 23–40.

Mott, N. L., Hans, V. P., & Simpson, L. (2000). What's half a lung worth? Civil jurors' accounts of their award decision making. *Law and Human Behavior, 24,* 401–420.

Muhl, C. J. (2001, January). The employment-at-will doctrine. *Monthly Labor Review,* 3–11.

Muller v. Oregon, 208 U.S. 412 (1907).

Mulvey, E. P., & Lidz, C. W. (1995). Conditional prediction: A model for research on dangerousness to others in a new era. *International Journal of Law and Psychiatry, 18,* 129–143.

Mundy, L. (1997, October, 26). Zero tolerance. *The Washington Post Magazine,* pp. 20–26.

Munsterberg, H. (1908). *On the witness stand: Essays on psychology and crime.* Garden City, NY: Doubleday.

Myers, L. B., & Brewin, C. R. (1998). Repressive copying and the directed forgetting of emotional material. *Journal of Abnormal Psychology, 107,* 141–148.

Myers, B., & Lecci, L. (1998). Revising the factor structure of the Juror Bias Scale. *Law and Human Behavior, 22,* 239–256.

Myers, J., Redlich, A., Goodman, G., Prizmich, L., & Imwindelried, E. (1999). Jurors' perceptions of hearsay in child sexual cases. *Psychology, Public Policy, and the Law, 4,* 1025–1051.

Myers, L. B., Brewin, C. R., & Power, M. J. (1998). Repressive coping and the directed forgetting of emotional material. *Journal of Abnormal Psychology, 107,* 141–148.

Narby, D. J., & Cutler, B. L. (1994). Effectiveness of voir dire as a safeguard in eyewitness cases. *Journal of Applied Psychology, 79,* 274–279.

Narby, D. J., Cutler, B. L., & Moran, G. (1993). A meta analysis of the association between authoritarianism and jurors' perceptions of defendants culpability. *Journal of Applied Psychology, 78,* 34–42.

National Advisory Commission on Criminal Justice Standards and Goals. (1973). *Task force report on corrections.* Washington, DC: U.S. Government Printing Office.

National Commission on Law Observance and Enforcement. (1931). *Report on lawlessness in law enforcement* (Vol. 11). Washington, DC: U.S. Government Printing Office.

Neil v. Biggers, 409 U.S. 188 (1972).

Neisser, U., & Harsch, N. (1992). Phantom flashbulbs: False recollections of hearing the news about Challenger. In E. Winograd & U. Neisser (Eds.), *Affect and accuracy in recall: Studies of "flashbulb" memories* (pp. 9–31). Cambridge: Cambridge University Press.

Nestor, P. G., Daggett, D., Haycosck, J., & Price, M. (1999). Competence to stand trial: A neuropsychological inquiry. *Law and Human Behavior, 23,* 397–412.

New facts about shaving revealed by lie detector! (1938, June 6). *Time.*

Newman, L. F., Duff, K., Schnopp-Wyatt, N., Brock, B., & Hoffman, Y. (1997). Reactions to the O.J. Simpson verdict: Mindless tribalism or motivated inference? *Journal of Social Issues, 53,* 547–562.

Nicholson, R. A. (1999). Forensic assessment. In R. Roesch, S. D. Hart, & J. R. P. Ogloff (Eds.), *Psychology and law: The state of the discipline* (pp. 121–173). New York: Kluwer/Plenum.

Nicholson, R. A., & Kugler, K. E. (1991). Competent and incompetent criminal defendants: A quantitative review of comparative research. Psychological Bulletin, 109, 355–370.

Nisbett, R. E., & Cohen, D. (1996). *Culture of honor: The psychology of violence in the South.* Boulder, CO: Westview.

Norris, F. H. (1992). Epidemiology of trauma: Frequency and impact on different potentially traumatic events of different demographic groups. *Journal of Consulting and Clinical Psychology, 60,* 409–418.

Novaco, R. W. (1994). Anger as a risk factor for violence among the mentally disordered. In J. Monahan & H. J. Steadman (Eds.), *Violence and mental disorder: Developments in risk assessment* (pp. 22–59). Chicago: University of Chicago Press.

O'Brien, D. (1985). *Two of a kind: The hillside stranglers.* New York: New American Library.

Ofshe, R. (1989). Coerced confessions: The logic of seemingly irrational action. *Cultic Studies Journal, 6,* 1–15.

Ofshe, R., & Leo, R. (1997). The decision to confess falsely: Rational choice and irrational action. *Denver University Law Review, 74,* 979–1122.

Ofshe, R., & Watters, E. (1994). *Making monsters.* Berkeley: University of California Press.

Ogloff, J. R. P. (1998). The risk assessment enterprise: Selective incapacitation of increased predictive accuracy. *Law and Human Behavior, 22,* 453–455.

Ogloff, J. R. P. (2000). Two steps forward and one step backward: The law and psychology movement(s) in the 20th century. *Law and Human Behavior, 24,* 457–484.

Ogloff, J. R. P., & Douglas, K. S. (1995). *The treatment of high-risk offenders: A literature review and analysis.* Ottawa, Canada: Department of Justice.

Ogloff, J. R. P., Roberts, C. F., & Roesch, R. (1993). The insanity defense: Legal standards and clinical assessment. *Applied and Preventative Psychology, 2,* 163–178.

Ogloff, J. R. P., & Vidmar, N. (1994). The impact of pretrial publicity on jurors: A study to compare the relative effects of television and print media. *Law and Human Behavior, 18,* 507–525.

Olczak, P. V., Kaplan, M. F., & Penrod, S. (1991). Attorneys' lay psychology and its effectiveness in selecting jurors: Three empirical studies. *Journal of Social Behavior and Personality, 6,* 431–452.

Olsen-Fulero, L., & Fulero, S. M. (1997). Commonsense rape judgments: An empathy-complexity theory of rape juror story making. *Psychology, Public Policy, and Law, 3,* 402–427.

Oncale v. Sundowner Offshore Services, Inc., 118 S. Ct. 998 (1998).

Orcutt, H. K., Goodman, G. S., Tobey, A. E., Batterman-Faunce, J. M., & Thomas, S. (2001). Detecting deception in children's testimony: Factfinders' abilities to reach the truth in open court and closed circuit trials. *Law and Human Behavior, 25,* 339–372.

Otto, A. L., Penrod, S. D., & Dexter, H. D. (1994). The biasing impact of pretrial publicity on juror judgments. *Law and Human Behavior, 18,* 453–469.

Palmore v. Sidotti, 104 S. Ct. 1879 (1984).

Parisi, N. (1982). The prisoner's pressures and responses. In N. Parisi (Ed.), *Coping with imprisonment* (pp. 9–16). Beverly Hills, CA: Sage Publications.

Partridge, A., & Eldridge, W. (1974). The second circuit sentencing study. Washington, DC: Federal Judicial Center.

Paternoster, R., & Kazyaka, A. M. (1988). The administration of the death penalty in South Carolina. *South Carolina Law Review, 39,* 245–414.

Pearson, J., & Thoennes, N. (1990). Custody after divorce: Demographic and attitudinal patterns. *American Journal of Orthopsychiatry, 60,* 233–249.

Peckham, R. (1985). A judicial response to the cost of litigation. *Rutgers Law Review, 37,* 253–271.

Pennington, N., & Hastie, R. (1993). The story model for juror decisionmaking. In R. Hastie (Ed.), *Inside the juror* (pp. 84–115). Cambridge: Cambridge University Press.

Penrod, S. D. (1990). Predictors of jury decision making in criminal and civil cases: A field experiment. *Forensic Reports, 3,* 261–277.

Penrod, S. D., & Cutler, B. (1999). Preventing mistaken convictions in eyewitness identification trials. In R. Roesch, S. D. Hart, & J. R. P. Ogloff, *Psychology and law: The state of the discipline* (pp. 89–118). New York: Kluwer Academic.

People v. McRae, 23 Crim. L. Rep. (BNA) 2507 (N.Y. Sup. Ct. 1978)

People v. Shirley, (1982). 31 Cal. 3d 18 55.

People v. Taylor, 522 N.E. 2d 131 (1990).

Perlin, M. L. (1990). Unpacking the myths: The symbolism mythology of insanity defense jurisprudence. *Case Western Reserve Law Review, 40,* 599–731.

Perlin, M. L. (1994). *The jurisprudence of the insanity defense.* Durham, NC: University of North Carolina Press.

Perlin, M. L. (1996). The insanity defense: Deconstructing the myths and reconstructing the jurisprudence. In B. D. Sales & D. W. Shuman (Eds.), *Law, mental health, and mental disorder.* Pacific Grove, CA: Brooks/ Cole.

Perlin, M. L. (2000). *The hidden prejudice: Mental disability on trial.* Washington, DC: American Psychological Association.

Peters, E. M. (1995). Prison before the prison: The ancient and medieval worlds. In N. Morris & D. J. Rothman (Eds.), *The Oxford history of the prison.* New York: Oxford University Press.

Peters, M. (1996). Evaluation of the impact of boot camps for juvenile offenders. Washington, DC: Office of Juvenile Justice and Delinquency Prevention.

Petersilia, J. (1994). Violent crime and violent criminals: The response of the justice system. In M. Costanzo & S. Oskamp (Eds.), *Violence and the law.* Thousand Oaks, CA: Sage Publications.

Petersilia, J., Turner, S., & Peterson, J. (1986). Prison versus probation in California: Implications for crime and offender recidivism (R-3323-NIJ). Santa Monica, CA: RAND.

Peterson, C., & Bell, M. (1996). Children's memory for traumatic injury. *Child Development, 567,* 3045–3070.

Pettigrew, T. F., & Martin, J. (1987). Shaping the organizational context for black American inclusion. *Journal of Social Issues, 43,* 41–78.

Pettigrew, T. F., & Meertens, R. W. (1995). Subtle and blatant prejudice in western Europe. *European Journal of Social Psychology, 25,* 57–75.

Phares, E. J. (1976). *Locus of control in personality.* Morristown, NJ: Learning Press.

Pickel, K. L. (1995). Inducing jurors to disregard inadmissible evidence: A legal explanation does not help. *Law and Human Behavior, 19,* 407–424.

Pinizzotto, A. J., & Finkel, N. J. (1990). Criminal personality profiling: An outcome and process study. *Law and Human Behavior, 14,* 215–233.

Platt, A., & Diamond, B. (1966). The origins of the "right and wrong" test of criminal responsibility and its subsequent development in the United States. *California Law Review, 54,* 1227–1260.

Podlesny, J. A. (1995). *A lack of operable case facts restricts applicability of the Guilty Knowledge Deception Detection Method in FBI criminal investigations.* Quantico, VA: Federal Bureau of Investigation.

Police and Criminal Evidence Act. (1986). London: HMSO.

Porter, S., Birt, A. R., Yuille, J. C., & Lehman, D. R. (2000). Negotiating false memories: Interviewer and rememberer characteristics relate to memory distortion. *Psychological Science, 11,* 507–510.

Porter, S., Yuille, J. C., & Lehman, D. R. (1999). The nature of real, implanted, and fabricated memories of emotional childhood events. *Law and Human Behavior, 23,* 517–537.

Poythress, N. J., & Brodsky, S. L. (1992). In the wake of a negligent release lawsuit: An investigation of professional consequences and institutional impact on a state psychiatric hospital. *Law and Human Behavior, 16,* 155–174.

Procunier v. Martinez, 416 U.S. 396 (1974).

Pruett, M. K., & Hoganbruen, K. (1998). Joint custody and shared parenting: Research and interventions. *Child and Adolescent Psychiatric Clinics of North America, 7,* 272–294.

Pryor, J. B., Giedd, J. L., & Williams, K. B. (1995). A social psychological model for predicting sexual harassment. *Journal of Social Issues, 51,* 69–84.

Pryor, J. D., & Whalen, N. (1997). A typology of sexual harassment: Characteristics of harassers and social circumstances under which sexual harassment occurs. In W. O. Donohue (Ed.), *Sexual harassment: Theory, research, and treatment.* Boston, MA: Allyn & Bacon.

Quinsey, V., Harris, G., Rice, M., & Cormier, C. (1998). *Violent offenders: Appraising and managing risk.* Washington, DC: American Psychological Association.

Radelet, M. L., Bedau, H. A., & Putnam, C. E. (1992). *In spite of innocence: Erroneous convictions in capital cases.* Boston: Northeastern University Press.

Rape Survivors Speak Out. (2001). www.rapesurvivors.com.

Reck v. Pate, 367 U.S. 433 (1961).

Regina v. Oxford, 9 Carr., & P. 525 (1840).

Reiman, J. (1998). *The rich get richer and the poor get prison.* Boston: Allyn & Bacon.

Ressler, R., Burgess, A., & Douglas, J. (1988). *Sexual homicide.* Lexington, MA: Lexington Books.

Rex v. Arnold, 16 How. St. Tr. 695 (1724), reprinted in *A complete collection of state trials.* (1812). Howell, T. B. (Ed.).

Rhodes v. Chapman, 452 U.S. 337 (1981).

Rideau, W., & Wikberg, R. (1992). *Life sentences: Rage and survival behind bars.* New York: Times Books.

Riggins v. Nevada, 112 S. Ct. 1810 (1992).

Ring v. Arizona, 122 S. Ct. 2428 (2002).

Risinger, D. M., Saks, M. J., Thompson, W. C., & Rosenthal, R. (2002). The Daubert/Kumho implications of observer effects in forensic science: Hidden problems of expectation and suggestion. *California Law Review, 90,* 1–56.

Roche, T. (2002, January 20). The Yates Odyssey, www.time.com.

Rock v. Arkansas, 107 S. Ct. 2704 (1987).

Roesch, R., & Golding, S. (1987). Defining and assessing competency to stand trial. In I. B. Weiner and A. K. Hess (Eds.), *Handbook of forensic psychology.* New York: Wiley.

Roesch, R., Golding, S. L., Hans, V. P., & Reppucci, N. D. (1991). Social science and the courts: The role of *amicus curiae* briefs. *Law and Human Behavior, 15,* 1–14.

Roesch, R., Zapf, P. A., Eaves, D., & Webster, C. D. (1998). *The Fitness Interview Test—Revised.* Burnaby, BC, Canada: Mental Health, Law, and Policy Institute, Simon Fraser University.

Rogers, R., & Ewing, C. P. (1992). The measurement of insanity: Debating the merits of the R-CRAS and its alternatives. *International Journal of Law and Psychiatry, 15,* 113–123.

Roper, R. (1980). Jury size and verdict consistency: "The line has to be drawn somewhere." *Law and Society Review, 14,* 977–995.

Rosenthal, R., & Jacobson, L. F. (1968). *Pygmalion in the classroom.* New York: Holt, Rinehart, & Winston.

Ross, L., & Nisbett, R. (1991). *The person and the situation.* New York: McGraw-Hill.

Rothenberg, P. S. (1995). *Race, class, & gender in the United States.* New York: St. Martin's Press.

Rothman, D. J. (1995). Perfecting the prison. In N. Morris & D. J. Rothman (Eds.), *The Oxford history of the prison.* New York: Oxford University Press.

Rotman, E. (1995). The failure of reform. In N. Morris & D. J. Rothman (Eds.), *The Oxford history of the prison.* New York: Oxford University Press.

Rowland, J. (1985). *The ultimate violation.* New York: Doubleday.

Ruback, R. B., & Wroblewski, J. (2001). The federal sentencing guidelines: Psychological and policy reasons for simplification. *Psychology, Public Policy, and Law, 7,* 739–775.

Sack, K. (1998, October 4). Fugitive in bombing may be charged with three more. *The New York Times,* p. 18.

St. Amand, M. D., & Zamble, E. (2001). Impact of information about sentencing decisions on public attitudes toward the justice system. *Law and Human Behavior, 25,* 515–528.

Saks, M. J. (1977). *Jury verdicts: The role of group size and social decision rule.* Lexington, MA: Lexington Books.

Saks, M. J. (1990). Expert witnesses, nonexpert witnesses, and nonwitness experts. *Law and Human Behavior, 14,* 291–313.

Saks, M. J. (1996). The smaller the jury, the greater the unpredictability. *Judicature, 79,* 263–266.

Saks, M. J., & Kidd, R. (1986). *Social psychology in the courtroom.* New York: Van Nostrand Reinhold.

Saks, M. J., & Marti, M. W. (1997). A meta-analysis of the effects of jury size. *Law and Human Behavior, 21,* 451–468.

Sales, B. D., & Shuman, D. W., (Eds.). (1996). *Law, mental health, and mental disorder.* Pacific Grove, CA: Brooks/Cole.

Salfati, C. G., & Canter, D. (1999). Differentiating stranger murders: Profiling offender characteristics from behavioral styles. *Behavioral Sciences and the Law, 17,* 391–406.

Sampson, E. E. (1975). On justice as equality. *Journal of Social Issues, 31,* 45–64.

Sandys, M., & Dillehay, R. C. (1995). First-ballot votes, predeliberation dispositions, and final verdicts in jury trials. *Law and Human Behavior, 19,* 175–195.

Schacter, D. L. (1996). *Searching for memory.* New York: Basic Books.

Schacter, D. L. (2001). *The seven sins of memory.* Boston: Houghton-Mifflin.

Schlegel, J. (1979). American legal realism and empirical social science: From the Yale experience. *Buffalo Law Review, 28,* 459–586.

Schlosser, E. (1999, December). The prison-industrial complex. *The Atlantic Monthly,* 51–77.

Schooler, J. W. (1994). Seeking the core: The issues and evidence surrounding recovered accounts of sexual trauma. *Consciousness and Cognition, 3,* 452–469.

Schuller, R. (1994). Applications of battered woman syndrome evidence in the courtroom. In M. Costanzo & S. Oskamp (Eds.), *Violence and the Law.* Thousand Oaks, CA: Sage Publications.

Schulman, J., Shaver, P., Colman, R., Emrick, B., & Christie, R. (1973, May). Recipe for a jury. *Psychology Today, 77,* 37–44.

Sears v. Rutishauser, 466 NE 2d 210 (Ill. 1984)

Sellin, T. (1980). *The penalty of death.* Beverly Hills, CA: Sage Publications.

Sentencing Project, The (2001). Rate of incarceration in selected nations. www.sentencingproject.org.

Serge, V. (1984). *Memoirs of a revolutionary.* London: Readers and Writers.

Sherman, L. W., Gottfredson, D., MacKenzie, D., Eck, J., Reuter, P., & Bushway, S. (1997). *Preventing crime: What works, what doesn't, what's promising.* Washington, DC: National Institute of Justice.

Shestowsky, D. (1999). Where is the common knowledge? Empirical support for requiring expert testimony in sexual harassment trials. *Stanford Law Review, 51,* 367–381.

Siegel, A., & Elwork, A. (1990). Treating incompetence to stand trial. *Law and Human Behavior, 14,* 57–65.

Siegel, L. J. (1998). *Criminology.* Belmont, CA: West.

Silberman, M. (1995). *A world of violence: Corrections in America.* Belmont, CA: West.

Silver, E., Cirincione, C., & Steadman, H. J. (1994). Demythologizing inaccurate perceptions of the insanity defense. *Law and Human Behavior, 18,* 63–70.

Simmons, R. J. (1997). *Employment discrimination and EEO practice manual.* Van Nuys, CA: Castle Publications.

Simon, R. J. (1967). *The jury and the defense of insanity.* Boston: Little, Brown.

Skeem, J. L., & Golding, S. L. (2001). Describing jurors' personal conceptions of insanity and their relationship to case judgments. *Psychology, Public Policy, and Law, 7,* 561–621.

Skolnick, J. H. (1961). Scientific theory and scientific evidence: An analysis of lie detection. *Yale Law Journal, 70,* 694–728.

Skolnick, J. H., & Fyfe, J. J. (1993). *Above the law.* New York: The Free Press.

Slade, M. (1994, February 26). Law firms begin reining in sexually harassing partners. *The New York Times,* p. B12.

Slobogin, C. (1997). Deceit, pretext, and trickery: Investigative laws by the police. *Oregon Law Review, 76,* 775–816.

Slobogin, C. (2000). An end to insanity: Recasting the role of mental illness in criminal cases. *Virginia Law Review, 86,* 1199–1223.

Slobogin, C., Melton, G. B., & Showalter, C. R. (1984). The feasibility of a brief evaluation of mental state at the time of the offense, *Law and Human Behavior, 8,* 305–321.

Smith, V. L. (1991). Impact of pretrial instruction on jurors' information processing and decision-making. *Journal of Applied Psychology, 76,* 220–228.

Smith v. United States, 148 F.2d 665 (1929).

Softley, P. (1980). *Police interrogation: An observational study in four police stations.* London, England: HMSO.

Sommers, S. R., & Ellsworth, P. C. (2001). White juror bias: An investigation of prejudice against black defendants in the American courtroom. *Psychology, Public Policy, and Law, 7,* 201–229.

Spanos, N. P., Burgess, M. F., Samuels, C., & Blois, W. O. (1999). Creating false memories of infancy with hypnotic and nonhypnotic procedures. *Applied Cognitive Psychology, 13,* 201–218.

Specialty Guidelines for Forensic Psychologists. (1999). In R. Roesch, S. D. Hart, & J. R. Ogloff (Eds.), *Psychology and law: The state of the discipline* (pp. 423–435). New York: Kluwer Academic/Plenum Publishers.

Spierenberg, P. (1995). The body and the state. In N. Morris & D. J. Rothman (Eds.), *The Oxford history of the prison.* New York: Oxford University Press.

Sporer, S. L., Penrod, S., Read, D., & Cutler, B. (1995). Choosing, confidence, and accuracy: A meta-analysis of the confidence-accuracy relation in eyewitness identification studies. *Psychological Bulletin, 118,* 315–327.

Springer, J. (2002, January 9). Kids drowned, mother faces execution, www.courttv.com.

Stack, M. K. (2002, March 13). Jury rejects insanity claim, convicts mother of murder. *Los Angeles Times,* pp. A1, A18.

Stack, M. K. (2002, March 16). Yates draws life sentence. *Los Angeles Times.* p. A14.

Stahl, P. M. (1994). *Conducting child custody evaluations: A comprehensive guide.* Thousand Oaks, CA: Sage Publications.

Stasser, G. (1992). Pooling of unshared information during group discussion. In S. Worchel, W. Wood, & J. Simpson (Eds.), *Group process and productivity* (pp. 48–67). Newbury Park, CA: Sage Publications.

State v. Dorsey, 539 P.2d 204 (N.M. 1975).

State of Oregon v. Hansen, 304 Or. 169, 176, 743 P.2d 157 (1987).

State v. Helterbridle, 301 N.W.2d 545, 547 (Minn. 1980).

State v. Scales, 518 N.W.2d 587–592 (1994).

Steadman, H. J., & Cocozza, J. J. (1974). *Careers of the criminally insane: Excessive social control of deviance.* Lexington, MA: Lexington Books.

Steadman, H. J., Mulvey, E., Monahan, J., Robbins, P. C., Appelbaum, P. S., Grisso, T., Roth, L. H., & Silver, E. (1998). Violence by people discharged from acute psychiatric inpatient facilities and by others in the same neighborhoods. *Archives of General Psychiatry, 55,* 393–401.

Steblay, N. (1992). A meta-analytic review of the weapon-focus effect. *Law and Human Behavior, 16,* 413–424.

Steblay, N., & Bothwell, R. K. (1994). Evidence for hypnotically refreshed testimony: The view from the laboratory. *Law and Human Behavior, 18,* 635–652.

Steblay, N., Dysart, J., Fulero, S., & Lindsay, R. C. L. (2001). Eyewitness accuracy rates in sequential and simultaneous lineup presentations: A meta-analytic comparison. *Law and Human Behavior, 25,* 459–474.

Stephan v. State, 711 P.2d 1156–1158 (1985).

Stephan, W. G. (1986). The effects of school desegregation: An evaluation 30 years after *Brown.* In R. Kidd, L. Saxe & M. Saks (Eds.), *Advances in Applied Social Psychology.* New York: Erlbaum.

Stern, V. (1998). *A sin against the future.* Boston: Northeastern University Press.

Strauss, M., & Gelles, R. (1988). How violent are American families? In G. Hotaling, D. Finkelhor, J. Kirkpatrick, & M. Strauss (Eds.), *Family abuse and its consequences* (pp. 14–36). Thousand Oaks, CA: Sage Publications.

Strier, F. (1999). Whither trial consulting: Issues and projections. *Law and Human Behavior, 23,* 93–115.

Strier, F., & Shestowsky, D. (1999). Profiling the profilers: A study of the trial consulting profession, its impact on trial justice and what, if anything, to do about it. *Wisconsin Law Review, 51,* 441–499.

Strodtbeck, F., & Hook, L. (1961). The social dimensions of a twelve-man jury table. *Sociometry, 24,* 397–415.

Strodtbeck, F., & Lipinski, R. (1985). Becoming first among equals: Moral considerations in jury foreman selection. *Journal of Personality and Social Psychology, 49,* 927–936.

Sunby, S. E. (1997). The jury as critic: An empirical look at how capital juries perceive expert and lay testimony. *Virginia Law Review, 83,* 1109–1188.

Tanford, J. A. (1990). The law and psychology of jury instructions. *Nebraska Law Review, 69,* 71–111.

Tanford, J. A. (1990). The limits of a scientific jurisprudence: The Supreme Court and psychology. *Indiana Law Journal, 66,* 137–173.

Tarasoff v. Regents of the University of California, 108 Cal. Rptr. 878 (Ct. App. 1973); reversed and remanded, 13 Cal. 3d 177 (1974); modified 17 Cal. 3d 425 (1976).

Taylor v. Louisiana, 419 U.S. 522 (1975).

Terpstra, D. E., & Baker, D. D. (1992). Outcomes of federal court decisions on sexual harassment. *Academy of Management Journal, 35,* 181–190.

Terrance, C. A., Matheson, K., & Spanos, N. P. (2000). Effects of judicial instructions and case characteristics in a mock jury trial of battered women who kill. *Law and Human Behavior, 24,* 207–230.

Thompson, J. (1999). *What Jennifer saw.* Interview. www.pbs.org.

Thompson, W. C. (1989). Death qualification after *Wainwright v. Witt* and *Lockhart v. McCree. Law and Human Behavior, 13,* 185–215.

Thornberry, T. P., & Jacoby, J. E. (1979). *The criminally insane: A community follow-up of mentally ill offenders.* Chicago: University of Chicago Press.

Title VII of the Civil Rights Act of 1964, 42 U.S.C. § 2000e *et seq.* (1964).

Toch, H. (1977). *Police, prisons, and the problem of violence.* Washington, DC: U.S. Government Printing Office.

Toch, H., & Adams, K. (1989). *Coping: Maladaptation in prisons.* New Brunswick, NJ: Transaction Press.

Tonry, M. (1996). *Sentencing matters.* New York: Oxford University Press.

Toobin, J. (1996, September 9). The Marcia Clark verdict. *The New Yorker,* pp. 58–71.

Townsend v. Swain, 372 U.S. 293 (1963).

Trans World Airlines, Inc. v. Hardison, 432 U.S. 63 (1977).

Tremper, C. R. (1987). Organized psychology's efforts to influence judicial policymaking. *American Psychologist, 42,* 496–501.

Triandis, H. C. (1996). The psychological measurement of cultural syndromes. *American Psychologist, 51,* 407–415.

Tripp, R. T. (1970). *The international thesaurus of quotations.* New York: Harper and Row.

U.S. Merit Systems Protection Board. (1995). Sexual harassment in the federal workplace: Trends, progress, continuing challenges. Washington, DC: Author.

Ulmer v. State Farm Fire & Casualty Co., 897 F. Supp. 299 (W.D. La.1995).

Uniform Marriage and Divorce Act, 9a U.L.A. 91 (1976).

United States v. Brawner, 471 F.2d 969 (D.C. Cir. 1972).

United States v. Goff, 6 F.3d 363 (6th Cir., 1993).

United States v. Scheffer, 118 S. Ct. 1261 (1998).

Valentine, P. W. (1999, February 14). 19 inmates moved in bid to bust drug ring. *The Washington Post,* pp. C1, 4.

Vanman, E. J., Paul, B. Y., Kaplan, D. L., & Miller, N. (1990). Facial electromyography differentiates racial bias in imagined cooperative settings, *Psychophysiology, 27,* 563–567.

Vidmar, N. (1998). The performance of the American civil jury: An empirical perspective. *Arizona Law Review, 40,* 849–899.

Vidmar, N., Lempert, R., Diamond, S., Hans, V., Landsman, S., MacCoun, R., Sanders, J., Hosch, H., Kassin, S., Galanter, M., Eisenberg, T., Daniels, S., Greene, E., Martin, J., Penrod, S., Richardson, J., Heuer, L., & Horowitz, I. (2000). Amicus brief: *Kumho Tire v. Carmichael. Law and Human Behavior, 24,* 383–400.

Vidmar, N., & Rice, J. J. (1993). Assessments of noneconomic damage awards in medical negligence: A comparison of jurors and legal professionals. *Iowa Law Review, 78,* 883–911.

Visher, G. (1987). Juror decision making: The importance of evidence. *Law and Human Behavior, 11,* 1–14.

Wainwright v. Witt, 105 S. Ct. 844 (1985).

Waldo, C. R., Berdahl, J. L., & Fitzgerald, L. G. (1998). Are men sexually harassed? If so, by whom? *Law and Human Behavior, 22,* 59–79.

Walker, L. (1979). *The battered woman.* New York: Harper & Row.

Walker, S. (1998). *Popular justice: A history of American criminal justice.* New York: Oxford University Press.

Wallerstein, J. S., & Blakeslee, S. (1989). *Second chances: Men, women, and children a decade after divorce.* New York: Ticknor and Fields.

Washington v. Harper, 494 U.S. 210 (1990).

Webster, C. D. (1998). Comment on Thomas Mathiesen's selective incapacitation revisited. *Law and Human Behavior, 22,* 471–476.

Wegner, D. M. (1994). Ironic processes of mental control. *Psychological Review, 101,* 34–52.

Weiner, B., Graham, S., & Reyna, C. (1997). An attributional examination of retributive versus utilitarian philosophies of punishment. *Social Justice Research, 10,* 31–452.

Weissman, H. N. (1991). Child custody evaluations: Fair and unfair professional practices. *Behavioral Sciences and the Law, 9,* 469–476.

Wells, G. L. (1978). Applied eyewitness testimony research: System variables and estimator variables. *Journal of Personality and Social Psychology, 36,* 1546–1557.

Wells, G. L. (2001). Police lineups: Data, theory, and policy. *Psychology, Public Policy, and Law, 7,* 791–801.

Wells, G. L., & Bradfield, A. L. (1998). "Good, you identified the suspect": Feedback to eyewitnesses distorts their reports of the witnessing experience, *Journal of Applied Psychology, 83,* 360–376.

Wells, G. L., Small, M., Penrod, S., Malpass, R. S., Fulero, S. M., & Brimacombe, C. A. E. (1998). Eyewitness identification procedures: Recommendations for lineups and photospreads. *Law and Human Behavior, 22,* 603–647.

Wells, G. L., Wright, E. F., & Bradfield, A. L. (1999). Witnesses to crime. In R. Roesch, S. D. Hart, & J. R. P. Ogloff, *Psychology and law: The state of the discipline* (pp. 53–87). New York: Kluwer Academic.

Werner, E. (1993). Risk, resilience, and recovery: Perspectives from the Kauai Longitudinal Study. *Development and Psychopathology, 5,* 503–515.

Wiener, R. L., Hackney, A., Kadela, K., Rauch, S., Seib, H., Warren, L., & Hurt, L. E. (2002). The fit and implementation of sexual harassment law to workplace evaluations. *Journal of Applied Psychology, 87,* 747–764.

Wiener, R. L., Hurt, L., Thomas, S., Sadler, M., Bauer. C., & Sargent, T. (1998). The role of declarative and procedural knowledge in capital murder sentencing, *Journal of Applied Social Psychology, 28,* 124–144.

Wiener, R. L., Watts, B. A., Goldkamp, K. H., & Gasper, C. (1995). Social-analytic investigation of hostile workplace environments: A test of the reasonable woman standard. *Law and Human Behavior, 19,* 263–281.

Wigmore, J. (1909). Professor Munsterberg and the psychology of testimony: Being a report of the case of *Cokestone v. Munsterberg. Illinois Law Review, 3,* 399–445.

Willams, L. M. (1994). Recall of childhood trauma: A prospective study of women's memories of child sexual abuse. *Journal of Consulting and Clinical Psychology, 62,* 1167–1176.

Williams v. Florida, 399 U.S. 78 (1970).

Williams, Bazille, et al. v. Alioto et al., 549 F.2d 136 (1977).

Wilson v. Seiter, 111 S. Ct. 2321 (1991).

Winick, B. J. (1996). Incompetency to proceed in the criminal process: Past, present, and future. In B. D. Sales & D. W. Shuman (Eds.), *Law, mental health, and mental disorder.* Pacific Grove, CA: Brooks/Cole.

Wissler, R. L., & Saks, M. J. (1985). On the inefficacy of limiting instructions. *Law and Human Behavior, 9,* 37–48.

Wolfgang, M. E., & Reidel, M. (1973). Rape, judicial discretion, and the death penalty. *Annals of the American Academy of Political and Social Science, 407,* 110–113.

Word, C. O., Zanna, M. P., & Cooper, J. (1974). The nonverbal mediation of self-fulfilling prophecies in interracial interaction. *Journal of Experimental Social Psychology, 10,* 109–121.

Wrightsman, L. S. (1999). *Judicial decision making: Is psychology relevant?* New York: Plenum.

Zapf, P. A., & Roesch, R. (1997). Assessing fitness to stand trial: A comparison of institution-based evaluations and a brief screening interview. *Canadian Journal of Community Mental Health, 16,* 53–66.

Zapf, P. A., & Roesch, R. (2000). Mental competency evaluations: Guidelines for judges and attorneys. *Court Review, 37,* 28–35.

Zeisel, H., & Diamond, S. S. (1978). The effect of peremptory challenges on jury and verdict: An experiment in a federal district court. *Stanford Law Review, 30,* 491–529.

Name Index

A

Abbott, J. H., 290
Abramson, J., 123, 124, 125, 127
Ackerman, M. C., 233
Ackerman, M. J., 233
Adams, K., 289
Adler, S., 129
Ajzen, I., 137
Alge, B. J., 265
Allison, J. A., 87
Alpert, J. L., 200
Anderson, A. B., 139
Anderson, D. C., 275, 282, 295
Anderson, M. C., 206
Appelbaum, P. S., 212, 238
Archer, D., 306
Arditti, J. A., 234
Aristotle, 260
Armstrong, P., 45
Arndt, J., 144, 168
Aronson, E., 139, 182
Ayduk, O. N., 139

B

Bachorowski, J., 219
Bailey, W. C., 306
Baker, D., 248, 250
Baldus, D., 304, 305
Baldwin, J., 166
Banks, C., 287, 288
Banks, S., 238
Bar-Hillel, M., 48, 64
Barkan, S. E., 193, 291, 297
Barland, G. H., 47
Barnard, G.W., 104
Baron, R. A., 261
Barratt, E. S., 220
Bastian, L., 242
Batson, J., 127
Batterman-Faunce, J. M., 208
Bazelon, D., 111
Bazerman, M. H., 264
Beale, C. R., 183
Beck, C. J. A., 237, 238
Becker, J. V., 88
Bedau, H., 308, 310
Behrman, B. W., 208
Bekerian, D. A., 94
Bell, M., 196

Belli, M., 129
Belnas, M., 296
Bennett, E., 146
Ben-Shakhar, G., 48, 55, 64
Berdahl, J. L., 243
Berman, A. L., 74
Berns, W., 277
Berry, S., 308
Bersoff, D. N., 8
Bianchi, K., 106
Billings, F. J., 205
Birt, A. R., 208
Blackburn, J. W., 264
Blakeslee, S., 230
Blois, W. O., 205
Blumenthal, J., 244
Bobecel, D. R., 265
Boeschen, L., 93
Bonnie, R., 104–105
Bonta, J., 220
Boone, J., 176
Borgida, E., 88, 90, 208
Bornstein, B. H., 168
Bothwell, R. K., 190
Bottcher, J., 296
Bottoms, B. L., 198, 208
Bottoms, S., 229
Bowers, K., 189
Bowers, W. J., 300, 304, 306
Bradfield, A., 182, 183, 186
Braid, J., 189
Brame, R., 297
Brandeis, L., 4
Bratt, C., 227
Braun, S., 249
Brehm, S. S., 144, 260
Brennan, W., 33
Brewin, C., 206
Bricklin, B., 234
Bridges, M., 226, 228, 230
Briggs, M. A., 44
Brigham, J. C., 29, 177
Brimacombe, C. A. E., 184
Brock, P., 137
Brodsky, S. L., 211
Broffit, B., 304
Brown, N., 58
Browne, A., 84
Bruce, W. M., 264

Bruck, M., 194, 197, 208
Brussel, J., 70–71
Buckey, R., 194
Buckhout, R., 178–179
Buckley, J., 38
Buffington-Vollum, J. K., 237
Bugliosi, V., 132
Bull, R., 176
Burgess, A., 68, 86, 87, 205
Burkhead, M., 300
Byrne, D., 261
Byrne, Z. S., 265

C
Campbell, D., 7
Campos, P. F., 12
Canter, D., 94
Cantor, N., 5
Caplan, L., 112
Caplow, T., 293
Carlsmith, K. M., 310
Carpenter, B. N., 234
Carroll, J., 8, 10, 142
Casey, J. O., 74
Cavoukian, A., 63
Ceci, S., 194, 197, 208
Charrow, R., 147
Charrow, V., 147
Christie, R., 130
Chung, S., 224
Cimerman, A., 62
Cirincione, C., 118, 120
Clark, M., 132
Clark, S. E., 208
Clayton, L. D., 152
Clear, T. R., 269, 275, 278
Cochran, C. C., 243
Cochran, R. F., 228
Cocozza, J., 214
Cohen, D., 286
Cole, G. F., 269, 275, 278
Conlon, A., 88, 93
Conlon, G., 45
Cooper, J., 146, 258
Cormier, C., 215
Costanzo, M., 140, 150, 153, 250, 267,
    274n, 275, 298, 301, 302, 305, 307,
    310
Costanzo, S., 153, 302
Cotton, R., 170–172, 177, 178, 181
Cropanzano, R., 265
Cuniff, M., 296
Currie, E., 274, 292, 310
Cutler, B., 134, 137, 172, 173, 174, 175,
    181, 188

D
Daggett, D., 101
Dane, F., 143
Daniels, S., 30, 161

Darley, J. M., 29, 310
Darrow, C., 129
Dauner, J., 124
Daunt, T., 308
Davey, S. L., 208
Davis, D., 77, 78, 93
Davis, S. L., 208
de Beaumont, G., 280, 309
DeBurger, J., 69
Dekle, D., 183
DeLisa, A., 134
Dershowitz, A. M., 301
de Tocqueville, A., 280, 309
Devine, D., 143, 152, 186
Devine, P. G., 259
Dewey, J., 5
Dexter, H., 142, 188
Diamond, B., 109
Diamond, S. S., 30, 129, 154, 162, 167
Dickens, C., 280
Diekmann, K. A., 264
Dillehay, R. C., 137, 153, 167
Dimitrius, J., 131
Dix, D., 279
Dodge, K., 219
Dodge, M., 84
Donaldson, S. I., 16
Donzinger, S., 269
Douglas, J., 67, 68
Douglas, K., 218, 220, 221
Dovidio, J., 257, 258
Downey, C., 146
Drapkin, I., 278
Drummond, E., 109
Dunford, B. B., 152
Durham, M., 110–112
Dutton, D., 82
Dutton, M., 85, 86
Dysart, J., 187

E
Eaves, D., 104
Ebbesen, E., 272–273
Edens, J. F., 237
Einhorn, J., 227
Eisenberg, T., 30
Ekman, P., 55
Elaad, E., 59
Eldridge, W., 271
Elkins, T. J., 266
Ellis, E. M., 231
Ellis, H. C., 176
Ellis, L., 154, 162
Ellison, K., 245
Ellsworth, P. C., 18, 26, 135, 143, 154,
    157, 160, 168, 282, 301, 303, 305
Elwork, A., 102
Emery, R., 236, 237
Eron, L. D., 306
Ery, F., 62

Estroff, S. E., 220
Eule, J., 110
Everington, C., 104
Ewing, C. P., 81, 84, 115

F
Fagan, J., 307
Faigman, D. L., 24, 30, 86, 90, 91
Fay, B., 62
Fein, S., 260
Felton, R., 81
Finckenauer, J. O., 297
Finkel, N., 72, 113, 116–117, 144, 145,
    261, 266
Fischer, K., 251, 252
Fischoff, B., 222
Fishbein, M., 137
Fisher, R., 192
Fiske, S., 44, 177, 248, 250, 251, 253, 260
Fitzgerald, L., 243, 251, 252
Fletcher, B., 286
Flin, R., 176
Follette, W., 77, 78, 93
Follingstad, D. R., 85
Fonda, H., 151
Foote, W. E., 243
Foster, J., 112
Fox, J., 68
Franklin, B., 189
Frazier, P., 88, 90, 93, 243
Freud, S., 3, 202
Friedman, L. M., 279, 280, 281
Fulero, S., 113, 150, 184, 187
Furedy, J., 55
Fyfe, J. J., 38, 64

G
Gaertner, S., 257, 258
Galanter, M., 30
Gale, J., 238
Galluccio, L., 179
Gartner, R., 306
Garven, S., 197, 198
Gasper, C., 244
Gatowski, S., 20
Gauld, A., 189
Gavin, P., 297
Geiselman, E., 192
Gelles, R., 80
Getman, J. G., 26
Giedd, J. L., 252
Gilmore, G., 299
Gindes, M., 231
Glaser, T., 88, 93
Glick, P., 250, 251, 253, 260
Goffman, E., 289
Goldberg, S., 8, 10, 11
Golding, S., 25, 100, 105, 120
Goldkamp, K. H., 244
Goldman, R., 58

Goodman, G., 198, 199, 208
Goodman-Delahunty, J., 146, 243, 251,
    254, 266, 267
Graham, G., 308–309
Graham, S., 270
Greenberg, J., 265
Greene, E., 30, 84, 146
Greenwood, P., 274
Griffin, P., 224
Grisso, T., 7, 28, 102, 212, 238
Gross, S. R., 282
Grove, W. M., 217
Gudjonsson, G., 42, 46, 53, 64
Gutek, B., 242, 243, 244, 245, 248
Guthrie, C., 165

H
Hackney, A., 267
Hafemeister, T. L., 7
Hagen, M., 21
Haney, C., 9, 10, 27, 130, 286, 287, 288,
    301, 302
Hans, V. P., 25, 30, 138, 143, 153, 154,
    161, 168
Hansen, M., 78, 240
Hanson, R. K., 220
Hare, R. D., 219
Harr, R., 286
Harris, G., 215, 223
Harris, T., 246
Harsch, N., 178
Hart, S. D., 22, 219, 238
Harvey, M., 89
Hastie, R., 149, 150, 152, 156
Haycosck, J., 101
Heilbrun, K., 212, 224
Henderson, M., 219
Herman, J. L., 93
Herrmann, M. S., 238
Hetherington, E. M., 226, 228, 230
Heuer, L., 30, 148
Hewstone, M., 219
Hickey, E. W., 68
Hill, P., 45
Hinckley, J., 112–114
Hofstede, G., 9
Hoganbruen, K., 226
Hoge, S. K., 105
Hollett, N. L., 238
Holmes, D., 202, 203
Holmes, O. W., 4–5, 11, 16
Holmes, R., 69
Holmstrom, L., 86, 87
Holst, V., 180
Holtzworth-Munroe, A., 93
Homant, R. J., 72, 73
Honts, C. R., 50, 53, 55
Hook, L., 151
Hopkins, A., 248
Horowitz, I., 30, 159

Horowitz, S., 50, 55
Hosch, H., 30
House-Higgins, C., 80
Hovland, A., 297
Hubler, S., 177
Huesmann, L. R., 306
Hunt, J. S., 208
Hunt, R. R., 176
Huntley, J. E., 140, 150, 249, 250, 267
Hurt, L. E., 267
Husband, T. H., 205
Huss, M. T., 143
Hyman, I., 204, 205
Hymes, R. W., 139

I
Iacono, W. G., 50, 52
Imwindelried, E., 199
Inbau, F., 38, 40, 61
Ingram, P., 200–202
Insabella, G. M., 226, 228, 230
Irvine, A. A., 44
Irving, B., 45
Isorena, T., 296

J
Jackson, J. L., 94
Jackson, L. A., 265
Jackson, T., 75–76
Jacobs, J. B., 286
Jacobson, L. F., 184
Jacoby, J., 214
James, W., 3, 5
Janofsky, M., 77
Jayne, B., 38
Jewell, R., 69–70
Jobes, D. A., 74
Johnson, C., 130
Johnson, M. K., 179
Johnson, R., 291

K
Kadela, K., 267
Kalven, H., 7, 150, 151, 157, 166
Kaplan, D. L., 258
Kaplan, M. F., 130, 151, 153
Kasian, M., 83
Kassin, S., 30, 33, 34, 39, 42, 43, 64, 137,
    158, 188, 260
Kaye, D. H., 24
Kazyaka, A. M., 304
Kebbell, M. R., 191
Keeney, M., 224
Kelly, J. B., 226, 231
Kennedy, D. B., 72, 73
Kerr, N., 139, 142, 151, 152
Ketcham, K., 202, 203, 208
Kevorkian, J., 159
Kidd, R., 135
King, N. J., 158

Kircher, J., 50, 53, 55
Kitzmann, K. M., 236
Knox, A., 176
Kolata, G., 27
Konecni, V., 272–273
Konopaske, R., 266
Koss, M., 80, 89, 93
Koutstaal, W., 179
Kovera, M. B., viii, 19, 142, 146
Kramer, G., 142
Krauss, D. A., 223, 238
Kravitz, D. A., 137
Kremnitzer, M., 48, 64
Kressel, D. F., 129, 131, 134, 168
Kressel, N. J., 129, 131, 134, 168
Krieger, L. H., 259
Krone, R., 308
Kropp, P. R., 238
Kugler, K. E., 101

L
LaBine, G., 222
LaBine, S. J., 222
LaFond, J. Q., 101
LaFortune, K. A., 234
Lamb, R. H., 211
Lancaster, A., 242
Landsman, S., 30, 165
Langan, P., 296
Larson, J. A., 50, 60
Lassiter, G. D., 44
Latham, G. P., 265
Laurence, J., 305
Law, M., 220
Lecci, L., 138
Lehman, D. R., 205, 208
Lelos, D., 103
Lempert, R. D., 30, 157
Lempert, R. O., 166
Leo, R., 34, 35, 36, 39, 41, 62, 64
Lerner, M. J., 136, 262
Leupnitz, D. A., 230
Levi, E., 150
Levin, J., 68
Lidz, C., 216
Liebeck, S., 160
Lieberman, J. D., 144, 168
Liebman, J. S., 307
Lindsay, D. S., 207
Lindsay, R. C. L., 187
Link, B. G., 220
Lipinski, R., 135
Lipsitt, P. D., 103
Liss, M., 230, 231, 237
Litwack, T. R., 215n
Llewellyn, K., 5, 12
Locke, E. A., 265
Lofquist, W. S., 138
Loftus, E., 172, 179, 202, 203, 208
Lowe, R. H., 264

Luginbuhl, J., 300
Lykken, D., 51, 52, 58, 59, 60, 63, 64
Lynch, M., 302
Lyon, D. R., 238

M
MacCoun, R., 30, 143, 152, 160, 161
MacDowell, D., 297
MacKenzie, D. L., 297
MacKenzie, M. M., 277
MacKinnon, C., 241
Major, B., 265
Malmquist, C. P., 203
Malpass, R., 177, 184, 186, 197
Mancini, T., 75–76
Mandela, N., 289
Manzo, J. F., 151
Marston, W. M., 47–48
Marti, M. W., 156
Martin, J., 30, 161, 253, 258
Martinson, R., 282
Matheson, K., 94
Matsumoto, D., 8
Matthews, S. G., 236
Mauer, M., 284, 285, 293
Mauro, R., viii, 135, 143, 157, 160, 303, 305
McAuliff, B., viii, 19
McConville, M., 46, 166
McGarry, A. L., 101, 103
McGrath, M., 73
McKelvey, B., 280, 281
McKenzie, I. K., 45
McKinley-Pace, M., 230, 231, 237
McMartin, P., 194, 197, 198
McNall, K., 39
McNaughton, D., 109–110
Meehl, P. E., 217
Meertens, R. W., 257
Meissner, C. A., 64, 177
Melton, G., 7, 23, 24, 26, 101, 114, 233
Mendoza-Dinton, R., 139
Menninger, K., 7
Mesmer, F. A., 189
Metesky, G., 70–71
Meza, E., 176–177
Michaels, K., 194, 195, 196
Milk, H., 114
Miller, C., 153
Miller, G., 7
Miller, N., 258
Mischel, W., 139
Moise-Titus, J., 306
Monahan, J., 23, 83, 214, 215, 216, 221, 238
Moon, D., 286
Moran, G., 134, 137
Morash, M., 286
Morris, N., 289, 291, 292
Moscone, G., 114

Moston, S., 33
Mott, N. L., 168
Mowery, R. L., 238
Muhl, C. J., 253
Mulvey, E., 216, 238
Mundy, L., 82
Munsterberg, H., 3–4
Murphy, B., 154, 162
Myers, B., 138
Myers, J., 199
Myers, L. B., 206

N
Narby, D. J., 137, 175
Neisser, U., 178
Nestor, P. G., 101
Neumann, K., 33
Newman, L. F., 139, 219
Nezu, C. M., 224
Nicholson, R. A., 101, 115, 234
Niedermeier, K. E., 151
Nietzel, M. T., 167
Nisbett, R. E., 217, 286
Norris, F. H., 92
Novaco, R. W., 219

O
O'Brien, D., 106
O'Connor, M., 244, 245
O'Connor, S. D., 246
Ofshe, R., 39, 41, 42, 62, 201
Ogloff, J. R. P., 22, 29, 113, 142, 212, 220
Olczak, P. V., 130
Olsen-Fulero, L., 150
Olshaker, M., 67
Olson, A. M., 243
Orcutt, H. K., 208
Orne, M., 106
Otto, A. L., 142

P
Palmer, J. C., 179
Parisi, N., 290
Partridge, A., 271
Patry, M., viii
Pascal, B., 260
Paternoster, R., 304
Patrick, C. J., 50, 52
Paul, B. Y., 258
Pearson, J., 236
Peckham, R., 165
Peebles, S., 83
Peel, R., 109
Pennington, N., 149, 150, 152–153, 156
Penrod, S., viii, 30, 130, 135, 142, 148, 152, 156, 172, 173, 174, 181, 184, 188
Perlin, M. L., 113, 118, 119, 120, 211
Peters, M., 296
Petersilia, J., 293, 294

Peterson, C., 196
Peterson, I., 27
Peterson, J., 294, 310
Peterson, R. D., 306
Petrila, J., 101, 233, 237
Pettigrew, T., 253, 257, 258
Pezdek, K., 180
Phares, E. J., 136
Phillips, J. S., 266
Pickel, K., viii, 144
Pinizzotto, A., 72
Plato, 277
Platt, A., 109
Poddar, P., 210
Podlesny, J. A., 60
Podolski, C. L., 306
Poole, B., 171–172, 178
Porter, S., 205, 208
Powell, L., 28
Poythress, N., 101, 211, 233
Price, J. M., 219
Price, M., 101
Prizmich, L., 199
Pruett, M. K., 226
Pryce, J., 152
Pryor, J., 250, 252, 253
Pryor, R., 185
Pulaski, C., 304
Putnam, C. E., 308

Q
Quinsey, V., 215

R
Rachlinski, J., 165
Radelet, M., 308
Rakos, R., 165
Raskin, D., 50, 53, 55
Rauch, S., 267
Read, D., 181, 207
Reagan, R., 112
Redlich, A., 199
Rehnquist, W., 19, 301
Reid, J., 38
Reifman, A., 168
Reilly, P., 61–62
Reiman, J., 294
Repucci, N. D., 25
Ressler, R., 68
Reyna, C., 270
Reyst, H., 242
Rice, M., 167, 215, 223
Richardson, C., 45
Richardson, J., 30
Rideau, W., 291
Riedel, M., 303
Riggins, D., 102–103
Risinger, D. M., 29
Robbins, P. C., 238
Roberts, C. F., 113

Robinson, P. H., 310
Roche, T., 108
Roesch, R., viii, 22, 25, 100, 101, 104, 105, 113, 120
Rogers, R., 115
Roper, R., 155
Rose, M., 154, 162
Rosenthal, R., 29, 184
Ross, L., 217, 264
Roth, L. H., 238
Rothenberg, P. S., 263
Rothman, D. J., 278, 279, 282
Rotman, E., 276
Rowland, J., 87
Ruback, R. B., 272, 273, 310
Rucker, L., 286
Rudolph, E., 70
Rudy, L., 208
Rupp, D. E., 265
Russell, B., viii

S
Sack, K., 70
Saks, M. J., 21, 22, 23, 24, 28, 29, 135, 145, 155
Sales, B., 93, 120, 223, 237, 238
Salfati, C. G., 94
Sampson, E., 261
Samuels, S. M., 205, 264
Sanders, J., 24, 30
Sandys, M., 153, 300
Savoie, R., 57
Sawyer, T., 41–42, 45
Scanlan, C. R., 44
Schacter, D. L., 179, 206
Schlegel, J., 5
Schlosser, E., 269, 286
Schmitt, K. L., 183
Schooler, J. W., 206
Schuller, R., 81, 84
Schulman, J., 130, 131
Schwartz-Kenney, B. M., 208
Scriven, M., 16
Sellin, T., 305
Serge, V., 289
Seying, R., 152
Shaver, L. D., 286
Shaver, P., 130
Shaw, J. S., 197
Sherman, L., 294–295
Shestowshy, D., 168, 267
Shoda, Y., 139
Showalter, C. R., 114
Shuman, D. W., 120
Siegel, A., 102
Siegel, L. J., 284–285, 291, 295
Silberman, M., 287, 290
Silver, E., 118, 120, 238
Simmons, R. J., 255
Simon, J., 293

Simon, R., 116, 150
Simpson, L., 168
Simpson, O. J., 58, 124, 131–132, 139
Skeem, J. L., 120
Skolnick, J. H., 38, 61, 64
Slade, M., 242
Slaw, R. D., 44
Slobogin, C., 46, 101, 114, 120, 233
Small, M., 184
Smith, H., 240
Smith, S., 32, 44–45
Smith, V. L., 148, 158
Softley, P., 33
Sommers, S. R., 168
Sontag, L., 302
Sourryal, C., 297
Spanos, N. P., 83, 94
Spence, J., 129
Spierenberg, P., 278
Sporer, S. L., 181
Springer, J., 96, 107
St. Amand, M. D., 310
Stack, M. K., 97, 301
Stahl, P. M., 235
Stasser, G., 152
Steadman, H. J., 118, 120, 214, 215, 216, 238
Steblay, N., 178, 187, 190
Steiner, B. D., 300
Stephan, W., 259
Stephenson, G., 33
Stern, V., 284, 292
Stevens, L. E., 248
Storvoll, E., 297
Strauss, M., 80
Strier, F., 133, 168
Strodtbeck, F., 135, 150, 151
Stueve, A., 220
Sukel, H., 34, 146
Sunby, S. E., 146
Swan, S., 251, 252

T
Tanford, J. A., 28, 147, 148
Tarasoff, T., 210
Taylor, J., 90
Taylor, S. E., 44, 177
Terpstra, D., 248, 250
Terrance, C. A., viii, 83, 94
Thoennes, N., 236
Thomas, C., 56
Thomas, S., 208
Thompson, D., 179
Thompson, J., 170–172, 177, 178, 181
Thompson, W. C., 29, 300
Thornberry, T., 214
Tobey, A. E., 208
Toch, H., 289, 290
Tonry, M., 271
Toobin, J., 131, 132

Tremper, C., 28
Triandis, H., 8
Tripp, R. T., 260, 261
Tulloch, W. F., 158
Tunnicliff, J. L., 208
Turner, S., 294

U
Ulmer, J., 57

V
Valentine, P. W., 291
Vanman, E. J., 258
Vidmar, N., 25, 30, 142, 154, 162, 167
Vinson, D., 131
Visher, G., 135

W
Wagstaff, G. F., 191
Waldo, C. R., 243
Walker, L., 80–81, 83
Walker, S., 280, 281
Wallerstein, J. S., 230
Warren, E., 6, 283
Warren, L., 267
Wasserman, A. L., 224
Watters, E., 201
Watts, B. A., 244
Weathers, J. E., 139
Webster, C., 104, 217, 218, 221
Wegner, D. M., 144
Weinberger, L. E., 211
Weiner, B., 270, 302
Weiner, N. A., 304
Weissman, N. H., 233
Wells, G., 27, 172, 173, 174, 182, 183, 184, 185, 186, 208
Werner, E., 232
West, V., 307
Whalen, N., 250, 252
White, D., 114
White, L., viii
Wickersham, G., 35
Wiener, R. L., 244, 267
Wigmore, J. H., 3
Wikberg, R., 291
Williams, K. B., 252
Williams, L., 203–204
Williamson, T. M., 33
Winick, B. J., 98, 102
Wissler, R. L., 145
Wistrich, A., 165
Wittig, M. A., 264
Wolfgang, M., 303
Woo, S., 176–177
Wood, J. M., 197
Woodworth, G., 304
Word, C., 258
Wright, E. F., 183
Wright, M., 74

Wrightsman, L. S., 30, 87, 137, 143
Wroblewski, J., 272, 273, 310
Wundt, W., 3
Wyer, M. M., 236

Y
Yates, A., 96–97, 107, 119, 301
Yates, R., 96
Yuille, J. C., 205, 208

Z
Zamble, E., 310
Zanna, M. P., 258
Zapf, P., 101, 104, 105, 120
Zeisel, H., 7, 129, 150, 151, 157, 166
Zender, J. P., 158
Zimbardo, P., 286, 287, 288
Zimmer, C., 220
Zuckerman, D., 304

Subject Index

A

ABA. *See* American Bar Association (ABA)
Abuse in interrogations, 35
Abusers
  murder of, defenses for woman for, 82–83
  traits of, 82
Ackerman-Schoendorf Scales for Parent Evaluation of Custody (ASPECT), 234
Actuarial predictions of violence, 214–215, 222–223
ADA. *See* Americans with Disabilities Act (ADA)
ADEA. *See* Age Discrimination in Employment Act (ADEA)
Adjudication Center, 24
Adjudicative competence, 104
Adversarial system, 12, 97, 126, 134
Adverse impact, 254–255
Advisors, psychologists as, 14–15
Advocacy versus objectivity, 12–13
Age Discrimination in Employment Act (ADEA), 254
Aggravated murder, 298
Aggravating factors, 122, 299, 302
Alcatraz, 275–276
Allen charge, 157
Alternative dispute resolution in child custody cases, 235–237
Alternative sentencing scheme, 273
American Bar Association (ABA), 5
  Code of Professional Responsibility, 12
American Bar Association Journal, 26
American Law Institute (ALI) insanity standard, 111–112, 116
American Psychological Association (APA), 7
  briefs, use of, 15
  Committee on Legal Issues (COLI), 24
  lobbying efforts of, 27
American Psychological Society (APS)
  briefs, use of, 15
  lobbying efforts of, 27
American Psychology-Law Society (AP-LS), 7–8, 184
Americans with Disabilities Act (ADA), 254
The American Jury (Zeisel), 7
Amicus curiae briefs, 24–26, 28
Amnesia, 106
Anderson v. General Dynamics, 256
Antidiscrimination laws, 259

APA. *See* American Psychological Association (APA)
AP-LS. *See* American Psychological-Law Society (APLS)
Apodaca, Cooper, & Madden v. Oregon, 156
Appeal, 147, 299
Approximate truth versus approximate justice, 9–11
APS. *See* American Psychological Society (APS)
Arizona project, 154, 162–164
Arizona v. Fulminante, 37
ASPECT. *See* Ackerman-Schoendorf Scales for Parent Evaluation of Custody (ASPECT)
Atkins v. Virginia, 299–300
Attorneys
  advocacy of, 12–13
  cross-disciplinary training, 22–24
  social science training, 22–24
Authoritarianism, 136–137

B

Ballew v. Georgia, 28, 155
Base rate of violence, 217
Batson v. Kentucky, 127
Battered Woman Syndrome (BWS), 79–86
  abuser, defenses for woman for murder of, 82–83
  abusers, traits of, 82
  criticisms of, 85–86
  hypervigilance, 82
  insanity defense, 83
  legal system, and, 82–85
  scientific validity of, 85–86
  self-defense, 82–83
  testimony, 83–84
  three-phase cycle, 80
  traits shared by battered women, 80–81
Baxstrom v. Herold, 214
Behavioral Sciences and the Law, 8
Belief in a just world, 136
Beyond a reasonable doubt, 112, 140–141
Biases
  expert witnesses, of, 22
  eyewitnesses at trial, exposing, 174–175
  hindsight, 222
  judges, of, 165

Biases (cont.)
  juries, of, 165
  Juror Bias Scale, 137–138
  own-race bias, 177
The Black Codes, 303
Blind lineup administrators, 184
Boot camp, 296
Bottoms v. Bottoms, 229
BPS. See Bricklin Perceptual Scales (BPS)
Brandeis Brief, 4
Bricklin Perceptual Scales (BPS), 234
Briefs, 15
  amicus briefs, 24–26, 28
Brown v. Board of Education, 6–7, 259
Brutalization effect, 306
Burch v. Louisiana, 156
Burden of proof, 112, 122, 140–141
Burlington Industries v. Ellerth, 242, 247
BWS. See Battered Woman Syndrome
  (BWS)

C
CADCOMP. See Computer Assisted Determi-
  nation of Competence to Proceed
  (CADCOMP)
Capital murder trial, 274. See also Death
  penalty, penalty phase
  bifurcation of, 299, 300
  research on, 300–301
Capital punishment. See Death penalty
CAST-MR. See Competence Assessment for
  Standing Trial for Defendants with Mental Retardation (CAST-MR)
CCTV. See Closed-circuit television (CCTV)
Challenges
  for cause, 125, 165
  peremptory. See Peremptory challenges
Change of venue motion, 142
Child custody arrangement
  Ackerman-Schoendorf Scales for Parent
    Evaluation of Custody (ASPECT), 234
  "best interests of child" standard,
    227–228, 230
  Bricklin Perceptual Scales (BPS), use of,
    234
  considerations in, 226–229
  continuity of care, 228
  joint custody, 225–226
  legal custody, 225
  mediation, 235–237
  parental competence as factor in,
    225–226
  Perception of Relationships Test (PORT),
    234
  physical custody, 225
  preferred custody arrangements, 228
  psychologist's contribution to decisions on,
    232–235
  sibling relationships, consideration of, 231
  sole custody, 226

standards, evolution of, 226–229
"tender years" doctrine, 227
Uniform Marriage and Divorce Act criteria
  for determining, 232
well-being of child, 228
Children
  at trial, jurors' reaction to testimony,
    198–200
  custody arrangements. See Child custody
    arrangement
  divorce, responses to, 229–232
  eyewitnesses, as, 183
  relationships to family after divorce, impor-
    tance of continuity of children's, 231
  resilient, 232
  sexual abuse, memories of. See Child sex-
    ual abuse, memories of
  testimony at trial, 198–200
Child sexual abuse, memories of, 193–207
  day care center cases, 194–198
  recovered memories. See Recovered mem-
    ories of sexual abuse
  testimony by children at trial, 198–200
  young children, 194–200
Civil Rights Act of 1964, 240
Civil Rights Act of 1991, 256
Civil trial, 138, 143
Civil Trial Bias Scale, 138
Class-action lawsuit, 276, 283
Clear and convincing evidence, 146
Clinical predictions of violence, 214–215,
  222–223
Clinical psychologists evaluations of compe-
  tence to stand trial (CST), 103–106
Clinical psychology, 2
Closed-circuit television (CCTV), 199–200
Closing arguments, 141
"Club Feds" prisons, 275
Coercion
  confessions, in. See Confessions
  polygraph as device of, 60–62
Coercive questioning, 196–198
Cognitive interview, 192–193
Cognitive psychology, 2
Cognitive test of insanity, 110
Cognizable groups, 126–127
COLI. See Committee on Legal Issues (COLI),
  APA
Coker v. Georgia, 303
Collins v. Brierly, 37
Colorado v. Connelly, 33
Committee on Legal Issues (COLI), APA
  amicus briefs, filing of, 24
Community service, 295
Compensatory damages, 138
  McDonald's coffee burn case, 160–161
Competence
  decisional competence, 104–105
  foundational competence, 104
  legal. See Legal competence

Competence Assessment for Standing Trial for Defendants with Mental Retardation (CAST-MR), 104
Competence to stand trial (CST), 98–99
  Competence Assessment for Standing Trial for Defendants with Mental Retardation (CAST-MR), 104
  Competency Assessment Instrument, 103–104
  Competency Screening Test, 103
  Computer Assisted Determination of Competence to Proceed (CADCOMP), 104
  evaluations, 100–101, 102
  Fitness Interview Test-Revised (FIT-R), 104
  MacArthur Structured Assessment of the Competencies of Criminal Defendants (MacSAC-CD), 105
  MacArthur Structured Assessment Tool-Criminal Adjudication (MacCAT-CA), 105
  pretrial hearing, 100
  restoring competence, 101–102
  tests and techniques for evaluating, 103–106
Competency Assessment Instrument, 103–104
Competency Screening Test, 103
Complex evidence, 145–146
Computer Assisted Determination of Competence to Proceed (CADCOMP), 104
Conditional prediction, 216
Conduit-Educator, expert witness as, 21, 22
Confessions
  coerced, 33–34, 37, 43
  eliciting, 32–34
  false. See False confessions
  power of, 32–34
  psychological techniques used to elicit, 37–41
  statistics on, 33
  trial, presentation of videotaped confession at, 43–44
  videotaped, 43–44
Confidence ratings, 186
Consensual relationship agreement, 240
Consultants
  jury, 131–132
  trial. See Trial consultants
Controllability, 270
Control Question Test (CQT), 50–51
Convict code in prisons, 290
Cooper v. Oklahoma, 98
Cooper v. Pate, 283
Coping strategies for sexual harassment, 251–252
CQT. See Control Question Test (CQT)
Crime scenes
  analysis of, 67
  categories of, 72
  recall of, eyewitness, 179–180

The Crime of Punishment (Menninger), 7
Criminal investigative analysis, 66
Criminal Justice and Behavior, 8
Criminal profiling. See Profiling
Cross-disciplinary training, 22–24
Cross-examination, 141, 175
Cross-racial identifications, 176–177
Cruel and unusual punishment, 99, 284, 298
CST. See Competence to stand trial (CST)
Culombe v. Connecticut, 35, 36
Cultural differences, 8
  study of, 9
Cultures of psychology and law
  bridging, 13–14
  clash of, 8–13
  defined, 8

D
Damages
  compensatory, 138, 160–161
  punitive, 138, 161
Dangerousness towards others, 212
Data versus rulings, 11–12
Daubert v. Merrell Dow Pharmaceuticals, Inc., 19, 23, 56, 57
Davis v. North Carolina, 35, 37
Day care center sexual abuse cases, 194–198
Death penalty, 278, 282, 292, 295, 297–309
  brutalization effect, 305–307
  deterrent to murder, as, 305–307
  errors and mistakes in cases, 307–309
  forms of execution, 298
  limits on, 299–300
  mental illness, for persons with, 299–300
  racial disparities, 303–305
  rape, for, 303–304
  states with, 298
  statistics on, 298
  Supreme Court decisions, 298–303
Death qualification, 300–301
Decisional competence, 104–105
Decision making, 2, 150–159
  juror models, 148–150
  jury deliberations, 150–159
  penalty phase, juries decision making during, 301–303
Defendant characteristics, effect on jurors of, 143
Defendant-juror similarity, 138–140
Deinstitutionalization movement, 211
Deliberations, jury, 150–159
Determinate sentencing, 271
Deterrence, 276
Developmental psychology, 2
Diagnostic and Statistical Manual of Mental Disorders, 4th edition (DSM-IV), 92–93
Diminished capacity defense, 113–114

Direct-examination, 141
Discrimination, workplace, 253–260
    adverse impact, 254–255
    antidiscrimination laws, 259
    categories of, 254
    damages for, 256
    discriminatory adverse action, 253–254
    disparate treatment, 254
    hostile environment, 254
    intent, 254
    protected categories, 254
    racial, 257–260
    reasonable accommodation, failure to pro-
        vide, 255–256
    religious, 256
Discriminatory adverse action, 253–254
Disorganized murderers, 68–69
Disparate treatment, 254–255
Dissemination of research findings, 26–27
Dissonance theory, 182
Distributive justice, 261–263
Divorce
    child custody arrangement. See Child cus-
        tody arrangement
    children's responses to, 229–232
    relationships to family, importance of conti-
        nuity of children's, 231
Dixon v. Attorney General of the Common-
    wealth of Pennsylvania, 214
DNA evidence, 132, 145, 308
Doctrine of stare decisis, 12
Double doctorate programs, 23
Drugs in prisons, 291–292
DSM-IV. See Diagnostic and Statistical Man-
    ual of Mental Disorders, 4th edition
    (DSM-IV)
Durham standard, 111, 116
Durham v. United States, 111
Dusky v. United States, 98, 100
Duty to protect laws, 210–211
Dynamic markers used in prediction of vio-
    lence, 219–220
Dynamite charge, 157

E
EEOC. See Equal Employment Opportunity
    Commission (EEOC)
EEOC v. Murphy Motor Freight Lines, Inc.,
    241
The Effect of Segregation and the Conse-
    quences of Desegregation: A Social
    Science Statement, 6
Electronic monitoring, 296
Ellison v. Brady, 245
Empiricism, 11
Employment at will, 253
Encoding, process of, 175–176
Equal Employment Opportunity Commission
    (EEOC), 241

Equal protection under the law, 6, 298
Estelle v. Smith, 102
Evaluation research, 15–17
Evaluators, psychologists as, 15–17
Evidence
    clear and convincing, 146
    complex, 145–146
    DNA. See DNA evidence
    exculpatory, 308
    Federal Rules of Evidence, 19
    impeachment, 145
    inadmissible, 143–145
    polygraphs, jurors' response to evidence
        from, 62–63
    probative, 77–78
    propensity. See Future violence, assess-
        ment of risk of
    psychological autopsy, used in, 74
    Rape Trauma Syndrome (RTS), research
        evidence on, 88
    risk assessment, jurors' reaction to,
        222–223
    social science evidence, effect of on judges
        of, 28
    social scientific, 4, 6
Evidence-driven style of deliberations,
    152–153
Expert testimony
    clinical and actuarial predictions of vio-
        lence, on, 223
    eyewitness identification, 188–189
    witnesses. See Expert witnesses
Expert witnesses
    biases of, 22
    considerations for and with, 20
    hired guns, as. See Hired gun, expert wit-
        ness as
    Rape Trauma Syndrome (RTS), testimony
        on, 89–90, 91
    roles assumed by, 21
    testimony, 18–22, 145–146
Eyewitnesses
    accuracy, use of research findings in
        improving, 183–189
    bias at trial, exposing, 174–175
    confidence ratings, 186
    improving accuracy of, 183–189
    instructions to, 185
    memories of. See Eyewitness memories
    testimony of, 172–174
Eyewitness memories, 175–183
    children, 183
    child sexual abuse. See Child sexual abuse,
        memories of
    cognitive interview as technique for refresh-
        ing, 192–193
    crime scenes, 179–180
    cross-racial identifications, 176–177
    encoding, process of, 175–176

hypnosis as technique for refreshing, 189–192
leading or suggestive comments, 179–180
preexisting expectations, 180–181
processes, 175–176
refreshing, techniques for, 189–193
retrieval, process of, 176
retrieval inhibition, 180
storage, process of, 176
unconscious transference, 178
weapons focus effect, 178
witness confidence, 181–183, 186
Eyewitness testimony
evaluating accuracy of, factors in, 173–174
impact of, 172–173

F

Fairness in the workplace, 260–266
distributive justice, 261–263
interpersonal justice, 261
perceptions of, research on, 264–266
procedural justice, 261
rewards, models for allocating, 261–264
salary discrepancies, male and female, 263–264
False confessions, 41–42, 45–46, 61
False memories, research on implanting, 204–207
False negatives, 213
False positives, 50, 213
Faragher v. Boca Raton, Fla., 242, 245, 247
Faretta v. California, 99
Farmer v. Brennan, 284
Federal Bureau of Investigation (FBI)
profiling, development of techniques for, 66–67
Profiling and Behavioral Assessment Unit, 66
Federal Judicial Center, 23
Federal Rules of Evidence, 19
Federal Violence Against Women Act, 82
Felony, 275
Finders of fact. *See* Judges; Juries
Fines, 295
Fitness Interview Test-Revised (FIT-R), 104
Ford v. Wainwright, 99
Foreperson of jury, 135, 151–152
Forfeiture of goods, 295
Formative evaluations, 16
Foundational competence, 104
Furman v. Georgia, 298–299
Future violence, assessment of risk of, 210–224
actuarial predictions, 214–215
base rate of violence, 217
clinical predictions, 214–215
dangerousness towards others, 211
difficulty in, studies illustrating, 214–215
duty to protect laws, 210–211
evidence, jurors' reactions to, 222–223
Historical, Clinical, and Risk Management-20 (HCR-20), 221
historical markers, 218–219
markers used in, 218–221
overprediction of violence, 214
predictions, 214–217
risk factors, list of, 218–221
risk management markers, 220–221
treatment to reduce risk, 223–224
two-by-two contingency table, 213
Violence Prediction Scheme (VPS), 221
Violence Risk Appraisal Guide (VRAG), 221

G

Gangs, prison, 291
Gatekeepers, judges as, 19–20
GBMI. *See* Guilty but mentally ill (GBMI)
Gender differences among jurors, 134
GKT. *See* Guilty Knowledge Test (GKT)
Godinez v. Moran, 100
Good cop/bad cop approach, 37–38
"Good from evil" test, 109
Gregg v. Georgia, 299
Griggs v. Duke Power Co., 255
Guided discretion statutes, 299
Guildford Four case, 45
Guilty but mentally ill (GBMI), 113–114
Guilty Knowledge Test (GKT), 58–60
Guilty mind, 108

H

Halfway houses, 297
Harassment
hostile environment, 241
quid pro quo, 241
sexual. *See* Sexual harassment
Harrisburg Seven case, 130–131
Harris v. Forklift Systems, Inc., 245, 246
Harvard Laboratory of Community Psychology, 103–104
HCR-20. *See* Historical, Clinical, and Risk Management-20 (HCR-20)
Hearsay, 199
Hedonistic serial killers, 69
Hillside Strangler case, 106
Hindsight bias, 222
Hired gun, expert witness as, 21, 118, 146
Historical, Clinical, and Risk Management-20 (HCR-20), 221
Historical markers used in prediction of violence, 218–219
Hostile environment harassment, 241
Hostile workplace environment, 254
House arrest, 296
Hung juries, 156, 157

Hypervigilance, 82
Hypnosis, 189–192

I
Identification
    correct, rate of, 173
    cross-racial, 176–177
    lineups. *See* Lineups
    mistaken, 172–173, 184–187
    videotaping, 188
    witness, expert testimony on, 188–189
Impeachment evidence, 145
Imprisonment, 274–277
    goals of, 276–277
Inadmissible evidence, 143–145
Incapacitation, 276, 293
Incompetence
    evaluations of, 100–101, 102
    faking, 106
    hospitalization for, 101–102
    legal competence. *See* Legal competence
Informational influence, 153
Inmates, prison. *See* Prisons
Insanity
    alternative test of, 117
    cognitive test of, 110
    competency concerns. *See* Legal compe-
        tence
    faking, 106
    jurors interpretation of, 115–117
    legal definition of, 107
    malingering, 106
    McNaughton Rule, 110
    Mental Screening Evaluation (MSE),
        114–115
    not guilty by reason of insanity (NGRI). *See*
        Not guilty by reason of insanity (NGRI)
    Rogers Criminal Responsibility Assessment
        Scales (R-CRAS), 115
    tests and techniques for assessing,
        114–115
Insanity defense, 107–114
    Battered Woman Syndrome (BWS), 83
    debate over, 118
    Durham case, 110–112
    evolution of, 108–109
    Hinckley case, 112–114
    McNaughton case, 109–110
    myths about, 118–119
Insanity Defense Reform Act, 113
Interpersonal justice, 261
Interrogations
    confessions from. *See* Confessions
    covert abuse used in, 35
    good cop/bad cop approach, 37–38
    lying by police during, 44–46
    maximization strategy, 39–40
    minimization strategy, 39–40
    "nine steps of interrogation," 38–39
    physical abuse used in, 35

polygraphs used in, 60–62
psychological techniques used in, 37–41
techniques used in, 34–41
Irresistible impulse, 110

J
Jackson v. Indiana, 101
Jackson v. State of Florida, 75
Jails, 274–275. *See also* Prisons
Johnson v. Louisiana, 156, 157
Johnson v. Zerbst, 99
Judges
    agreement with juries, 166–167
    biases of, 165
    characteristics of, 29
    gatekeepers, as, 19–20
    instructions as source of juror confusion,
        146–148, 302–303
    juries compared to, 164–167
    juror confusion, instructions as source of,
        146–148
    social science evidence, effect of, 28
Juries. *See also* Jurors
    advantages of, 167
    agreement of judges with, 166–167
    Allen charge, 157
    Arizona project, 154, 162–164
    assembling, process of, 123–127
    biases of, 165
    criticisms of, 160
    deliberations, 150–159, 175
    discussion of case during trial, 122,
        162–164
    diversity in, 127
    dynamics of, 150–159
    dynamite charge, 157
    foreperson, 135, 151–152
    hung, 156, 157
    impartiality of, 123–127
    instructions to, 146–148, 302–303
    judges compared to, 164–167
    majority, power of, 151, 153
    majority-rule, 156, 157
    mock, 132–133
    morality-based decisions, 153
    nullification by, 158–159
    open conflict stage of deliberation process,
        153
    orientation stage of deliberation process,
        152–153
    panel, 124–125
    penalty phase, decision making during,
        301–303
    reconciliation stage of deliberation process,
        153
    reform ideas, 160–164
    scientific jury selection, 129–132
    selection of, strategies for, 128–134
    shadow, 133
    shotgun instruction, 157

size of, 154–156
stacking, 126, 132
stages in deliberation process, 152–154
unanimous verdicts, requirement for,
    156–158
venire, 124–125
Juror Bias Scale, 137–138
Jurors. *See also* Juries
    attitudes about legal system, 137–138
    biases of, 165
    capital cases, 299
    challenges, 125–126
    challenges for cause, 125
    characteristics and attitudes as predictors of
        verdicts, 134–140
    children at trial, reaction to testimony by,
        198–200
    cognizable groups, 126–127
    complex evidence, effect of, 145–146
    confusion, judge's instructions as source of,
        146–148
    death qualified, 300–301
    death sentence cases, 299
    decision making, models, 148–150
    defendant characteristics, effect of, 143
    defendant-juror similarity, 138–140
    eligible, primary sources for identifying,
        123–124
    excusals for, 124–125
    exemptions, 124–125
    expectations on, legal system, 141
    gender differences, 134
    general personality tendencies, 135–137
    inadmissible evidence, effect of, 143–145
    information processors, as biased,
        141–150
    insanity, interpretation of, 115–117
    judge's instructions as source of confusion,
        146–148
    key jurors, 151
    models of decision making, 148–150
    panel, 124–125
    peremptory challenges. *See* Peremptory
        challenges
    polygraph evidence, response to, 62–63
    pretrial publicity, effect of, 142
    risk assessment evidence, reaction to,
        222–223
    scientific jury selection, 129–132
    selection of, strategies for, 128–134
    sources for identifying eligible, 123–124
    stereotypes used in selection of, 129
    strong jurors, 151
    unbridled discretion of, 299
    undue hardship or extreme inconvenience,
        excusal for, 124–125
    venire, 124–125
    verdicts, characteristics and attitudes as pre-
        dictors of, 134–140
    verdicts, items affecting, 141–150

    voir dire, 125–126
    voter lists, 124
Jury pool, 124
Jury selection, 123–127
    Harrisburg Seven case, 130–131
    O.J. Simpson case, 131–132
    scientific, 129–132
Jury Selection and Service Act, 123
Juveniles, competence evaluations of, 102

K
Key jurors, 151
Kumho Tire Co. Ltd. v. Carmichael, 25

L
Law and Human Behavior, 8
Law and Society Review, 8
Leading or suggestive comments, 179–180
Legal competence
    competence to stand trial (CST). *See* Com-
        petence to stand trial (CST)
    concerns regarding, 97–98
    defendant's responsibilities, 98
    incompetent defendants, 100–103
    issues surrounding, 99
    meaning of, 97–100
Legal fictions, 5
Legal Realism movement, 4–6
    principles of, 5
    social science and, 6
Legal system
    amicus curiae briefs, 24–26, 28
    differences between psychology and,
        9–13
    expert testimony. *See* Expert witnesses
    jurors attitudes about, 137–138
    pathways for influencing, 18–27
    psychology, influence of, 28–29
Legislatures and public policy, influencing, 27
Liability, 138
Lie detection. *See* Polygraphs
Likelihood to Sexually Harass (LSH) scale,
    252–253
Likert format scale, 137
Limiting instructions, 146–148
Lineups
    blind lineup administrators, 184
    eyewitnesses, instructions to, 185
    sequential, 187–188
    unbiased, 185–186
    videotaping, 188
Litigation crisis, 138
Lockett v. Ohio, 299
Lockhart v. McCree, 301
Locus of control, 136
*Lopez v. Laborers International Union
    Local 18,* 255
LSH scale. *See* Likelihood to Sexually Harass
    (LSH) scale
Lying by police, 44–46

M

MacArthur Structured Assessment of the
    Competencies of Criminal Defendants
    (MacSAC-CD), 105
MacArthur Structured Assessment Tool-
    Criminal Adjudication (MacCAT-CA),
    105
MacCAT-CA. *See* MacArthur Structured
    Assessment Tool-Criminal Adjudication
    (MacCAT-CA)
MacSAC-CD. *See* MacArthur Structured
    Assessment of the Competencies of
    Criminal Defendants (MacSAC-CD)
"Mad Bomber" profiling case, 70–71
Madrid v. Gomez, 276
Majority-rule juries, 156, 157
Malingering, 106
Malpractice, 161
Mandatory sentencing, 271
Manson v. Braithwaite, 173
Maryland v. Craig, 199
Maximization strategy, 39–40
McClesey v. Kemp, 304
McDonald's coffee burn case, 160–161
McGuckin v. Smith, 284
McNaughton Rule, 110, 111, 113, 116
Mediation in child custody cases, 235–237
Medina v. California, 98
Memories
    child sexual abuse, of. *See* Child sexual
        abuse, memories of
    eyewitness. *See* Eyewitness memories
    false, research on implanting, 204–207
    repressed. *See* Recovered memories of sex-
        ual abuse
    sexual abuse, recovered memories of. *See*
        Recovered memories of sexual abuse
Mens rea, 108
Mental illness
    amnesia, 106
    competency concerns. *See* Legal compe-
        tence
    execution of prisoners with, 299–300
    faking, 106
    guilty but mentally ill (GBMI), 113–114
    malingering, 106
    prisoners with, treatment of, 284
Mental Screening Evaluation (MSE), 114–115
Minimization strategy, 39–40
Minnesota v. Mack, 191
Miranda rights, 35–36, 99
Miranda v. Arizona, 35–36
Misdemeanor, 274
Mission-oriented serial killers, 69
Mistaken identification, 172–173
    rules for reducing, 184–187
Mitigating factors, 122, 300, 301, 302
Mock juries, 132–133
Mock witness procedure, 185–186
Models of juror decision making, 148–150

Monetary restitution, 295
Morality-based decisions by juries, 153
Morrow v. Maryland, 106
Motion for change of venue, 142
MSE. *See* Mental Screening Evaluation (MSE)
Muller v. Oregon, 4
Murderers
    death penalty for. *See* Death penalty
    disorganized, 68–69
    organized, 68
    serial killers. *See* Serial killers

N

National Judicial College, 24
Natural law, 4
Negligence, 122, 147, 210, 222
Neil v. Biggers, 173
NGRI. *See* Not guilty by reason of insanity
    (NGRI)
1996 Atlanta Summer Olympics bombing
    profiling case, 69–70
Nonviolent criminals, 275
Normative influence, 153
Not guilty by reason of insanity (NGRI)
    alternatives to, 113–114
    Hinckley case, 112–114
    issues, 119–120
    McNaughton case, 109
    sentences of persons found, 118–119
Nullification, jury, 158–159

O

Objectivity versus advocacy, 12–13
O.J. Simpson case
    Guilty Knowledge Test (GKT), 58
    jury consultants, 131–132
    jury panel, 124
    jury selection, 131–132
    similarity-leniency hypothesis, 139
*Oncale v. Sundowner Offshore Services,
    Inc.,* 245, 246–247
On the Witness Stand (Munsterberg), 3–4
Opening statements, 140–141
Organized murderers, 68
Own-race bias, 177

P

PACE. *See* Police and Criminal Evidence Act
    (PACE)
Palmore v. Sidotti, 228
Panel, jury, 124–125
Parental competence as factor in child custody
    arrangement, 225–226
PCT. *See* Positive Control Test (PCT)
Pelican Bay Prison, 276
Penalty phase of capital murder trials,
    299–303
People v. Hickey, 227
People v. McRae, 37
People v. Shirley, 191

People v. Taylor, 90
Perception of Relationships Test (PORT), 234
Peremptory challenges, 125, 127, 130, 165
Perjury, 308
    suborning, 13
Philosopher-Advocate, expert witness as, 21
Plaintiff, 140
Police
    confessions to. *See* Confessions
    good cop/bad cop approach, 37–38
    interrogations. *See* Interrogations
    lying by, 44–46
    suspects, competency issues of, 99
Police and Criminal Evidence Act (PACE), 45
Polygraph Protection Act of 1988, 49
Polygraphs
    accuracy rates, 54–56
    coercion device, as, 60–62
    Control Question Test (CQT), 50–51
    countermeasures, 53
    countries using, 47
    development of, 47–49
    ethical concerns, 54
    evidence from, jurors' response to, 62–63
    false positives, 50
    future of, 63–64
    Guilty Knowledge Test (GKT), 58–60
    legal status of, 56–57
    machine used, 49–50
    person being tested, problems relating to,
        52
    Postive Control Test (PCT), 51–52
    preemployment screening, 49
    problems associated with, 52–54, 64
    questioning procedures, 50–52
    Relevant-Irrelevant Test (RIT), 50
    research on accuracy of, 54–56
    results, admissibility of, 56–57
    scoring, 51
    self-stimulation strategies, 53
    standardization, lack of, 53
PORT. *See* Perception of Relationships Test
    (PORT)
Postive Control Test (PCT), 51–52
Post Traumatic Stress Disorder (PTSD),
    92–93
Power distance, 11
Power-oriented serial killers, 69
Precedents, 11
Predictions of violence. *See* Future violence,
    assessment of risk of
Preexisting expectations, 180–181
Prejudice, 257–260
Preponderance of the evidence standard,
    122, 141, 146
Pretrial publicity, 142
Preventative detention, 212
Prisonization, 286
Prisons, 16, 269–270
    alternatives to, 295–297

"Club Feds," 275
convict code, 290
cost of, 292–293
culture of, 286–292
deterrence as goal of, 276
double-celling, 283, 289
drugs in, 291–292
effectiveness of, 292–295
1800's, in, 278–281
evolution of, 277–282
gangs, 291
gender differences in prisoners, 285–286
imprisonment, 274–277
incapacitation as goal of, 276, 293
inmates. *See* subhead: prisoners
jails, 274–275
life in, 288–289
medical care for prisoners, 293
medical model, 281
New York system, 279
1900's, in, 281–282
Pennsylvania system, 279, 280
power disparities in, 287–288
prisoner classification schemes, 281
prisoner rights, 283–284
prisoners, medical care for, 293
prisoners, statistics on, 284–286
probation, 295–296
purpose of, 275
racial statistics of prisoners, 286
rape in, 290–291
reforms, 282
rehabilitation as goal of. *See* Rehabilitation
retribution as goal of, 276–277, 293–294
scared straight program, 296
serious mental illness, treatment of prison-
    ers with, 284
shock incarceration as alternative to,
    296–297
state and federal, 275
statistics on, 284–286
supermax, 275–276
terms used to describe, 276
threats of violence in, 290–291
violence in, 290–291
Privileged communications, 211
Probation, 295–296
Probative evidence, 77–78
Procedural justice, 261
Procunier v. Martinez, 283
Profiling
    crime scenes. *See* Crime scenes
    criminal investigative analysis, 66
    famous cases, 69–71
    "Mad Bomber" case, 70–71
    1996 Atlanta Summer Olympics bombing,
        69–70
    process of, 66–68
    psychological autopsy. *See* Psychological
        autopsy

Profiling (*cont.*)
  racial, 76–77
  research on, 72–73
  retroclassification, 66
  signature aspect of crime, 67, 72
  stereotyping, 76–78
  studies on, 72–73
  techniques, 66–67
Program evaluation, 15
Progressive movement, 4
Propensity evidence. *See* Future violence,
    assessment of risk of
Proportionality, 270–274
Proximate cause, 122
Psychiatric symptomatology, 219–220
Psychological autopsy, 73–76
  accidental death, 74–75
  evidence used in, 74
  goal of, 74
  legal status of, 75–76
  suicide, 74–75
Psychologists
  advisors, as, 14–15
  child custody decisions, contribution to,
    232–235
  cross-disciplinary training, 22–24
  duty to protect requirement, 210–211
  evaluators, as, 15–17
  legal training, 22–24
  reformers, as, 17–18
  roles played by, 14–18
  trial consultants, as, 15
Psychology
  areas of, 2
  courts, influence on, 28–29
  culture of, 8–13
  empiricism and, 11
  historical overview, 3–8
  objectivity, 12–13
Psychology, Public Policy, and Law, 8
Psychology Today, 26
Psychopaths, 219
PTSD. *See* Post Traumatic Stress Disorder
    (PTSD)
Punishment, goals of, 16
Punitive damages, 138, 161

Q
Quid pro quo harassment, 241

R
Racial discrimination in death penalty,
    303–305
Racial discrimination in workplace, 257–260
Racial profiling, 76–77
Rape
  death penalty for, 303–304
  prisons, in, 290–291
Rape myths, 89

Rape shield laws, 92
Rape Trauma Syndrome (RTS), 86–92
  expert testimony, 89–90, 91
  phases of, 86–87
  research evidence on, 88
  symptoms, 88–89, 90–91
  testimony in court, 89–92
R-CRAS. *See* Rogers Criminal Responsibility
    Assessment Scales (R-CRAS)
Reactance theory, 144
Realist movement. *See* Legal Realism move-
    ment
Reasonable accommodation, failure to pro-
    vide, 255–256
Reasonable doubt, 122, 141, 146, 152
Reasonable woman standard, 245
Reck v. Pate, 35
Recovered memories of sexual abuse,
    200–207
  creation of memories, 202–207
  false memories, research on implanting,
    204–207
  implantation of memories, 202–207
  Ingram case, 200–202
  relaxation techniques, 203
  visualization techniques, 203
Recross, 141
Redirect, 141
Reformers, psychologists as, 17–18
Regina v. Oxford, 109
Rehabilitation, 7, 16, 277, 279, 281, 282,
    294–295
Relaxation techniques, 203
Relevant-Irrelevant Test (RIT), 50
Religious discrimination, 256
Remittitur, 161
*Report on Lawlessness in Law Enforce-
    ment,* 35
Repressed memories. *See* Recovered memo-
    ries of sexual abuse
Residential community corrections centers,
    297
Resilient children, 232
Restitution, monetary, 295
Retribution, 276–277, 293–294
Retrieval, process of, 176
Retrieval inhibition, 180, 206
Retroclassification, 66
Revised Legal Attitudes Questionnaire
    (RLAQ), 137
Rex v. Arnold, 109
Rhodes v. Chapman, 283
Riggins v. Nevada, 102–103
Ring v. Arizona, 300
Risk factors used in prediction of violence,
    218–221
  dynamic markers, 219–220
  historical markers, 218–219
  risk management markers, 220–221

RIT. *See* Relevant-Irrelevant Test (RIT)
RLAQ. *See* Revised Legal Attitudes Question-
    naire (RLAQ)
Rock v. Arkansas, 191
Rogers Criminal Responsibility Assessment
    Scales (R-CRAS), 115
RTS. *See* Rape Trauma Syndrome (RTS)
Rulings versus data, 11–12

S
Scared straight program, 296
Science translation brief, 24
Scientific jury selection, 129–132
Sears v. Rutishauser, 22
Self-defense, 82–83
Sentencing decisions, 270–274
    attributions about criminals, and, 270
    disparities, 270–271
    guidelines, 271–274
Sentencing Reform Act of 1984, 271
Sequential lineups, 187–188
Serial killers, 66–67
    characteristics of, 68–69
    Hillside Strangler, 106
    incompetence, faking, 106
    malingering, 106
    profiling. *See* Profiling
    types of, 69
Sexual abuse, child. *See* Child sexual abuse,
    memories of
Sexual discrimination law, 240–242
Sexual harassment
    causes of, 250–251
    Boeing case, 248
    coping strategies, 251–252
    current status of law, 246–250
    effects of, 251–252
    gender harassment, 246–247
    lawsuits, 247–250
    legal boundaries of, 244–245
    Likelihood to Sexually Harass (LSH) scale,
        252–253
    Mitsubishi case, 249–250
    prevalence and perceptions of, 242–244
    preventing, 252–253
    Price Waterhouse case, 248
    psychology of, 250–253
    reasonable person standard, 244–245
    reasonable victim standard, 245
    reasonable woman standard, 245
    studies of, 242–244
Sexual Harassment of Working Women
    (MacKinnon), 241
Shadow jury, 133
Shock incarceration, 296–297
Shotgun instruction, 157
Signature aspect of crime, 67, 72
The Silence of the Lambs, 66
Similarity-leniency hypothesis, 138–140

Simpson, O.J. *See* O.J. Simpson case
Smith v. United States, 110
Social psychology, 2, 10
Social scientific evidence, 4
    Legal Realism movement and, 6
Standard of proof, 98, 146
Stare decisis, doctrine of, 12
State of Oregon v. Hansen, 78
State v. Dorsey, 56
State v. Helterbridle, 91
State v. Scales, 46
Stephan v. State, 46
Stereotypes used in selection of jurors, 129
Stereotyping, 76–78
Storage, process of, 176
Strong jurors, 151
Suborning perjury, 13
Suggestive comments, 179–180
Summative evaluations, 16
Supermax prisons, 275–276
Supreme Court decisions in death penalty
    cases, 298–303
Swearing contests, 37
Syndromes, 79–93
    Battered Woman Syndrome (BWS). *See*
        Battered Woman Syndrome (BWS)
    Post Traumatic Stress Disorder (PTSD),
        92–93
    Rape Trauma Syndrome (RTS). *See* Rape
        Trauma Syndrome (RTS)

T
*Tarasoff v. Regents of the University of Cali-
    fornia,* 210–211, 222
Taylor v. Louisiana, 123
"Tender years" doctrine, 227
Testimony
    Battered Woman Syndrome (BWS), 83–84
    children at trial, by, 198–200
    closed-circuit television (CCTV), by,
        199–200
    expert. *See* Expert witnesses
    eyewitness, 172–174
    Rape Trauma Syndrome (RTS), 89–92
Threat/control-override (TCO) symptoms,
    220
Three-strikes laws, 274, 278, 284
Title VII, 240, 241, 253
Townsend v. Swain, 35
Trans World Airlines, Inc. v. Hardison, 256
Trial
    competence to stand trial (CST). *See* Com-
        petence to stand trial (CST)
    expert testimony. *See* Expert witnesses
    polygraph results, admissibility of, 56–57
    procedure, 140–141
    testimony by children at, 198–200
    videotaped confessions presented at,
        43–44

Trial consultants
  efficacy of, 133–134
  psychologists as, 15
  use of, 132–133
Truth in sentencing laws, 293
Twinkie defense, 114
Two-by-two contingency table, 213

U
Ulmer v. State Farm, 57
Ultimate issue, 113
Unanimous jury verdicts, 156–158
Unbiased lineups, 185–186
Uncertainty avoidance, 9
Unconscious transference, 178–179
Uniform Marriage and Divorce Act, 232
United States v. Brawner, 112
United States v. Goff, 272
United States v. Scheffer, 56
University of Chicago Jury Project, 150

V
Venire, 124–125
Verdict-driven style of deliberations, 152
Verdicts
  arriving at, dynamics behind, 150–159
  items affecting juror, 141–150
  juror characteristics and attitudes as predictors of, 134–140
Videotaped
  confessions, 43–44
  identification procedures, 188
Violence
  assessment of risk of future. See Future violence, assessment of risk of
  treatment to reduce risk of, 223–224

Violence Prediction Scheme (VPS), 221
Violence Risk Appraisal Guide (VRAG), 221
Visionary serial killers, 69
Visualization techniques, 203
Voir dire, 125–126, 165, 175
Voter lists, 124
VPS. See Violence Prediction Scheme (VPS)
VRAG. See Violence Risk Appraisal Guide (VRAG)

W
Wainwright v. Witt, 300
War on drugs, 285
Washington v. Harper, 284
Water cure, 35
Weapons focus effect, 178
Whores of the Court (Hagen), 21
Williams Bazille et al. v. Alioto et al., 77
Williams v. Florida, 155
Wilson v. Seiter, 283
Witness confidence, 181–183, 186
Witnesses
  examinations of, 141
  expert. See Expert witnesses
  eyewitnesses. See Eyewitnesses
  mock witness procedure, 185–186
  questioning of, 32
Workplace law
  discrimination. See Discrimination, workplace
  fairness. See Fairness in the workplace
  sexual discrimination, 240–242
  sexual harassment. See Sexual harassment
Wrongful convictions, 172, 308

TO THE OWNER OF THIS BOOK:

We hope that you have found *Psychology Applied to Law* useful. So that this book can be improved in a future edition, would you take the time to complete this sheet and return it? Thank you.

School and address: _____

_____

Department: _____

Instructor's name: _____

1. What I like most about this book is: _____

_____

_____

2. What I like least about this book is: _____

_____

_____

3. My general reaction to this book is: _____

_____

_____

4. The name of the course in which I used this book is: _____

_____

5. Were all of the chapters of the book assigned for you to read?_____

   If not, which ones weren't? _____

6. In the space below, or on a separate sheet of paper, please write specific suggestions for improving this book and anything else you'd care to share about your experience in using this book.

_____

_____

_____

_____

OPTIONAL:

Your name: _____ Date: _____

May we quote you, either in promotion for *Psychology Applied to Law*, or in future publishing ventures?

Yes: _____ No: _____

Sincerely yours,

Mark Costanzo

BUSINESS REPLY MAIL

FIRST CLASS   PERMIT NO. 34   BELMONT, CA

POSTAGE WILL BE PAID BY ADDRESSEE

NO POSTAGE
NECESSARY
IF MAILED
IN THE
UNITED STATES

ATTN: *Marianne Taflinger*

WADSWORTH/THOMSON LEARNING
10 DAVIS DRIVE
BELMONT, CA   94002-9801